electronic day trading 101

electronic day trading 101

SUNNY J. HARRIS

John Wiley & Sons, Inc.

New York • Chichester • Weinheim • Brisbane • Singapore • Toronto

Copyright © 2000 by Sunny J. Harris. All rights reserved.

Published by John Wiley & Sons, Inc.

Published simultaneously in Canada.

This publication is designed to provide accurate and authoritative information in regard to the subject matter covered. It is sold with the understanding that the publisher is not engaged in rendering professional services. If professional advice or other expert assistance is required, the services of a competent professional person should be sought.

Material in this book is for educational purposes only. It should not be assumed that the methods, techniques, or indicators presented in this book will be profitable or that they will not result in losses. Past results are not necessarily indicative of future results. This is not a solicitation of any offer to buy or sell. Trading and investing are speculative and include risk of loss. Hypothetical or simulated performance results have certain inherent limitations. Unlike an actual performance record, simulated results do not represent actual trading. Also, since the trades may not have been executed, the results may have under- or over-compensated for the impact, if any, of certain market factors, such as lack of liquidity. Simulated trading programs in general are also subject to the fact that they are designed with the benefit of hindsight. No representation is being made that any account will or is likely to achieve profits or losses similar to those shown.

Library of Congress Cataloging-in-Publication Data:

Harris, Sunny J.
    Electronic day trading 101 / Sunny J. Harris.
      p. cm .—(Wiley online trading for a living)
    Includes index.
    ISBN 0-471-36210-7 (cloth : alk. paper)
    1. Electronic trading of securities.   2. Investments—Computer network resources.
 I. Title: Electronic day trading one hundred one. II. Title: Electronic day trading one hundred one. III. Title. IV. Series.
HG4515.95 .H37 2000
332.64'0285—dc21

                                           99-046207

Printed in the United States of America

It is with great hope for the future that
I dedicate this book to my grandson,
Liam Asher Littlejohn,
who just turned 3 years old.

Education is our hope for the future and
this book is meant as an educational primer.
Share education with your children and
love them as much as I love Liam
and your life will be filled with joy.

The general who wins a battle makes many calculations in his temple before the battle is fought. The general who loses a battle makes few calculations beforehand.

—*Sun Tzu in* The Art of War

contents

preface

Human nature! What a continual marvel. Everyone wants something for nothing, or at least fairly cheap. Quick fixes, free lunches, easy riches—and the *For Dummies* books to tell you how to do it in 21 minutes.

That is what this book is *not* about. Although *Electronic Day Trading 101* does address that very same audience, it is with a great deal of concern for these people that I write this book. It is my hope that you will read this book and realize several things: Trading is not for everyone; trading can lose you lots of money; and yet trading can make you lots of money if you plan, study, and work hard.

Authors always thank their families for being supportive and tolerating their submersion into the work. I am no exception. In addition to Howard, I am eternally grateful to Dr. Gina Maraio, Shelby Harris, Colby and Liam Littlejohn, Fred Yates, and Mae Evans for giving me the time to write and for assisting me with the details along the way. I can't help but wonder, however, if we authors are a bit nearsighted in our recognition of their thankless service. Perhaps our families are really quite pleased that we have something to do that keeps us out of their hair.

electronic day trading 101

chapter 1

before you begin

The universal regard for money is the one hopeful fact in our civilization, the one sound spot in our social conscience. Money is the most important thing in the world. It represents health, strength, honor, generosity and beauty as conspicuously as the want of it represents illness, weakness, disgrace, meanness and ugliness.

—*George Bernard Shaw, 1856–1950*

Why on Earth do you want to do this? Trading is certainly the most difficult profession there is. Let me take this opportunity to tell you that at least 80% of all those who start trading today will have lost their trading capital within the first 12 months. Most people would make more money working for minimum wage than trading!

It is the specific job of those who already know how to day trade to take your money. That's how we make profits. Markets exist because people disagree about the future direction of stocks and commodities. You think it's going up; I think it's going down—or vice versa. We take opposite sides of the trade. One of us wins, the other loses. And believe me, I will put all the computing power, experience, and education I have into trying to be the one who wins.

definition:

> **day trading**   The rapid buying and selling of shares, followed by closing all positions before the end of the trading session. Day traders do not carry overnight positions. Day trading is typically based on real-time data.

Don't think you can read this book and begin day trading. Like any new job, this one requires a tremendous amount of education. You wouldn't wake up today and decide to build a house without spending time on training and apprenticeship in the areas of carpentry, masonry, or plumbing. What would make you think you can be a successful trader with any less experience?

All the books you can buy on trading, and there are hundreds, will only serve to plant ideas and theories in your mind. You cannot be a successful trader until you have made these ideas your own, by testing and trying them. Before you can make money as a trader, you have to lose money.

If you come to this profession like a gambler, you will ultimately give your fortune to the market. There is no place in the trading business for hope. Becoming a successful trader takes years of study and hard work. If you gamble in the market, you have no one to blame but yourself when your money is all gone.

If you still are interested in day trading, let's get going. If not, you probably read this first page in the bookstore and didn't buy the book anyway.

introduction

The stock markets have been an open-outcry auction from the beginning of time—until recently! Many of the non-U.S. markets have been converting to electronic trading over the past 10 years or so. The U.S. markets, however, have been reluctant to make the switch, telling the floor traders that their jobs would never disappear. That is probably the main reason we are not fully electronic, yet.

The times they are a changin'. More and more frequently I see signs of computerized trading creeping into the pits, as well as into the home. It used to be against policy to have any computers in the trading pits; now floor traders have handheld terminals, cell phones, and all manner of electronic equipment. Trading back-offices are computerized. Real-time quotes, once only available to professionals at great expense, are available over the Internet for $79 per month. You can listen to the sounds of the pits using RealAudio over the Internet. Hopefully, soon the U.S. exchanges will join the rest of the world in abandoning the trading pits in favor of computerizing the entire process.

At this point in time you can enter some trades directly from your computer to the exchange's computer, but most trading is still done through an open-outcry auction.

definitions:

    auction   A public sale of items to the highest bidders.

    open outcry   A method of public auction in which verbal bids and offers are made in the trading pits or rings. More to the point, a system of trading in which people standing in pits frantically wave and shout out orders (Figure 1.1).

pit   The area on the exchange trading floor where futures trading takes place. The area is generally octagonal with steps descending into the center. Traders stand on the various steps, which designate the contract month they are trading. When viewed from above, the trading area looks like a pit (Figure 1.2).

The futures industry is entering the electronic trading arena through a negotiated TKO arrangement. Futures exchanges are pairing pit traders with electronic traders, allowing both processes to exist side by side. Just recently, the Chicago Board Options Exchange (CBOE) announced that it too was pursuing an ambitious plan to develop parallel paths for open-outcry and screen-based trading. In its press release, the CBOE carefully stated:

> At the same time, CBOE will develop a separate screen-based system to complement, not to supplant, floor-based trading. CBOE will begin next year to move less actively traded stock options to a screen-based trading system. Exchange officials said the screen-based system will also be used to facilitate "after hours" trading which is expected to commence in the middle of next year.

Sounds like the beginning of a much-needed transition to me.

The National Association of Securities Dealers Automatic Quotation (Nasdaq), however, is the stellar example of electronic trading.

figure 1.1   activity in an open-outcry trading pit

figure 1.2   how a trade takes place in the pit

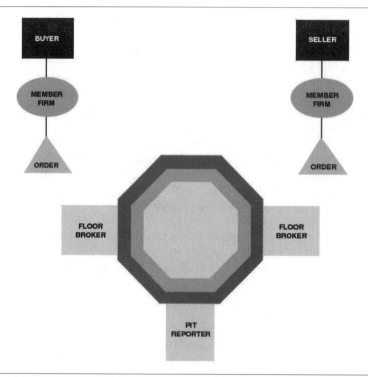

Once the exchange for the little guys, the Nasdaq now experiences heavier trading volume than the New York Stock Exchange (NYSE)—and the Nasdaq is not a floor-based auction!

Without a doubt, the widespread use of the Internet has changed our way of life. In the near future, nearly every aspect of your life will have some component that you conduct over the Internet. Fast phone lines and modems have allowed this revolution, and it will continue its exponential growth as hardware ceases to be a limiting factor.

online trading versus screen-based trading

What is the difference between online trading and screen-based trading? Can't you enter your NYSE trades online?

Online trading is using electronic means to transmit an order to the floor of the exchange. Currently, when you use your computer to enter a trade to buy shares of stock on the NYSE, the order goes from your computer to another computer, and then to a device (either a fax, a computer screen, or a handheld device) in or near the exchange trading pit. Although that transaction occurs in seconds, it is not fast enough for people who want to engage in speed trading.

You can do online trading from the Internet with most brokerage firms. If your brokerage firm doesn't have online trading already, they will soon.

Online trading is essentially a way to deliver your message to your broker, that you wish to place an order. Online trading doesn't usually require any special software, just an Internet browser.

Speed trading is the electronic equivalent of *scalping*. Scalpers, traditionally, were the guys in the pits who could quickly buy and sell any stock (or commodity), looking for just a sixteenth, an eighth, or a quarter point profit. Scalpers make it up in volume. Scalpers provide a valuable service to the markets, they create liquidity.

definition:
> **liquidity**   Liquidity is the ease with which a market can absorb volume buying and selling without dramatic fluctuations in price.

Speed traders are scalpers who are not in the pit. *Speed trading* is my own word for the process, but I'm hoping the description will stick. Speed traders trade from their computer screens, at home or at one of the day trading salons around the country. Speed traders are also making it up in volume, looking for small moves in large quantities.

Day trading salons are available in most major cities around the United States (Figures 1.3 and 1.4). For a list of day trading salon branch offices, take a look in Appendix B.

Speed traders execute their trades from a computer screen (Figure 1.5), by clicking on a price, or by filling in an electronic form (Figure 1.6). The public is demanding screen-based trading! The popularity of online brokers and electronic day trading speaks clearly and loudly. The exchanges will have to respond and react to the demand side of the equation (Figure 1.7).

At the same time, the Chicago Mercantile Exchange (CME) announced the introduction of its newest futures contract, the E-Mini Nasdaq 100 Index. What is that? If you want to day trade the Nasdaq 100 Index, rather than individual stocks, this futures contract just might be the ticket. (For more information, see www.cme.com/news/e_nasdaq1.html.) Again, this new contract is being established on a side-by-side basis, allowing both electronic and open outcry trading.

figure 1.3   trading salon locations

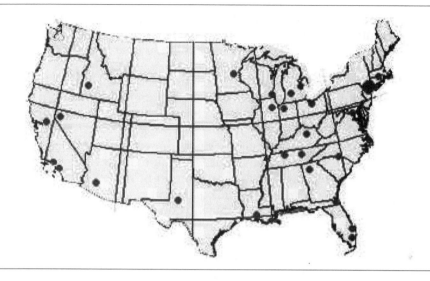

figure 1.4   a day trading salon at All-Tech in New Jersey

figure 1.5 a typical Level II screen

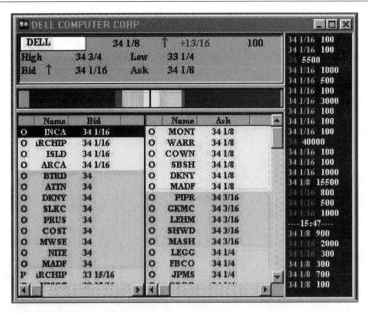

Source: Quote.com QCharts. Reprinted with permission.

figure 1.6 a typical electronic trading form

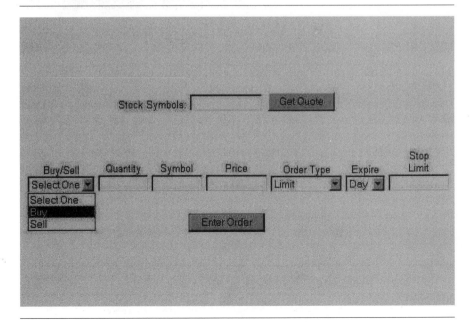

figure 1.7   trading from home

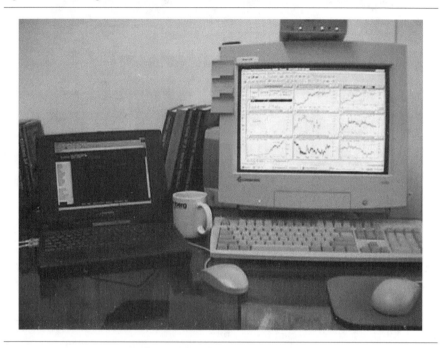

introduction to trading

This book, *Electronic Day Trading 101,* is the collection of years of study and experimentation, condensed into an easy-to-use guide for the newcomer. *Electronic Day Trading 101* is like an overview class: You will learn about the existence of concepts, but will not necessarily learn the concepts in depth. You will, however, learn where to look for information on each of these concepts, so that you may explore in-depth and develop your knowledge base further if a particular topic appeals to you. I've drawn liberally from the work of others, using quotes and telling you where you can find more information on the subject.

Electronic Day Trading 101 could have been subtitled *Everything You Ever Wanted to Know about Day Trading but Were Afraid to Ask* because we'll be covering many very basic questions (and their answers), which students are often afraid to ask in a large class for fear of asking dumb questions.

There are thousands of professional money managers in the world: bankers, stock brokers, insurance brokers, real estate agents, art dealers, coin dealers, antique dealers, accountants, attorneys, and so on. Any one of these professionals will be happy to tell you that his (whenever I use the masculine pronoun I use it generically, implying his/her throughout this book) specialty is the only one that will stead you well for the long-term outlook. In other words, they're all salesmen. All of these professionals have one goal foremost: to increase their own take-home pay.

There is no such thing as altruism. We all have personal motives for doing good deeds, whether it be attention getting, reward seeking, or monetary. For instance, I'm not writing this book just for kicks and because I want to see you make a lot of money—I'm writing it so you'll purchase the book, and as an aside, I'm writing about a subject that I believe will assist you in making a lot of money. This is a trade: I get something of value and you get something of value. That's what this whole book is about, trading: the perceived fair exchange of one item or service for another item or service in the hopes that both parties benefit.

Electronic Day Trading 101 is not for the aforementioned professionals—they already know it all. This book is written for everyone else. I will show you the ropes, pulling from many different resources. I will introduce you to concepts that you may want to study in-depth.

the market

The market goes up and the market goes down. That's about all there is to it. Your job, as a trader, is to catch those swings at just the right time and price to profit from the movement. Buy low, sell high is the adage. Your job is simply to determine what is low and what is high. That's the tough part.

Throughout this book, the word *market* will refer to anything that one person wants to buy and another person wants to sell. If I have a car that I want to sell and you want to purchase, then that's the market.

The action of negotiating for the price at which we are willing to complete this transaction is called *trading*. Trading, when it involves just two people, is a negotiation process. Trading, when it involves more than two people, is an auction process. Sellers are looking for the highest bidder and buyers are looking for the lowest offer.

definitions:

ask   The lowest price at which someone is willing to sell a security.

bid   The highest price someone is willing to pay for a security.

The securities markets are, at their basic level, a way for companies to raise money for expanded growth. Initially, a company may be owned by a few individuals; these individuals own all the stock of the company. As the company grows, it may decide it needs funds to expand further. The company can borrow the funds (and pay them back over time), or it can sell part of the stock of the company. Selling stock to the public is known as going public. Making an initial public offering (IPO) provides the opportunity for individuals in the general public to buy shares of the company. When the public buys shares of the company, the company receives cash in exchange for letting others own a percentage of the company.

further study

If you want to know more about IPOs, take a look at these web sites:

- www.ipocentral.com
- www.ipodata.com
- www.dsm.com
- www.gaskinsco.com
- www.ipomaven.com
- www.netresource.com
- quote.bloomberg.com/markets/ipocenter.html

Whether we are talking about the NYSE, the Nasdaq, the American Stock Exchange (Amex), the Over-the-Counter Exchange (OTC), or any of the other exchanges, the purpose of a securities market is primarily to allow businesses to acquire investment capital. (As this book was in progress, the Nasdaq and the Amex merged, forming the Nasdaq-Amex.)

When you trade with purpose, you are not a gambler. You are providing a service. The service you provide is to enhance the liquidity of the markets so that businesses can expand and grow.

why trade?

There is only one reason to trade—to make money! If you are trading for any other reason, stop. I say that over and over as I lecture around the world, and I still find people who trade for the excitement or the challenge. Be careful what you ask for.

Everyone is looking for the next greatest money-making gimmick. Trading, in one form or another, has been the money maker for eons. It was trading that led to the discovery of the New World as explorers were looking for better trading routes. It was trading euphoria (greed) followed by a trading panic (fear) in the Tulip Panic of 1636.

At this moment in history, electronic trading is making its debut, and is the most talked about facet of trading. The only aspect that is new to this endeavor is the speed with which we can receive information and execute trades.

exchanges

An exchange is an organization that provides or maintains a marketplace. We think of an exchange being a huge organization consisting of all those folks on the floor, but that is not it. An exchange is generally a small organization that keeps things orderly. An exchange is usually a corporation; it is not a government body, though many people think of it as such. The folks on the floor of the exchange are self-employed or employed by brokerage firms. They pay the exchange for the privilege of having a seat, which gives them the right to trade on the floor.

Traditionally, exchanges provided physical locations for trading to take place. The traditional markets have been floor based, operating in a specific building, on a physical trading floor. In a floor-based market, all trades for a particular stock are channeled through a single person, called a *specialist*. All buy and sell orders for that particular stock pass through the specialist.

definition:
> **specialist** A member of a stock exchange through whom all trades in a given security pass.

For floor-based markets, specialists function to match buy orders with sell orders. Specialists also trade for their own accounts and establish the public quote for the stock. Specialists generally know every order in their book.

As long as the buy and sell orders are approximately balanced, this works fine. When a large block order comes in for a stock, and the floor specialist is unable to match it, he may send the trade off the floor to a broker/dealer firm. When a buyer or seller is found to take the other side of the trade, it is then brought back to the specialist to complete the trade execution in his book.

An exchange provides for orderly markets. It organizes and creates methods for buyers and sellers to come together.

Have you ever used one of the online auctions, like eBay or uBid? eBay and uBid are exchanges. eBay provides a means for people who have something to sell to engage in an online auction with participants who wish to buy. Like all auctions, the highest bidder wins. For all we know, eBay could be just a one-person shop consisting of a programmer who set up the web site. The function of eBay (the exchange) is to bring buyers and sellers together. eBay performs two functions: electronic record keeping and advertising. These are the same two functions any exchange performs.

I believe that in the not too distant future, most exchanges will function in much the same manner as eBay. There will be no physical floor where people stand around and yell out their bids and offers. Even at physical auctions like Sotheby's (www.sothebys.com), no one yells out; bidders simply hold up their card, which has their unique number on it and the auctioneer nods in acknowledgment. In further compliance with the information age, the auction houses are online with electronic auctions.

Furthermore, exchanges will evolve as the online brokers and direct-access brokers have evolved, first as electronic exchanges that you access through your browser or computer program, and then as direct-access exchanges where you have instant access to all exchanges and all traders around the world.

In time, it won't matter whether you are trading the U.S. exchanges or any of the multitude of exchanges around the world. You will be entering your trades for Russian stocks, Swiss stocks, and Japanese stocks from the same computer screen you enter your orders for U.S. stocks.

At present, when we talk about direct-access day trading, we are talking about stocks. The only reason we limit our discussion to stocks is that while the other exchanges offer electronic order delivery methods, they do not offer direct-access electronic execution. Never fear; they will. Competition from the Nasdaq, now the most heavily traded exchange, will dictate online as well as direct-access trading for all the exchanges.

The best way for you to find information about each exchange is to visit their web site. I list the various exchanges in Appendix J for your convenience. You may not need them just now, but in time you will.

screen-based exchanges

A screen-based exchange is order driven rather than quote driven. A screen-based exchange does not operate from a physical trading floor with an *auction;* rather, it operates electronically from computer screens by *negotiation.*

definitions:

>**auction**   A competitive bidding method for selling an asset to the highest bidder.

>**negotiation**   The process whereby the purchase price is determined by a public offering.

Simply put, in an auction everyone is screaming and yelling in competition and prices are driven up or down in the process. In a negotiation, if you see a price you like, you take it. Price changes based on the public's willingness to buy or sell.

The primary U.S. screen-based exchange, Nasdaq, has been in operation as an electronic exchange since 1971. In 1995, the cry for electronic futures exchanges was answered with the creation of Globex by the CME. Globex provides screen-based trading in the hours while the auction floor is closed.

Electronic exchanges have reduced spreads and transaction costs, over their floor-based counterparts. Orders to an electronic exchange are received from a *computer screen,* into the exchange's computer, time-stamped, and immediately processed for a potential match. That's what we mean by screen-based.

GLOBEX®$_2$

GLOBEX$_2$ is the electronic trading system of the Chicago Mercantile Exchange (CME). GLOBEX$_2$, an automated order entry and matching system, provides institutional and other investors a worldwide network for futures and options trading virtually 24 hours per day (Figures 1.8 and 1.9). Developed on the Paris Bourse's NSC trading system, GLOBEX$_2$ replaced the original GLOBEX system in 1997—the first global electronic trading system—which was launched in 1992.

Beginning in 1997, the CME launched a series of smaller-sized electronically traded products, called "E-mini's," including an E-mini S&P 500, E-mini Nasdaq 100, E-mini Euro FX, and E-mini Japanese yen. These products provide retail customers convenient and cost-effective access to some of the most popular futures and options products. The CME also offers side-by-side electronic and open outcry trading of its most actively traded interest rate product—Eurodollars.

figure 1.8 GLOBEX Market Watch screen

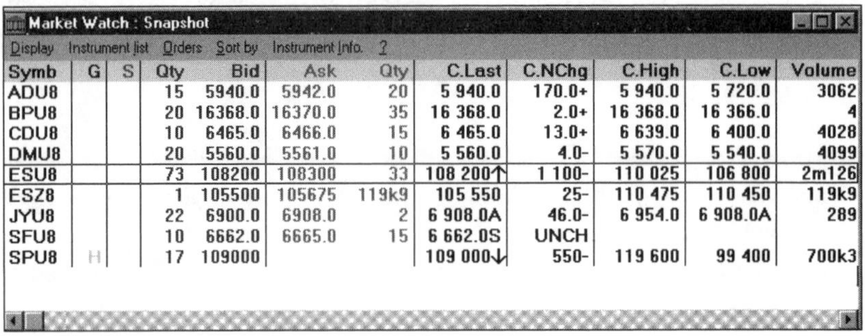

Market Watch : Snapshot

Display Instrument list Orders Sort by Instrument Info. ?

Symb	G	S	Qty	Bid	Ask	Qty	C.Last	C.NChg	C.High	C.Low	Volume
ADU8			15	5940.0	5942.0	20	5 940.0	170.0+	5 940.0	5 720.0	3062
BPU8			20	16368.0	16370.0	35	16 368.0	2.0+	16 368.0	16 366.0	4
CDU8			10	6465.0	6466.0	15	6 465.0	13.0+	6 639.0	6 400.0	4028
DMU8			20	5560.0	5561.0	10	5 560.0	4.0-	5 570.0	5 540.0	4099
ESU8			73	108200	108300	33	108 200↑	1 100-	110 025	106 800	2m126
ESZ8			1	105500	105675	119k9	105 550	25-	110 475	110 450	119k9
JYU8			22	6900.0	6908.0	2	6 908.0A	46.0-	6 954.0	6 908.0A	289
SFU8			10	6662.0	6665.0	15	6 662.0S	UNCH			
SPU8	H		17	109000			109 000↓	550-	119 600	99 400	700k3

Source: GLOBEX Market Watch. Reprinted with permission.

figure 1.9 GLOBEX₂ terminal screen

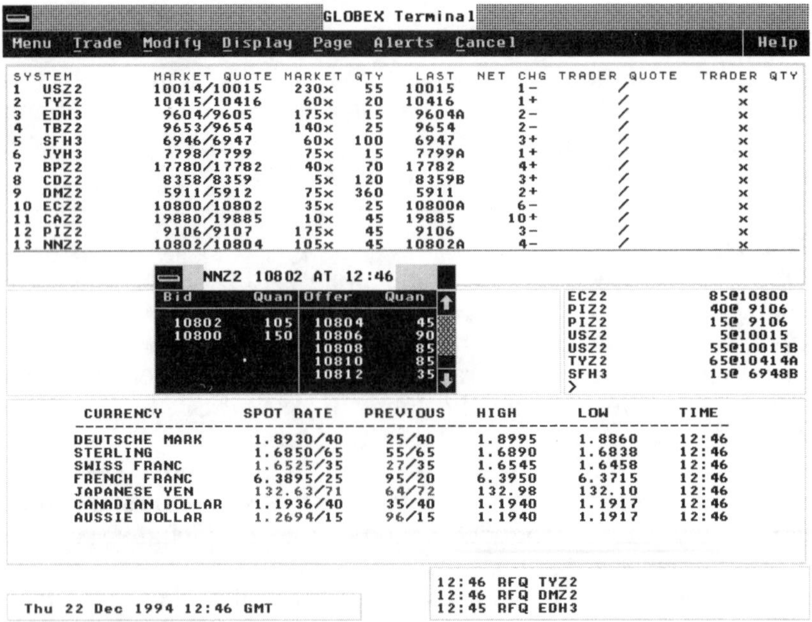

GLOBEX Terminal

Menu Trade Modify Display Page Alerts Cancel   Help

SYSTEM		MARKET QUOTE	MARKET QTY	LAST	NET CHG	TRADER QUOTE	TRADER QTY
1	USZ2	10014/10015	230× 55	10015	1 -	/	×
2	TYZ2	10415/10416	60× 20	10416	1 +	/	×
3	EDH3	9604/9605	175× 15	9604A	2 -	/	×
4	TBZ2	9653/9654	140× 25	9654	2 -	/	×
5	SFH3	6946/6947	60× 100	6947	3 +	/	×
6	JYH3	7798/7799	75× 15	7799A	1 +	/	×
7	BPZ2	17780/17782	40× 70	17782	4 +	/	×
8	CDZ2	8358/8359	5× 120	8359B	3 +	/	×
9	DMZ2	5911/5912	75× 360	5911	2 +	/	×
10	ECZ2	10800/10802	35× 25	10800A	6 -	/	×
11	CAZ2	19880/19885	10× 45	19885	10 +	/	×
12	PIZ2	9106/9107	175× 45	9106	3 -	/	×
13	NNZ2	10802/10804	105× 45	10802A	4 -	/	×

NNZ2 10802 AT 12:46

Bid	Quan	Offer	Quan
10802	105	10804	45
10800	150	10806	90
		10808	85
		10810	85
		10812	35

ECZ2	85@10800
PIZ2	40@ 9106
PIZ2	15@ 9106
USZ2	5@10015
USZ2	55@10015B
TYZ2	65@10414A
SFH3	15@ 6948B
>	

CURRENCY	SPOT RATE	PREVIOUS	HIGH	LOW	TIME
DEUTSCHE MARK	1.8930/40	25/40	1.8995	1.8860	12:46
STERLING	1.6850/65	55/65	1.6890	1.6838	12:46
SWISS FRANC	1.6525/35	27/35	1.6545	1.6458	12:46
FRENCH FRANC	6.3895/25	95/20	6.3950	6.3715	12:46
JAPANESE YEN	132.63/71	64/72	132.98	132.10	12:46
CANADIAN DOLLAR	1.1936/40	35/40	1.1940	1.1917	12:46
AUSSIE DOLLAR	1.2694/15	96/15	1.1940	1.1917	12:46

12:46 RFQ TYZ2
12:46 RFQ DMZ2
12:45 RFQ EDH3

Thu 22 Dec 1994 12:46 GMT

Source: GLOBEX Market Watch. Reprinted with permission.

In 1999, the CME, Paris Bourse, Singapore International Monetary Exchange (SIMEX), Brazil's BM&F, and the Montreal Exchange joined their trading systems under the GLOBEX Alliance, allowing cross-exchange product access on one trading screen and providing other cost savings through cross margining agreements.

Nasdaq

A screen-based exchange, such as Nasdaq, does not conduct itself within the confines of a single physical trading floor. A screen-based market takes place in a highly competitive electronic trading environment.

Referring back to the eBay example, where is eBay? Nowhere. Everywhere. You and I can compete against each other in a real-time auction, while I am in California and you are in New York. We are competing over our computer screens through the Internet.

Screen-based market systems are commonly used in the world's largest stock markets, including Tokyo, London, Paris, Taipei, Toronto, Zurich, and Sydney. Doesn't it strike you as strange that I did not mention the U.S. markets? On most of our exchanges, we are behind the times.

The only U.S. fully screen-based exchange is Nasdaq. Trading began on the Nasdaq in 1971, with the introduction of the world's first electronic market. By 1980, Nasdaq was displaying inside quotations on-screen, the result of which was that spreads between bid and ask prices decreased.

definitions:

inside quotation   The difference between the best bid and best ask among all securities is the highest bid and lowest offer being quoted among all of the market makers competing in a security. Because the spread is the aggregate of individual market maker spreads, it is narrower than an individual dealer spread or quote.

inside market   The highest bid and the lowest ask prices among all market makers competing in a security; the best bid and ask prices for a security. See BBO (following).

best ask   The lowest quoted offer of all competing market makers to sell a particular stock at any given time.

best bid   The highest quoted bid of all competing market makers to buy a particular stock at any given time.

bbo   From all of the market maker and electronic communications network (ECN) bids and offers, Nasdaq calculates the highest bid and the lowest offer, and publishes that information on the Nasdaq Workstation and through information vendors around the world. They call this the inside market, or best bid and offer (BBO).

In 1984 Nasdaq introduced the *Small Order Execution System* (SOES^{SM}). The SOES was designed to automatically execute small orders against the best quotations. The effect of SOES was to allow the public to enter orders ahead of computer trading programs, especially during times when markets were fast and congested. By 1994, Nasdaq surpassed the NYSE in trading volume, more than likely due to its access through electronic means. Note that 1994 was also the year that the Internet boom began, as web sites began to spring up everywhere.

When direct-access trading first became popular, the trading salons were fondly called "SOES houses," and the day traders who traded there were called "SOES bandits."

The recent merger of the Nasdaq with the Amex to form the Nasdaq-Amex heralds the beginning of great mergers and alliances yet to come. In a recent presentation at a National Press Club luncheon, Frank Zarb, chairman and CEO of the NASD presented his visions of a digital stock exchange. He spoke about Nasdaq extending its trading hours, extending its global alliances beyond Nasdaq-Japan, and alliances with the Hong Kong and Australian Stock Exchange. He also expressed interest in Nasdaq initiating a screen-based futures exchange, which could extend into international futures trading.

At the same time, in June of 1999, the Deutsche Mark futures pit at the CME closed—no more floor traders. It's happening, folks. Now is the time to prepare.

In the Nasdaq market, *there is no single specialist* through whom all orders flow. Instead, Nasdaq allows multiple market participants to trade stock through a sophisticated computer network that links buyers and sellers all around the world.

These market participants are divided into two groups: *market makers* and *electronic communications networks* (ECNs).

definitions:

market maker The Nasdaq member firms that use their own capital, research, retail, and/or systems resources to represent a stock and compete with each other to buy and sell the stocks they represent.

electronic communications network (ECN) Any electronic system that widely disseminates to third parties orders entered by an exchange market maker or OTC market maker, and permits such orders to be executed against in whole or in part.

The acronym ECN just means *electronic communications network.* Out of context, these three words together mean that a bunch of computers are sending and receiving messages electronically. In the context of day trading, however, an ECN is a brokerage firm that accepts electronic orders, checks for in-house matches, and then posts the bid or ask electronically in Nasdaq as an ECN quote. Because the posting comes from the ECN, the identity of the originating client is disguised. What you will see on the screen is the name of the ECN, not the name of the client.

Practically speaking, an ECN is an electronic brokerage that receives and transmits orders on behalf of clients and for its own accounts. There are more than 500 member firms that act as Nasdaq market makers. One of the major differences between the Nasdaq stock market and other major markets in the United States is Nasdaq's structure of *competing market makers*. Each market maker competes for customer order flow by displaying buy and sell quotations for a guaranteed number of shares. Once an order is received, the market maker will immediately purchase for or sell from its own inventory, or seek the other side of the trade until it is executed, often in a matter of seconds.

Specialists, on other exchanges, know all the orders in their book, because all orders for a particular stock come through the single specialist. Market makers are only aware of the cards in their hand, because there are other market makers competing for the same stock.

In addition to committing capital to buy and sell shares of a company's stock, many market maker firms offer a full range of other services to investors, including research reports, and advertising to seek buyers and sellers through retail and institutional networks.

linked ECNs

The Securities and Exchange Commission (SEC) makes a distinction between linked and nonlinked ECNs. A linked ECN displays its best prices in Nasdaq and allows subscribers to access those prices through the Nasdaq Workstation. A linked ECN displays its best prices and sizes along with its market maker identifier (MMID). Nasdaq appends a unique fifth-character identifier (#) to the right of the ECN's MMID to distinguish the quote from one displayed by a market maker.

The linked ECNs currently include Instinet (INCA), Island (ISLD), B-Trade (BTRD), Terra Nova (TNTO), Attain (ATTN), BRUT (BRUT), and Spear, Leeds and Kellogg (REDI).

SelectNet Broadcast is an ECN under the SEC's definition, but it is not a linked ECN. That means that SelectNet orders are not included in the Nasdaq quote montage and do not set the inside market. (The quote montage is the color-coded screen with the bids on one side and the asks on the other.)

fractions

One more thing, before you begin. You had better know your fractions. Sometimes, in the heat of the moment, your brain clutches and you can't even remember your name.

When you are looking at two columns of numbers that are flickering as they reflect rapid buying and selling of stocks, you will be faced with stress akin to that of a traffic controller. Keep the Maalox handy. Looking at Figure 1.10, you will see an example of fractions as they come onto the Level II screen. Quick, is $\frac{11}{16}$ bigger or smaller than $\frac{3}{4}$?

When you are speed-trading for sixteenths and eighths, you better know that $\frac{5}{8}$ is more than $\frac{9}{16}$ right off the top of your head! Table 1.1 is a table of fractions, both reduced and ordinary. (By reduced, I mean that $\frac{8}{16}$ is equivalent to $\frac{1}{2}$.)

On the monitors of the computer stations at All-Tech in New Jersey, I saw a device that I now have on my monitors, as well. You can make this device for yourself, or you can copy and enlarge it from Table 1.2 in this book. All you need is a strip of paper about 8 inches long and 1 inch high.

figure 1.10   fractions—Level II screen

Sym	COVD							
Q	66 5/8	H	68 1/8	L	63 5/8	T	65 1/8	N
TT		TI		TIV	2,207	TS	3800	V	1,060,400

	MMID	Bid	Size	Time		MMID	Ask	Size	Time
	REDI	64 1/4	1,000	07/16 15:45		BRUT	66	100	07/16 15:52
	BRUT	62	1,200	07/16 15:55		REDI	66 1/4	1,000	07/16 14:10
L	MSCO	64 7/8	500	07/16 16:10	L	NITE	65 1/8	200	07/16 16:10
L	NITE	64 7/8	200	07/16 16:10	L	INCA		300	07/16 16:10
L	MASH		200	07/16 16:10	L	MASH		100	07/16 16:10
L	BEST		100	07/16 16:10	L	SLKC		100	07/16 16:10
L	NFSC	64 3/8	100	07/16 16:10	L	USCT	65 5/8	1,000	07/16 16:10
L	HRZG	64 3/8	100	07/16 16:10	L	SHWD	65 11/16	300	07/16 16:10
L	GSCO	64 5/16	200	07/16 16:10	L	DBKS	65 3/4	100	07/16 16:10
L	SNDS	64	100	07/16 16:10	L	MSCO	65 13/16	500	07/16 16:10
L	SHWD	64	100	07/16 16:10	L	HRZG	66	1,500	07/16 16:10
L	MONT	63 3/4	500	07/16 16:10	L	NFSC	66	100	07/16 16:10
L	LEGG	63 11/16	100	07/16 16:10	L	FBCO	66	100	07/16 16:10
L	DBKS	63 5/8	100	07/16 16:10	L	JEFF	66 1/4	100	07/16 16:10
L	FBCO	63 1/2	100	07/16 16:10	L	GSCO	66 5/16	200	07/16 16:10

table 1.1   fractions—reduced and ordinary

Ordinary Fraction	Reduced Fraction	Decimal Equivalent
$\frac{1}{16}$		0.125
$\frac{2}{16}$	$\frac{1}{8}$	0.125
$\frac{3}{16}$		0.1875
$\frac{4}{16}$	$\frac{1}{4}$	0.250
$\frac{5}{16}$		0.3125
$\frac{6}{16}$	$\frac{3}{8}$	0.375
$\frac{7}{16}$		0.4375
$\frac{8}{16}$	$\frac{1}{2}$	0.5
$\frac{9}{16}$		0.5625
$\frac{10}{16}$	$\frac{5}{8}$	0.625
$\frac{11}{16}$		0.6875
$\frac{12}{16}$	$\frac{3}{4}$	0.75
$\frac{13}{16}$		0.8125
$\frac{14}{16}$	$\frac{7}{8}$	0.875
$\frac{15}{16}$		0.9375
$\frac{16}{16}$		1.0

table 1.2   order of fractions

1	1	3	1	5	3	7	1	9	5	11	3	13	7	15	1
16	8	16	4	16	8	16	2	16	8	16	4	18	8	16	

table 1.3   fractions per share

		200	500	600	800	1,000	1,500	2,000
$\frac{1}{32}$	.0313	6	16	19	25	31	47	63
$\frac{1}{16}$	.0625	13	31	38	50	63	94	125
$\frac{3}{32}$	.0938	19	47	56	75	94	141	188
$\frac{1}{8}$	.1250	25	63	75	100	125	188	250
$\frac{5}{32}$	.1563	31	78	94	125	156	234	313
$\frac{3}{16}$	.1875	38	94	113	150	188	281	375
$\frac{7}{32}$	.2188	44	109	131	175	219	328	438
$\frac{1}{4}$	.2500	50	125	150	200	250	375	500

(continued)

table 1.3   Continued

$\frac{9}{32}$	.2813	56	141	169	225	281	422	563
$\frac{5}{16}$	.3125	63	156	188	250	313	469	625
$\frac{11}{32}$	.3438	69	172	206	275	344	516	688
$\frac{3}{8}$	.3750	75	188	225	300	375	563	750
$\frac{13}{32}$	.4063	81	203	244	325	406	609	813
$\frac{7}{16}$	.4375	88	219	263	350	438	656	875
$\frac{15}{32}$	.4688	94	234	281	375	469	703	938
$\frac{1}{2}$	.5000	100	250	300	400	500	750	1,000
$\frac{17}{32}$	.5313	106	266	319	425	531	797	1,063
$\frac{9}{16}$	.5625	113	281	338	450	563	844	1,125
$\frac{19}{32}$	.5938	119	297	356	475	594	891	1,188
$\frac{5}{8}$	.6250	125	313	375	500	625	938	1,250
$\frac{21}{32}$	.6563	131	328	394	525	656	984	1,313
$\frac{11}{16}$	.6875	138	344	413	550	688	1,031	1,375
$\frac{23}{32}$	.7188	144	359	431	575	719	1,078	1,438
$\frac{3}{4}$	.7500	150	375	450	600	750	1,125	1,500
$\frac{25}{32}$	.7813	156	391	469	625	781	1,172	1,563
$\frac{13}{16}$	.8125	163	406	488	650	813	1,219	1,625
$\frac{27}{32}$	.8438	169	422	506	675	844	1,266	1,688
$\frac{7}{8}$	.8750	175	438	525	700	875	1,313	1,750
$\frac{29}{32}$	.9063	181	453	544	725	906	1,359	1,813
$\frac{15}{16}$	.9375	188	469	563	750	938	1,406	1,875
$\frac{31}{32}$	.9688	194	484	581	775	969	1,453	1,938

When the exchanges all become electronic, it will be easy to change from trading in sixteenths to trading in decimals. Presumably, trading in decimals will also add even more liquidity to the markets. Until that time, this little reminder device works well. If you want to get more information, keep this little crib sheet by your side. You can see what the fraction comes to when you trade from 200 to 2,000 shares at a time (Table 1.3).

chapter 2

getting started

A man must make his opportunity, as oft as find it.
—*Francis Bacon, 1561–1626*

Whether you are a long-term investor, a short-term trader, a day trader or a speed trader, there are certain basics you must know. Every carpenter, no matter how skilled and how master a craftsman, has a set of basic tools. This book is about the basic tools of speed trading, so as we move along, the information in subsequent chapters will be more specific to that area of specialty. For now, we need to cover some of the basics.

Before you can learn strategies for speed trading and strategies for trade execution, you need to memorize a few basic terms. At first, the terminology and buzz words of this industry will seem foreign to you, as they did at one time to us all. The only way to approach this issue is to memorize the words and know that, over time, they will become integrated in your neurology, and you will have embraced them as your own buzzwords.

history lesson

During the Crash of 1987, there was a lack of liquidity in the markets. Customers called their brokers frantically, only to be met with busy signals and unanswered phones. Nasdaq market makers, required to buy stocks for their own account when no buyers can be found, did not answer their phones. After the Crash, the Securities and Exchange Commission (SEC) implemented a regulation to protect the little guys, called the *Small Order Execution System.* Commonly referred to as the SOES, it was in place prior to the 1987 Crash but was not enforced. After the Crash, market makers who did not take SOES orders within 17 seconds were punished by being "SOESed out" for 20 days.

the Level II screen

As you sit in your chair, whether at home or at a day-trading salon, and view your computer monitor, you will be confronted with a barrage of information. The monitor screen you look at will look something like Figure 2.1. Unless you know how to interpret the information on the

figure 2.1   a Level II screen of Intel stock

Source: Quote.com QCharts. Reprinted with permission.

screen, it is just useless letters and numbers, albeit colorful. Most of the information that appears on the screen, commonly referred to as a *Level II screen,* relates to who is bidding and who is asking, what their price is, and how much they want.

who

On the left side of the screen you see bids, and on the right side you see asks. Before each bid or ask price you see a mnemonic that tells you who is presenting the bid or ask. There are three or four letters in each mnemonic that uniquely represent the market maker or electronic communications network (ECN) from whom the bid or ask came. This mnemonic is called the market maker identifier (MMID).

The mnemonic for the market maker or ECN is in the left column of the bid montage and in the left column of the ask montage. Notice in the enlargement in Figure 2.2, you can see the MMIDs on the ask side of the screen. In the top row we see ISLD, followed by NITE, REDI, NFSC, MWSE, INCA, and so on. The mnemonic ISLD stands for Island, Datek's ECN. Likewise, NITE stands for Knight Securities, Inc.; REDI stands for Spear, Leeds and Kellogg; and so it goes. As you become accustomed to seeing the Level II screens and watching the MMIDs change instantaneously, you will begin to develop a feel for who trades and how.

figure 2.2   another Level II screen

Source: Quote.com QCharts. Reprinted with permission.

There are, at present, only a few ECNs, so we can list them all later in this chapter. There are over 500 market makers, however, so we will list only the top, most active ones.

what

Each Level II screen will be displaying the montage for a single stock. In Figure 2.1, the stock being quoted is INTC. In Figure 2.2, the stock being quoted is SEEK. The montage will show all the competing players for a single stock.

To view quotes on a second stock, you would open a second screen. You might have several screens open, watching several stocks at a time. Doing so can become confusing. As in all types of trading, I suggest you specialize. Find a few stocks that are active and move well, and take profits on these few regularly. The human mind can only follow seven things at a time.

Figure 2.3 shows a screen with multiple Level II screens on it. This is what your computer monitor would look like if you were following multiple stocks.

how much

The color bands or background colors behind the Level II data change to highlight the best bid and ask quotes. *Yellow* signifies the highest bid or lowest ask quote (inside market); *green* signifies the next best quote (first outer); *dark blue* signifies the second best quote (second outer); *light blue* signifies the third best quote (third outer); *red* signifies the fourth best quote (fourth outer).

Most speed-trading software allows you to change these colors to your own preference. I would suggest staying with the defaults, so that when you look at anyone else's screen you will be instantly familiar with what you see (Figure 2.4).

Within each band of color, you will see the bid and ask prices— bids on the left of the montage and asks on the right. The color coding facilitates your instant recognition of how much the negotiators are willing to pay.

Nasdaq Levels I, II, and III

We keep talking about Level II screens, without having defined what Level II is. Let's get to that detail now.

A *Level I screen* is a snapshot of time, price, bid, and ask, along with the size of the bid and ask. Although the screen shows real-time information, it shows only the current inside market and size. That is, you get

figure 2.3 multiple Level II screens

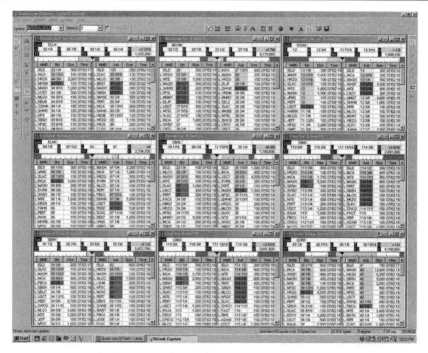

Source: Quote.com QCharts. Reprinted with permission.

figure 2.4 color preferencing for Level II screens

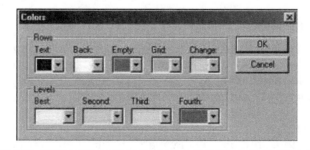

figure 2.5   Level I information

Title	Symbol	Net	Volume	Bid	Ask	Bid Size	Ask Size	B Bid	B Ask
Allegheny Teledyne	ALT	unch	104,500	22 3/4	23	100	1000	22 7/8	23
Alcoa Inc	AA	-1 1/2	1,081,200	62 1/16	62 1/2	100	5000	62 1/8	62 1/2
American Electric Po AEP	+ 5/16	575,900	36 9/16	36 5/8	2500	100	36 9/16	36 5/8
Amer Express	AXP	-1 7/8	248,700	137 1/16	137 7/16	100	100	137 1/8	137 3/8
Amern General Corp	AGC	+ 1/8	211,200	78 1/2	78 5/8	2000	1200	78 1/2	78 5/8
American Intl Group	AIG	-3/4	308,100	120 11/16	120 7/8	1000	2500	120 11/16	120 7/8
Ameritech Corp	AIT	+1 1/16	386,800	71 7/8	72 1/4	100	2500	72 1/16	72 1/4
Autonation Inc	AN	-1/4	123,200	16 3/8	16 1/2	100	200	16 3/8	16 7/16
At&T Corp	T	+ 13/16	1,950,800	57 3/8	57 7/16	7500	1100	57 3/8	57 7/16
Atlantic Richfield	ARC	-1 1/8	189,200	86 1/8	86 1/4	700	3000	86 1/8	86 1/4
Avon Products	AVP	+ 1/8	178,500	55 15/16	56 1/8	3100	5000	55 15/16	56 1/8
Baker Hughes Inc	BHI	-1/16	300,100	33 1/16	33 1/4	100	100000	33 1/8	33 1/4
Bank Of America Cor BAC	-3/16	853,100	74 15/16	75 1/8	2400	100	74 15/16	75
Baxter International	BAX	+ 1/4	270,700	58 7/8	59	2000	500	58 7/8	59
Bell Atlantic Corp	BEL	unch	574,700	62	62 1/4	300	100	62	62 1/16
Bethlehem Steel Corp BS	109,900	7 9/16	7 5/8	13500	28000	7 9/16	7 5/8
Black & Decker Corp	BDK	-1 1/16	200,600	61 5/16	61 3/8	700	11300	61 5/16	61 3/8
Boeing Co	BA	-7/8	466,500	42 7/16	42 1/2	2500	24000	42 7/16	42 1/2
Boise Cascade	BCC	+ 1/8	103,100	44 7/8	45	100	6000	44 15/16	45

to see the best bid and best ask, along with their size, but you don't know what else is behind it. Your retail broker looks at a Level I screen when he sells you Nasdaq stock. A Level I screen might look like Figure 2.5.

The *Level II screen* allows you to see the depth of the bid and ask prices. In addition to seeing the current inside market, you can view a list of bids and asks waiting in the queue. A Level II screen shows you the depth of information, but only on a single stock. Retail traders can use the Level II screen to see support and resistance levels to a stock's price (Figure 2.6).

Level III service is for National Association of Securities Dealers (NASD) member firms acting as market makers. A Level III screen includes all the features of the Level II screen, plus it allows the market maker to enter quotations, direct or execute orders, and send information.

ECNs

An ECN is a private communications network allowing the public investor to broadcast prices on the Nasdaq. This gives the ability to bypass market makers and, thus, to buy and sell directly with other traders. Electronic communications networks do not accept SOES orders.

The benefits of using an ECN have been traditionally bestowed upon institutions, but are now available to individuals trading at home and at day-trading salons. These benefits include:

- Avoiding spreads when trading directly with other customers
- Trading after hours
- Representing trades in the markets "just like the big boys"
- Maintaining anonymity
- Trading without revealing how much you have left

As an individual, you will go through a brokerage firm that acts as an intermediary, to get to an ECN. When you trade at a day-trading salon or subscribe to direct-access services, like Quote.com, AB Watley, or Attain, you pay them to act as your intermediary broker.

Archipelago (ARCA or ARCHIP) is an ECN that acts as a finder to seek the best method of execution, whether it is a market maker or another ECN. There is a fee associated with each ECN's execution of your order. The fee may be different for the various ECNs. Find out the details about preferencing and using Archipelago from your broker.

Table 2.1 lists the most active ECNs that the Archipelago will send you to.

figure 2.6 Level II information

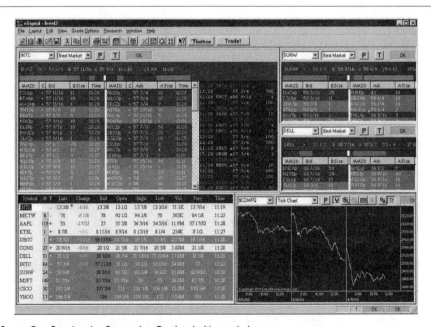

Source: Data Broadcasting Corporation. Reprinted with permission.

table 2.1 ECNs	
ECN	Mnemonic
All-Tech Investment Group	ATTN
Bloomberg Trade Book	BTRD
Brass Utility LLC	BRUT
Instinet	INCA
Island (Datek)	ISLD
Next Trade	NXTD
NexTrend	TRND
Spear, Leeds and Kellogg	REDI
Terranova Trading LLC	TNTO

In Appendix A, you will find a comprehensive listing of ECNs, with their addresses and contact information. There, also, is a description of their services. For now, just know that an ECN is your portal into direct-access trading with other traders, and with market makers.

market makers

Market makers are the firms, usually brokerage firms, that trade for their own accounts and place customer orders. They compete against each other, and they compete against you. Market makers also place your orders in the market. They use their own capital to buy and maintain an inventory in a company's stock. When a market maker receives an investor's order to buy shares in a particular stock, it sells those shares to the customer from its existing inventory. If necessary, it will buy enough shares from other market makers to complete the sale.

There are more than 500 market makers. In Appendix D is a list of the most active market makers—the ones you are most likely to encounter. As you become accustomed to seeing the names (mnemonics) flit up and down on your Level II screen, you will develop a feel for who the big traders are and how they trade.

SuperDOT

The acronym DOT stands for *direct order turnaround*. The SuperDOT system is the New York Stock Exchange's answer to Nasdaq's Level II. SuperDOT is an order delivery mechanism. It electronically links member firms directly to a stock's specialist on the floor of the exchange.

The specialist can fill the orders from his own inventory, manually pair up orders, or place the order on his limit order book.

SuperDOT gives individual investor orders of less than 2,100 shares priority over all larger institutional orders. Direct-access brokerage firms provide the SuperDOT mechanism for their customers to access non-Nasdaq stocks.

Although SuperDOT is electronic and fast, it is not direct access. It is still just a method of communicating with the exchange floor. Hopefully, in the near future, electronic direct access to the NYSE computers will be available, bypassing the specialists on the floor and going directly to other traders, like Nasdaq.

the book

An electronic ledger is kept for all trading transactions. This ledger matches all buys with all sells, and it is commonly called *the book*. There are lots of books: the Archipelago book, the Island book, the National book, and so forth. Each specialist has his limit order book. So, when you hear someone refer to "the book," just know that it is their own electronic ledger.

software

Software for online and direct-access trading comes in two flavors: *order entry* and *analysis*. Most of the software specific to this relatively new field is for order entry. The analysis software that is available is, for the most part, not yet tailored to speed trading. Most analysis software is still for day trading and longer-term applications.

Each day-trading salon will either have its own order-entry software for you to use, or will have software that interfaces with RealTick III, and thus to the ECNs. If you opt to trade at home, rather than going to one of the salons each morning, there is software they will license to you for that purpose.

You will want your broker to train you in the use of the order-entry software they provide. Essentially, the software will be like a Level II screen with capabilities for you to click on a price, or press a key on your keyboard, and have the order instantly executed. Most day-trading salons also offer training seminars, often lasting a week or more, that not only educate you about the use of their software, but about specific day-trading techniques. It is the goal of these seminars to make you a successful day trader. They want to keep you coming back.

As for analysis software, that is a topic about which I could write another book. In Chapter 5, "Analyzing Your Data," I devote a section to software that will assist you in creating and analyzing trading methodologies.

opening your account

Setting up an electronic trading account is no different from setting up a traditional trading account. You fill out a bunch of forms, sign away all your rights, sometimes get a notary to verify that you are you, and send the forms to the broker. Even though you will be opening an electronic account, there is still no such thing as an electronic signature. Each brokerage, whether direct-access or online, will have its own set of forms for you. You can either request the forms online at their web site (Figure 2.7), or you can call them on the phone.

Once your forms have been received by the brokerage firm, they will set up an account for you and mail you the account number and any associated documents. If you sent them money with the account forms, you are ready to go; if not, you will need to send them money now. After the brokerage firm has received your money and it has cleared the banks, they will let you begin trading.

time frame

Your time frame, as a day trader, could be just about anything, as long as you close your trades before the end of the day. If you hold your positions overnight, you are no longer considered a day trader—you become a position trader.

Whether you consider yourself a speed trader, staying in trades for only a few minutes at a time, or a short-term day trader, using 1-, 5-, or 15-minute data, you should assess the rhythm of the market you intend to trade before you lock in on a time frame.

Any research you do should incorporate Potential Hourly Wage (PHW) analysis, before you settle on a style or a time frame. In *Trading 101—How to Trade Like a Pro,* I describe PHW in depth. If you want to know more about the technique, you should read it there. If you would like just a quick overview of PHW, keep reading—it's in Chapter 8, "Developing Your Own Approach."

execution style

Execution styles and strategies are very personal. I have met and talked with well over a thousand traders, and found that no one of them trades like any other one.

figure 2.7 requesting forms from InvestIN Brokerage

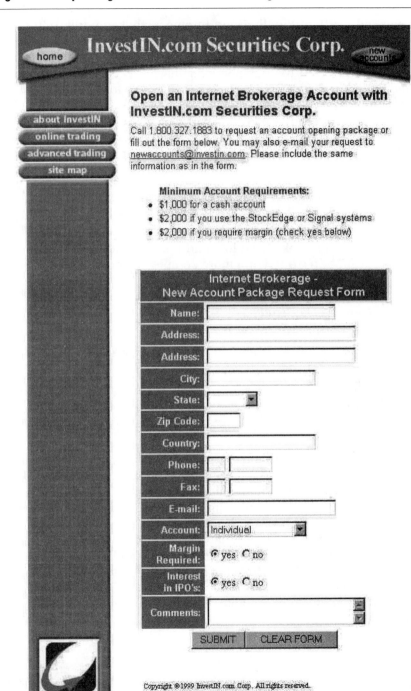

I would caution you, first and foremost, that the only thing that matters, ultimately, about your strategy is whether it makes money. How can you know that it makes money? By thorough testing with programs that allow you to back-test over historical data. *Trading 102— Getting Down to Business* is devoted to techniques for creating, testing, and analyzing your strategies.

There are several books that you can buy if you want to know more about canned strategies. Each of these books covers techniques, systems, and strategies that you might want to investigate. Please remember, however, that any technique has its winning and losing phases. Before you trade any system, you must test, test, and test again. You must know the system's statistics backward and forward. Then, paper-trade first, to see that what you told the computer is what you thought you told the computer.

The following books have lots and lots of trading strategies that you might want to try out. For a more complete list of books related to day trading, consult the Bibliography.

• *High-Impact Day Trading*	Robert M. Barnes
• *The Compleat Day Trader II*	Jake Bernstein
• *The Electronic Day Trader*	Marc Friedfertig
• *How to Get Started in Electronic Day Trading*	David Nassar
• *Electronic Trading TNT*	Joe Ross and Mark Cherlin
• *Stock Patterns for Day Trading*	Barry Rudd

Throughout the other books on speed trading, I have come across one technique that seems to be universal. Speed traders are in this business for a fast buck. Minutes can seem like an eternity. The technique is to enter your exit order immediately after your entry order. When looking for a 16th or an 8th, it can happen in a flash that you don't even see. If you buy 1,000 shares at 30 and immediately enter an order to sell them at 30⅛, you might get that order filled in seconds. On 1,000 shares, that's $125 in the blink of an eye. The speed trader's goal is to do that 30 times a day.

What happens if you are able to do that 30 times a day? Did you run that calculation yet?

$$30 \times \$125 = \$3,750$$

That's pretty close to the ultimate goal. For me, the ultimate goal is $1 million a year. I would consider that a decent return for a trader. If you

table 2.2 achievable steps

No. of Trades	Dollars per Trade	Net per Day
30	$135	$4,050
20	$200	$4,000
10	$400	$4,000
5	$800	$4,000
4	$1,000	$4,000
2	$2,000	$4,000
1	$4,000	$4,000

don't set a goal, you will never achieve it. For a goal to be attainable, it must be broken down into achievable steps. There are approximately 250 trading days in a year. One million dollars a year is then $4,000 per day. You could make a table for yourself, showing several ways to achieve your goal—it could like Table 2.2.

Remember, in your calculations, that you have to pay fees: brokerage fees, exchange fees, ECN fees, Island fees, and Archipelago fees all have to be taken out of the dollars-per-trade figure before you run your calculations.

Also, you must remember that you will not be a winner each and every day that you trade. Some days will be losing days. That's just the way this business is. Therefore, to have an average of $4,000 per day net, you must make more on your winning days to cover for the losses on your losing days. How much? It depends on your ratio of winning trades to losing trades. The sections on software and evaluating your performance will tell you more about this topic.

order types and terminology

On your trading screen you will see selection boxes, pull-down menus, or radio buttons indicating the types of orders your broker will accept. Figure 2.8 is a fairly typical online order-entry screen. Other typical direct-access order screens are shown in Figure 2.9 (*a* and *b*).

You will notice several things from these screens. Initially, you might be overwhelmed by the amount of information popping out at you, but if we look at it one piece at a time it will become familiar.

The first decision you must make is *what* stock you want to buy or sell. You will either enter the stock symbol manually, or it will be

figure 2.8   an online order screen

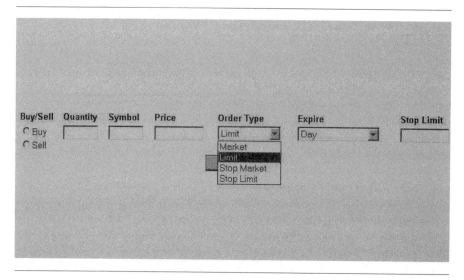

entered for you by the software. The box on the form will be labeled "Symbol" or "Stock Symbol." It is typically the third box on the form because of the way brokers are accustomed to placing and receiving orders, but it is the first part of your decision tree. If you don't know the symbol for the stock you are interested in, there are symbol lookup capabilities at most brokers' web sites. If you can't find one right away, go to the first page of The Money Mentor, at www.moneymentor.com.

Next, you must decide whether you want to *buy* or to *sell* the stock. This is usually in the first box on the form, and is sometimes represented as *B* or *S* in shorthand.

How many is the next question you will answer. Often, in trading salons, you may preset a default of 1,000, 500, or 100 in this box. The box is typically marked "shares" or "quantity."

Order type is probably the most confusing part of the order form to most new traders. The order types accepted by most brokerage firms are as follows: market, market on close, limit, stop, stop market, stop limit, market if touched, open range only, closing range only, and order cancels order. Not all of these order types are accepted by all brokers. Furthermore, not all of these order types are accepted by Nasdaq or Level II brokers. Check with your broker as to the validity of any order types. Following is an explanation of the more common order types:

figure 2.9 direct-access order screens (a and b)

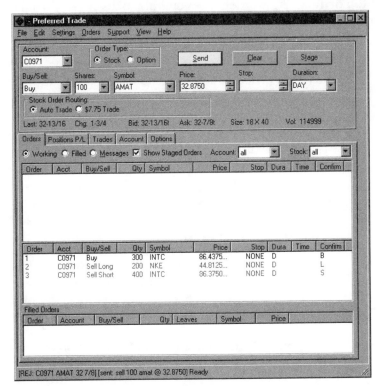

(a)

(b)

Source: Preferred Trade. Reprinted with permission.

Market. A market order instructs the broker to buy or sell stock for you right away at the best price available in the current market. When you enter a buy market order, you want to purchase the stock for the best sell price in the market—the ask. Likewise, by entering a sell market order, you are indicating that you want to the sell the stock for the best buy price in the market—the bid. If a stock's price is moving rapidly, a market order can be filled at a significantly different price than the quote that was indicated upon entry.

Limit. A limit order sets a price limit beyond which you do not want to place the trade. A buy limit order sets an upper limit price, above which you do not want to buy the shares. Similarly, a sell limit order sets a lower limit, below which you do not want to sell. By using a limit order, you eliminate the risk of an unwanted transaction price, but you take a chance that, because there might not be buyers or sellers at your limit price, you will not get an execution. The order can only be executed if the market reaches or betters that price.

Stop orders. Stop orders are generally placed away from the current price on a stock, and are only activated if and when the stock trades at, or trades through, the stop price.

- **Sell stop** orders are entered below the current price.
- **Buy stop** orders are entered above the current price.
- **Stop market** orders specify an activation price. When the stock trades at, or trades through, the activation price, the stop order converts to a market order and is executed at the best available price as soon thereafter as possible. There is no assurance that the execution price will be equal to, or even near, the stop price.
- **Stop limit** orders specify two prices: the activation price and the limit price. When the stock trades at the activation price, or trades through it, the order converts to a limit order and is executed at the limit (or better, if available). There is no assurance that the limit order will be executable because a stock might very well penetrate the stop and the limit, in which case the risk of not being filled arises, just as with a regular limit order.

Possibly, the easiest question to answer is *duration* or *order expiration*. For how long do you want this order to be presented? Usually the last box in the group, duration determines whether your order expires at the end of the day or continues into the next day. Following is a list of the types of order expiration:

Day order

- *9:30 A.M. to 4:00 P.M. EST business days.* Order participates in the current normal trading session. Will not participate in after-hours trading sessions.
- *4:00 P.M. to 5:15 P.M. EST business days.* Order participates in the next normal trading session only. Will not participate in the current after-hours session.
- *After 5:15 P.M. and before 9:30 A.M. business days and all day Saturday/Sunday.* Order participates in the next normal trading session only. Will not participate in after-hours sessions.

GTC (good 'til canceled)

- *9:30 A.M. to 4:00 P.M. EST business days.* Order participates in that day's normal trading session, plus subsequent normal trading sessions. No after-hours participation.
- *4:00 P.M. to 5:15 P.M. EST business days.* Order participates in next normal trading session, plus subsequent normal trading sessions. No after-hours participation.
- *After 5:15 P.M. and before 9:30 A.M. business days and all day Saturday/Sunday.* Order participates in the next normal trading session, plus subsequent normal trading sessions. No after-hours participation.

Day + after-hours

- *9:30 A.M. to 4:00 P.M. EST business days.* Order participates in the current normal trading session, and will also participate in that day's after-hours session.
- *4:00 P.M. to 5:15 P.M. EST business days.* Order participates in the current after-hours session only.
- *After 5:15 P.M. and before 9:30 A.M. business days and all day Saturday/Sunday.* Order participates in the next normal trading session, plus the subsequent after-hours session.

GTC + after-hours

- *9:30 A.M. to 4:00 P.M. EST business days.* Order participates in the current trading session, plus subsequent normal and after-hours sessions.

- *4:00 P.M. to 5:15 P.M. EST business days.* Order participates in the current after-hours session, plus subsequent normal and after-hours sessions.
- *After 5:15 P.M. and before 9:30 A.M. business days and all day Saturday/Sunday.* Order participates in the current trading session, plus subsequent normal and after-hours trading sessions.

chapter 3

theories and strategies

Life is too short to learn German.

—*T. L. Peacock*

Keep it simple! If the goal of trading is to make money, and if a simple strategy is available that makes money, why not use it? Too many people in this business are convinced that they must create their own unique strategy to be successful. Wrong! Use one that works and get to it.

If you invest the time and the money to taking a day-trading class from one of the day-trading salons, or one of the educators (listed in Appendix F), you will get some of the best trading tips available. Furthermore, you will learn some of the latest and most consistently successful trading strategies. Take the time to invest the $3,000 to $5,000 and the several weeks it takes to go through the hands-on training. It is well worth it. Education is not expensive; lack of education is.

Having learned some of their strategies, use them. You will learn specific tricks, peculiar to speed traders, which will steadily turn profits. Don't worry that these strategies are not invented by you. Your goal is not to outsmart the market, but to take home money.

fundamental analysis

Fundamental analysis is the analytical method by which only the sales, earnings, and the value of a given tradable's assets may be considered.

definition:

> **fundamental analysis**   The theory that holds that stock market activity may be predicted by looking at the relative data and statistics of a stock as well as the management of the company in question and its earnings.

Fundamental analysis relies on the study of reports to predict price trends; it addresses what a stock *should* sell for. In trading stocks, for instance, fundamental analysts rely on quarterly earnings reports; they look at reports about the company's products and personnel; and they study reports about that sector of the economy and that industry in general.

To my mind, these are all just reports generated by humans striving to create a picture that satisfies their boss, or the board of directors, or their stockholders. I've been on boards of directors. I know what happens in those meetings. That's why I rely strictly on technical analysis.

Quoting from Steven B. Achelis in *Technical Analysis from A to Z:*

> If we were all totally logical and could separate our emotions from our investment decisions, then fundamental analysis, the determination of price based on futures earnings, would work magnificently. And since we would all have the same completely logical expectations, prices would change only when quarterly reports or relevant news was released.

That said, the line between technical and fundamental analysis is becoming thinner. With fundamental facts available in data format through data providers, we can now analyze most of the fundamental data on a technical basis. Still, I would not rely on boardroom numbers for analysis. There are, however, some numbers that are statistics, not opinion, such as number of shares outstanding, percent owned by institutions, beta, float, dividend, and earning per share growth rate. These numbers are now available through datafeeds like Quote.com, and they can be used as technical indicators.

Fundamental analysis may well constitute part of your background research on which stocks to trade, but during a speed-trading session, believe me, you will not have time to pay attention to anything but price.

sources of fundamental data

For your evening activity, get accustomed to obsessing about trading research. For the first few years, you will think of little else but trading. Part of your research activity may well be spent reading about companies or sectors. You might do your research through traditional paper vehicles, you might use the Internet, or you might use software.

Investor's Business Daily (IBD) frequently runs a section called "Investor's NewsWire." Although this section is actually advertorial in nature, it is devoted to corporate announcements. In section A, *IBD* supplies "Earnings News," "New Issues," and psychological data. Section B of *IBD* covers "The Economy," and it includes reports on economic data and corporate news. To order a free two-week trial of *IBD,* come to The Money Mentor: www.moneymentor.com

The Value Line Investment Survey is still available in the traditional binder format, at a minimal annual cost. *Value Line* updates you weekly with their printed charts and fundamental information, as well as their ratings of stocks and industry reviews. The selected *Value Line* portfolio always seems to outperform the market, and they still provide their views on the economy and projections for one-, three-, and five-year time frames.

In addition to the traditional print medium, *Value Line* offers Windows-based software with capabilities for viewing, sorting, screening, graphing, and preparing reports on individual equities. The *Value Line* CD includes a host of fundamental information on each of the stocks in their universe. At their web site, you can download a demo of the software: www.valueline.com

Software products like Quote.com's QCharts and Omega Research's TradeStation now collect and analyze fundamental data. You can import and export data from their datafeeds and from Omega's HistoryBank.com.

There are thousands of web sites that can connect you with all the fundamental data you could ever need. I would suggest several places for you to start:

The Money Mentor	www.moneymentor.com ⏐ Economy
ABC News	www.abcnews.com
Boston Globe	www.boston.com/globe/
C-Span	www.c-span.org
CBS Market Watch	cbs.marketwatch.com
CNN	www.cnn.com
CNNfn Industry Watch	www.cnnfn.com
Edgar	www.edgar-online.com
Financial Times	www.ft.com
Fox News	www.foxnews.com
Hoover's Online	www.hoovers.com
Investment Company Institute	www.ici.org
IPO Central	www.ipocentral.com
Market Central	www.mktctl.com
MSNBC Headlines	www.msnbc.com

Nando Times	www.nando.net
New York Times	www.nytimes.com
Nightly Business Report	www.nbr.com
Quote.com	www.quote.com
USA Today	www.usatoday.com
VectorVest	www.vectorvest.com
Washington Post	www.washingtonpost.com
Zacks Investment Research	www.zacks.com

technical analysis

Technical analysis is the study of prices. Technical analysts study supply and demand for securities and commodities based on trading price and, sometimes, volume. Using charts and modeling techniques, technicians attempt to identify price trends in a market.

My research leads me to believe that all the information I'll ever need is in price. The price of the underlying instrument already reflects opinion, rumor, volume, volatility, news, and fundamentals, before it ever gets to my computer screen. Everything "the big boys" know about a stock, using all their computers and research teams, is already in price before I see it.

If the big boys are buying, I want to be a buyer; if the big boys are selling, I want to be a seller. It's that simple. On a much shorter time frame, you will find yourself doing this with the market makers. They will be the big boys in the speed-trading arena.

Generally, technical analysts use charts of price to learn about price behavior and price patterns, but this is not always so. Some great technical analysts never look at a chart, but rather do their analysis on the numbers alone.

Consider the following list of closing prices for COVD:

64.375, 65.125, 65, 65.75, 66.375, 66, 66.0625, 66.5, 66.9375, 67, 67.75, 67.25, 67.5, 66.875, 67.375, 68.125, 68.75, 67.5, 67.25, 65.625, 66.125, 66.5, 66, 66.5625, 68.0625, 68, 68.375, 67.5, 66.5, 65.875, 66.5625, 67.5, 66.25, 66, 65, 64.6875, 65.1875, 64.8125, 64.5, 64.5, 64.375, 64.75, 65.375, 65.75, 65.6875, 65.75, 65.125.

Do you see anything? I don't.

How about that old adage "A chart is worth a thousand numbers"? Look at Figure 3.1. Now, do you see anything? The number sequence from the preceding list of COVD closing prices is found in the center of the chart. Now, I can see several things: an uptrend, a possible head-

figure 3.1   same data, showing head-and-shoulders pattern

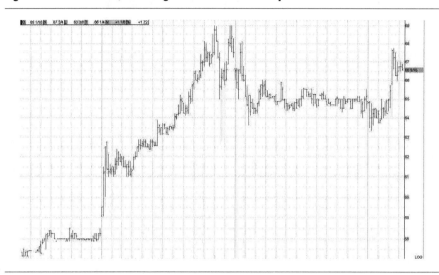

and-shoulders pattern, a downtrend, a range, and a bounce. Whether you chart by hand or using a computer, technical analysis is easier with a picture.

The chart in Figure 3.1 is of five-minute data. You can use technical analysis on any time frame. A chart, is a chart, is a chart.

Market technicians use specific chart formations to identify potential future moves. Classic chart patterns include head-and-shoulders, triangles, flags, pennants, gaps, reversals, support-and-resistance, cup-and-handle, and more. To really know the market, you should be able to readily identify these patterns as they occur. My favorite book on technical analysis is by John Murphy, *Technical Analysis of the Futures Markets.* Ignore the title of this book; it is not just about futures. For a truly intense look at technical analysis, *Trading Systems and Methods* by Perry Kaufman is my favorite book. In addition to the book, the formulas and techniques from Kaufman's book are available on a CD-ROM, for those who use computers to analyze the markets. The CD-ROM is available through The Money Mentor and through financial book vendors.

With what frequency and reliability classic chart patterns foretell future market moves is yet to be determined. Calculating the statistics in a comprehensive and cohesive way is a boring and gargantuan endeavor, not yet undertaken by anyone. Just such an endeavor is what

I propose to undertake for my PhD dissertation. Maybe someday we will know how often the classic chart patterns work.

pattern recognition

Pattern recognition is a study of how current prices (open, high, low, and close) relate to prices of immediately previous bars. For instance, you may have heard of The Ross Hook, the 1-2-3 high, the 1-2-3 low, pivot points, or the works of Larry Williams. All of these techniques involve pattern recognition. Proponents of this work believe that certain patterns set up future, predictable moves. The best books to begin your research into pattern recognition methods would be:

- *The Definitive Guide to Futures Trading,* Larry Williams
- *Stock Patterns for Day Trading,* Barry Rudd
- *Electronic Trading TNT I–IV,* Joe Ross and Mark Cherlin

As with any and all methodologies, test before trying!

Speaking of testing, in the area of pattern recognition, there is one program that no one else can hold a candle to: Pattern Smasher by Kasanjian Research. To be reviewed in an upcoming issue of *Traders' Catalog & Resource Guide,* this software allows you to define patterns in bar charts and then search the entire market for stocks that meet the criterion. In addition, the program comes with a set of predefined patterns for you to use, and has the most well-done manual I have ever seen from any software vendor. The program is elegant, sophisticated, and easy to use! If this one interests you, call Ed Kasanjian in Blue Jay, California, at 1-909-337-0816, or e-mail to support@kasanjianresearch.com.

strategies

The combination of techniques from fundamental and technical analysis, along with the recognition of very short-term bar patterns, will put you way ahead of the crowd. Learn how to do something well, and then do it over and over again. Don't worry about fancy techniques. Just remember what your goal is and how many trades at what profit level you need to reach your goal.

Just briefly, Table 3.1 lists other goals to which you might aspire. How many trades per day, at what profit level, do you need to reach your goal?

table 3.1   setting goals

Annual Income	Daily Income
$750,000	$3,000
$500,000	$2,000
$250,000	$1,000

You cannot watch everything. You probably can't keep an eye on more than between 5 and 10 stocks. Even that many will be difficult, if you are actually trading them. Some of the day-trading techniques I have come across are:

- Trade only the Dow Jones 30 Industrials.
- Trade only Nasdaq stocks.
- Trade only the Internet stocks in the ISNET index.
- Eliminate stocks that already moved if you are trading for 8ths or 16ths.
- Trade only stocks that already moved.
- Look for a wide bid-ask spread.
- Look for the biggest point movers.

Again, test before trying! When you go to day-trading school (whether through a day-trading salon or an independent educator), they will show you any number of techniques for capturing small profits repeatedly. I don't know whether they work consistently, and neither do you. The only way you will know is if you back-test these strategies over historical data, and even then you will not know what the future will bring.

Why test, then? Because it is the best you can do. In *Trading 102—Getting Down to Business,* I cover testing procedures at length. Chapter 3 of that book is about the design and testing of mechanical trading systems; Chapter 10 is about back-testing and optimizing your system.

time frames

The time frame in which you trade will be determined by several factors. First and foremost, what's your day job? How do you support yourself while you are learning to be a successful trader? If you are retired and independently wealthy, you can trade in any time frame you like; if you work from 9 to 5, then you should not consider electronic day trading at this time. Day trading, and especially speed trading, means you need to be sitting in front of your computer every minute from the time the market opens until the time it closes.

Second, what is your nature? Are you an adrenaline junkie who drinks lots of coffee and can't wait for the next challenge, or are you mellow and prefer a life of relaxation and no hassles? If you prefer a life of relaxation, you won't find it in a day-trading atmosphere.

Next, you must consider the nature of the market you want to trade. Each market has its own rhythm. Some markets ask to be traded intraday, and often, some reveal only a few good trades each year. Pick your markets carefully and match them to your personality.

long-term versus short-term

Beginning traders often want to know just exactly how many days or months constitute *long-term*. To me, these words are both relative. Long-term, in my personal trading, is about three days. If I hold a position that long, it is approaching a record-length trade under my system. Yet, if I were a bond trader and made trades weekly instead of hourly, long-term would be a matter of weeks or months. In real estate ventures, what's long-term? Years. For a speed trader, long-term means an hour.

day trading

Real-time data is data you receive while it's happening. If you want to be a day trader, or a speed trader, real-time data is mandatory. The trades you place will sometimes only be minutes in duration.

The only delay you should experience with a real-time datafeed is the amount of time it takes to transmit to and from the satellite—just a few seconds. Of course, this is in an ideal world.

In the real world, you will experience delays. Computers will be down; networks will crash; the backbone of the Internet will be unavailable; lightning will strike. Be prepared. Even the most fail-safe, redundant computer systems will fail from time to time.

One of the hazards of doing business this way is the technology. Has your car ever failed you? Before you stake your life's savings and all your investment strategies on speed trading, have backup systems in mind for times when the technology hiccups. I do much of my trading over the Internet. For times when the access to my broker is down, for whatever reason, I asked for backdoor entrances to my trading account. They were kind enough to give me eight separate ways to get through. Then, in case all else failed, they gave me a phone number with which I should be able to reach a broker. Luckily for me, I have never had to use any of these.

As a business-planning tool, I always examine the worst case. What if all the backdoors failed, and I couldn't get to my broker on the phone? It could happen. I would need to know beforehand just how bad the exposure to the market would be and how much I could afford to lose. Part of your risk planning must be to assume that the worst can happen, more than once. Make sure that you are not overtrading, so that at any given moment you could afford to lose everything you have in the market.

speed trading

Speed trading is scalping. It is much like arbitrage.

definition:

arbitrage A financial transaction where an arbitrageur (arb) simultaneously purchases in one market and sells in another where there is a slight price differential. Often, it is a full hedge, and therefore, a risk-free transaction. Arbs play an important role in keeping markets liquid and efficient.

scalp To trade quickly for small gains.

Speed traders attempt to catch 16ths and 8ths as a stock moves up or down. Enough of those in a day, in large enough volume, will eventually net you lots of bucks—or, at least, that's the goal.

holding overnight

Holding a trade overnight (fondly referred to as *taking a trade home*) eliminates you from the strict classification of day trader. Day traders can sleep at night. Day traders have no positions open at the end of each day. Position traders worry the night away (Figure 3.2).

Nevertheless, there will be times when you will take a trade home. You may find yourself wishing and hoping, sitting on a small loss you are unwilling to take, or sitting on a large gain you hope will become larger. You may even be rethinking your philosophy about the frequency and rapidity with which you should be trading.

I would caution you to avoid the wishing and hoping. Stick with your rules. The only event that should cause you to abandon your rules is to replace them with new rules that have been thoroughly tested and proven to be better.

momentum

Traditionally, momentum is a gauge of price activity as compared with price a defined length of time ago. For instance, technicians often talk about the 10-day momentum of a stock. That means they are compar-

---

figure 3.2   day traders at work

---

ing the price today with the price 10 days ago. The formula for calculating momentum would be:

$$M = C - C_{10}$$

where

C is the closing price of today, and C_{10} is the closing price of 10 days ago.

In computer programs, you cannot use a subscript as written in this text, so programmers developed a shorthand notation to mean the same thing. Not all programmers think exactly alike, and there is no standard notation, so you will see a variety of representations:

- C[0] – C[10]
- C – C10
- C – Ref(C,–10)

all meaning the same thing.

Momentum, in physics, means mass times velocity, or the impetus of a moving object. Thus follows the axiom that things moving tend to keep moving, and things not moving tend to stay not moving. Physicists and engineers say it a little differently than that, but that's what it means.

In speed trading, we look for the upside momentum of ECNs and market makers moving their bids or offers higher. Conversely, downside momentum is reflected in ECNs and market makers moving their bids or offers lower.

Speed traders like to use jargon that rolls off the tongue as fast as the trades roll off their fingertips. Some of the terms you will hear and begin to use are defined below, using MMID to mean both market maker and ECN. The following terms often indicate upside momentum:

definitions:

ask to bid   The MMID was willing to sell at the current offer, but is now willing to buy on the bid.

high bid   Improving the highest price willing to be paid for the stock. This movement changes the inside market price.

joins bid   Improving the bid and being willing to buy at the current bid. This movement indicates that there are now more buyers on the bid, but does not change the inside market price.

up off ask   Was willing to sell at the current offer, but leaves and is now willing to sell at a higher price. This movement indicates there are now fewer sellers on the offer, but does not change the inside market price.

ticks up   Improving the underlying bid.

The following terms often indicate downside momentum:

definitions:

bid to ask   Was willing to buy on the current bid, but now willing to sell on the offer.

down off bid   No longer willing to buy on the current bid, thus lowering bid. This movement indicates that there are now fewer buyers on the bid, but does not change the inside market price.

down to ask   The MMID was willing to sell at a higher price, but is now willing to sell at the current offer. This movement indicates that there are now more sellers on the offer, but it does not change the inside market price.

drops bid   The MMID leaves the bid, thus the current bid moves lower. This movement changes the inside market.

low offer   MMID offers to sell lower than the current asking price. This movement changes the inside market price.

ticks down   MMID lowers the underlying offer.

Watching the Level II screens can be as hypnotic as watching raindrops bounce off the sidewalk in a downpour. The stacatto rhythm of MMIDs flitting up and down your screen is not only hypnotic, it is difficult to learn to follow. Invest in your education.

When you take your EDAT training, whether through a software vendor, an educator, or a day-trading salon, you will learn elementary strategies for pulling consistent profits out of the market. Keep in mind, of course, that by *consistent,* I do not mean you will always be a winner! You *will* have losses, and lots of them. The trick is to keep your losses small and your wins large.

Watching the MMIDs is like playing a complex bridge hand. Your bid could be a signal to your partner and your competition, or it may be a fake out. You will learn from others and develop your own ways to interpret the action on the Level II display. One basic approach is to watch key players as they position themselves relative to the inside bid and ask. Sometimes you can determine whether they are buyers or sellers and how much they are trying to buy and sell, just by watching the display. *The Electronic Day Trader,* by Friedfertig and West, goes into this and other techniques for interpreting the Level II display.

the gap

Some speed traders use the size and direction of any gaps that occur when trading opens in the morning to signal a trade. The only thing that will tell you whether this is a valid strategy is historical testing followed by actual trading.

Take a look at the chart in Figure 3.3. Just to the right of the center of the chart, there is a gap in the price data. On July 2, CMGI closed at 114⅜. On the next trading day, July 6, CMGI opened at 118½. That means there was nearly a 4-point gap first thing in the morning.

If your strategy were based on analyzing the gaps, you might play into this strength. One idea to test would be to buy the gap and hold for a specific number of minutes. Another could be to buy the gap only after the first 15 minutes, and only if price broke the high of the opening range. Either way, on this chart, CMGI continued to show strength, until reaching a high of 126 at 11:30 A.M. If your play had been to buy strength after the first 15 minutes, and sell weakness before noon, your 1,000 shares of CMGI would have netted you a cool 2 points, at least, for a profit of $2,000. That might be a good time to go home.

figure 3.3   one minute chart with morning gap

Source: NexTrend. Reprinted with permission.

That sort of play would be a day trading technique. A speed-trading technique would have lasted for a much shorter time period, and would probably not have made quite the profit. The speed-trading technique, however, would have you exposed to the market for only a very small increment of time.

time of day

There are time periods during each day that seem to be more volatile than others. Conversely, there are other time periods during each day when it seems that everyone has gone home. Analyzing stocks, and the market in general, to determine which time frames lend themselves to your style of trading can go a long way toward system development.

If your style of speed trading relies on capturing 16ths and 8ths, you will more than likely be looking for stocks that are not particularly volatile, but show steady momentum. There might be specific times during the day when the markets statistically exhibit this behavior more frequently than not. Similarly, if you are looking for a point or more of profit in your trade, on a day trading basis, you will want to find the volatile time periods, for high-momentum trades.

shorting

What do you do when the market is generally going down, rather than up? Although it hasn't happened for any extended periods in recent history, markets do get into bear phases historically. It will probably happen again.

When the market, or your stock, is going down, you can still profit. To profit from a downward move in a stock, you need to sell at a high price and buy at a low price, in that order. However, you can't sell a stock you haven't already bought—or can you? Selling short means exactly that. You are essentially borrowing a stock from the broker's inventory, promising that you will buy it back later.

the shortlist

Before you can borrow the stock from the broker, it must be in his inventory. Each morning, at your local day trading salon, a new short-

---

figure 3.4   a shortlist

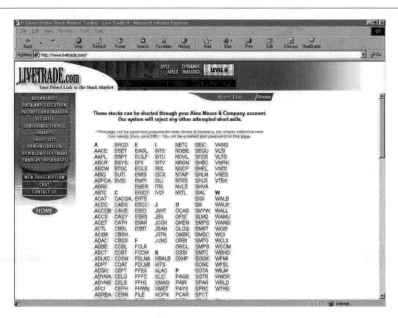

Source: LiveTrade.com. Reprinted with permission.

---

list is generated by the broker. (This list will not likely be the same at your broker and mine.) If you are speed trading at home, you can usually get the shortlist online from your broker (Figure 3.4).

To see an example of a shortlist online, go to www.livetrade.com and click on the menu button "Short List." There you will find a list of the stocks you can borrow from Alex Moore and Company. In addition to knowing whether you can borrow the stock from your broker, you must remember a little roadblock, called the *uptick rule.*

uptick rule

Nasdaq's short sale rule prohibits member firms from entering short sales in securities at or below the current inside bid. A short sale on a down bid is permitted if the sale is at least a 16th above the current inside bid. An opening bid is a down bid if it is lower than the previous day's closing bid, or the same as the previous day's closing bid, if that closing bid was a down bid.

All that means is, if the stock is falling, you can't sell short until it rises slightly. That rule is to prevent, or at least forestall, crashing markets.

chapter 4

sources of information and data

Where observation is concerned, chance favors only the prepared mind.

—*Louis Pasteur, 1822–1895*

I have been trading since 1981. Over the years, I have seen tremendous growth in the trading industry. Since starting my then-small-company in the fledgling computer industry in the 1970s, we have been saying that we were entering first the information age and then the communications age. Nowhere is this more clear than in the instantaneous transmission of data from the floor of the exchanges to your desktop. It's through the ether, no less—the EtherNet.

We are fast coming to a time (some exchanges kicking and screaming all the way) when all trading will be done electronically, with open-outcry auction just a memory in antiquity. These are exciting times we live in.

When I first began using my computers to trade, no one seemed quite sure how to get the data from the airwaves to the computer. There was regular confusion about who was responsible for what part of the handshaking. Now, the integration of data transmission and software manipulation is seamless. Click a few buttons as instructed by setup screens, and you are on your way.

Ten years ago we at-home traders all sported satellite dishes on the roof or big tan receiver boxes on our desktops. Now, the trend is toward Internet-based data transmission, which means you can get your data any time, any place—just log on to your Internet account. Stock market data is no longer limited to big cities with broadcast transmitters! The progression has been truly amazing—and, we've only just begun.

There is very little that matters as much to your successful trading as good data—especially if you are a speed trader! If your data is off by seconds, and your trade only lasts seconds, what do you have? Garbage in, garbage out.

If you are speed trading, your data will likely come from your direct-access broker. Before signing up, ask about the speed of their datafeed. Do they have ISDN lines, T1 lines, T3 lines, or what?

a personal example

Just yesterday, I had the momentary thrill of a lifetime. I was holding a stock overnight that had been at 7.5—MZON. As I was flipping through the screens (that generally means pressing the Page Down key on the keyboard), I saw that MZON was now at 76.25! I thought I had the IPO run-up of the century, for a split instant.

To confirm my newfound riches, I checked the same chart on two other real-time feeds. I keep three real-time datafeeds in the office. Not to say that I mistrust any particular datafeed, but I find that having redundant systems is important in most walks of life.

Of course, my riches crumbled instantly as I discovered that the real number for MZON was 7.625, not 76.25. Oh well, easy come, easy go.

The example, nevertheless, is real. What if that number had printed in my historical data—the data I use for testing theories? What theories might have been structured around that piece of bad data?

two flavors of data

For your second-by-second trading, you will be using real-time data. That data will stream into your computer over high-speed lines. The data you use for testing your theories will be historical data, either saved from your real-time feed, or purchased from an alternate source.

Be willing to pay for your data. You are in this business to make money. Please do not begrudge others with the same goal. It costs a lot of money to provide you with accurate and clean data, both in hardware and personnel time.

Nowhere is the adage "you get what you pay for" more true than in the acquisition of data. Your trading decisions are directly influenced by the accuracy of your data. If you think you'll save money by collecting your own data, or by finding a free source on the Internet or by paying some discounted price for shareware, FORGET IT. And don't trade data with your buddies.

The money you lose by making bad decisions with bad data will far outweigh any savings you made on the purchase of cheap data. As with any business tool, buy the best you can afford. You are trading to make money. This is a business. You are a capitalist. As a capitalist, you must pay for the goods and services you receive, to keep other capitalists providing those goods and services. This business is market driven, like the software business. If you pay someone to do good work, they'll do it; otherwise, you'll be whining that you have bad data and can't make good trading decisions. Data is available somewhere on almost anything. The data must be input and maintained by someone, and you'll get what you pay for.

data vendors

The list of data vendors in Appendix H is as complete as it can be at this writing. Before the three months pass that constitute the editing, publishing, and binding time, there will be more data vendors, especially for day-trading data.

Possibly the best source of historical data is your live, real-time datafeed. Most datafeeds allow you to export the data to disk. This will be your source of historical data to use for back-testing.

Real-time data for day trading and speed trading is no longer dear. A few years ago, real-time data cost me close to $1,000 per month. Now, you can subscribe to real-time services for as little as $25 per month. Most real-time data vendors make use of the Internet for their cost-effective delivery method. Also, surprisingly, these data vendors typically provide charting and/or analytical software for free, as part of the data service.

eSignal	www.dbc.com
Genesis Financial Data Services	www.gfds.com
iqChart	www.iqc.com
NexTrend	www.nextrend.com
PAWWS Financial Network	www.pawws.com
PCQuote	www.pcquote.com
Quote.com	www.quote.com

Until recently, there was a vendor of historical tick data called Tick Data, Inc. They were bought out by *Futures Magazine* Group and within a year ceased doing business. Apparently, the tick data business is fraught with error correction headaches. To my knowledge, there is only one vendor from whom you can purchase historical tick data for stocks. (There are several vendors who carry tick data for futures contracts.) Although at this writing they were still working on cleaning their datafiles and checking them for accuracy, they should be done by press time. In any case, it's your only bet, so call Genesis Financial Data Service at 1-800-808-3282.

Many data vendors supply daily data for stocks, futures, and mutual funds. The list in Appendix H will help you locate the data you will need.

periodicals

In the fledgling arena specific to day trading and speed trading, there are few periodicals devoted to the subject. It is almost as though the subject matter changes too fast to get printed. In fact, this book will likely be out of date before it goes to press. (Never fear, I am available for questions. Please call.) Your best bet for magazines and newspapers are the following:

- *Traders' Catalog & Resource Guide*
- *Barron's*
- *Bloomberg Personal Finance*
- *Futures Magazine*
- *Individual Investor*
- *Investors Business Daily*
- *Omega Magazine*
- *Smart Money*
- *Technical Analysis of Stocks and Commodities*
- *Wall Street & Technology*
- *Wall Street Journal*

web sites

The Internet will be your best source of information, both in the form of data and subject matter. You can find nearly anything you can imagine on someone's web site.

Through the use of your favorite search engine (AltaVista, Excite, Go, GoTo, Infoseek, Lycos, MSN, Yahoo, and so on), you can find millions (literally) of web sites with information about money, trading, and investing. Only the judicious use of Boolean operators like AND and OR will narrow down your search to something meaningful.

In the appendix of this book I have done some of that work for you. Take the time to browse through the web sites I have selected. The beauty of the Internet is that most of these web sites will point you to other web sites, and you will form your own list of favorite resources. As you do, e-mail me your links (sunny@moneymentor.com), and I'll provide them as resources at The Money Mentor for all to share. To click through a host of day-trading links, join us on The Money Mentor's Day Traders page.

list servers, forums, chat rooms, and discussion groups

Bulletin board services (BBSs) are often small enterprises maintained (loosely) by a single individual. Some, on the other hand, are corporate or government in nature and have financial backing. Many of the small BBSs come and go within weeks or months. Frequently, your local weekly computer rag will list other BBS numbers in the back.

Often, BBSs will maintain collections of information that you can download for free. This can be a way to get started and to discover if you enjoy the process of research before you begin trading. Data acquired for free should not be relied on to make trading decisions, but can be a useful practice tool.

To venture out into BBS land, first go to www.bbsnets.com. There, you will find links to thousands of BBS services that contain a wealth of information.

A *list server* is essentially an interactive e-mail list. When you join a list, you select whether to receive individual messages or a digest. As a member of a list, you will receive e-mails from other list members, and you may, in turn, communicate with the list's members. You can select lists by topic of interest. Communicating through a list server preserves some measure of anonymity, and allows you to view messages offline.

The ultimate catalog of lists is at www.lsoft.com/lists/listref.html. This site lets you search through more than 25,000 list servers, by topic, by statistics, or by country.

Forums, chat rooms, and discussion groups are the interactive equivalent of the older listserver concept. (For simplicity, let me call them all chat rooms.) Chat rooms allow you to communicate directly with other participants without checking your e-mail. You enter a chat room on the Internet and, through your keyboard, chat with the other people who are in attendance. Most chat rooms are free, though some investment chat rooms require a membership, and have an associated fee. Some of the more prominent investment chat rooms are:

- www.ino.com
- www.moneymentor.com/chat.htm
- abcnews.go.com
- chat.go.com
- www.atlanticfinancial.com/chat.htm
- www.frontiernet.net
- www.investorama.com
- www.marketcentral.net/chat/
- www.motleyfool.com
- www.msnbc.com
- www.stockresearch.com
- www.thewebinvestor.com

chapter 5

analyzing your data

> Prognostics do not always prove prophecies—at least the wisest prophets make sure of the event first.
>
> —*Thomas Walpole, 1785*

Although getting data into your computer is certainly a critical component of the process, what you do with it once it is there will govern your success as a trader. Your interpretation of the markets will be based entirely on your understanding and use of your historical data.

The more you know about classic analysis techniques, the better able you will be to branch off into specialties of your own. Learn as much as you can from the masters before you adventure into creating your own independent strategies.

what is true?

Inductive reasoning is the use of specific facts to form a general conclusion. *Deductive reasoning* is the use of general information to form specific conclusions. In creating a trading system, you will use both types of reasoning. You will deduce from your overall view of markets some specifics you believe to be true. From these specifics you will attempt to make generalizations that hold true both in historical situations and in future situations.

You will stare at a chart for hours, repeatedly asking yourself, "What is true?" You will not be able to answer your question with a solid 100% answer like "The market *always* does . . . ," because the market doesn't. However, you will be able to statistically evaluate your chances of observing a pattern that repeats x% of the time. When x is large enough, you've found something that's true of the market.

Another way to look at market action is through patterns and statistics. Maybe you are not comfortable with the indicators found in most of the technical analysis software packages. Maybe you don't have or don't want a computer. Maybe you prefer to work with daily data after the market closes and believe there is some predictive value in pattern recognition.

Patterns in the market are presented in words, based on the five pieces of information you can find in the *Wall Street Journal* or *Investors Business Daily:* open, high, low, close, and volume. Pattern recognition involves a process of asking yourself repeatedly: "What is true of this data?" If I give you a number sequence like 1,2,3,4, you can observe that data and probably tell me what number comes next. If I give you the sequence 1,1,2,3,5, you might be harder pressed to observe the data and recognize the pattern.

To discover patterns in the market, you can begin in one of three ways:

- Write down each thing that you observe to be true of the current day's data as compared with yesterday's data.
- Write down each thing that you observe to be true of yesterday's data as compared with today's data.
- Read several books by Larry Williams (such as *The Definitive Guide to Futures Trading,* Volumes 1 and 2), and make use of the thousands of patterns he has already discovered and published.

Patterns are presented like this:

- Open of today is higher than close of yesterday.
- We have had three consecutive down closes.

and patterns are analyzed statistically to measure their probability of success and repetition.

In *The Definitive Guide to Futures Trading,* Volume 2, Larry Williams presents patterns thus:

If we have 3 consecutive down closes in the S&P, you have a 64.6% probability of an up day tomorrow.

If yesterday closes up and today's open gaps higher, we will close above yesterday's close about 60% of the time. If we open down we will close below yesterday's close about 70% of the time.

Personally, I find looking at a chart with a moving average on it easier than attempting to recognize patterns. It is a matter of personal preference, though, with one process being a digital approach and the other being analog.

If you are interested in analyzing patterns, there is no software more suited to the task than PatternSmasher by Kasanjian Research in Blue Jay, California (Figure 5.1). Give them a call at 1-888-220-9789. With PatternSmasher, you can find a lot of true things about the market really fast! It is then up to you to conduct the historical testing with other software, like TradeStation or MetaStock, to generate performance data and optimization reports.

potential hourly wage

The backbone of all my work is a technique I call Potential Hourly Wage™ (PHW™). You can learn about the technique in depth from *Trad-*

---

figure 5.1   the PatternSmasher program from Kasanjian Research

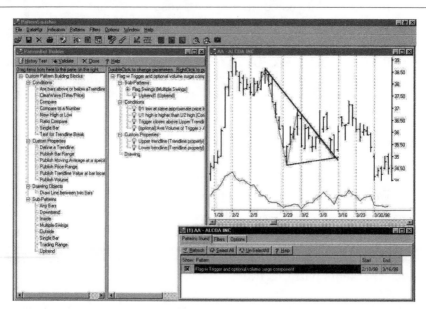

Source: PatternSmasher. Reprinted with permission.

figure 5.2   meaningful highs and lows

Source: Omega Research TradeStation. Reprinted with permission.

ing 102—Getting Down to Business, or by taking my correspondence course, *Solving the Puzzle.*

As a review of the process, basically we always want to know whether trading is worth it. Can we make more money trading than working at McDonald's? To deduce this, we will perform the analysis in three steps:

1. Mark meaningful highs and lows.
2. Calculate the maximum profit.
3. Calculate PHW (40% of the maximum).

By *meaningful highs and lows,* I mean moves that you might be able to catch, and moves that are wide enough to produce a profit. Using the grey circles in Figure 5.2 as an illustration of the process, Table 5.1 is used to calculate the maximum possible profit. Clearly, if you marked different highs and lows than I did, you will get a different value for the maximum profit. Because the outcome is only an approximation of potential, I like to use round numbers to calculate the input as well. The numbers for highs and lows in Table 5.1 are, thus, approximations.

Table 5.1 represents 10 days of perfect trading. Let's say we were trading 100 shares at a time. That would require a minimum $14,000

table 5.1   maximum profit potential

Buy or Sell	High	Low	Profit
S	140	120	20
B	128	120	8
S	128	122	6
B	128	122	6
S	128	110	18
B	118	110	8
			66

account to start. Sixty-six points on 100 shares would be $6,600 in 10 days. That number represents a 47% return on investment (not annualized). That's step 2.

Next, we acknowledge that we will never pick all the tops and bottoms by taking 40% of the maximum number (66) for a resultant roughly 26 points. That would still represent $2,600 profit, for a 19% return. None of this stage of the analysis tells us whether it is really possible to achieve this goal. All we're doing here is sketching out a goal.

The next step in your data analysis is to determine whether it is possible to find or invent indicators that will assist you in buying at or near the goal and selling at or near the goal.

looks like a duck, walks like a duck

There should be no pride-of-ownership syndrome evident in your market analysis. You don't have to be Welles Wilder (well-known author and originator of the ADX indicator) and invent new and proprietary indicators. Your goal, don't forget, is to make money. Do you really care whether you do it with some brilliant new technique you can name after yourself, or whether you do it with something simple like moving averages? You shouldn't. *The more elegant solution to any problem is always the simplest solution.* Simple solutions tend to work over time. Complicated solutions tend to fail as new data creates new and unforeseen situations. Be careful not to fit your answers too closely to the data under observation.

Always follow the market, because the reality is you can't lead it. The market is always right, and will do whatever it wants to, independent of your predictions. *Dancing backward with your eyes closed* is the best way to respond to the markets. To that end, moving averages are great—they follow the trend and slowly change as market conditions change. In my own work, I use some pretty fancy moving averages that change themselves dynamically and that are based on exponential moving averages. I like this area of concentration because the exponential averages react quickly to changes in the market and still smooth out erratic market swings.

For now, and for the simplicity of this exercise, we'll take a look at two exponential moving averages, shown in Figure 5.3. Notice that the grey line and the black line cross back and forth over each other. The point at which they cross can be considered a trigger for buying or selling. If you vary the inputs in your software, making the averages longer or shorter, you will change the places at which they cross. This variation of inputs is sometimes called *optimization*.

There are many other indicators besides the exponential moving averages. Some that I find useful are:

- ADX
- MACD
- Momentum
- On-balance volume

figure 5.3   exponential moving averages (9,18)

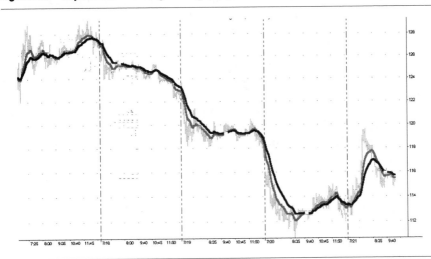

- Percent change
- RSI
- Stochastics

Your day-trading software may or may not include these indicators. Ask the vendor which indicators are provided. The object of the indicator game is to find some combination of indicators that will do a decent job of matching the PHW points you have marked.

There are many, many books devoted to the analysis of indicators, and I have mentioned some of them already. You can devote your life's work to the endeavor—or you can get about trading. All you need is one good indicator.

software

Software for speed trading and day trading comes in two flavors: order-entry and analysis. Order-entry software is the interface between you and the broker or exchange. Analysis software is your toolbox for reviewing and studying market trends, patterns, and indicators.

order-entry software

It seems that most of the software specific to speed trading is built on top of Townsend Analytics, Ltd.'s RealTrade™, and TAL Trading Tools. Other vendors, especially data vendors, are beginning to develop their own software, which includes not only the data display capability, but analytical capabilities as well. Most notably, Quote.com and NexTrend offer data and software not based on TAL. Please don't misconstrue this as disparaging Townsend's software. It is still the leader, and it is extremely powerful. Specifics, including addresses and phone numbers where possible, about the software and vendors have been included in Appendix G.

Your choice of broker will determine your default order-entry software. More than likely, your broker will not provide more than one order-entry technology. The software packages I have come across for this task are the following:

- A-T Attitude
- Attain
- The Executioner
- NexTrend Analysis
- On-Site Trader

- QCharts
- RealTrade
- Rocket Trade
- TradeCast
- Ultimate Trader
- The Watcher

analysis software

Order-entry software assists you in entering your orders. You already know what you want to trade and when. Analysis software helps you determine what and when. A few analysis packages allow you to perform historical back-testing.

You already know that I insist on your knowing your methodology inside and out before you trade. Analysis software is one of the tools you will use to accomplish the "know your system" part.

If you trade at a salon, you may not have access to their computers, other than to use their data and order-entry software. Some salons have analysis software for you to use, but most do not. This means that you must do your own analysis, usually not during market hours. If you want to do analysis during market hours, you might consider taking a laptop computer with you to the day-trading salon. (If you work remotely, this of course is not a problem.)

There are hundreds of analytical software products that will produce charts for traders. The vendors of these products are listed in *Traders' Catalog & Resource Guide*. In Appendix G of this book, I have listed information about the software vendors whose products are more likely to be useful to day traders and speed traders.

The obvious advantage to using software over doing your analysis by hand is speed. The drawback to using software, especially in the beginning of your training, is that you don't get a feel for the market you are studying like you do when you create all your charts by hand.

When racing sports cars, one first looks at the track, then walks the track several times, then drives the track slowly before considering actually driving the track with any speed. Walking the track allows your body's memory to incorporate distance and curves into its neurology.

If you begin your trading career by making all your charts by hand, your neurology will suggest theories for trading systems later on when you do your research. Something happens in your subconscious when you draw one bar at a time over a long time frame, which reveals itself later as *intuition*.

Therefore, even if all your trading and research is going to be computerized, start by making your charts with pencil and paper. After your subconscious is attuned to the market, you can begin to work with computerized charts. If you begin with computer-generated charts, you'll find that you miss the nuances of the market and can't quite ever seem to find a system that really works.

As in televised cooking shows where they mix up the batter and then take a finished cake out of the oven, let's skip to the point in time when you are intimately familiar with the markets you have been studying. That could be several months or several years. By that time, you will know what type of charting interests you, and you can intelligently select software to perform the charting function.

What software will not do is generate ideas. You must hold brainstorming sessions. Customarily, brainstorming sessions are conducted in a room with a white-board and markers; a person who acts not as a moderator, but as a clerk to write down the ideas; and all the people involved in a project. A question is brought under consideration, and everyone speaks freely as ideas come to mind. As a trader, you will have brainstorming sessions with yourself. Write down all possible research avenues as they occur to you. I always keep a small six-ring binder with me in which to write these notes. You never know when these ideas will pop to the surface.

Your analysis software will help you answer the question, "Does this theory work?" Before trading actual dollars, you must know whether you are likely to make a profit. The analysis software packages that address the problem by generating performance statistics are:

- MetaStock
- SuperCharts
- TradeStation
- Window On Wallstreet

For specific testing methods and suggestions, you should read both *Trading 101* and *Trading 102*.

chapter 6

education: seminars, conferences, and study guides

Education is not expensive; lack of education is!

Perhaps one of the most meaningful educational experiences you can have to prepare you for the day-trading business is to actually trade. That is a Catch-22 if ever there was one. You don't want to trade until you know how, but you can't learn how without doing it. Of course, you don't want to trade before you know how, because you don't want to give too much money back to the markets. Let me admonish you once again: Don't trade until you have established every reason to believe that your endeavor will be financially successful.

You have made a good start, by reading this book. You are spending a little bit of time and energy on your education. Please do not think that this is the only book you need to read on the subject, although it should make a good first one.

Learn from the success of others. Find traders who are actually doing what you want to do and ask them about their techniques. They probably won't tell you much specifically, but you might get a few hints. For instance, I spent a full day sitting by a prominent day trader in Texas. I observed quietly. As the day wore on, I began to ask a few questions. As his trading for the day began showing significant profits, he started revealing a few of his techniques. The primary component of his strategy was to buy new highs. If a stock was at a new 52-week high, he would buy for the intraday move and exit at the end of the day. That's a pretty specific, yet simple, technique. Would I trade his technique? Not without testing it first on a multitude of stocks over a long period of historical data! If I tested it over the historical data and it proved to be a profitable strategy, would I trade it? You bet. There is no need to try improving a good thing.

Barring observation of other traders, what else can you do to gain experience and knowledge? Several things. First and easiest is to explore the Internet. There are web sites devoted to day trading and speed trading. Next, you read all the books you can get your hands on. Third, it would be good for you to go to traders' club meetings in your area, and to go to seminars and conferences. There you can ascertain whether a particular broker or software vendor matches your style and preferences without first purchasing their products and services. Then, you should consider committing to formal education through one of the trading salons or independent educators specializing in day trading and speed trading.

Don't believe everything you read. That pertains to the Internet as well as books and periodicals. The only things that will give you some measure of confidence in your strategy are your own independent historical tests.

informative web sites

Electronic day trading is the hot topic, for the moment. New web sites spring up every day touting their wares and skills. Entering "day trading" in your favorite search engine brings up millions of matches. It would not be possible to even begin listing them all. In Appendix E, I list some of the more useful web sites that offer education about day trading. At the Money Mentor, we keep a more complete list, so please feel free to visit.

These web sites are a good starting point for education about trading, day trading, and speed trading:

- www.investor.nasd.com
- www.undergroundtrader.com
- www.worldwidetraders.com
- www.winningdaytraders.com

There are more web sites listed in Appendix E.

educators

Often, the day-trading salons that offer you brokerage will also offer education. It is in their best interest to help you make money. If you don't become a profitable trader, you will stop trading and they will lose your commissions and fees.

In addition to the trading salons, there are independent educators. Typically, a day-trading seminar will cost you from $3,000 to $5,000 and will take a week or more of your time. Before signing up, ask for a syllabus so you can get an idea of the subject matter and techniques you will be learning. Ask about the teachers. Are they traders? Were they traders? What was their track record? Also, ask if you can repeat the training at no cost if you need to.

Much of the other reference material I have isolated to Appendix F. I feel so strongly about the necessity of trading education that I am listing these educators here in the text. Here are some of the educators you should call first:

All-Tech Training Group, Inc.   www.traintotrade.com
160 Summit Ave.
Montvale, NJ 07645

All-Tech Training Group, Inc. (ATG), offers an intensive training program in Montvale, New Jersey, and Seattle, Washington, consisting of four phases of training.

Market Wise Trading School   www.getmarketwise.com
6343 West 120th Ave., Ste. 200
Broomfield, CO 80020

Founded by David Nassar, author of *How to Get Started in Electronic Day Trading,* this school has a CD-ROM narrated by Mr. Nassar. Market Wise Stock Trading School specializes in EDAT training. No matter what discipline (momentum, intraday, swing, short-term, or longer-term) you choose to pursue, you learn the use of direct-access execution with Nasdaq market makers and NYSE specialists.

Nasdaq   www.nasd.com
80 Merritt Blvd.
Trumbull, CT 06611

The NASD Institute for Professional Development provides educational programs for financial industry professionals.

On-Site Trading, Inc.   www.onsitetrading.com
98 Cutter Mill Rd., Ste. 100
Great Neck, NY 11021

Provides several methods and complimentary training in New York. Also offers simulation mode software.

OptiMark Technologies, Inc.   www.optimark.com
10 Exchange Place Ctr.
Jersey City, NJ 07302

The web-based OptiMark Nasdaq Trader Course is a self-paced course where current or potential OptiMark users can learn about the advantages and uniqueness of the system. This web-based course will allow you to learn how OptiMark is integrated with the Nasdaq Stock Market and how the OptiMark Trading System works. You will also have the opportunity to simulate profile entry and see the results of a matching cycle. You will see how easy it is to enter simple and sophisticated trading strategies and learn how the patented OptiMark matching process works.

Pristine Day Trader   www.pristine.com
7–11 S. Broadway, Ste. 210
White Plains, NY 10601
1-800-340-6477
Fax: 1-914-682-7640

Boot camps and seminars for day traders.

RT2 Trader   www.rttrading.com
InvestIN
Infomart Ste. 2016
1950 Stemmons Fwy.
Dallas, TX 75207

Seminars are offered in Dallas and London training facilities. Cost for the five-day course is $1,950. The course is hands-on and limited to six participants.

Sagamore Trading Group   www.learn2trade.com
1446 Old Northern Blvd.
Roslyn, NY 11576
1-888-773-9306

Offering a message board and a day-trading handbook, this web site also offers free information to enhance your learning.

Sceptre Trading   **www.sceptretrading.com**
1-214-826-2466

Sceptre offers a comprehensive day-trading course based on the book *Stock Patterns for Day Trading,* by Barry Rudd, the course's founder. They offer a one-week and a two-week course, as well as a home-study course.

Traders Edge   **www.tradersedge.net**
20 Broad St., 17th Flr.
New York, NY 10004

Learn from Marc Friedfertig and Gerge West, the authors of *The Electronic Day Trader.* Broadway Consulting Group's Tradersedge.net is a leading provider of day-trading educational services. Tradersedge.net offers informative books, an intensive seminar, and a weekly day-trading chat room on the Internet.

Trading School   **www.TradingSchool.com**
P.O. Box 1831
Duarte, CA 91010
1-626-963-2057

Whether you are a beginner, an experienced trader, or an aggressive investor, our hands-on workshops, online courses, and educational materials can assist you in your quest for knowledge and experience. We train day traders, short-term momentum traders, and aggressive investors. Individuals come from all over the United States and around the world to attend our workshops.

seminars and conferences

Day trading and speed trading are still new enough in the marketplace that we have not been flooded with ads and conferences. At this point, the only conference specific to day trading (of which I am aware) is the *First Annual International Day-Trading Expo.* This conference is to take place in Orange County, California, in September of 1999. Stock, option, and futures traders at all levels of experience are invited to attend the Expo. This book will go to press after the conference is already over, but if all goes well, there will be a second annual expo, and the boom in day trading will continue. To learn more about this conference and any future conferences they might conduct, check out their web site at www.daytradingexpo.com.

Although the Day-Trading Expo is devoted to the subject, there are other conferences for traders of all kinds. Attending these seminars

and conferences will expose you to a variety of techniques and philoso-
phies about short-term and long-term trading. I highly recommend
each of these conferences for gathering the most information in one
place.

Technical Analysis Group (TAG)   **www.ino.com/tag/**
1-800-538-7424 or 1-410-867-7424
M–F, 9:30 A.M. to 7:00 P.M. EST

Founded by Tim Slater, these seminars have been held every year since
1978. With time this conference only gets better! This is the ultimate
gathering place for gurus and enthusiastic students. I have gone every
year since 1986 (except for the one year that Southwest Airlines
wouldn't allow my dog onboard)—and I always learn something.

Omega World   **www.omegaresearch.com**
Omega Research
8700 W. Flagler St., Ste. 250
Miami, FL 33174
1-800-327-3794

Omega World will hold its third annual conference June 8 to 11, 2000, in
New York City. Previous conferences were held in Las Vegas and
Orlando. An exceptional conference for users of TradeStation and Super-
Charts (and potential users), this annual event is a comprehensive sys-
tem trading conference.

Futures South and Futures West   **www.futuresmag.com**
250 S. Wacker Dr., Ste. 1150
Chicago, IL 60606
1-800-221-4352

Futures holds two conferences per year, one on each coast. The spring
conference on the right coast and the fall conference on the left coast
offer exciting workshops for beginning, intermediate, and advanced
traders. The title of this conference is a bit of a misnomer. Futures
South and Futures West both offer techniques and strategies valuable
to stock traders as well.

FIA Expo   **www.fiafii.org**
2001 Pennsylvania Ave. NW, Ste. 600
Washington, D.C. 20006

Held every year in Chicago, usually in November, this conference is the
largest futures industry event in the world. The FIA Expo offers the
widest variety of exhibits showcasing the latest products and services.

Seminar sessions address brokerage issues, trading systems and strategies, and users' needs. This is the venue at which vendors unveil their newest products.

educational software

I have only found four sources for day-trading software that are specifically for education. Two are mentioned in the preceding "Educators" section: MarketWise Training and OnSite Trading. The other sources for educational software are:

Online Trading Academy   **www.tradingacademy.com**
4199 Campus Dr., Ste. G
Irvine, CA 92612

This web site offers online training as well as a free introduction to a day-trading seminar. They offer a one-week online boot camp and a 10-day Advanced Online Trading Immersion Course.

SpecTrader+ by Cavlogix Corporation
2601 Elliott Ave., Ste. 1341
Seattle, WA 96121
Fax: 1-206-441-6455
E-mail: spectrader@cavlogix.com

This $34.95 software can be used as a simulation to try out your trading skills. The program is stimulating, offers three skill levels, and lets you measure and test your skills agains random market situations. The most you stand to lose is $34.95.

You might wisely consider all trading software to be educational in nature. There is no "sure thing." With that in mind, let me list a few more sources of trading software.

AbleSys Corp.	www.ablesys.com
InvestorLinks	www.investorlinks.com
SimpleX	www.prime-line.com
TradeTutor	www.tradetutor.com
Zagury Directory	www.zagury.com

clubs

It can be of enormous value for you to network with others who are attempting to do the same thing you are. It is amazing how much others have to share, and how many roadblocks you can avoid by making new friends. Often, these clubs will invite guest speakers who can enhance your learning and help point you in new directions.

Day Traders of Orange County   www.worldwidetraders.com

This group is the first of its kind in the United States, offering biweekly meetings in Orange County, California. The group typically has 200 active traders in attendance and includes a presentation by a guest speaker. Meetings are held on the second and fourth Saturdays of every month at 9:00 A.M.

American Association of
Individual Investors (AAII)   www.aaii.org

With groups in most major cities, the AAII holds monthly meetings of interest to traders and investors of all kinds. To see if there is a club in your area, go to www.aaii.org/loclchap/chaptermap/ and click on your area.

chapter 7

electronic brokerage

There are only two qualities in the world: efficiency and inefficiency; and only two sorts of people: the efficient and the inefficient.

—*George Bernard Shaw, 1856–1950*

At this point in time, there is still a distinction between online (or electronic) brokers and direct-access brokers. That will probably not always be true. More than likely, the online brokerage firms will all begin to offer direct-access programs in the near future.

So, what's the difference? *Online brokerage* simply means that you can place your trades (orders) through your Internet browser, but the trade does not necessarily get immediately executed. There will be a slight delay—sometimes seconds, sometimes minutes—before your trade is presented on the floor of the exchange to be filled. Online brokerage is still going through the open-outcry process.

Direct-access brokerage means that your order is placed immediately when you push the button, through the computer itself, not through a person on the floor. Direct access is (or has been) also referred to as Small Order Execution System (SOES) trading, Level II trading, day trading, and electronic trading, and I am now calling it speed trading.

A third possibility exists: *direct-investment plans,* where you buy shares of a company, not through an exchange, but through the company, or the company's broker, itself. Direct-investment plans are commonly referred to as dividend reinvestment plans (DRIPs). In the past, you would call each company separately for an enrollment application. For your convenience, you can now call the Direct Stock Purchase Plan Clearinghouse at 1-800-774-4117 to receive a comprehensive list of companies that offer DRIPs.

If DRIPs interest you, check out Charles B. Carlson's newsletter, *The DRIP Investor,* or on the Internet you can get information at http://www.netstockdirect.com. I have included information about DRIPs here because they offer another way around the middleman, not because they lend themselves to the day-trading or speed-trading style.

exchanges versus brokers

The old Chinese curse, "May you live in exciting times," certainly is true now, with respect to trading. Exchanges and brokerages change nearly every day, as they vie for market share and explore electronic possibilities. Recently, I read this entry in the Chicago *Sun-Times* (emphasis mine):

> June 25, 1999
>
> The Chicago Board Options Exchange detailed a reorganization it announced last week, which includes the formation of a transition team and the creation of a new division. Last week, in moves to protect its turf as the nation's leading market for stock options, it said it will shift some business from its trading floor *to a computer network* next year. CBOE Executive Vice President Richard DuFour was named to lead the transition team, and Edward Joyce, also executive vice president, will head the newly formed Business Development division. The exchange said it plans to transfer by mid-2000 its less actively traded options. They would be moved to a *screen-based system* that also would be used if the stock markets extend their hours into the evening. (© 1999 Chicago *Sun-Times.*)

I am of the firm belief that exchanges and brokerages will be indistinguishable to the average person within five years. Even as I write this, Island (Datek's ECN) is applying to become an exchange.

online and electronic brokers

Because a picture can explain so much, let me show you the difference between *electronic direct-access trading* (EDAT) and *online trading.* Figure 7.1 shows the order-entry screen for a popular online trading broker, Datek. From this screen, on your computer, you can enter a buy or

figure 7.1   an online trading order-entry screen

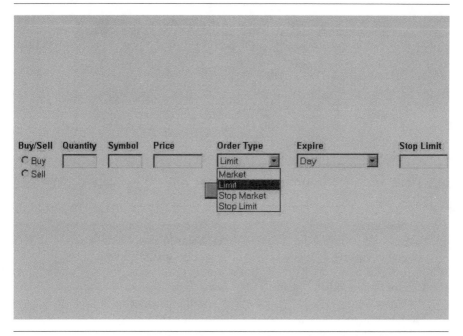

sell order. You fill in the blanks, using your mouse and your keyboard, and click the Enter Order button. The order is then sent to the trading floor of the exchange, to a specialist (or market maker in the case of a Nasdaq stock) who then fills the order. By e-mail, or by checking the "Filled Orders" screen, you will receive notification that your order has been processed and you will be able to see the price at which the order was filled.

If you are in a hurry to see your fill, go immediately to the "Daily Transactions" or "Messages" screen, or even to your "Portfolio" screen. With my broker, the trade confirmation is always there before I get there—no waiting time. There is some delay, however, if you wait for the automatic e-mail to reach you.

Although nearly every stock brokerage offers an electronic order-entry option, only a few futures brokers offer electronic order entry (Figure 7.2). Historically, the stumbling block to online futures orders has been the extreme margin you are allowed and the broker's inability to keep your equity up-to-date on a real-time basis. This, too, is chang-

figure 7.2   electronic futures order entry

COMMODITY ORDER TICKET							
B/S	Qty	Symbol	Month	Year	Modifier	Price	GTC
⊙ Buy ○ Sell	10	SP	Z	1997 ▾	Market ▾		☐
Optional Row for **Option Orders** Only				○ Call ○ Put	Strike Price		
Optional Row for OCO (One Cancels Other) Orders Only				(n/a) ▾			

ing. Here are a few futures brokers that offer the online order-entry alternative:

Access-Direct	www.access-direct.com
Alaron	www.alaron.com
American Futures & Options	www.optionsbroker.com
Best Direct	www.pfgbest.com
Capitol Commodity Services	www.ccstrade.com
DH Financial	www.dhfinancial.com
First American Discount	www.fadc.com
Futuresweb Trading Group	www.futuresweb.com
Jack Carl Futures	www.jackcarl.com
Lind-Waldock	www.lind-waldock.com
NetFutures	www.netfutures.com
Paragon Investments	www.paragoninvestments.com
Price Futures Group	www.pricegroup.com
Rand Financial Services	www.rand-usa.com
Transitions Trading	www.transitionstrading.com
XPRESSTRADE	www.xpresstrade.com
ZAP Futures	www.zapfutures.com

The distinction between online, or electronic, order entry and direct access is whether the order gets delivered to the exchange floor for execution in the open-outcry auction. If the trade goes directly to the computers, bypassing the floor altogether, then it is direct access.

EDAT brokers—direct access

A direct-access trading screen (EDAT) bypasses specialists and the exchange floor altogether. Through direct access, you are negotiating

figure 7.3 an EDAT screen

with market makers and other traders. Figure 7.3 is an example of an EDAT order screen.

Which online broker is best? That's probably between you and the broker. Your service and your requests will be a matter of personal taste and performance history. To look at an independent assessment of online brokerage, you should visit Gomez Advisors at www.gomez.com to view their Internet Broker Scorecard.

chapter 8

developing your own approach

When you come to a fork in the road, take it.

—*Yogi Berra, 1925–*

Over the years, I have developed a couple of approaches that give me peace of mind and some sense of statistical assurance that hanging in there will ultimately lead to greater profits than losses. In this chapter, I will share those ideas with you.

If you examine the long-term results of all the professional traders and divide by the number of traders, you will find that the average return is close to zero. Not only do the professional money managers not beat the average 9% per year experienced by the stock market, but they end up flat, on average. If the pros can't do it, how can you?

There are a few pointers I would like you to know, that will help you beat the pros. Although there is never any guarantee of profits in an endeavor as risky as trading, there are a few ways you can give yourself an edge.

The first thing you need to know: plan your work, and then work your plan. The likelihood of you following an approach that you have designed and thoroughly tested is small. The likelihood of you following an approach that someone else developed and you haven't tested is next to nil. In addition, the likelihood of your making a profit in the long term, if you don't have a systematic approach, is also nil.

stock selection

Whether your day trading is in stocks or in futures (commodities), you cannot trade them all. Somehow, you will need to narrow down your purview to a manageable few.

Another Catch-22 presents itself. How do you know what stocks to trade if you haven't developed the filter? Also, how do you develop the filter if you don't know what to look for? Easy answer. We go back to the Potential Hourly Wage™ (PHW™) analysis. We don't really care what we trade, we just care that it makes us money, right?

indexes and industries

One quick, first-pass answer to the filter could be to concentrate on a well-defined stock group. For instance, if we only traded the Dow Jones 30 Industrials, we would be watching the 30 most watched stocks in the United States. In fairly short order, you would become familiar with the rhythm exhibited by these stocks. You would develop a feel for how fast or slowly they trade. If you watched each of the stocks in various time frames, you would be able to analyze which of the time frames would generate the most potential profit.

Let's evaluate a single stock from the Dow Jones 30 Industrials. I am not doing what most educators do, which is to pick an example that perfectly fits my intent. I decided to grab GE because it is well known and has been around for a long time. We are going to look at a variety of time frames in the figures that follow.

With each chart, you must perform the same PHW analysis:

1. Mark the ideal highs and lows.
2. Calculate the ideal profits.
3. Take 40% of the ideal.

Notice two things from Figures 8.1 through 8.5, please:

- The longer the time frame, the more days are represented on the chart.
- As your time frame gets longer, you take fewer trades per day.

As part of any rational analysis of trading potential, you should also take a look at the ultimate question: Is trading more lucrative than buy-and-hold?

figure 8.1   GE on a 1-minute time frame

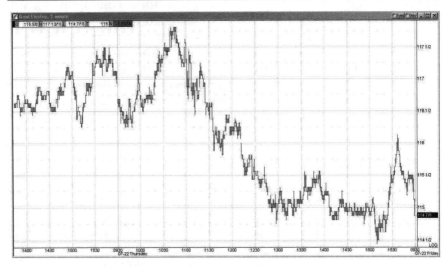

Source: Quote.com QCharts. Reprinted with permission.

figure 8.2   GE on a 5-minute time frame

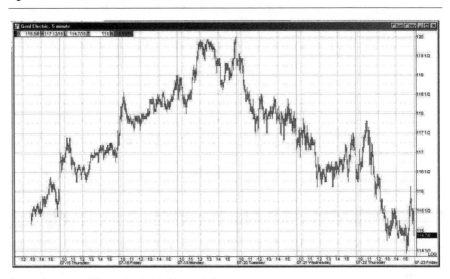

Source: Quote.com QCharts. Reprinted with permission.

figure 8.3   GE on a 10-minute time frame

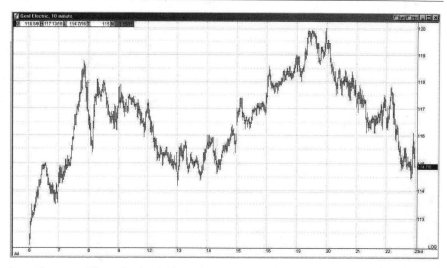

Source: Quote.com QCharts. Reprinted with permission.

figure 8.4   GE on a 15-minute time frame

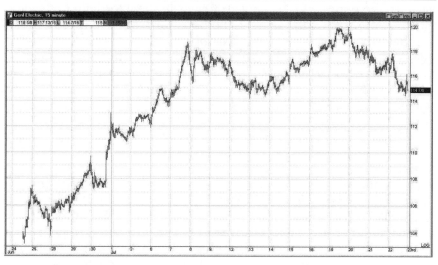

Source: Quote.com QCharts. Reprinted with permission.

figure 8.5 GE on a 30-minute time frame

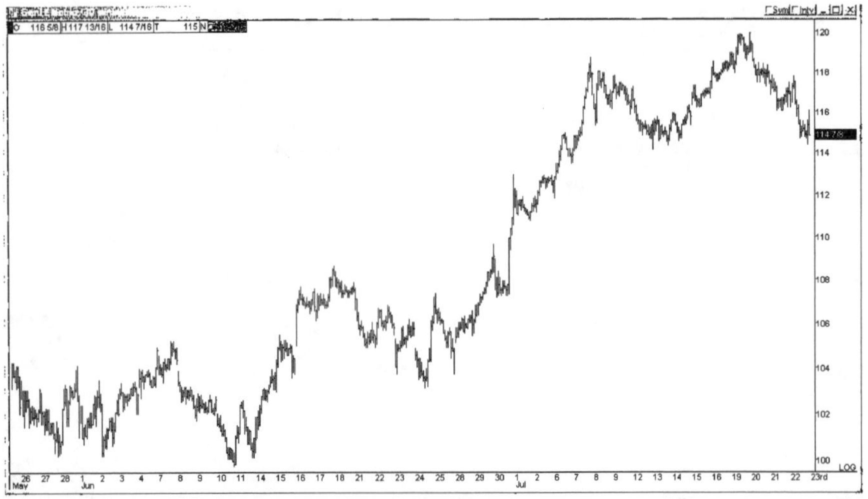

Source: Quote.com QCharts. Reprinted with permission.

If you find a time frame in any of the charts above that appeals to you, and if trading in that time frame gives you a decent PHW, then it is time to set about the task of finding a systematic approach that will consistently net you the PHW you are looking for. Let me refer you again to the books with trading strategies in them for help in developing an approach. As for specific methods for testing and proving any approach, I'll again refer you to *Trading 102.*

Many speed traders like to trade the stocks in the Dow 30 because they are not as volatile as, for instance, the Internet or high-tech stocks. With the more seasoned stocks in the Dow 30, you can more reliably pick off 8ths and 16ths, as the stocks are not typically as volatile.

The current list of Dow 30 stocks is in Appendix K.

ISDEX

If it's volatility you are looking for, consider specializing in the stocks of the Internet Index, the ISDEX. The current list of 48 ISDEX stocks, in Appendix L, represents some of the most volatile stocks around. If you are looking at price multiples, these stocks are out of fundamental bounds. If it is price you analyze, these are exciting stocks foretelling an even more exciting future. Don't get me started, I could talk for days about the future of the Internet and electronic communication.

A 5- to 10-point swing in a day is not unusual for an Internet stock. A move of 10% in a single day in an Internet stock is not unusual, but would be cause for alarm in one of the Dow 30 stocks. If you want to ride this one, hold on tight. At some point, something else will take over as the bleeding-edge favorite.

Nasdaq

There are thousands of stocks in the Nasdaq. Of course, you can't specialize in them all. If you want to isolate a few, there are several approaches you can take. First, a quick look at the Nasdaq-100 Index (see Appendix M) will help you bring the list to a more manageable 100 stocks. How do you know, though, that these are the stocks that will make you the most money? You don't.

There is software and there are web sites that you can use to filter down the stocks you want to watch. On the Nasdaq web site, at screening.nasdaq-amex.com/, you can access their stock-screening algorithm to narrow down your search with your own selection criteria (see Figure 8.6).

Largely, you will be using the trial-and-error approach for the first pass at this part of your research. You want your screen to isolate a small enough subset that you can manage to follow the stocks in a meaningful way. You also want the screen to isolate stocks that have a high enough PHW to meet your goal. You just have to try a few. When you have used PHW frequently, you will develop a feel for it, just like anything else. You will begin to look at a stock chart and know whether it will have the trading frequency you feel comfortable with, and whether 40% of the ideal moves will fit within your profit requirements.

stock-screening software

There are other software products that will assist you in narrowing your search. Although the Nasdaq stock-screening capabilities are limited, there are several products that offer you nearly unlimited filtering capabilities. Two products that are forerunners in their flexibility and broad-spectrum capabilities are:

- PatternSmasher by Kasanjian Research
- Telechart 2000 by Worden Brothers

Both products allow you to construct your own formulas and to have the program run through thousands of stocks to find the few that meet the criteria.

figure 8.6   Nasdaq-Amex stock screening

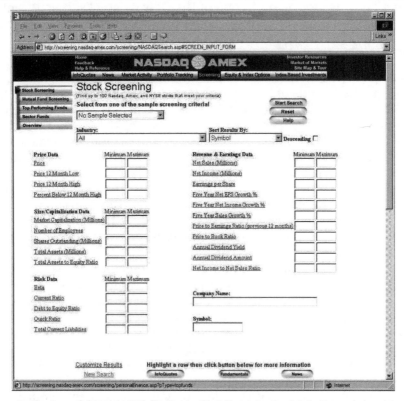

Source: Nasdaq-Amex. © Copyright 1999, The Nasdaq Stock Market, Inc. Reprinted with permission of the Nasdaq-Amex Market Group.

Again, you will first rely on the trial-and-error approach for defining patterns with which to filter. Both programs come with a set of predefined patterns with which you can begin. A drawback to these programs is that they both work on daily data, not real-time data, at this juncture.

big movers

One theory worth examining is another approach to the momentum theory. A body at rest tends to stay at rest; a body in motion tends to stay in motion. If this were true of stocks, then it might be worth running a quick screen each morning at the opening of the market (on real-time data, of course) to see what is hot.

My favorite tool for quick, real-time screening of stocks is a little program by Quote.com, called QCharts. Available for free when you sign up for their Internet datafeed, QCharts is incredibly powerful. Designed with the speed trader and day trader in mind, QCharts allows you to create dynamically updating windows, so you can watch for things like:

- Very short term up
- Percent gainers
- Point gainers
- Volume
- Number of trades
- Trade rate
- Unfilled gaps
- Unusual volume
- Largest range
- Most volatile
- New yearly highs
- New yearly lows

Certainly, it would be worth investigating whether any of these screens is a harbinger of stock action for the remainder of the day.

research

Both a technique for screening stocks down to a manageable few and for gaining some knowledge about the company itself, you might want to delve into elements of fundamental stock research.

Let's go back to Quote.Com's QCharts software. Probably the easiest way to get an overview of fundamentals is by creating a Quote Sheet with columns for fundamental data. QCharts lets you double-click on any column to immediately sort by the values in the column. QCharts also provides a link to the Market Guide profile, which affords you an overview of the fundamentals and a brief business summary of the company.

There are other Internet sites you can use to conduct your research:

Multex Investor Network   www.multex.com

Multex.com is an online investment research network serving asset managers, investment banks, brokerage firms, corporations, and individual investors.

Reuters   www.reuters.com

Reuters provides financial information products that deliver news and prices to customer screens. They provide datafeeds and the software tools to analyze the data.

Wall Street Research   www.wallstreetresearch.net

Wall Street Research Group provides information on small- and micro-cap stocks.

Zacks Investment Research   www.zacks.com

Look here for an amazing amount of fundamental data and other resources: Earnings Surprises, SEC Filings, Earnings Calendar, Insider Trading Info, Company News, Edgar Filings, and more.

conclusion

The process of designing, testing, and proving a system can be time consuming and tedious. However, this process is your insurance. Without this investment of time and effort, you are doing nothing more than gambling.

chapter 9

trading as your business

Our life is frittered away by detail . . . Simplify, simplify.
—*Henry David Thoreau, 1817–1862*

How much is $1 million dollars? How many dollars per hour is it? How many dollars per day? How much money do you want to make per year? How much is that per day? Per hour? If you are serious about trading, you had better know everything about how to get from *A* to *Z*. Without a clearly defined goal, you won't get there.

Trading is a very serious business. This endeavor can become all-consuming (with more tentacles than an octopus), encompassing your personal time as well as your allotted work time.

Trading is the only business I know of that pays you sometimes and, at other times, you pay it. With most jobs, you can expect a paycheck; with trading, you can lose everything you have!

There is only one goal in trading: to make money. Certainly, an important element of your business will be that you enjoy what you do, but you can enjoy your efforts and not make a profit. When treating it like a business, every step you take must be to further your primary goal: making money. When you consider purchasing another computer, ask whether it will add to or subtract from the business's bottom line. When you want another piece of trading software, ask whether it will add to or subtract from the bottom line. When you begin looking at new offices, ask whether it will add to or subtract from the bottom line.

Often, we busy ourselves with the trappings and forget that the bottom line is of prime importance. A new camera does not make you a better photographer. The purchase of new trading software, office equipment, and business trappings will not make you a better trader. Hard work and study will improve your photography and your trading skills. Consider adding to your education before adding to your inventory.

Make your plan and stick to it. Set out your goals for this business as you would for any other business. Create long-term timelines for expansion based on worst-case scenarios, rather than pie-in-the-sky, hopeful scenarios. Be detailed in your specifications, pretending that you must present your plan to your banker or a venture capitalist for funding.

getting down to business

One of the main reasons that traders fail is not their lack of trading skills, but their lack of business skills. Traders aren't the only ones who suffer from this dilemma. Physicians, in medical school, receive an enormous amount of scientific information, but very little information about running their practice from a business standpoint. Young attorneys are taught to argue the law, but not to run a business. This is true of most technical schooling.

Having the best education and talent for your current or previous profession is not enough to guarantee your success in trading. You might be a highly trained attorney, accountant, or engineer, and have been tremendously successful at it, but that does not insinuate that you will become equally as successful as a trader. To become a successful trader, plan on spending as much time obtaining the appropriate education for the job as you would spend becoming educated for any other profession. If you plan to run a successful trading business, in addition to developing a proven, profitable trading system, you must develop the skills of running a business, which requires just as much education as you devoted to your current profession.

setting goals

All too often, I hear wanna-be traders saying that they expect to generate 100%+ profits every year through trading. They've heard stories about traders like Hillary, who turn $1,000 into $100,000, and these wanna-be traders think that this is exactly what will happen to them. Because Hillary did it, they believe they, too, can read the *Wall Street Journal* and get rich.

Please, don't set this as your goal. Be realistic. There are several ways to form realistic trading goals by asking yourself some common-sense questions. What does an average retail business make? What does the average professional trader make? What does the Dow Jones Industrial Average make? What does the S&P 500 Index make?

how much is enough?

What would you expect to make as net profit if you started up a new business with a product to sell? All too often, we forget that trading is a business and act more like gamblers. Remember that this is your new, start-up business and treat it as such.

Let's set our business net profit target at that of the average business in the United States. The U.S. Bureau of the Census reports that the average small business owner reports a 9.7% return on the business, before taxes, for 1998. Let's use 10%, then, as our goal. If your after-expenses trading profits are 10% or higher, you are doing as well as the average American business.

Performing as well as the average business would be a reasonable goal for a new trader. Furthermore, it is a difficult, though attainable, target. Sure, there are a few traders who make it to the 100% annual level. There are also a few athletes who make it to the Olympics.

The Dow Jones, over the long term, makes about a 9% return per year. Your stockbroker will tell you that a buy-and-hold approach to investing will, in the long run, net you more return than any other scheme. How many times have I heard ". . . a $10,000 investment 25 years ago would currently be worth $802,000." That is because these figures have been compounded, assuming that all the money was left in the account and reinvested during that 25 years.

compounding

Lest you become discouraged, it is time to engage in some wishful planning. What happens to a $20,000 trading account if you can make an annual return of 30%? Have you any idea just how much that is? What if you can make more than 30% per year? Table 9.1 illustrates your potential.

money, money, money

Trading capital is one of your business assets; it is your inventory. Do not confuse your trading capital with your office expenses, nor with

table 9.1   hypothetical investment of $20,000*

	30%	40%	50%
Year 1	$26,897	$29,642	$32,641
Year 2	$36,174	$43,933	$53,274
Year 3	$48,650	$65,115	$86,949
Year 4	$65,429	$96,509	$141,909
Year 5	$87,995	$143,039	$231,609
Year 6	$118,344	$212,002	$378,008
Year 7	$159,160	$314,214	$616,944

* Annual rates of return compounded monthly.

your personal finances. They must be kept very separate in your mind and in your accounting.

Do not confuse your trading profits with your net profits. You are running a small business, remember? You trading profits are your gross profits, from which you must subtract your expenses. Data doesn't come to you for free and neither does a computer. Taxes and telephone are additional expenses you must consider. Let's break the components of your business into budget items, so we can analyze income and expenses.

costly shortcuts

There are essentials in your business, around which you probably should not try to make shortcuts. Both in the long and the short run, these tools will be time savers for you and, thus, will save you money.

A good answering machine can act as a substitute for a receptionist for a long time. This is especially true if you have a computer you can devote to answering the phone, so that you can assign voice-mail boxes to segregate functions, like requests for information, trading fills, and personal calls. Telephony applications (like SuperVoice and Visual Voice) are comparatively inexpensive and act as a great buffer for filtering out distractions.

A clerical person to do your filing, typing, errands, and data entry can increase your efficiency an order of magnitude. In the beginning, you probably won't need this person full-time, so contact a local temp agency and get someone to come in two afternoons a week. It's too easy for you to confuse busyness with productivity. Spending your time doing clerical functions makes you feel like you worked hard, but it doesn't get you further along in your research and trading.

Your computer equipment is your main tool. If you are trying to force an old clunker to do the job for which you need a Pentium, you will be spending most of your time acting as a hardware expert. A used or reconditioned monitor can be had for $80; a new Pentium with all the bells and whistles can be as little as $800, if you have a repair shop build it for you from parts. Buy two; they're cheap.

Your market data is probably the last place you should cut corners. As they say: "Garbage in, garbage out." If you feed your system inaccurate data, you will be getting erroneous results upon which you intend to base your entire business. How smart is that? Don't get your data from your friends. Rely on highly reputable data vendors, and pay for their best service. Don't cut corners here!

budgeting

As a philosopher, statistician, and armchair psychologist, I have noticed that the folks who start a new business by renting prime office space and furnishing it with the best of the best are usually out of that office within a year. The cautious new entrepreneur who begins in the garage, on the other hand, and accumulates furnishings (often used) as needed, taking on only those expenses his profits will cover, is far more likely to succeed in the long run.

There is a delicate balance between being extravagant and being parsimonious. As Benjamin Franklin said, "Penny wise, pound foolish." If you base your business plan on savings, rather than increasing income, you are planning backward.

Avoid poverty consciousness. Take stock of your *musts* and your *wants.* Adequate desk space and a comfortable chair are important; plush surroundings are not. Having a computer with enough power and storage that you can get your research done without fighting the hardware is imperative; having the latest, greatest, top-of-the-line computer is not.

Paramount in your planning: *Don't spend money you don't have.* Trading is not likely to produce a steady monthly income, especially in the beginning. It has its ups and downs. There are months with no income. In fact, there are months with negative income. So, don't go out on a limb and get loans (or even extend yourself loans via credit cards) against income you anticipate, but don't yet have.

Assign a dollar value to your own time. There are occasions when it is inappropriate for you to do the work yourself. If you know what the value of your own time is, you can more easily determine these occasions. For instance, let's say that your goal is to make $100,000 your first year, and that to do so, you must do the research, testing, and trading yourself. Using an estimated 2,000 hours per year, your time is worth $50 per hour. Every task you do that takes you away from your stated priorities is an expense to the company. If you do the filing and telephone answering, and you spend three hours a day doing it, you are costing the company $150 per day, by getting behind in your scheduled goal. You will end the year being 750 hours, or $37,500, away from your goal. You would be better off paying a temp service $10 per hour to do your clerical work, while you concentrate on your primary goal. Always aim toward making the highest and best use of your time. Your time is your most expensive commodity.

income

Anticipate and plan; set your goals high and your expectations low. Try to be realistic and, at the same time, hopeful. If you want to make $1 million a year, that's not unreasonable, just break that goal down into its daily equivalent. Having done that, then begin to analyze what it would take to generate that much income on a daily basis, above your expenses. At every step along the way, you must ask, "What does it take?" and "Am I willing to do what it takes?"

Assuming you take weekends off and two weeks' vacation per year, there are then 250 working days in a year. To make $1 million in that year, you must produce a net profit of $4,000 each and every day—above your losses! If one day you lose $2,000, the next day you must make $6,000. Breaking this down a bit further, if you can make $500 per day net trading one S&P contract, then you must trade eight contracts to make $1 million in a year. Eight S&P contracts, at today's $15,000 margin requirement, would be $120,000 in your account, just to cover the margin. I recommend having a minimum of twice the margin in your account before you even think about trading, which would mean you would need $240,000 to make your million. That is, if you can find a sure way to make $500 per contract to start with.

Whatever your goal, keep a progress chart. If you want to establish a workout program, keep a log of your routine and when you increase repetitions, frequency, or weight in your training. If you want to lose weight, make a chart for the year, with realistic weight milestones, and plot your actual weight against it daily. If you want to make $1 million a year, keep a chart of your goal and plot your actual progress on a weekly basis toward that goal.

Some weeks, your dot will be over the line, some weeks it will be under. However, as long as you are making progress in the right direction and staying near your goal line, you are doing the right thing.

outgo

In any business, you will have fixed costs (FC) and variable costs (VC). Fixed costs remain the same month after month, independent of how many widgets you make or how many trades you take. Variable costs vary directly with the number of widgets or trades. For instance, commission is a VC, which rises and falls according to the number of contracts or shares you are trading. Your rent is an FC, staying the same every month, regardless of how much you trade.

Your total costs (TC) are the sum of your FCs and your VCs. Your break-even point (BE) is where your TCs are equal to your total income. In analyzing your business and its potential for success, you will need to find your BE point. How much trading profit must you bring in to cover all your costs? How much trading capital is necessary to generate this trading profit?

expense worksheet

Keep yourself honest. Write down your estimates of your business's monthly fixed and variable expenses. Tables 9.2 and 9.3 show a format that should help in this effort. What other expenses are you likely to incur? Keep careful track of your ledgers, either by hand, using spreadsheet software, or using an accounting program like Quicken or Quick-Books.

table 9.2   fixed costs

Item	Monthly Expense
Your salary	$3,000
Wages for temp help	$1,000
Rent	$1,000
Utilities	$300
Telephone	$300
Insurance	$100
Shipping and postage	$100
Data service fees	$300
Taxes and licenses	$100
Legal fees	$100
Accounting fees	$100
Total estimated fixed costs	**$6,400**

table 9.3   variable costs

Item	Monthly Expense
Travel	
Seminars and conferences	
Education and books	
Magazine subscriptions	
Office supplies	
Computer maintenance and upgrades	
Software	
Historical data	
Total estimated variable costs	

your trading business plan

There are many ways you can get help structuring a basic business plan. Every bookstore carries several books on the subject, including formats you can mimic. Jian software makes a combined book and software product, called BizPlanBuilder, which will walk you through the process step by step. Browsing the Internet, you will be able to find both shareware and retail software to help you get more ideas for your business plan. Two great sites for shareware downloads are www.download.com and www.zdnet.com.

chapter 10

discipline

There's this perception that if you worry a lot and you look busy and stressed out, then you'll be more successful. You talk about how little sleep you get and how tense you are and how you're not getting the appreciation you deserve and how hard you're working. You think this is somehow feeding into your success and your career, and that's just not true.

Any success that you have in your career is despite your being all bothered and annoyed and stressed-out—not because of it.

—Richard Carlson

Scurrying about will not make you a better trader. The frantic pace of speed trading will not make you successful. Studying will help; planning will help; having a tested and proven system will do half the job; however, having the discipline to actually follow the system is probably the most important component of being a successful trader. The most difficult part of trading, without a doubt, is following your system.

If I gave you every rule for my trading methodology, and I told you that it made 100% per year, within a matter of weeks you would stop following it. Why? Because you won't have the confidence it takes to withstand the losing periods.

The only way you can gain this confidence is through extensive testing of a system that you have either designed yourself, or that you fully understand. You must know every statistic and measurement introduced in this book inside and out, backward and forward. You must be intimately familiar and comfortable with how many losing trades you are likely to experience in a row before your system starts winning again.

Even armed with all this information, you will still have trouble following your system. You must bolster your ego and your positive intentions on a daily basis.

There are people who specialize in working with traders' psychology. They are experts in dealing with the problems that face this industry every day. I generally refer people to Adrienne Toghraie (1-919-851-8288, or adtoghraie@aol.com) for coaching in this area. Also, check out her new book, *Real People, Real Traders.*

If you want to access a full list of traders' coaches, I keep it on The Money Mentor, under psychology.

Post-it® Notes

There are many little tools you can use to keep your focus trained on following your system. Most of these tools are pretty simple, but you'll be surprised how well they work.

Start your own collection of motivational sayings. When you realize you have violated a trading rule, write a positive reinforcement on a Post-it Note, and stick it on your monitor. When you find one of those pearls of wisdom in a book, write it on a Post-it Note and stick it to your monitor.

Move the notes around every few days, reading each one carefully as you move it. Notes that stay in the same place become part of the surroundings and get ignored.

Talk to a coach versed in neurolinguistic programming so that you only give yourself positive notes, not negative ones.

hard hat area

As a new trader, I found it difficult to stay with my system when it was in drawdown. I knew what my statistics said, I had done all the testing, and I believed it would work. Still, I had a hard time pulling the trigger when the going was tough. I felt like Chicken Little with the sky falling in around me.

Because I was able to describe my fear as "things falling" (like my equity curve), I decided to go to the hardware store and purchase a hard hat. I even painted my name on the front of the hard hat to make it look official. The investment of time made the object more of a trigger for me. When the going got tough, I just put on my hard hat to help remind me to stick with the system.

pointers

All traders face losing days. All traders face drawdown periods. All traders get discouraged sometimes. To assist you in sticking with your plan, remember these simple pointers:

- Know your system.
- Trust your system.
- Follow your system without hesitation or second-guessing.
- Don't make excuses to rationalize losses.
- Stay focused and control your emotions; this is a business.
- Think independently, especially if you are trading in an environment with other traders.
- Let the market tell you what it's doing, you will never tell it what to do.
- Avoid greed and fear; there is always another trade.
- Don't let a bad trade ruin your day.
- Don't get married to a stock or a position. Take small losses and let profits run.
- Don't try to get back at the market. Follow your business plan.

chapter 11

evaluating your performance

Well, if I called the wrong number, why did you answer the phone?
—*James Thurber, 1894–1961*

At the very least, you must know the profit or loss of each trade you make. Keeping a running total of your profits and losses keeps you honest. Gamblers talk about their big wins, but they never tell you about their losses. Trading is not gambling, it is a profession, so keep good books.

For *every* trade you make, you must record the price at which you entered the trade and the price at which you exit. From these two numbers you compute your profit or loss.

definition:

    profit   The difference between the price at which you sell something and the price at which you bought it, less any transaction costs.

If your trade was long (that is, you bought and then sold in that order), then your profit is calculated as:

$$\text{Profit} = \text{exit price} - \text{entry price}$$

If your trade was short (that is, you sold and then bought in that order), then your profit is calculated as:

$$\text{Profit} = \text{entry price} - \text{exit price}$$

I cannot stress this strongly enough: Keep good books. I don't care whether you use plain white paper and a pen, green ledger paper, or a computer, but keep track of everything you do. Otherwise, you're just gambling and you have no statistics upon which to base subsequent calculations that can improve your performance. An example of keeping track of your trades in a spreadsheet is shown in Figure 11.1. This is the very least you must know; however, it is not really enough. We math types call this *necessary, but not sufficient.* You can keep better statistics than these, and thereby have more confidence in your trading.

Your equity is the cumulative amount of money you have made or lost trading. In the spreadsheet above, we could add a column to the right of "Profit" and call it "Equity." The figures in the equity column would be calculated by adding all your profits and subtracting all your losses, and keeping a running total.

The more you know about your trading statistically, the more able you will be to follow your system, or your plan, during periods of drawdown.

definition:

   drawdown   The reduction in account equity as a result of a trade or series of trades.

In practice, we measure drawdown from the highest equity high to the lowest equity low. Looking at this number answers the question: "How bad can it be?" What's your worst case?

---

figure 11.1   spreadsheet for tracking your trades

Entry Date	Entry Time	Entry Price	Exit Date	Exit Time	Exit Price	Profit

useful statistics

In addition to keeping track of your equity and your drawdown, there are several other numbers you should compute. Many of the financial software products will calculate these statistics automatically for you as part of their portfolio modules.

Figure 11.2 shows an example of the information available from a performance summary from TradeStation™ (Omega Research). Study the information on the performance summary. There's a lot to be learned. The total net profit *is not* the most important number. We know that if the system is profitable (has a positive mathematical expectation), we can maximize the profit through money management; so as long as the total net profit is positive, we can improve it.

Professional traders can make a good living with systems that show 40% or more profit as long as the ratio of the average win to the average loss is high enough to generate a positive mathematical expectation. Because the "Percent profitable" figure shows that 63% of the trades are profitable, that's acceptable. We can calculate that number

---

figure 11.2 TradeStation performance summary

TradeStation System Report

TradeStation System Report - Solar_1 SP U9-15 min. (5/3/99-7/6/99)

Performance Summary: All Trades

Total Net Profit	$30,375.00	Open position P/L	($500.00)
Gross Profit	$44,225.00	Gross Loss	($13,850.00)
Total # of trades	8	Percent profitable	63.00%
Number winning trades	5	Number losing trades	3
Largest winning trade	$15,675.00	Largest losing trade	($10,050.00)
Average winning trade	$8,845.00	Average losing trade	($4,616.67)
Ratio avg win/avg loss	1.92	Avg trade (win & loss)	$3,796.88
Max consec. Winners	3	Max consec. losers	3
Avg # bars in winners	92	Avg # bars in losers	71
Max intraday drawdown	($14,825.00)		
Profit Factor	3.19	Max # contracts held	1
Account size required	$14,825.00	Return on account	204.89%

Summary | Trades | Analysis | Annual | Monthly | Weekly | Daily | Win l Loss | Time | Graphs | Settings

Created with TradeStation 2000i by Omega Research © 1999

Source: Omega Research TradeStation. Reprinted with permission.

ourselves by taking the total number of winning trades (5) and dividing by the total number of trades (8).

When evaluating an idea, or theory, for its long-term potential, I like to have a quantitative measure of the theory. With a quantitative measure, I can compare systems with each other. In a sense, I can give each system a score. Here's what I look at:

- Mathematical expectation (*ME*)
- Percent profitability (*P*)
- Ratio of the average profitable trade to the average losing trade (*P/L* ratio)
- Profit factor (*PF*)
- Return on account (*ROA*)

I call these my *Cardinal Profitability Constructs*™ (CPC™). If a system I have designed passes muster through this rigorous set of CPC conditions, after already passing through the first set of tests, I'm ready to trade it.*

The qualifying conditions I look for in the CPC numbers are these:

- $ME > 0.0$.
- $P \geq 35\%$.
- $(P/L \text{ ratio}) \times (PF) \geq 3.0$.
- $ROA \geq 20\%$.

All well and good, you say, but where do we get those numbers? Okay, hang on just a little bit here, we're going to do some mathematics. Nothing strenuous, though, so don't stop reading.

Often, the statistics you need to form the CPCs are included in the standard reports of your technical analysis software. Even so, you should be able to calculate them yourself and understand the underlying concepts.

ME: mathematical expectation
Mathematical expectation tells us whether we should expect to win or lose in the long run. We calculate *ME* using this formula:

---

* Please note that I am not saying that this level of CPC numbers will guarantee success. I am suggesting that this is a vigorous test, and one I use in my own system evaluation.

$$ME = [(1 + A) * P] - 1$$

where
> P = Probability of winning
> A = (Amount you can win)/(Amount you can lose)

CPC Index™

How high does the P/L ratio need to be? It depends. Many technicians say that the ratio needs to be 2 or greater and that the PF needs to be 2 or greater. Although I agree that it would be comforting, I believe you can still show a profit with numbers a bit smaller. I found a multiplicative relationship between these two numbers and P, which I use to evaluate my own trading. When these three numbers are multiplied together, we have a single number that I call my CPC Index number, for Cardinal Profitability Construct. If one number is high enough, the others can be lower and still have the result be the same. For instance, Table 11.1 demonstrates the relationship of the numbers.

Finally, I look at the maximum consecutive losers and the average number of bars in losers to see whether my emotional makeup and personality can stand the heat in this kitchen. Looking at Figure 11.2 again, there are three losers in a row before encountering a winning trade. That's not too bad emotionally. There are 71 bars, on average, in each losing trade, whereas the winners, on average, last for 92 bars. I think I can handle that.

is it broken?

How much is enough? Are you still on track? Has the system failed? How do you compare with other traders? How do you compare with the instrument itself? How does your actual trading compare with your system's hypothetical trading?

table 11.1 CPC index

% Profitable	Ratio	Profit Factor	CPC Index
63%	1.92	3.19	3.86
50%	2.0	2.0	2.0
45%	2.0	2.22	2.0
40%	2.0	2.5	2.0

Have you asked yourself these questions? If you haven't, you should! You should know your system inside and out, backward and forward. You should be intimately familiar with the statistics that illustrate which ways your system can succeed and which ways it can fail.

Of course, don't forget that nothing ever performs exactly in the future as it did in the past. You can flip a coin 50 times and get 50 heads. Statistically, however, you should see results similar to those of the model.

keeping track

With good bookkeeping, you can stay ahead of the game. If you keep close account of your trades, your tests, and your mistakes, you'll be ahead of 90% of the traders against whom you are competing.

At the very least, you must know whether your trade was a buy or a sell, when the trade was made, and what you were trading. Figure 11.3 shows a handy little form I use to keep up-to-date with the essentials. Actually, I make this form on my computer (using a spreadsheet), and I print out hundreds of them. I then keep these records in a three-hole-punch binder, as well as entering the information into the spreadsheet in the computer. I find that the double-entry method still works best for me. It's easy to get flustered, or not to have the spreadsheet running at the time you place the trade. Then, you could lose track of whether you are long or short; it's embarrassing to have to ask your broker to tell you.

figure 11.3 keep track of your orders

Date	Time	Buy Sell Cancel	Qty	Symbol	Price	Ticket
06/22/1999	10:30 am	BUY	1000	EGGS	12 5/8	C-400-123-4456

measurements

There is no end to the ways you can analyze your success (or failure). You can run statistics from now until doomsday, but the only thing that really matters in the end is whether you are turning a profit. We will go over a few important measurements here, but if you are interested in fully examining your performance, PSP (by Rina Systems) does a thorough job.

VAMI

VAMI is an acronym for Value-Added Monthly Index. Professional traders compare their performance with each other using this statistic. The reason it is so widely used is that it allows us to compare apples with apples.

If you are trading a $50,000 account and your friend is trading a $1,000,000 account, how can you meaningfully compare your successes and failures?

VAMI represents the growth of $1,000 invested at the start of the track record based on historical monthly rates of return (ROR). The formula for its calculation is:

$$VAMI_{i+1} = VAMI_i \times (1 + ROR)$$

Thus, we would take the percentage return made on your actual account and apply it to the theoretical $1,000 account. Your friend would be doing the same calculations with his account. Therefore, each month you would be able to compare apples with apples. Figure 11.4 is a spreadsheet illustration of the method.

average time to recovery

The number of months it takes you to recover from the low point in your equity decline is your *time to recovery.* You will experience more than one drawdown in your trading career. The average time to recovery is the average of each of those recoveries.

Why is this information important? If your trading seems to be going along great, and you hit a catastrophic drawdown, the significance of that drawdown can be measured by your time to recovery. If it only takes you a month to recover, then your loss was not such a big deal. If, however, it takes you the rest of the year to get back to even, then the drawdown was pretty significant.

figure 11.4 *VAMI* **calculation**

	Beginning	P/L	ROR	Ending	VAMI $1,000
January	$50,000	$1,000	2.0%	$51,000	$1,020
February	$51,000	$2,000	3.9%	$53,000	$1,060
March	$53,000	$1,000	1.9%	$54,000	$1,080
April	$54,000	$(500)	−0.9%	$53,500	$1,070
May	$53,500	$3,000	5.6%	$56,500	$1,130
June	$56,500	$(1,500)	−2.7%	$55,000	$1,100
July	$55,000	$1,200	2.2%	$56,200	$1,124
August	$56,200	$1,500	2.7%	$57,700	$1,154
September	$57,700	$1,800	3.1%	$59,500	$1,190
October	$59,500	$(900)	−1.5%	$58,600	$1,172
November	$58,600	$1,500	2.6%	$60,100	$1,202
December	$60,100	$750	1.2%	$60,850	$1,217
ANNUAL TOTAL		$10,850	21.7%		

Now, let's say that you've had five periods of drawdown. If the average time to recovery of those five was a month or two, you're still an exceptional trader. One bad experience does not ruin your track record, but if the average of all your adverse events is bad, you'd better take another look at your system.

conclusion

One more thought before we move on. As you design and test your theories, always remember that it takes longer to recover from bad trades than it does to make them. If you lose money on several trades in a row, your bankroll will have decreased. Thus, the power you have to make money is diminished. If your system makes 30% per year, you will have reduced the principal upon which you can make that 30%. Why am I admonishing you now? Because most of the people who call me for help do so after they've lost much of their money, not before. Do your homework before you trade, not after.

chapter 12

record keeping and taxes

A little neglect may breed mischief, . . . for want of a nail, the shoe
was lost; for want of a shoe the horse was lost; and for want of a
horse the rider was lost.

—*Benjamin Franklin, 1706–1790*

If there were one single piece of advice I could give you about taxes,
it would be, "Don't trade for the tax man!" By that I mean, paying taxes
is a good thing. The more profit you make, the more taxes you are
going to pay. Think about it: The way to pay less taxes is to make less
money.

Nevertheless, you don't really want to pay more taxes than you
owe. Striking a balance between too much and too little necessitates
the proper keeping of records. In this chapter, we are going to take a
look at a little of each.

your trading records

As you test your theories and, subsequently, as you begin trading, you
will generate massive amounts of papers. Keeping track of what it all
means can become a full-time job.

Like using separate computers, I like to use separate file cabinets.
I keep all of my testing theories and results in a location away from
other kinds of paperwork.

Document each test or set of tests before you run them and, again, after you run them. First document what you are going to do, and then document the results of what you did. Remember that you are a researcher and you don't want to prejudice your outcomes with preconceived notions. Next year, or the year after, when you come back to review your efforts, you will have forgotten what you did. If you have kept an accurate record, you will be able to reconstruct your thought process and avoid duplicating your effort.

It is often helpful to create an index or table of contents to your filing system, so you can find things by glancing rather than rummaging.

Keep another file cabinet or drawer for your trading confirmations, statements, and account balances. Your real-time trading results will be important to you for several reasons, not the least of which is taxes. You will want to keep summaries of your real-time trading results, which will include weekly, monthly, or annual results in tabular format.

Your real-time results will be important to you if you ever want to manage money for someone else. They will also be important for you to compare with your theoretical performance.

Keep all your trading results together in one place—and, keep them organized.

income and outgo

In another section, drawer, or drawers, keep your accounts receivable and accounts payable. In the beginning of your trading business, you may not have any accounts receivable, but create the section anyway. Keep careful track of all your receipts, and become acutely aware of the balance between your spending and your trading income.

If your trading is like gambling, you will remember the big wins and not the accumulation of small losses. When you add *all* your wins and losses together, is the net result positive or negative?

Your losses are not your only expense. If you are driving to a trading salon, you are putting miles on your car and expending gas and oil. You probably spend money on paper and office supplies. You probably have a computer or software that you use for your trading research. You might have real-time data to pay for. Chances are you are paying for Internet access. All these things are part of your trading business. They add up. You must know the bottom line: Does this job pay more than minimum wage?

taxes

Taxation for traders can be a complicated issue. Most tax accountants are well qualified to deal with long-term investors, but not versed in the nuances of day traders and speed traders. Choose your accountant carefully through an interviewing process. Ted Tesser, of Waterside Financial, has written books on how to deal with the tax obligations you will face as a trader. You would do well to read his works, including *The Serious Investor's Tax Survival Guide.*

On the Internet, you will find resources for other tax preparers and consultants:

SmartMoney   **www.smartmoney.com**

Includes a section on Tax Tips for Day Traders.

Green & Company, Inc.   **www.greencompany.com**

The leading tax expert for online traders. Includes Trader Tax Guides, Trader Tax Solution Packages, and Trader Tax Preparation service.

appendixes

It is my hope that this book will be your reference guide for months, or years, to come. Yes, you will get past the learning phase, and hopefully you will go on to make lots and lots of money. To that end, these appendixes are to supply you with the reference materials you will need as you grow and become more proficient.

It would be physically impossible to print an appendix to this book that was up-to-date. The electronic information age we are in changes daily. For current resources, please visit The Money Mentor at www.moneymentor.com.

appendix a

ECNs

All-Tech Investment Group ATTN
160 Summit Avenue
Montvale, NJ 07645
1-888-328-8246
www.attain.com

All-Tech Investment Group, Inc., is respected as one of the pioneers of direct-access electronic stock trading. For the past 10 years, All-Tech fought for investor fairness and a level playing field environment for individual market participants. All-Tech's struggle against a system that favored market makers and the brokerage community at the expense of the average investor has been widely highlighted in financial publications.

All-Tech CEO, Harvey Houtkin, has been an outspoken proponent for the reform of investing rules and regulations that provide the individual investor with fair and equal opportunities to participate in the financial markets. Mr. Houtkin's pursuit of these ideals earned him the nickname "The Original SOES Bandit"; he was criticized by the same market makers and brokerage firms that would be investigated by the Securities and Exchange Commission (SEC) and the Justice Department and would eventually pay almost $1 billion to settle a class action lawsuit alleging price fixing. Mr. Houtkin is now referred to as "The Father of Electronic Stock Trading" and has authored two books on stock trading.

Bloomberg Tradebook LLC BTRD
499 Park Avenue
New York, NY 10022
1-212-318-2200
www.bloomberg.com

Bloomberg TRADEBOOK provides institutional equity traders, agency brokers, and market makers innovative access to multiple sources of liquidity. Bloomberg TRADEBOOK embraces the rules and helps traders consolidate all sources of liquidity on one electronic platform. Bloomberg TRADEBOOK represents your orders in the National Quote Montage and interacts with general order flow across the Nasdaq system or specifically accesses liquidity from individual market makers or electronic communications networks (ECNs).

In May of 1999, Bloomberg announced its formation of a SuperECN strategic partnership with Investment Technology Group (ITG), Inc., providing all the benefits of B-Trade (BTRD) plus the electronic crossing system of the ITG platform.

An electronic crossing system offers liquidity by electronically matching buy and sell orders at a derived price, such as the market midpoint, at discrete times during the day.

Instinet (a Reuters Company) INCA
875 Third Avenue
New York, NY 10022
1-212-310-9500
www.instinet.com

One of the oldest after-hours markets, Instinet Corporation has long allowed subscribing institutions to match bids and asks for any stock listed on the 17 participating exchanges around the world. Instinet Corporation is a member of these 17 exchanges, and is a registered broker headquartered in New York. Instinet is an agency broker, founded in 1969, and acquired by Reuters Group PLC in 1987.

Instinet is neutral and does not compete with clients' orders by buying or selling for its own account. (Remember that specialists and market makers can buy and sell for their own accounts.) Instinet provides anonymity to its client, allowing them to enter the market without revealing strategy, profile, or identity to the market place. The advantage of anonymity is clear when you are a big player and don't want others bidding up the price as you enter a large order.

As a broker, Instinet charges a fee for each transaction. Instinet fundamentally changed the way institutional trading was conducted when it allowed clients to view the order pad and, thus, to secure the best price instantly.

Using Instinet, clients execute their own trades globally, in their own local currency. Through the Instinet terminal, all client orders worldwide are displayed simultaneously. Yet, if necessary, Instinet can deal in traditional telephonic communication.

Island (ISLD)
50 Broad Street, 6th Floor
New York, NY 10004
1-212-231-5000
www.isld.com
info@isld.com

Island, headquartered in New York City and owned by Datek, was founded in 1996 to be an electronic meeting place for institutions and brokerages to display and match stock orders. Island began representing orders in the Nasdaq Stock Market's quote montage on January 17, 1997, and now has close to 200 subscribing brokerage firms.

Island is registered as an ECN with the SEC under Rule 17a23. Island is also a registered member of the National Association of Securities Dealers (NASD) and Securities Investor Protection Corporation (SIPC).

NexTrade ECN
1-727-423-5495
www.invest2000.com

The NexTrade ECN and ProTrade software are uniquely positioned to provide firms the ability to generate income on the limit order book, and at the same time, to handle compliance liabilities and market responsibilities that go along with limit order handling.

NexTrend (TRND)
251 West Renner Parkway, Suite 200
Richardson, TX 75080
1-972-470-9265
www.nextrend.com
sales@nextrend.com

New to the ECN scene, NexTrend offers a full analytical solution without any secondary costs. Whereas most of the day-trading salons either use third-party software, or base their software on Townsend's RealTick III, NexTrend has created a stand-alone, non-browser-based package to address the complete speed-trading problem. *NexTrend Electronic Trading*, to be launched in late 1999, will enable users to instantly enter electronic trades on direct order-entry systems, such as Nasdaq (SOES), New York Stock Exchange (DOT), London Stock Exchange (SETS), ECNs, and broker/dealer links directly to the trading floors.

Spear, Leeds & Kellogg (REDI)
120 Broadway, 6th Floor
New York, NY 10271
1-212-433-7000
www.slk.com

Spear, Leeds & Kellogg (SLK) offers to its customers a proprietary computer interface called REDIPlus®. REDIPlus, a 32BIT Windows point-and-click system, is designed specifically for the sophisticated trader. REDIPlus builds upon the success of the SLK REDI® System (Routing and Execution Dot Interface), which was originally developed in 1992.

REDIPlus supports multiple computer-to-computer interfaces, allowing customers to benefit from Spear, Leeds & Kellogg connections to various exchanges. REDIPlus integrates order routing to the NYSE/Amex/REDIBook® (SLK ECN)/Selectnet/SOES/SLK Nasdaq. These routing capabilities are combined with user-friendly terminal screens (NASD Level II), P&L/Position Management, Market Monitor, and Quotation Services.

Terra Nova Trading LLC (TNTO)
Empire State Building
350 Fifth Avenue, Suite 630
New York, NY 10118
1-212-279-7800
www.terranovatrading.com

Providers of The Executioner and Terra Nova Trader software. Terra Nova does not sell order flow, they route your orders directly to Nasdaq and the exchange floors. Terra Nova is the creator of the Archipelago ECN. Terra Nova provides comprehensive order routing, including Archipelago, Instinet, Island, SOES, several DOT execution systems, as well as Selectnet broadcast.

appendix b

direct-access brokers and trading salons

There are direct-access brokers, with trading salons, in many major cities throughout the United States. See the map shown in Figure B.1.

figure B.1   direct-access brokers and trading salons

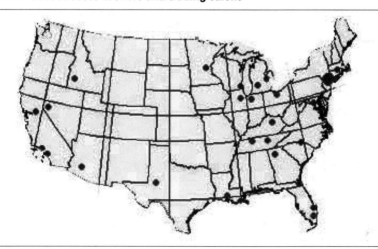

branch office locations

All-Tech Investment Group, Inc. (Attain)　　　　www.attain.com

Montvale, NJ
(Corporate Headquarters)
160 Summit Ave.
Montvale, NJ 07645

Albany, NY
296 Washington Ave. Extension
Albany, NY 12203

Atlanta, GA
3525 Piedmont Rd., Ste. 215
Atlanta, GA 30305

Boca Raton, FL
7601 North Federal Hwy., Ste. B240
Boca Raton, FL 33487

Livingston, NJ
25 South Livingston Ave., 2nd Flr.
Livingston, NJ 07039

Chicago, IL
1400 East Lake Cook Rd., Ste. 130
Buffalo Grove, IL 60089

Dallas, TX
4900 Beltline Rd., Ste. 250
Dallas, TX 75240

Detroit, MI
30700 Telegraph Rd., Ste. 2675
Bingham Farms, MI 48025

Edison, NJ
1090 King Georges Post Rd., Ste. 503
Edison, NJ 08837

Flushing, NY
41–60 Main St., Ste. 208
Flushing, NY 08873

Fort Worth, TX
Water Gardens Place
100 East 15th, Ste. 520
Forth Worth, TX 76102

Garden City, NY
500 Old Country Rd.
Garden City, NY 11530

Kansas City, KS
5360 College Blvd., Ste. 100
Overland Park, KS 66211

Knoxville, TN
5204 Kingston Pike
Knoxville, TN 37919

New York City, NY
61 Broadway, Ste. 1115
New York, NY 10003

Oklahoma City, OK
4141 Northwest Expwy., Ste. 150
Oklahoma City, OK 73116

Portland, OR
9650 S.W. Beaverton-Hillsdale Hwy.
Beaverton, OR 97005

Seattle, WA
1130 140th Ave., N.E.
Bellevue, WA 98005

San Diego, CA
6310 Greenwich Dr., Ste. 140
San Diego, CA 92122

Stamford, CT
Phillips Mansion
666 Glenbrook Rd., Ste. LL-B
Stamford, CT 06906

Tulsa, OK
4111 South Darlington, Ste. 120
Tulsa, OK 74135

Falls Church, VA
7700 Leesburg Pike, Ste. 304
Falls Church, VA 22043

Westchester, NY
2500 Westchester Ave., Ste. 102
Purchase, NY 10577

Broadway Trading   www.broadwaytrading.com

Broadway Trading, LLC, specializes in day trading. Broadway offers online executions through the use of the Watcher, a program that provides the individual trader with the ability to place orders directly into an order-entry system. After firm approval, these orders are immediately sent to the market for execution or posted on the Island ECN. Orders can be filled in less than a second. Broadway Trading offers hands-on training on the use of the systems it provides.

New York, NY
50 Broad St., 2nd Flr.
New York, NY 10004
Phone: 1-212-328-3555
Fax: 1-212-377-1562

Castle Online   www.castleonline.com

Offers proprietary JavaTrader execution software. Timely executions and fast confirmations. Trading on: Nasdaq exchange w/SOES, Selectnet, and ECN executions; NYSE exchange through the SuperDOT system; Amex exchange.

Corporate Headquarters
45 Church St.
Freeport, NY 11520

TradingRoom A
Phone: 1-800-661-5133
1-516-868-8812
Fax: 1-516-868-5131

TradingRoom B
Phone: 1-800-891-1003
1-516-868-0981
Fax: 1-516-868-0228

Cornerstone Securities   www.protrader.com

Austin, TX (Corporate Offices)
504 Lavaca, Ste. 1000
Austin, TX 78701
Phone: 1-512-479-7300
Fax: 1-512-479-7301

Scottsdale, AZ
4725 North Scottsdale Rd., Ste. 210
Scottsdale, AZ 85251
Phone: 1-480-423-1700
Fax: 1-480-954-5353

Irvine, CA
2081 Business Center Dr., Ste. 230
Irvine, CA 92612
Phone: 1-714-475-4228
Fax: 1-714-475-4231

La Jolla, CA
4130 La Jolla Village Dr., Ste. 300
La Jolla, CA 92037
Phone: 1-858-587-9677
Fax: 1-858-587-9476

San Jose, CA
4675 Stevens Creek
Suite 200
Santa Clara, CA 95051
Phone: 1-408-615-5305

Los Angeles, CA
10880 Wilshire Blvd., Ste. 200
Los Angeles, CA 90024
Phone: 1-310-446-8989
Fax: 1-310-446-8990

Denver, CO
201 Filmore Dr., Ste. A
Denver, CO 80206
Phone: 1-303-321-1091
Fax: 1-303-316-7822

Jacksonville, FL
7411 Fullerton St., Ste. 109
Jacksonville, FL 32256
Phone: 1-904-519-2111
Fax: 1-904-519-2181

Atlanta, GA
3355 Lenox Road, Ste. 440
Atlanta, GA 30326
Phone: 1-404-266-2562
Fax: 1-404-266-8566

Lexington, KY
3070 Lakecrest Circle, Ste. 300
Lexington, KY 40513
Phone: 1-606-296-2542
Fax: 1-606-224-4063

Cleveland, OH
6100 Rockside Woods Blvd., Ste. 215
Independence, OH 44131
Phone: 1-216-901-9600
Fax: 1-216-901-9690

Austin, TX
1717 West 6th St., Ste. 310
Austin, TX 78703
Phone: 1-512-472-0877
Fax: 1-512-472-0878

Houston, TX
3355 West Alabama, Ste. 750
Houston, TX 77098
Phone: 1-713-627-3788
Fax: 1-713-627-3789

Greenwich, CT
283 Greenwich Ave., 2nd Floor
Greenwich, CT 06830
Phone: 1-203-862-9260
Fax: 1-203-862-9364

Tampa, FL
4830 West Kennedy Blvd., Ste. 865
Tampa, FL 33609
Phone: 1-813-287-1184
Fax: 1-813-287-2484

Chicago, IL
200 S. Wacker, Ste. 3969
Chicago, IL 60606
Phone: 1-312-382-1230
Fax: 1-312-382-1231

Long Island, NY
1300 Veterans Memorial Hwy., 2nd Flr.
Hauppauge, NY 11788
Phone: 1-516-231-7777
Fax: 1-516-231-0009

Nashville, TN
1800 Galleria Blvd., Ste. 1650
Franklin, TN 37067
Phone: 1-615-771-9206
Fax: 1-615-771-9078

Dallas, TX
9400 North Central Expressway, Ste. 320
Dallas, TX 75231
Phone: 1-214-739-8191
Fax: 1-214-739-8194

San Antonio, TX
1020 NE Loop 410, Ste. 330
San Antonio, TX 78209
Phone: 1-210-822-8723
Fax: 1-210-822-0519

Market Wise   **www.marketwise.com**

Broomfield, CO
6343 West 120th Ave., Ste. 200
Broomfield, CO 80020
Phone: 1-303-439-8442

Englewood, CO
6551 S. Revere Parkway
Englewood, CO 80111
Phone: 1-303-799-8445

Baton Rouge, LA
2351 Energy Dr., Ste. 1009
Baton Rouge, LA 70808
Phone: 1-225-932-2337

Tampa, FL
4890 W. Kennedy Blvd., Ste. 500
Tampa, FL 33609
Phone: 1-813-288-8181

San Francisco, CA
22 Second St., Ste. 500
San Francisco, CA 94105
Phone: 1-415-348-WISE

MaxTrade Financial Services   www.maxtrading.com

A Level II online investment company that offers Realtick III software. Site includes online chat room, link to download software (free demo), and bookstore.

MAX Trade, L.L.C.
560 Kirts Blvd., Suite 118
Troy, MI 48084
Phone: 1-248-362-2650
Toll Free: 1-888-741-8733
Fax: 1-248-362-2678

Momentum Securities Management Company   www.soes.com/home.html

Momentum Securities Management Company (Momentum Securities), and its affiliated companies, including its securities broker/dealer, Momentum Securities, Inc., are leaders in virtually every aspect of the electronic day-trading industry, proprietary software development, and order delivery systems. Founded in Texas in 1995, Momentum Securities has become one of the largest electronic day-trading organizations in terms of total trading volume in the country, with its home office in Houston (Galleria Area) and branch offices in North Houston, Austin, Dallas, Tyler, Plano; Irvine, California; Atlanta, Georgia; Chicago, Illinois; and Milwaukee, Wisconsin. E-mail: info@soes.com

Austin, TX
609 Castle Ridge Rd., Ste. 222
Austin, TX 78746
Phone: 1-512-347-1700
Fax: 1-512-347-1900

Houston, TX
1800 Bering, Ste. 750
Houston, TX 77057
Phone: 1-713-706-3300
Fax: 1-713-977-7975

Dallas, TX
3811 Turtle Creek Ctr., Ste. 1320
Dallas, Texas 75219
Phone: 1-214-520-2115
Fax: 1-214-520-9505

Houston, TX
17776 Tomball Pkwy., Ste. 33
Houston, TX 77064
Phone: 1-281-970-5444
Fax: 1-713-977-7975

Irvine, CA
4199 Campus Dr., Ste. F
Irvine, CA 92612
Phone: 1-949-854-4040

Tyler, TX
202 South Broadway
Tyler, TX 75702
Phone: 1-903-597-2887
Fax: 1-903-597-0560

Plano, TX
1800 Preston Park Blvd., Ste. 101
Plano, TX 75093
Phone: 1-972-769-9555
Fax: 1-972-769-9455

OnlineTradingInc.com

Boca Raton, FL
2700 North Military Trail, Ste. 200
Boca Raton, FL 33431
Phone: 1-800-995-1076
Fax: 1-561-995-0606

Hudson, OH
44 Clinton St.
Hudson, OH 44236
Phone: 1-330-342-8557
Fax: 1-330-650-1074

Pittsburgh, PA
4955 Steubenville Pike, Ste. 130
Pittsburgh, PA 15205
Phone: 1-888-506-7644
Phone: 1-412-506-2000
Fax: 1-412-506-1985

West Chester, OH
8992 Cincinnati Dayton Rd.
West Chester, OH 45069
Phone: 1-513-755-7470
Fax: 1-513-755-7480

Boston, MA
The Pilot House, Lewis Wharf
Boston, MA 02110
Phone: 1-888-267-4320
Phone: 1-617-854-3700
Fax: 1-617-854-3709

Osterville, MA
8 West Bay Rd. (Cape Cod)
Osterville, MA 02655
Phone: 1-877-428-3444
Phone: 1-412-506-2000
Fax: 1-508-428-3444

Troy, MI
2690 Crooks Rd., Ste. 409
Troy, MI 48084
Phone: 1-248-244-1191
Fax: 1-248-244-1194

RT Trading   www.rttrading.com

Discount brokerage specifically for day traders: Level II, Instinet, Island, SOES, Archipelago, ABN-Amro. No payment for order flow.

RT Trading (InvestIN.com)
Phone: 1-214-939-0110
Toll Free: 1-800-327-1883
Fax: 1-214-939-0116

InvestIN.com Securities Corp.
Infomart—Ste. 2016
1950 Stemmons Frwy.
Dallas, TX 75207

InvestIN Securities Ltd.
International Finance Center, Ste. 502
25 Old Broad Street
London EC2N 1HN UK

Self Trading Securities, Inc.   www.selftrading.com

Self Trading Securities, Inc., is an Austin, Texas-based brokerage firm
that specializes in electronic day trading. Clients use the fastest, most
reliable execution and quotation systems available to trade Nasdaq- and
NYSE-listed securities. By using the strategies and techniques they've
learned through direct interaction with experienced traders, STS clients
attempt to leverage a relatively modest amount of capital into significant
percentage gains. In addition to providing the best possible tools and
resources, STS also provides superior ongoing service and support.

Austin, TX (Corporate Office)   **San Antonio, TX**
620 RR620 #201   110 Broadway, Ste. 150
Austin, TX 78734   San Antonio, TX 78205
Phone: 1-512-263-2769   Phone: 1-210-475-9751
Fax: 1-512-263-2141

Ft Wayne, IN
105 W. Wayne St.
Ft. Wayne, TX 46802
Phone: 1-219-424-5521
Fax: 1-219-426-8358

TrendTrader LLC   www.trendtrader.com

Specializing in "remote" electronic order routing and execution for institutions, day traders and retail investors. New clients may trade 200-
share lots for $10.00 during the first week of software use.

Trend Trader LLC
15030 N. Hayden Rd., Ste. 120
Scottsdale, AZ 85260
Phone: 1-602-948-1146
Fax: 1-602-948-1195

appendix c

online/electronic brokers

AccuTrade   **1-800-494-8939**

figure C.1   www.accutrade.com

Minimum Deposit	$5,000
Online Commission	$29.95
Real-Time Quotes	$20/mo
Futures	
Stocks	✔
Options	✔
Mutual Funds	✔

Source: AccuTrade. Reprinted with permission.

BestDirect   **1-800-759-0062**
(A Division of Peregrine Financial Group, Inc.)

figure C.2 www.pfgbest.com

Source: BestDirect. Reprinted with permission.

Minimum Deposit	$10,000
Online Commission	
Real-Time Quotes	Discount for eSignal
Futures	
Stocks	✔
Options	✔
Mutual Funds	✔

Charles Schwab

1-800-435-4000

figure C.3   www.schwab.com

Minimum Deposit	$2,500
Online Commission	$29.95 up to 1,000 shares
Real-Time Quotes	
Futures	
Stocks	✔
Options	✔
Mutual Funds	✔

Source: Schwab. Reprinted with permission. Note: Schwab in no way endorses any of the trading or investment strategies outlined in this book.

Datek   **1-888-GO-DATEK**

This broker enters more than 50% of all electronic orders in the Nasdaq stock market each day, and offers online trading for just $9.99 per execution. Datek Online uses an automated, intelligent order-routing system to place your orders in the best venue. Your orders route directly to NYSE, Amex, and Nasdaq. Datek also represents your Nasdaq orders on The Island Electronic Communication Network—the second largest ECN.

E*TRADE

1-800-ETRADE-1

figure C.4   **www.etrade.com**

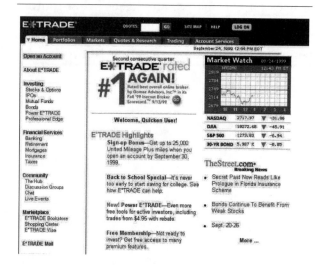

Minimum Deposit	$1,000
Online Commission	$4.95 and up
Real-Time Quotes	free
Futures	
Stocks	✔
Options	✔
Mutual Funds	✔

Source: E*TRADE. E*TRADE is a registered trademark of E*TRADE Securities, Inc. etrade.com is a trademark of E*TRADE Securities, Inc. Used by permission. All rights reserved.

FCNIS (Bank One)

1-888-THE-NET2

figure C.5   www.fcnis.com

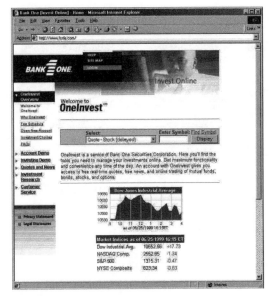

Source: FCNIS (Bank One). Reprinted with permission.

Minimum Deposit	
Online Commission	$19.95
Real-Time Quotes	free
Futures	
Stocks	✔
Options	✔
Mutual Funds	✔

LindWaldock

1-800-445-2000

figure C.6 www.lind-waldock.com

Source: LindWaldock. Reprinted with permission.

Minimum Deposit	$5,000
Online Commission	$19–29
Real-Time Quotes	500 Snap-shots/ month free
Futures	✔
Stocks	
Options	
Mutual Funds	

Preferred Trade   1-888-889-9178

figure C.7   www.preferredtrade.com

Minimum Deposit	$1,000
Online Commission	$7.75
Real-Time Quotes	free
Futures	
Stocks	✔
Options	✔
Mutual Funds	✔

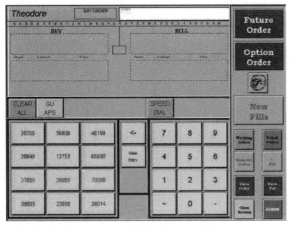

Source: Preferred Trade. Reprinted with permission.

Rand-USA's Theodore   1-800-842-RAND

figure C.8   www.rand-usa.com

Minimum Deposit	
Online Commission	
Real-Time Quotes	
Futures	✔
Stocks	
Options	
Mutual Funds	

Source: Rand-USA's Theodore. Reprinted with permission.

SureTrade

1-401-642-6900

figure C.9 www.suretrade.com

Minimum Deposit	$0
Online Commission	$7.95
Real-Time Quotes	100/day free
Futures	
Stocks	✔
Options	✔
Mutual Funds	✔

Source: SureTrade. © 1999–2000 SureTrade, a Fleet Financial Group company. All rights reserved. Reprinted with permission.

Wall Street Access

1-800-925-5781

figure C.10 www.wsaccess.com

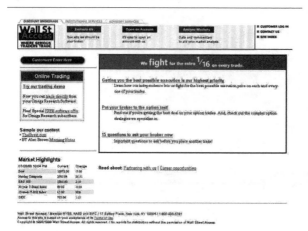

Minimum Deposit	
Online Commission	$25
Real-Time Quotes	100 free/ trade
Futures	
Stocks	✔
Options	✔
Mutual Funds	✔

Source: Wall Street Access. Reprinted with permission.

TD Waterhouse webBroker

1-800-934-4410

figure C.11 www.tdwaterhouse.com

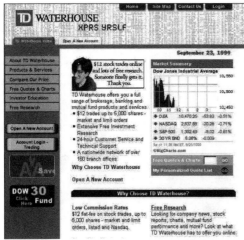

Minimum Deposit	$1,000
Online Commission	$12.00
Real-Time Quotes	100 free/day
Futures	
Stocks	✔
Options	✔
Mutual Funds	✔

Source: TD Waterhouse. © 1999 TD Waterhouse Investor Services, Inc. All rights reserved. Member NYSE, SIPC. Reprinted with permission.

Web Street Securities, Inc.

1-800-WEB-TRADe

figure C.12 www.webstreetsecurities.com

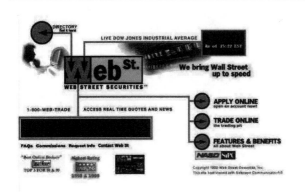

Minimum Deposit	$0
Online Commission	$14.95
Real-Time Quotes	free
Futures	
Stocks	✔
Options	✔
Mutual Funds	✔

Source: Web Street Securities, Inc. Web Street logo © 1999, Web Street Securities, Inc.™ All rights reserved. Logo appears courtesy of Web Street Securities, Inc.

XPRESSTRADE   1-800-947-6228

figure C.13   www.xpresstrade.com

Minimum Deposit	$5,000
Online Commission	$20
Real-Time Quotes	free to account holders
Futures	✔
Stocks	
Options	
Mutual Funds	

Source: XPRESSTRADE. Reprinted with permission.

ZAP Futures   1-800-441-1616

figure C.14   www.zapfutures.com

Minimum Deposit	$5,000
Online Commission	$20
Real-Time Quotes	eSignal
Futures	✔
Stocks	
Options	
Mutual Funds	

Source: ZAP Futures. Reprinted with permission.

appendix d

market makers

There are more than 500 market makers. Here, we list some of the most active, and thus more likely for you to encounter.

Mnemonic	Market Maker
ABSB	Alex Brown & Sons, Inc.
AGIS	Aegis Capital Corp.
BEST	Bear Stearns & Co., Inc.
BTSC	BT Alex Brown Securities
CANT	Cantor Fitzgerald & Co.
CHGO	Chicago Corp.
CJDB	J Lawrence Deutsche Bank
COST	Costal Securities
COWN	Cowen & Co.
DAIN	Dain Bosworth, Inc.
DEAN	Dean Witter
DLJP	Donaldson Lufkin Jenrette
DMGL	Deutsche Morgan Grenfell
DOMS	Domestic Securities
EXPO	Exponential Capital Markets
FACT	First Albany Corp.
FAHN	Fahnestock & Co.

Mnemonic	Market Maker
FBCO	First Boston Corp./Credit Suisse
FPKI	Fox-Pitt, Kelton, Inc.
GRUN	Gruntal & Co., Inc.
GSCO	Goldman Sachs & Co.
GVRC	GVR Co.
HMQT	Hambrecht & Quist, Inc.
HRZG	Herzog, Heine, Geduld, Inc.
JEFF	Jefferies Co., Inc.
JPMS	J.P. Morgan
KEMP	Kemper Securities, Inc.
LEHM	Lehman Brothers
MADF	Bernard Madoff
MASH	Mayer & Schweitzer, Inc.
MHMY	M.H. Meyerson & Co., Inc.
MLCO	Merril Lynch
MONT	Montgomery Securities
MSCO	Morgan Stanley & Co.
MSWE	Midwest Stock Exchange
NAWE	Nash Weiss & Co.
NEED	Neddham & Co.
NMRA	Nomura Securities Intl.
OLDE	Olde Discount Corp.
OPCO	Oppenheimer & Co.
PERT	Pershing Trading Co.
PIPR	Piper Jaffray
PRUS	Prudential Securities
PUNK	Punk Ziegel & Knoell
PWJC	Paine Webber Inc.
RAGN	Ragen McKenzie Inc.
RPSC	Rauscher Pierce
RBSF	Robertson Stephens & Co.
SALB	Salomon Brothers
SBNY	Sands Brothers & Co., Ltd.
SELS	Furman Selz Inc.
SHWD	Sherwood Securities Corp.
SNDV	Soundview Financial
SWST	Southwest Securities
TSCO	Troster Singer Corp.
TUCK	Tucker Anthony, Inc.
TVAN	Teevan & Co., Inc.
UBSS	UBS Securities
WARB	S.G. Warburg & Co., Inc.
WEAT	Wheat First Securities
WEDB	Wedbrush Morgan Sec.
WEED	Weeden & Co. LP
WERT	Wortheim, Schroder

appendix e

web sites

A quick pass through any of the popular search engines will take you to thousands of trading and day-trading web sites. Here are a few that I consider to be important for you to investigate further:

Big Charts   **www.bigcharts.com**

Big Charts is a comprehensive and easy-to-use investment research site, providing access to professional-level research tools like interactive charts, quotes, news, industry analysis, and intraday stock screeners.

Broadway Trading   **www.broadwaytrading.com**

Broadway Trading, LLC specializes in providing Nasdaq executions for individuals who want to day trade for a living. Founded by Marc Friedfertig, previously a member of the American Stock Exchange and author of *The Electronic Day Trader,* Broadway Trading, LLC is an introducing broker/dealer that clears through Datek Online Brokerage Services.

CBS MarketWatch   **www.marketwatch.com**

Rated by Barron's as one of the top web sites for investors, the DBC Online web site joins forces with CBS News to create this active web site. With DBC quotes and news, CBS MarketWatch serves nearly two million pages of data and news each business day. Topics include:

Short-term trading	U.S. stocks
Futures and options	Personal finance
Global investing	Letters to the editor

Charles Schwab Investment Forums   www.forum.schwab.com

Lively online discussions with well-known investment experts and business leaders. Topics include:

Online chats with notables, such as Terry Savage, Gill Cyester, Nancy Evans, Walter Updegrave, Mark Riepe, and Robert Bennin	Check web site for schedule of events

CyBerCorp.com   www.cybercorp.com

Charting, RealTime/Level II, Risk and Back Office management, software, and more. Formed in 1995 in Austin, Texas, CyBerCorp is an Electronic Trading Technology Group, which develops high-end, real-time electronic stock-trading and execution systems for day traders and active investors.

Day Trader Mercantile Co.   www.daytradermerc.com

Merchandise for day traders: pins, shirts, mouse pads, and more.

Day Traders   www.daytraders.org

Billed as the Number 1 chat room for professional stock traders on the Internet.

Day Traders On-Line   www.daytraders.com

Day Traders On-line provides two main services: short-term market research for subscribers and a service that provides intraday plays.

Day Traders of Orange County   www.worldwidetraders.com

Biweekly meetings and information for short-term stock, option, and currency traders. Learn profitable trading techniques by networking with other successful short-term investors. The goal of each meeting—to go away with at least one new trading idea or strategy.

Day Trading Stocks   www.daytradingstocks.com

Day-trading learning center. Free day-trading resources including chat room, Island book viewer, trading links, and daily stock picks for all day traders. Topics include:

Active trader   The final frontier
Trader   Stocks
Cons of day trading   Alert trading
Day traders

DBC   www.dbc.com

Data Broadcasting Corporation focuses its considerable database and technology resources on meeting the financial information needs of the individual and professional investment community through Internet-delivered products and services.

DirecTrade, Inc.   www.d-trade.com

Internet-based trading at $18.50 per ticket plus fees. Branch office of Terra Nova Trading, LLC.

The Elite Trader   www.elitetrader.com

Online training course, community message board, links to brokerage, software, and books.

Electronic Traders Association   www.electronic-traders.org

The Association promotes the interests of electronic day traders in Washington, D.C., by engaging policy makers about the benefits of electronic trading. Their mission is to ensure that policies adopted in Washington represent the interest of the electronic trading industry and of all small public investors nationwide.

Equity Trading   www.equitytrading.com

A branch of Terra Nova Trading, LLC, the Equity Trading web site offers education and seminars.

Executioner   www.theexecutioner.com

Instant executions for the active trader.

FuturesWeb   www.futuresweb.com

Another financial futures information portal.

Harbor Remote   www.daytrading.net

Offers professional trading systems and services to traders worldwide. Provides day-trading technology, training, and capital. Remote-access trading, competitive commissions. Instant executions directly through SelectNet, Island, Instinet, and SuperDOT. Broker/dealer member of the

Philadelphia Stock Exchange. Trades cleared through Spear, Leeds & Kellogg.

Hoovers Online   www.hoovers.com
Company profiles and free access to 8,500-plus records on public and private companies.

Individual Investor Online   www.iionline.com/boards
News, message boards, analysis, opinions, research. Topics include:
                        Stocks, A–Z   Individual stocks

INO.com   www.ino.com
INO's comprehensive web site for futures and options traders offers MarketForum.com, with lively discussions, hot topics, and guest experts.

Internet Stock Report   www.internetnews.com
News search, stock quotes, information on IPOs.

Internet Stocks   www.internetstocks.com
Publishes the Weekly Web Report, news, and research.

InterQuote Stock Services   www.interquote.com
Real-time and 15-minute-delay stock quotes.

Investor's Edge   www.irnet.com
Market summary and charts, news, commentary, StockPoint.com.

InvestorSEEK.COM   www.investorseek.com
Hundreds of financial and investment sites and services.

Investorville.com   www.investorville.com
Full-resource, upcoming IPOs.

InvesTrade Discount Securities   www.investrade.com
Deep-discount electronic stock brokerage firm. Charges one flat rate for electronic stock trade executions, with no limit on size.

IPO Central   www.ipocentral.com
In-depth information on more than 13,500 companies, including a corporate description, financial information, key officers, competitors, and more.

LiveStreet.com   www.livestreet.com

Created by Wall Street professionals for clients who are interested in trading their portfolio online. Real-time access to live dynamic updating quotes, streaming live-market information. Executions through Terra Nova Trading LLC.

Market Guide   www.marketguide.com

The Market Guide Investment Center provides timely and accurate company reports, quotes, news, price charts, and stock-screening tools, as well as industry, sector, and company rankings on over 9,800 equities.

MAXTrade, LLC   www.maxtrading.com

MaxTrade software lets you turn your home or office into a virtual trading floor. MaxTrade specializes in active trading of Nasdaq and listed securities. MaxTrade is based on RealTick III and routes with ARCA through Terra Nova Trading.

MB Trading, Inc.   www.mbtrading.com

We are proud to present the most powerful Internet-based, professional-level, Y2K-compliant order-entry trading platform available today. Our data is provided by Townsend Analytics via your normal Internet connection. You may also opt for a virtual private network (VPN). The MBTrader gives the full capabilities of RealTick III and the ARCA system. ARCA is an electronic order-routing system that assists a day trader in maximizing the efficiency of an execution. ARCA reduces partial fills and increases speed of order entry and execution by memorizing the most active market makers on any particular Nasdaq stock. MBTrader allows immediate order routing via our ECN, TNTO, and ISLD.

Money Mentor, The   www.moneymentor.com

The Money Mentor is the primary directory for everything financial. In-depth information on investing, trading, day trading, market analysis, brokerage, financial software, data services, quotes, charts, technical analysis, free quotes and data, real-time data, newsletters, advisory services, investment bookstore, education, and searchable yellow pages.

The Momentum Trader   www.mtrader.com

Learn day trading in Momentum Trader's online day-trading chat room. Day-trading class taught daily in our interactive day-trading chat room. Learn to day trade like the professionals by learning from Ken Wolff's daily day-trading lessons.

Motley Fool   **www.fool.com**

Online forum for the entertainment and education of the individual investor.

Nasdaq Newsroom   **www.nasdaqnews.com**

The Nasdaq-Amex newsroom is designed to provide media professionals with timely information about Nasdaq and the markets in general.

Nasdaq Trader   **www.nasdaqtrader.com**

Provides the trading community and market data vendors with trading data, information on Nasdaq products and trading services, the Nasdaq Symbol Directory, the Daily List, and news about the Nasdaq Stock Market.

NetFutures   **www.netfutures.com**

Electronic order entry for futures at $9.99 per side flat fee.

NET Worth   **networth.galt.com/**

Free quotes; requires registration.

NexTrade   **www.invest2000.com**

ECN using Pro-Trade software.

NexTrend   **www.nextrend.com**

NexTrend was the first financial market information provider to create its business and technology specifically to deliver totally integrated market information, professional analysis, and trading services over the Internet. NexTrend Analysis provides quotes, professional charting, online portfolio valuation, news, and fundamentals.

Online Daytraders.com   **www.onlinedaytraders.com**

This site was designed for both the novice and professional trader, with one thing in mind—profits.

Online Investing   **www.onlineinvesting.net**

By Doug Gerlach, the author of *The Complete Idiot's Guide to Online Investing*.

Online Investor, The   **www.theonlineinvestor.com**

New SEC filings, IPO calendar, stock buybacks, splits, mergers and buyouts, earnings calendar.

Online Trading Academy   www.onlinetradingacademy.com

Online Trading Academy is a cutting-edge training firm focusing on training products and services geared toward stock day traders. Includes "Electronic Trading Guide to Nasdaq Level II." Offices in Irvine, California.

Pacific Day Trading, Inc.   www.day-trade.com

Branch of Terra Nova Trading, LLC. Traders cleared through Southwest Securities Corp. Day trade through your own computer terminal.

PAWWS   www.secapl.com/cgi-bin/qs

Unlimited free quotes.

PCQuote   www.pcquote.com

Twenty-minute delay; free unlimited quotes.

Premier Internet Trading   www.pitonline.com

A branch of Terra Nova Trading, LLC. Powered by RealTick III, PIT offers institutional and individual traders instant access to trade initiation on OTC and listed exchanges.

Performance Stocks   www.performance-stocks.com

Model portfolio with hot stocks, great returns, big gains, and the performance of hot IPOs, hot Internet stocks, great technical stocks, and hot fundamental value and growth plays.

Phactor.com   www.phactor.com

Day-trading tools, tips, tutorials, resources.

Polar Trading   www.polartrading.com

Internet-based training through seminars, self-paced modules, and structured courses in Internet-based trading.

Quicken   www.quicken.com

News, investments, mortgages, taxes, banking, credit, and small business information.

Quote.com   www.quote.com

Real-time charts and quotes, fundamental and technical, plus QCharts, their powerful online charting software.

Remote Trading International   **www.remotetraders.com**

At RTI, we provide our clients with the equipment and knowledge necessary to day trade from their own personal computers, at the location of their choice.

Silicon Investor   **www.siliconinvestor.com**

Topics include:

Banking and finance	Market trends and strategies
Brokerages/investment	Mutual funds
Resources	Overvalued stocks
Futures and commodities	Short-term traders
Initial public offerings	Web/information stocks
Internet financial connection	

The Small Investor's Software Company   **www.smallinvestors.com**

Affordable Technical Analysis and Charting Software and Free Market timing analysis for Small Investors.

StockMaster   **www.stockmaster.com**

Topics include:

Market update	Portfolios
Most active	Big gainers/losers
Funds	Rates

StockPoint   **www.stockpoint.com**

Stockpoint, a unit of Neural Applications Corporation, is the online industry's leading provider of personalized information-driven solutions for individual and professional investors. Stockpoint offers investors an online environment in which they can analyze, manage, and trade their holdings using the most comprehensive information and the most advanced web technologies available.

Stock Rumors   **www.stockrumors.com**

Buzz and Bits, quotes, Wall Street Beat, message boards.

StockTrade.net   **www.stocktrade.net**

Lieber & Weissman Securities LLC ("LWS") is an SEC-registered broker/dealer and PHLX member firm. LWS was founded to provide professional traders with the latest proprietary trading technology, as well as leveraged trading capital and clearing services.

Talk City   **www.talkcity.com/communities**

Chat rooms of all types. Click on your special interest. Topics include:

Business and finance   BizCenter

TechStock Investor   **www.techsto.com**

Top 10 stocks.

TechStocks   **www4.techstocks.com**

Takes you to Silicon Investor.

TechWeb   **www.techweb.com**

By clicking on the Finance button, this site brings you all the latest high-tech financial news.

Thomson Investors Network   **www.thomsoninvest.net**

Market edge.

Townsend Analytics, Ltd.   **www.taltrade.com**

Whether you're a professional broker-dealer or you're new to the stock market, Townsend Analytics, Ltd. has a product for you. TAL Trading Tools, our open-architecture trading platform for Microsoft Windows, encompasses a broad range of individual products. Townsend Analytics, Ltd. (TAL) was incorporated in 1987 and, from the beginning, specialized in Microsoft Windows applications. The release of Windows 3.11 vindicated this choice, and the advent of NT provided the robust operating system that allowed us to transform our servers into devices capable of supporting hundreds of simultaneous users. Our state-of-the-art client applications continue to meet the demanding needs of the very active trader, and we are committed to ongoing development based on the latest technical advances and the needs of our customers.

Trader-Talk   **www.wwfn.com/investor-chat.html**

Topics include:

Broker discussion forum   Pitbull investor discussion
Point-and-figure charting   Mutual fund trading

Traders' Catalog & Resource Guide   **www.traderscatalog.com**

This quarterly magazine is the only printed financial yellow pages directory. Half resource and half articles, its eclectic style has been its trademark since inception in 1991. Published by Sunny Harris & Associates, Inc., the resource of this magazine can also be found at The Money Mentor, www.moneymentor.com.

Traders Resource www.tradersresource.com

The information resource center for active stock traders.

TrendTrader www.trendtrader.com

Specializes in remote electronic order routing and execution to SOES, Selectnet, ECN, and DOT for institutions and day traders. Trade from your office or home.

Underground Level II Day Traders Handbook www.undergroundtrader.com/

Online day-trading chat room, handbook, and training. Our main service is the Underground Trading Pit. This is our interactive, Java-based trading chat room where live, real-time trading alerts are called throughout the day utilizing the tools and principles in the *Underground Level II Daytraders Handbook* and hosted by the author, Jay Yu, and several other top traders. Our goal is to profit from market volatility while minimizing risk and preserving capital using our indicators and techniques. We are speculators, not gamblers. By tempering our calls with solid tools and indicators, we maintain consistency and our customers profit as they learn.

Wall Street Voice www.wsvoice.com

Research reports for individual investors.

Winning DayTraders www.winningdaytraders.com

Real-time stock recommendations, market analysis, news alerts, trading auditorium. Newsletter and consulting services.

World Wide Financial Network www.wwfn.com

Quotes, articles, real-time charts, corporate information, business headlines, hot stocks, world markets, globex, stock screening.

Yahoo!chat chat.yahoo.com

A wide variety of chat rooms on every imaginable subject.

Zeus www.zeus-holdings.com

Our goal is to provide the short-term trader with the most concise, real, and effective trading advice out there.

appendix f

clubs, seminars, conferences, and educators

As would befit a community of online traders, the most exciting clubs for day traders and speed traders are online. There are a few clubs with physical locations, and at this writing the First Annual International Day Traders Expo is being organized. More than likely, by this time next year, there will be a day-trading club in most major cities and more conventions and seminars will be directed to this audience.

professional organizations

The *Electronic Traders Association* is the voice of electronic day traders, proprietary traders, and public investors nationwide. The Association promotes the interests of the industry in Washington, D.C., by engaging policy makers about the benefits of electronic trading. Their mission is to ensure that policies adopted in Washington represent the interests of the electronic trading industry, and, more importantly, of all small public investors nationwide. The ETA accomplishes its mission by promoting the accessibility of the securities marketplace for all investors, by promoting price competition in the marketplace and by promoting investor fairness and confidence in the marketplace. ETA's regular activities include educating the press and policy makers about our industry, representing the industry in rule-making and other regulatory proceedings at the SEC and other federal agencies, and working with these parties to ensure fair and reasonable policies affecting the industry.

Electronic Traders Association **www.electronic-traders.org**
1800 Bering, Suite 750
Houston, Texas 77057
(713) 706-3300
Fax (713) 977-7975

clubs

Day Traders of Orange County www.daytrading.org

Meets the second and fourth Saturdays of each month near Orange County Airport. Their biweekly meetings are for active short-term traders to share strategies and tools for investing and day trading in stocks, options, futures, commodities, and currencies. Each meeting has between 200 and 210 active traders in attendance. Their membership exceeds 250 full-time traders and is growing. Visit their web site for details.

educators

Often, the day-trading salons that offer you brokerage will also offer education. It is in their best interest to help you make money. If you don't become a profitable trader, you will stop trading and they will lose your commissions and fees.

All-Tech Training Group, Inc. www.traintotrade.com

All-Tech Training Group (ATG), Inc., offers an intensive training program in Montvale, New Jersey, and Seattle, Washington, consisting of four phases of training: basics, trading strategies, paper trading, and supervised live trading.

NASDAQ www.nasdaq.com

Offers an investment lesson on the web site.

Nasdaq Trader nasdaqtrader.com

Nasdaq trading data provides the trading community with a centralized and efficient means of obtaining updates and valuable market information, including monthly share volume reports, IPO trading statistics, Nasdaq 100 Index, Nasdaq Financial 100 Index, and Nasdaq performance overviews.

OptiMark Technologies, Inc.   www.optimark.com

The web-based OptiMark Nasdaq Trader Course is a self-paced course where current or potential OptiMark users can learn about the advantages and uniqueness of the System. This web-based course will allow you to learn how OptiMark is integrated with the Nasdaq stock market and how the OptiMark Trading System works. You will also have the opportunity to simulate profile entry and see the results of a matching cycle. You will see how easy it is to enter simple and sophisticated trading strategies and learn how the patented OptiMark matching process works.

Pristine Day Trader   www.pristine.com
7–11 S. Broadway, Ste. 210
White Plains, NY 10601
1-800-340-6477
Fax: 1-914-682-7640

Boot camps and seminars for day traders.

RT2 Trader   www.rttrading.com

Seminars are offered in Dallas and London training facilities. Cost for the five-day course is $1,950. The course is hands-on and limited to six participants.

Sceptre Trading   www.sceptretrading.com
1-214-826-2466

Sceptre offers a comprehensive day-trading course based on the book *Stock Patterns for Day Trading,* by Barry Rudd, the course's founder. They offer a one-week and a two-week course, as well as a home-study course.

Sagamore Trading Group   www.learn2trade.com
1446 Old Northern Blvd.
Roslyn, NY 11576
1-888-773-9306

Market commentary, economic calendar, message boards, and a valuable *Traders' Handbook.*

Traders Edge   www.tradersedge.com
27 W. Beaver Creek Rd.
Richmond Hill, ON L4B 1M8
Canada

Learn from Marc Friedfertig and Gerge West, the authors of *The Electronic Day Trader*. Training available in Toronto. Also offers investment portfolio manager software.

Tradersedge.net   206.252.211.97

Broadway Consulting Group's Tradersedge.net is a leading provider of day-trading educational services. Tradersedge.net offers informative books, an intensive seminar, and a weekly day-trading chat room on the Internet.

Trading School   www.tradingschool.com
P.O. Box 1831
Duarte, CA 91010
1-626-963-2057

Whether you are a beginner, an experienced trader, or an aggressive investor, our hands-on workshops, online courses, and educational materials can assist you in your quest for knowledge and experience. We train the day trader, short-term momentum trader, and aggressive investors. Individuals come from all over the United States and around the world to attend our workshops.

appendix g

software vendors

Software for online and direct-access trading comes in two flavors: order entry and analysis. Most of the software specific to this relatively new field is for order entry. The analysis software that is available is, for the most part, not yet tailored to speed trading. Most analysis software is still for day trading and longer-term applications.

analysis software

Advanced GET   **www.tradingtech.com**
689 W. Turkeyfoot Lake Rd.
Akron, OH 44319
1-330-645-0077
Real-time Elliott Wave analysis.

figure G.1   Advanced GET screen

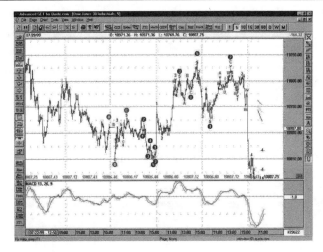

Source: Advanced GET. Reprinted with permission.

A-T Financial®   www.atfi.com

A-T Attitude® for the Internet is a professional trading tool that delivers a complete picture of the market so you can make informed investment decisions. It features unlimited real-time continuous quotes with custom tickers and alerts; real-time Nasdaq Level II; dynamic time of sale and quote, options analytics, real-time news, and historical data and charts. The software links to Preferred Trade for executions.

figure G.2   A-T® Attitude screen

Source: A-T Attitude.® Reprinted with permission.

MetaStock www.equis.com

Equis International, Salt Lake City, UT

1-801-270-3130

End-of-day or real-time analysis of stocks, commodities, options, indices, and mutual funds. You can create, test, optimize, and automate your trading systems.

figure G.3 MetaStock screen

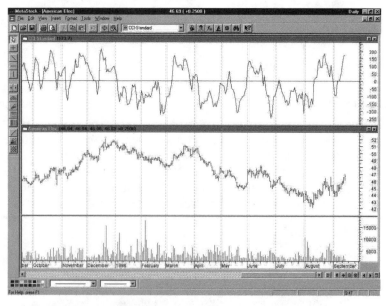

Source: Equis MetaStock. Reprinted with permission.

NexTrend Analysis www.nextrend.com

251 W. Renner Pkwy., Ste. 200

Richardson, TX 75080

1-972-470-9265

Another product developed specifically for speed traders is by Nex-Trend. Again, this product is stand-alone, not using Townsend's RealTick tools. NexTrend has their own real-time datafeed and is also an ECN.

figure G.4 NexTrend Analysis window

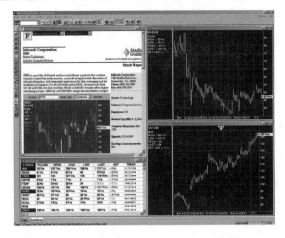

Source: NexTrend Analysis. Reprinted with permission.

PatternSmasher

www.kasanjianresearch.com

Kasanjian Research
P.O. Box 4608
Blue Jay, CA 92317
1-888-220-9789
1-909-337-0816

Kasanjian's latest product, PatternSmasher, looks for various types of patterns and pattern formations in your data with drag-and-drop building blocks.

---

figure G.5 PatternSmasher screen

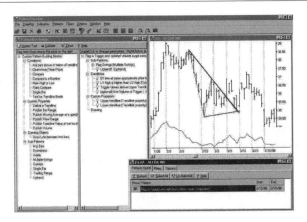

Source: PatternSmasher. Reprinted with permission.

Professional Trade Advisor www.stelar.com
Elliott Wave analysis with predictive technology.

figure G.6 Professional Trade Advisor screen

Source: Professional Trade Advisor. Reprinted with permission.

QCharts www.quote.com
One product that defies this caveat is QCharts, by Quote.com. They are
rapidly developing this product with the Level II trader in mind. QCharts
currently provides 12 of the most popular indicators on 12 different time
frames (including ticks), and provides a real-time look at the Island book.
QCharts is built on VisualBasic and the Quote.com datafeed, and it does
not use Townsend's RealTick. To enter trades from QCharts, you double-
click on the price you want to hit, and your trade will be connected to
Preferred or CyBerX for execution.

figure G.7 QCharts technical window

Source: Quote.com QCharts. Reprinted with permission.

figure G.8 QCharts fundamental window

Broadcom Corp 'A' - Fundamentals					
Title	Broadcom Corp 'A'	Symbol	BRCM	Exchange	NASDAQ
Industry Name	Semiconductors	Dividend	0.00	Return On Equity	28.513
Sector Name	Technology	Earnings	484	Return On Assets	24.565
Industry Code	1033	E/S Growth Rate	196.992	Gross Margin	57.070
Financials Date	03/31/99	Sales/Share	2.683	Pretax Margin	27.980
		Cash Flow/Share	-0.142	Operating Margin	26.017
Last	115 3/4	Book Val/Share	2.602	Inventory Turnover	11.930
1-Year High	124 1/4	Revenue/Employee	642,509	Asset Turnover	1.351
1-Year Low	23 1/2	Revenue Growth Rate	182.040	Receivables Turnover	9.320
% In Yearly Range	91.56	Current Ratio (QTR)	4.583	Debt Equity Ratio (QTR)	0.000
Beta		Quick Ratio (QTR)	3.898	LT Debt Equity Ratio (QTR)	0.000
Volume	1,063,200	Institutional Owned %	18.634	Short Int	0.798
65-Day Avg Vol	2,163,898	Inside Owned %	39.647	Short Int Prev	0.691
Shares Outstanding	92.456	Insider Purchased	0.000	Short Int Ratio	0.311
Float	55.800	Insider Sold	0.756		

Source: Quote.com QCharts. Reprinted with permission.

TradeStation   www.omegaresearch.com
Omega Research
8700 W. Flagler St., Ste. 250
Miami, FL 33174
1-800-327-3794, x5546
1-305-485-7499, x5546

The standard in back-testing and automation software, TradeStation has been around since 1991. The software continues to grow with the market to meet traders' ever-changing needs. TradeStation's EasyLanguage programming tools let you create and test nearly every strategy you can imagine.

figure G.9   TradeStation screen

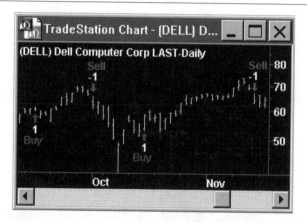

Source: Omega Research TradeStation. Reprinted with permission.

order-entry software

Most of the software products used for direct-access trading are based on the RealTick software toolbox from Townsend Analytics. As such, they provide essentially the same services: the Level II screen, a few charts with indicators, and trade entry.

Attain   www.attain.com

Attain ECN's software is based on RealTick III. You can work your own order, hit bids, take offers, or trade in between spreads.

figure G.10   Attain screen

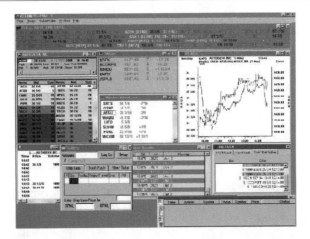

Source: Attain. Reprinted with permission.

AB Watley   **www.abwatley.com**

Ultimate Trader offers real-time, dynamically updating exchange-fed data. Service levels 2 through 4 give you the ability to place your orders directly into the various exchanges and ECNs.

figure G.11   AB Watley screen

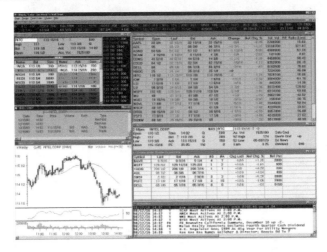

Source: AB Watley. Reprinted with permission.

OnSite Trader www.onsitetrading.com

Leading provider of stock-trading services targeted to both the on-premises and remote trader.

---

figure G.12 On-Site Trading, Inc. screen

Source: On-Site Trading, Inc. Reprinted with permission.

QCharts by Quote.com
3375 Scott Blvd.
Ste. 300
Santa Clara, CA 95054
1-800-498-8068

In addition to a powerful charting package, a simple double-click takes you to direct-access execution screens like Preferred Trade and CyBerX. QCharts is definitely a product developed with the speed trader in mind.

figure G.13 Preferred Trade screen

figure G.14 CyBerX Trade screen

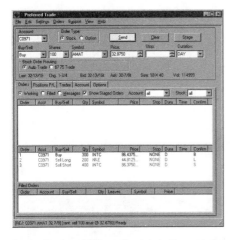

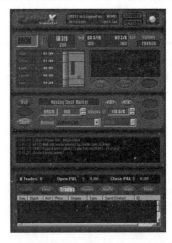

Source: Quote.com QCharts. Reprinted with permission.

Source: Quote.com QCharts. Reprinted with permission.

RealTick III   www.taltrade.com

RealTick III is the software toolbox from Townsend Analytics. Most Level II order-entry systems are based on RealTick III. In addition to offering the toolbox, Townsend allows users Level II access through RealNet, their own software, which includes RealTick III and full charting software.

figure G.15 RealTick by Townsend Analytics

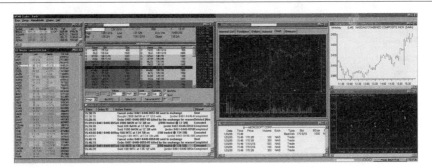

Source: Townsend Analytics. Reprinted with permission.

Rocket   **www.netfutures.com**

An Internet futures-trading system, Rocket is an electronic order-entry and fill-reporting system. It helps manage orders, reduce paperwork, and thereby, hopefully, it reduces errors. Rocket connects to the Chicago Mercantile Exchange's TOPS order-routing system. It takes orders from your PC and delivers them directly to the floor, and delivers your fills back to your PC.

figure G.16   Rocket order screen

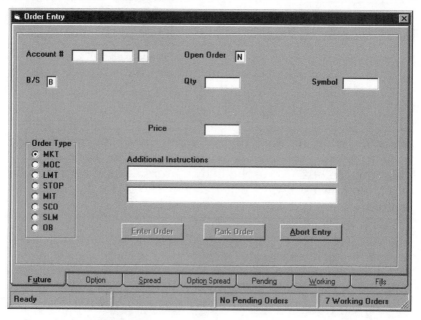

Source: Rocket. Reprinted with permission.

Terra Nova Trading, LLC   www.terranovatrading.com
The Executioner, LLC
7–11 South Broadway, Ste. 217
White Plains, NY 10601

Terra Nova Trader (TNT) allows you to create an unlimited number of custom pages.

figure G.17   TNT Trader 2 screen

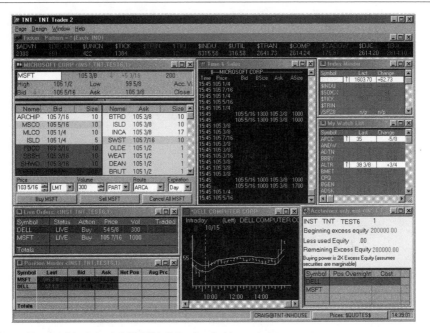

Source: Townsend Analytics, Ltd. Real Tick III. Reprinted with permission.

TradeCast   www.tradecast.com
3355 W. Alabama, Ste. 880
Houston, TX 77098

The Watcher   **www.broadwaytrading.com**
Broadway Trading, LLC
50 Broad St., 2nd Flr.
New York, NY 10004
1-212-328-3555
Fax: 1-212-377-1562

This trading system provides individuals with instant access to information and fast, low-cost executions. Monitor your positions, account activity, and access the Island ECN.

appendix h

data vendors

Consult the individual data vendor for details on their services and products.

Bonneville Market Information (BMI) 1-800-255-7374

BMI offers over 110,000 real-time and delayed quotes on equities, bonds, futures, options, mutual funds, and indexes, along with a variety of informative news and weather services through FM and satellite services.

Commodity Systems, Inc. (CSI) 1-800-274-4727

CSI provides daily updates and historical data on commodities, stocks, options, indexes, and mutual funds.

Data Broadcasting Corp. 1-800-527-0722, ext. 719

DBC is the nation's leader in providing real-time market data to the individual investor. DBC transmits quotes on over 65,000 stocks, options, and commodities. The Signal receiver brings quotes to your PC via FM, cable, or satellite.

Data Transmission Network Corp. (DTN)   **1-800-475-4755, ext. 361G**

DTN offers 15-minute delayed quotes on stocks and bonds, real-time index quotes, as well as quotes on mutual funds, futures, precious metals, and a business news service.

Dial Data   **1-718-522-6886**

Since 1972, leading institutional investors and thousands of individuals have relied on Dial/Data for its industry-standard database of daily and historical securities prices for U.S., Canadian, European, and Pacific Rim exchange-traded equities, futures, equity options, mutual funds, bonds, government issues, money markets, indexes, and stock dividends.

Genesis Financial Data Services   **1-800-808-3282**
www.gfds.com

Genesis offers two data packages: historical data from 1968 on 140-plus commodities and historical data from 1970 on 8,000 stocks. With the package, you get their Navigator data management software, which allows you to convert the data between more than 10 formats.

Genesis also offers SnapQuotes on U.S. futures at no additional charge for current subscribers. SnapQuotes are real-time for Chicago exchanges and 20-minute-delayed for NYSE, available by snapshot every 10 minutes.

In addition to data, Genesis offers a graphical platform for followers of Larry Williams' Money Tree course, making it easy to pinpoint fakeouts, oops patterns, and more.

Pinnacle Data Corp.   **1-800-724-4903**

Pinnacle specializes in hard-to-find historical data. With their free communications software, you can download index and breadth data, continuous futures contracts, and commitment of trader reports.

Prophet Information Services, Inc.   **1-800-772-8040**

Prophet gives you historical data back to 1968, customized updating capability, high-speed modem access, and a vast selection of stocks and futures from around the world.

Stock Data Corp.   **1-410-280-5533**

Stock Data has historical data by diskette or modem for the NYSE, Amex, and Nasdaq.

TeleChart 2000   **1-919-408-0545**

Fast databank updates and stock scanning, at a very low price.

Telerate Systems, Inc.   **1-201-938-4000**

Telerate offers dial-up, modem access to their global information network.

Telescan, Inc.   **1-800-324-8246**

Telescan has current and historical quotes on stocks, mutual funds, indexes, and options, which you can import to spreadsheet and charting programs.

appendix i

downloadable data

technical data

Some of the Internet sites we have found that supply technical data are:

DBC Quote Server	www.dbc.com/quote.html
Ford Investor Services	www.fordinv.com
Investor's Edge	www.irnet.com
InterQuote Stock Services	www.interquote.com
Quote.com	www.quote.com
PCQuote	www.pcquote.com
PAWWS	www.secapl.com/cgi-bin/qs
E*Trade Quote Server	www.etrade.com
NET Worth	networth.galt.com
StockPoint	www.stockpoint.com
Lombard Public Access Quotes	www.lombard.com/PACenter/index.html

fundamental data

Some of the Internet sites we have found that supply fundamental data are:

DBC Quote Server   **www.dbc.com/quote.html**

Economic Time Series   **www.economagic.com**
Interest rates, consumer credit, industrial production, capacity utilization, Federal Reserve, retail sales, building permits, Consumer Price Index, Producer Price Index.

EDGAR Database   **www.sec.gov**
*E*lectronic *D*ata *G*athering, *A*nalysis, and *R*etrieval system performs automated collection, validation, indexing, acceptance, and forwarding of submissions by companies and others who are required by law to file forms with the U.S. Securities and Exchange Commission (SEC). Its primary purpose is to increase the efficiency and fairness of the securities market for the benefit of investors, corporations, and the economy by accelerating the receipt, acceptance, dissemination, and analysis of time-sensitive corporate information filed with the agency.

Financial Data Finder   **www.cob.ohio-state.edu**
Banks, commodities, equity, exchanges, financial institutions, investments, market and economy, mergers, venture capital.

Fundamental Data   **www.economics.harvard**
                                                .edu/~jrappa/download.htm

Insider Holdings at IPO   **linux.agsm.ucla.edu/ipoinside/**
                                                ipoinsideaccess.html
The information on the Internet changes every few minutes. At present, at least, it is in an exponential growth phase. To see updated information relating to this chapter, come to The Money Mentor's EDAT 101 site at www.moneymentor.com/edat101.htm. We'll do our best to keep up!

appendix j

exchanges

American Stock Exchange. Access Amex fast quotes, company listings, options and derivatives information, and the latest stock news.
www.amex.com/

Amsterdam Stock Exchange. Find opening, high, low, and closing prices of yesterday's Dutch stocks.
www.aex.nl/

Arizona Stock Exchange (AZX), Inc. Formed in 1990 to operate the Arizona Stock Exchange, an electronic single-price auction trading system. AZX uses state-of-the-art telecommunications and computer, bringing everyone together electronically. Bringing traders together at the same time—and at a single price—avoids the spreads, market impact, and random turbulence common in continuous markets.
www.azx.com

Asuncion Stock Exchange
www.pla.net.py/bvpasa

Athens Stock Exchange
www.ase.gr

Australian Stock Exchange (Amex). Investor services and products plus market news.
www.asx.com.au/

The Barcelona Stock Exchange
www.borsabcn.es

Bavarian Stock Exchange
www.bayerischeboerse.de

Beijing Commodity Exchange
bcewww.cnfm.co.cn

Belgian Futures and Options Exchange
www.belfox.be

Bermuda Stock Exchange (BSX). The Bermuda Stock Exchange (BSX) is the world's first fully electronic offshore securities market. The BSX is recognized internationally as an attractive, open market for the listing of securities and international investment funds. The BSX has been in operation since 1971 as the only stock exchange in Bermuda, and in the past three years has rapidly developed as an international offshore equities market specializing in listing capital market instruments. More than 248 equities, funds, debt issues, and depositary programs currently list on the BSX, with a total market capitalization (excluding investment funds) in excess of $92 billion. The success of the BSX lies in global access to its electronic trading and settlement systems.
www.bsx.com

Bilbao Stock Exchange
www.bm30.es/socios/empresas/bolsa_es.html

Bolsa de Comercio de Santiago, Chile. Stock exchange of Santiago, Chile. In Spanish.
www.bolsantiago.cl/

Bolsa de Madrid. Stock exchange of Madrid, Spain. In Spanish.
www.bolsamadrid.es/

Bolsa de Valores do Rio de Janeiro. Rio de Janeiro stock exchange. In Portuguese.
www.bvrj.com.br/

Bolsa Electronica de Chile. Bolsa de Valores.
www.bolchile.cl

Bolsa Mexicana de Valores. Mexican stock exchange. In Spanish.
www.bmv.com.mx/

Boston Stock Exchange
www.bostonstock.com

The Bratislava Stock Exchange
www.bsse.sk

Brazilian Futures Exchange
www.bbf.com.br

Brussels Stock Exchange
www.stockexchange.be

Budapest Commodity Exchange
www.bce-bat.com

Capital Market Supervisory Agency
www.indoexchange.com/bagong/general/bapepam/bapepam.html

Caracas Stock Exchange
www.caracasstock.com

Chicago Board of Trade   Futures exchange news, quotes, products, and services.
www.cbot.com/

Chicago Board Options Exchange (CBOE).   Online site for the CBOE, and also a source of market data, quotes, and the basics of options.
www.cboe.com/

Chicago Mercantile Exchange.   An online international marketplace for managing financial risk and allocating assets. Futures and options news, quotes, products, and trading.
www.cme.com/

Chicago Stock Exchange.   The second largest U.S. stock exchange, the Chicago Stock Exchange (CHX) opened for trading on May 15, 1882. The initial list of securities (82 bonds and 52 stocks) was highly concentrated on regional issues, including Chicago Gas Light & Coke Company (now Peoples Energy) and First National Bank of Chicago. Many railroad companies became early listings as Chicago became the rail hub of the United States. Today, The Chicago Stock Exchange has more than 4,000 issues available for trading. 1998 was a record-breaking year with over 9 billion shares traded and 16 million trades executed. The total value of these transactions, over $298 billion, solidified the Exchange's position as the second-largest stock exchange in the United States.
www.chicagostockex.com

Citrus Fruit and Commodity Futures Market of Valencia
drac.medusa.es/fcm/index.html

Coffee, Sugar & Cocoa Exchange.   Information and opportunities about coffee, sugar, cocoa, milk, cheddar cheese, nonfat dry milk, but-

ter futures, and options markets, as well as milk futures and options contracts.
www.csce.com/

Colombo Stock Exchange
www.lanka.net/cse

Commodities and Futures Exchange
www.bmf.com.br

Commodity Exchange of Ljubljana
www.eunet.si/commercial/bbl/bbl-ein.html

Copenhagen Stock Exchange
www.xcse.dk

Czech Capital Market The Prague Stock Exchange. In Czechoslovakian and English.
stock.eunet.cz/

EASDAQ (European Association of Securities Dealers Automated Quotation—EASDAQ-SA). The EASDAQ stock market operates across 14 European countries with one regulatory structure, one rule book, and one seamless trading and settlement system.
www.easdaq.be

Finnish Option Exchange
www.foex.fi

Finnish Options Market
www.som.fi

German Stock Exchange
www.exchange.de

Guayaquil Stock Exchange
www.bvg.fin.ec

Helsinki Exchanges Stock Exchange. In Helsinki, Finland. In Finnish and English.
www.hex.fi/

Hong Kong Futures Exchange. A derivatives market in the Asia Pacific region.
www.hkfe.com/

International Petroleum Exchange (IPE). A commodity market that deals in futures contracts (Brent and Dubai crude oil, gas oil, leaded and unleaded gasoline, naphtha and heavy fuel oil), as well as in options (Brent crude and gas oil). It offers the facilities for making an exchange of futures for physicals.
www.ipe.uk.com

International Securities Exchange (ISE). In development since 1996, trading on the first electronic options exchange is slated to begin in January of 2000. Funded by Adirondak Partners, the exchange will use Swedish OM electronic exchange technology on Compaq's OpenVMS Alpha Server system.

Istanbul Stock Exchange
www.ise.org

Italian Derivatives Market
www.borsaitalia.it

Italian Stock Exchange
www.borsaitalia.it

Jakarta Stock Exchange (JSX). The JSX is seeking to establish itself as one of the principal capital markets in the Asia Pacific region. To attract investors and promote liquidity, fast and reliable information is paramount. Below, you will find a list of the information services the JSX presently provides. A priority in designing these services has been the idea that technological sophistication must be put to the service of the JSX participants' information needs, as well as to those of the general public.
www.jsx.co.id

The Jamaica Stock Exchange
www.jamstockex.com

The Johannesburg Stock Exchange
www.jse.co.za

Kansai Agricultural Commodities Exchange
www.kanex.or.jp

Kansas City Board of Trade. General information, trading, and reports from the KCBT.
www.kcbt.com/

Korea Stock Exchange
www.kse.or.kr

Kuala Lumpur Stock Exchange
www.klse.com.my

Lima Stock Exchange
www.bvl.com.pe

Lisbon Stock Exchange. Companies, bonds, prices, and exchange index. In Portuguese and English.
www.bvl.pt/

Ljubljana Stock Exchange.   Slovenian stock exchange. In English.
www.ljse.si/html/eng/kazalo.html

London International Financial Futures & Options Exchange (London FOX).   This exchange, which includes the former London Commodity Exchange (LCE), is the leading exchange in Europe for soft commodities (for example, cocoa, coffee, sugar, rubber, potatoes, and grain).
www.liffe.com

London Metal Exchange (LME).   The LME is the London market for trade in metals and the world futures and cash market for trades in nonferous metals, such as aluminum, aluminum alloy, copper, lead, nickel, tin and zinc. There are also exchange-traded options, available on all futures contracts apart from aluminum alloy. 24-hour market.
www.lme.co.uk

The London Securities and Derivatives Exchange (OMLX)
www.omgroup.com

London Stock Exchange.   News, information on trading, and how to use the market.
www.londonstockex.co.uk/

Luxemborg Stock Exchange
www.bourse.lu

Madrid Stock Exchange
www.bolsamadrid.es

MATIF: Marche a Terme International de France.   The international French futures and commodities exchange.
www.matif.fr/indexN4.htm

MEFF Renta Variable.   A leading options and futures market in Europe.
www.meffrv.es/

MEFF: Spanish Financial Futures & Options Exchange.   Exchange and clearinghouse in Spain for trading of futures and options contracts on interest rates.
www.meff.es/

MICEX/Relis Online
www.relis.ru

Mid America Commodity Exchange (MIDAM).   An exchange in Chicago that deals in futures and options contracts in a variety of commodities. It offers, among others, minicontracts in metals, meats, and grains. The MIDAM is affiliated to the CBOT, and a number of its futures and options contracts are traded on the floor of the CBOT.
www.midam.com

Minneapolis Grain Exchange (MGE).   A commodity market for grain, dealing in futures contracts for spring wheat and white wheat, and, on the cash market, for barley, maize, drum wheat, flaxseed, oats, rye, soy beans, spring wheat, and sunflower seeds. It offers the world's only seafood futures contracts (White and Black Tiger shrimp).
www.mgex.com

Montreal Exchange
www.me.org

Nagoya Stock Exchange
www.iijnet.or.jp/nse-jp/e-home.htm

The Namibian Stock Exchange
www.nse.com.na

NanoCaps Exchange.   Large cap, mid cap, small cap, microcap? Nope, we're Nanocap! Nanocaps are SEC-reporting companies for securities not listed on Nasdaq or an exchange. The Nanocap Community offers a full range of services—designed exclusively for Nanocaps: free real-time (no delay) open-order display, trade match history, a comprehensive Nanocap company database, chat and discussion groups.
www.nanocaps.com

The Nasdaq Stock Market
www.nasdaq.com
www.nasd.com

National Association of Securities Market Participants.   (NAUFAR)
www.rtsnet.ru

The National Stock Exchange of India
www.nseindia.com./

New York Cotton Exchange (NYCE). The oldest commodity exchange in New York (founded in 1870) and the world's prime market for cotton futures and options. The NYCE also trades in liquified propane gas futures.
www.nyce.com

New York Mercantile Exchange (NYMEX).   The NYMEX in its current form was created in 1994 by the merger of the former New York Mercantile Exchange and the Commodity Exchange of New York (COMEX). Together they represent one of the world's largest markets in energy and precious metals. It deals in futures (and options) in oil products (such as crude oil, heating oil, leaded regular gasoline, natural gas, and propane) and in rare metals (such as platinum and palladium). It also deals in gold and silver, aluminum and copper, sharing with the London Metal Exchange a dominant role in the world metal trading. The trade

of crack spread allows investors to construct their own spread combinations.
www.nymex.com

New York Stock Exchange (NYSE).   The world's largest equities market, with a total market capitalization of nearly $12 trillion. The NYSE is an auction market, also known as "The Big Board."
www.nyse.com

New Zealand Futures & Options Exchange
www.nzfoe.co.nz/

New Zealand Stock Exchange
www.nzse.co.nz

Nigerian Stock Exchange
www.mbendi.co.za/exng.htm

Occidente Stock Exchange
www.bolsadeoccidente.com.co

Option Traders Combination
www.otc.nl/

Osaka Securities Exchange
www.ose.or.jp

Oslo Bors.   Stock exchange of Oslo, Norway. In Norwegian.
www.ose.no/

Pacific Stock Exchange (PCX).   The Pacific Exchange has two trading floors, one in San Francisco and one in Los Angeles.
www.pacificex.com/

Paris Stock Exchange
www.bourse-de-paris.fr

Philadelphia Stock Exchange (PHLX).   News and exchange information.
www.phlx.com/

The Riga Stock Exchange
www.lanet.lv/business/rfb

Russian Exchange.   General information and news. In English and Russian.
www.re.ru/

Sao Paulo Stock Exchange
www.bovespa.com.br

Securities Exchange of Barbados
www.caribft.com

Shanghai Metal Exchange
www.sme.com

Siberian Stock Exchange
www.sse.nsk.su

Singapore Commodity Exchange Ltd
www.sicom.com.sg

Singapore International Monetary Exchange Ltd
www.simex.com.sg

South African Futures Exchange. South African currency exchange
and derivatives.
www.safex.co.za/

The Spanish Options Exchange
www.meffrv.es/

St. Petersburg Futures Exchange
www.futures.ru/

St. Petersburg Stock Exchange
lse.spb.su

Stock Exchange of Hong Kong. Regulations, services, jobs, and market information.
www.sehk.com.hk

Stock Exchange of Singapore. Trade securities, find information and
get the latest news.
www.ses.com.sg/

The Stock Exchange of Thailand
www.set.or.th

Stockholm Stock Exchange Ltd
www.xsse.se

Stuttgart Stock Exchange
www.boerse-stuttgart.de/

Surabaya Stock Exchange
www.bes.co.id

Swiss Exchange. Swiss stock exchange offering news and trading
information. In English, German and French.
www.bourse.ch/

Swiss Options and Financial Futures Exchange AG
www.bourse.ch

Sydney Futures Exchange Ltd
www.sfe.com.au

Taiwan Stock Exchange
www.tse.com.tw

Tallinn Stock Exchange Estonia
www.tse.ee

Tehran Stock Exchange
www.neda.net/tse

Tel-Aviv Stock Exchange
www.tase.co.il/

Tokyo Grain Exchange
www.tge.or.jp

Tokyo International Financial Futures Exchange
www.tiffe.or.jp/jpn.html

Tokyo Stock Exchange
www.tse.or.jp

Toronto Stock Exchange. Market overview, investor services, and financial news.
www.tse.com

Vancouver Stock Exchange. Official site for the Vancouver stock exchange.
www.vse.ca/

Vienna Stock Exchange. Cash market.
www.vienna-stock-exchange.at/boerse

Warsaw Stock Exchange
www.atm.com.pl/~gielda

The Winnipeg Commodity Exchange
www.wce.mb.ca

Zagreb Stock Exchange. Official home page of the Zagreb stock exchange. In English.
www.zse.hr/

appendix k

Dow Jones 30 Industrials

Dow Jones Industrial Average as of July 20, 1999

Company Name	Symbol	Price	Weighting %
AlliedSignal, Inc.	ALD	64.8125	2.977
Aluminum Co. of America	AA	60.4375	2.776
American Express Co.	AXP	135.6875	6.234
AT & T Corp.	T	54.5625	2.506
Boeing Co.	BA	45.4375	2.087
Caterpillar Inc.	CAT	60.6875	2.788
Chevron Corp.	CHV	91.7500	4.215
Citigroup Inc.	C	49.2500	2.262
Coca-Cola Co.	KO	63.6250	2.923
DuPont Co.	DD	70.9375	3.259
Eastman Kodak Co.	EK	74.2500	3.411
Exxon Corp.	XON	77.0000	3.537
General Electric Co.	GE	117.3750	5.392
General Motors Corp.	GM	66.8750	3.072
Goodyear Tire & Rubber Co.	GT	57.2500	2.630
Hewlett-Packard Co.	HWP	111.2500	5.111

Company Name	Symbol	Price	Weighting %
International Business Machines Corp.	IBM	127.5625	5.860
International Paper Co.	IP	54.8750	2.521
J.P. Morgan & Co.	JPM	34.1250	6.162
Johnson & Johnson	JNJ	95.8125	4.402
McDonald's Corp.	MCD	42.7500	1.964
Merck & Co.	MRK	69.0000	3.170
Minnesota Mining & Manufacturing Co.	MMM	89.9375	4.132
Philip Morris Cos.	MO	37.8750	1.740
Procter & Gamble Co.	PG	90.2500	4.146
Sears, Roebuck & Co.	S	43.6875	2.007
Union Carbide Corp.	UK	45.1250	2.073
United Technologies Corp.	UTX	70.2500	3.227
Wal-Mart Stores Inc.	WMT	46.4375	2.133
Walt Disney Co.	DIS	27.6250	1.269

appendix I

ISDEX—the Internet Stock Index

Company	Symbol	Focus
24/7	TRSM	Ad network
@Home	ATHM	Cable Internet services
Amazon	AMZN	E-tailer of books, music, video
America Online	AOL	Consumer online services
Axent	AXNT	Web security software
Broadcast.com	BCST	Web audio-video aggregator
Broadcom	BRCM	Broadband chips
Beyond.com	BYND	Software retailer network
Broadvision	BVSN	Web marketing software
CDnow Inc	CDNW	E-tailer for music
CheckPoint Software	CHKP	Web security software
Cisco	CSCO	Leading Internet routing firm
CMG Info	CMGI	Internet venture firm
CNET	CNET	Web and cable content
Concentric	CNCX	Internet services provider
Cybercash	CYCH	Digital currencies
Cyberian Outpost	COOL	PC/technology e-tailer
DoubleClick	DCLK	Web advertising

Company	Symbol	Focus
E*Trade	EGRP	Web stock trades
Earthlink	ELNK	Internet services provider
eBay	EBAY	Leading personal auction service
Egghead	EGGS	E-tailer of software/hardware
Excite	XCIT	Navigation services
Exodus	EXDS	Web hosting data centers
GeoCities	GCTY	Websteader/free Web sites
Go2Net	GNET	Content, search, and business communities
Infoseek	SEEK	Navigation services
Infospace.com	INSP	Content and commerce wholesaler
Inktomi	INKT	Network caching, search wholesaler
ISS Group	ISSX	Security software
Lycos	LCOS	Navigation services
Mindspring	MSPG	Internet services provider
Network Associates	NETA	Internet security software
Network Solutions	NSOL	Domain name registrar
ONSALE	ONSL	Web auctions
Open Market	OMKT	Internet commerce software
Preview Travel	PTVL	Web-based travel services
PSINet	PSIX	Internet services provider
RealNetworks	RNWK	Internet streaming media software
Security Dynamics	SDTI	Internet security software
Security First	SONE	Web banking software
Sportsline	SPLN	Web-based sports news
USWeb	USWB	Turnkey Web business services
Verio	VRIO	Internet services provider
Verisign	VRSN	Web digital ID issuer
Vocaltec	VOCLF	IP telephony software
Yahoo	YHOO	Navigation services
XOOM.com	XMCM	E-Commerce community

appendix m

Nasdaq 100 Index

The Nasdaq 100 Index reflects Nasdaq's largest companies across major industry groups, including computer hardware and software, telecommunications, retail/wholesale trade, and biotechnology.

Nasdaq 100 as of July 21, 1999

Company Name	Symbol	% of Index
3Com Corporation	COMS	0.45
Adaptec, Inc.	ADPT	0.32
ADC Telecommunications, Inc.	ADCT	0.67
Adobe Systems Incorporated	ADBE	0.5
Altera Corporation	ALTR	1.03
Amazon.com, Inc.	AMZN	1.27
American Power Conversion Corporation	APCC	0.52
Amgen Inc.	AMGN	1.65
Andrew Corporation	ANDW	0.12
Apollo Group, Inc.	APOL	0.16
Apple Computer, Inc.	AAPL	0.96
Applied Materials, Inc.	AMAT	1.3

Company Name	Symbol	% of Index
At Home Corporation	ATHM	1.13
Atmel Corporation	ATML	0.19
Autodesk, Inc.	ADSK	0.11
Bed Bath & Beyond Inc.	BBBY	0.66
Biogen, Inc.	BGEN	1.3
Biomet, Inc.	BMET	0.53
BMC Software, Inc.	BMCS	0.98
Cambridge Technology Partners, Inc.	CATP	0.07
CBRL Group Inc.	CBRL	0.06
Centocor, Inc.	CNTO	0.36
Chiron Corporation	CHIR	0.53
Cintas Corporation	CTAS	0.81
Cisco Systems, Inc.	CSCO	6.68
Citrix Systems, Inc.	CTXS	0.51
CMGI, Inc.	CMGI	0.98
CNET, Inc.	CNET	0.34
Comair Holdings, Inc.	COMR	0.18
Comcast Corporation	CMCSK	1.32
Compuware Corporation	CPWR	0.7
Comverse Technology, Inc.	CMVT	0.53
Concord EFS, Inc.	CEFT	0.52
Conexant Systems, Inc.	CNXT	0.57
Corporate Express, Inc.	CEXP	0.05
Costco Companies, Inc.	COST	0.86
Dell Computer Corporation	DELL	3.58
Dollar Tree Stores, Inc.	DLTR	0.23
Electronic Arts Inc.	ERTS	0.3
Electronics for Imaging, Inc.	EFII	0.22
Fastenal Company	FAST	0.15
First Health Group Corp.	FHCC	0.06
Fiserv, Inc.	FISV	0.44
Food Lion, Inc.	FDLNB	0.21
Genzyme General	GENZ	0.5
Herman Miller, Inc.	MLHR	0.14
Immunex Corporation	IMNX	1.17
Intel Corporation	INTC	7.07
Intuit Inc.	INTU	0.65
JDS Uniphase Corporation	JDSU	0.8
KLA-Tencor Corporation	KLAC	0.66
Level 3 Communications, Inc.	LVLT	1.37
Lincare Holdings Inc.	LNCR	0.13
Linear Technology Corporation	LLTC	1.23
LM Ericsson Telephone Company	ERICY	0.66
Lycos, Inc.	LCOS	0.54

Company Name	Symbol	% of Index
Maxim Integrated Products, Inc.	MXIM	1.15
MCI WORLDCOM, Inc.	WCOM	5.53
McLeodUSA Incorporated	MCLD	0.33
Microchip Technology Incorporated	MCHP	0.19
Micron Electronics, Inc.	MUEI	0.07
Microsoft Corporation	MSFT	15.45
Molex Incorporated	MOLX	0.24
Network Associates, Inc.	NETA	0.22
Nextel Communications, Inc.	NXTL	1.89
Northwest Airlines Corporation	NWAC	0.22
Novell, Inc.	NOVL	1.03
NTL Incorporated	NTLI	0.71
Oracle Corporation	ORCL	2.12
PACCAR, Inc	PCAR	0.47
PacifiCare Health Systems, Inc.	PHSY	0.24
PanAmSat Corporation	SPOT	0.75
Parametric Technology Corporation	PMTC	0.49
Paychex, Inc.	PAYX	0.68
PeopleSoft, Inc.	PSFT	0.44
QUALCOMM Incorporated	QCOM	2.64
Quantum Corporation	QNTM	0.49
Quintiles Transnational Corp.	QTRN	0.54
Qwest Communications International Inc.	QWST	1.17
Reuters Group PLC	RTRSY	0.19
Rexall Sundown, Inc.	RXSD	0.05
Ross Stores, Inc.	ROST	0.17
Sanmina Corporation	SANM	0.4
Siebel Systems, Inc.	SEBL	0.64
Sigma-Aldrich Corporation	SIAL	0.34
Smurfit-Stone Container Corporation	SSCC	0.43
Staples, Inc.	SPLS	0.9
Starbucks Corporation	SBUX	0.59
Stewart Enterprises, Inc.	STEI	0.11
Sun Microsystems, Inc.	SUNW	2.21
Synopsys, Inc.	SNPS	0.44
Tech Data Corporation	TECD	0.16
Tellabs, Inc.	TLAB	1.36
USA Networks, Inc.	USAI	0.61
VERITAS Software Corporation	VRTS	0.93
VISX, Incorporated	VISX	0.64
Vitesse Semiconductor Corporation	VTSS	0.47
Worthington Industries, Inc.	WTHG	0.09
Xilinx, Inc.	XLNX	1.15
Yahoo! Inc.	YHOO	1.54

appendix n

Nasdaq stocks

Symbol	Company Name	Sector
ATEN	@Entertainment, Inc.	Telecommunications
CTAC	1-800 Contacts, Inc.	Industrial
FBCV	1st Bancorp	Other Finance
FBER	1st Bergen Bancorp	Other Finance
SRCE	1st Source Corporation	Other Finance
SRCEO	1st Source Corporation	Other Finance
SRCEP	1st Source Corporation	Other Finance
TFSM	24/7 Media, Inc.	Industrial
TCCC	3CI Complete Compliance Corporation	Industrial
COMS	3Com Corporation	Computer
TDSC	3D Systems Corporation	Computer
TDFX	3Dfx Interactive, Inc.	Industrial
TDDDF	3Dlabs Inc., Ltd.	Computer
THDO	3DO Company (The)	Industrial
TDXT	3DX Technologies, Inc.	Industrial
KIDE	4 Kids Entertainment Inc.	Industrial
FFTI	4Front Technologies Inc.	Computer
SEVL	7th Level, Inc.	Computer

Symbol	Company Name	Sector
IFLY	800 Travel Systems, Inc.	Transportation
JRJR	800-JR Cigar, Inc.	Industrial
EGHT	8×8, Inc.	Computer
ELUXY	A B Electrolux	Industrial
VOLVY	A B Volvo	Industrial
SHLM	A. Schulman, Inc.	Industrial
ACMR	A.C. Moore Arts & Crafts, Inc.	Industrial
ACLNF	A.C.L.N. Limited	Transportation
ACSEF	A.C.S. Electronics Limited	Industrial
ADAM	A.D.A.M. Software, Inc.	Computer
ASVI	A.S.V., Inc.	Industrial
AAON	AAON, Inc.	Industrial
ASHE	Aasche Transportation Services, Inc.	Transportation
ASTM	Aastrom Biosciences, Inc.	Industrial
AATT	Aavid Thermal Technologies, Inc.	Computer
SKFRY	AB SKF	Industrial
ABACF	Abacan Resource Corporation	Industrial
ABDR	Abacus Direct Corporation	Industrial
ABIX	Abatix Environmental Corp.	Industrial
ABAX	ABAXIS, Inc.	Industrial
ABBBY	ABB AB	Industrial
ABCB	ABC Bancorp	Other Finance
ABCR	ABC Rail Products Corporation	Industrial
ABGX	Abgenix, Inc	Biotechnology
AANB	Abigail Adams National Bancorp, Inc.	Other Finance
ABBK	Abington Bancorp Inc.	Bank
ABMD	ABIOMED, Inc.	Industrial
ABTE	Able Telcom Holding Corp.	Industrial
ABRX	ABR Information Services, Inc.	Industrial
ABRI	Abrams Industries, Inc.	Industrial
AXAS	Abraxas Petroleum Corporation	Industrial
ABTC	ABT Building Products Corporation	Industrial
ACRI	Acacia Research Corporation	Other Finance
ACLE	Accel International Corporation	Other Finance
ACLY	Accelr8 Technology Corporation	Computer
ACLR	Accent Color Sciences, Inc.	Computer
ACNFC	Accent Software International	Computer
AABC	Access Anytime Bancorp, Inc.	Bank
ACCS	Access Health, Inc.	Industrial
AWWC	Access Worldwide Communications, Inc.	Industrial
AKLM	Acclaim Entertainment, Inc.	Industrial
ACMI	AccuMed International Inc.	Industrial

Symbol	Company Name	Sector
AACE	Ace Cash Express, Inc.	Other Finance
ACEC	ACE*COMM Corporation	Industrial
ACET	Aceto Corporation	Industrial
ACIT	ACI Telecentrics, Incorporated	Industrial
ACMTA	ACMAT Corporation	Insurance
AVCC	Acorn Holding Corp.	Other Finance
ACRN	Acorn Products, Inc.	Industrial
ACRG	ACR Group, Inc.	Industrial
AGAM	Acres Gaming Incorporated	Industrial
ACRO	Acrodyne Communications, Inc.	Industrial
ACSY	ACSYS, Inc.	Industrial
ACTM	ACT Manufacturing, Inc.	Computer
ANET	ACT Networks, Inc.	Industrial
ACTT	ACT Teleconferencing, Inc.	Industrial
ACTL	Actel Corporation	Industrial
ACTN	Action Performance Companies, Inc.	Industrial
APII	Action Products International, Inc.	Industrial
AAGP	Active Apparel Group, Inc.	Industrial
ACVC	Active Voice Corporation	Industrial
ATVI	Activision, Inc.	Industrial
ACRT	Actrade International, Ltd.	Industrial
ACTU	Actuate Software Corporation	Computer
IATV	ACTV Inc.	Telecommunications
ACXM	Acxiom Corporation	Computer
ADAC	ADAC Laboratories	Industrial
ADGO	Adams Golf, Inc.	Industrial
ADPT	Adaptec, Inc.	Computer
ADCT	ADC Telecommunications, Inc.	Industrial
ADDM	ADDvantage Media Group, Inc.	Industrial
ADEX	ADE Corporation	Industrial
ADECY	Adecco S A c/o Adecco Services, Inc.	Industrial
ADLAC	Adelphia Communications Corporation	Telecommunications
ADTK	Adept Technology, Inc.	Industrial
AFLX	ADFlex Solutions, Inc.	Computer
ADMTC	ADM Tronics Unlimited, Inc.	Industrial
AAABB	Admiralty Bancorp, Inc.	Bank
ADBE	Adobe Systems Incorporated	Computer
ACCOB	Adolph Coors Company	Industrial
ADRN	Adrenalin Interactive Inc.	Industrial
ADLRF	Adrian Resources Corporation	Industrial
ADTN	ADTRAN, Inc.	Industrial
AFBC	Advance Financial Bancorp	Bank

Symbol	Company Name	Sector
ADVP	Advance ParadigM, Inc.	Industrial
AASI	Advanced Aerodynamics & Structures, Inc.	Industrial
ACSC	Advanced Communication Systems, Inc.	Industrial
ADTC	Advanced Deposition Technologies, Inc.	Industrial
ADIC	Advanced Digital Information Corporation	Computer
AESP	Advanced Electronic Support Products, Inc.	Industrial
AEIS	Advanced Energy Industries, Inc.	Computer
AERTA	Advanced Environmental Recycling Tech.	Industrial
AFCI	Advanced Fibre Communications	Telecommunications
ADVH	Advanced Health Corporation	Industrial
ADLT	Advanced Lighting Technologies Inc.	Industrial
AMVC	Advanced Machine Vision Corporation	Industrial
ADMS	Advanced Marketing Services, Inc.	Industrial
ADMG	Advanced Materials Group, Inc.	Industrial
ANSI	Advanced Neuromodulation Systems, Inc.	Industrial
APOS	Advanced Polymer Systems, Inc.	Industrial
ARTT	Advanced Radio Telecom Corp.	Telecommunications
ATPX	Advanced Technical Products, Inc.	Industrial
ATIS	Advanced Tissue Sciences, Inc.	Industrial
ADVNA	ADVANTA Corp.	Other Finance
ADVNB	ADVANTA Corp.	Other Finance
ADVNZ	ADVANTA Corp.	Other Finance
ALSI	Advantage Learning Systems, Inc.	Computer
AMSO	Advantage Marketing Systems, Inc.	Industrial
DINE	Advantica Restaurant Group, Inc.	Industrial
ADVS	Advent Software, Inc.	Industrial
AGIS	Aegis Communications Group Inc.	Industrial
AEHR	Aehr Test Systems	Industrial
AEPI	AEP Industries Inc.	Industrial
AERN	AER Energy Resources, Inc.	Industrial
AERL	Aerial Communications Inc.	Telecommunications
AERS	Aero Systems Engineering, Inc.	Industrial
ARVX	Aerovox Incorporated	Industrial
ATRM	Aetrium Incorporated	Industrial
AFCX	AFC Cable Systems, Inc.	Industrial
AFFI	Affinity Technology Group, Inc.	Computer
AFFX	Affymetrix, Inc.	Industrial
AFPC	AFP Imaging Corporation	Industrial
AFED	AFSALA Bancorp, Inc.	Other Finance
ATAC	Aftermarket Technology Corporation	Industrial
AGAI	AG Associates, Inc.	Industrial
AGBGC	Ag-Bag International Limited	Industrial

Symbol	Company Name	Sector
AGCH	Ag-Chem Equipment Co., Inc.	Industrial
AGPH	Agouron Pharmaceuticals, Inc.	Biotechnology
ABTX	AgriBioTech, Inc.	Industrial
AGNU	Agri-Nutrition Group, Ltd.	Industrial
AGTO	Agritope, Inc.	Industrial
AHLS	AHL Services, Inc.	Industrial
ACNAF	Air Canada	Transportation
AEIC	Air Express International Corporation	Transportation
AIRM	Air Methods Corporation	Transportation
AIRT	Air Transportation Holding Company, Inc.	Transportation
ASII	Airport Systems International, Inc.	Industrial
AAIR	AirTran Holdings, Inc.	Transportation
AKRN	Akorn, Inc.	Industrial
AKSY	Aksys, Ltd.	Industrial
AKZOY	Akzo Nobel N.V.	Industrial
ALAB	Alabama National BanCorporation	Other Finance
ALDNF	Aladdin Knowledge Systems Limited	Industrial
ALAN	Alanco Environmental Resources Corporation	Industrial
ALRS	ALARIS Medical, Inc.	Industrial
ALBK	ALBANK Financial Corporation	Bank
ALBC	Albion Banc Corp.	Other Finance
ALCD	Alcide Corporation	Industrial
ALDA	Aldila, Inc.	Industrial
ALEX	Alexander & Baldwin, Inc.	Transportation
ALXN	Alexion Pharmaceuticals, Inc.	Biotechnology
ALFA	Alfa Corporation	Insurance
ACEL	Alfacell Corporation	Industrial
ALGSF	Algoma Steel, Inc.	Industrial
ALGO	Algos Pharmaceutical Corp.	Biotechnology
ALNT	Aliant Communications Inc.	Telecommunications
ALCO	Alico, Inc.	Industrial
MASK	Align-Rite International, Inc.	Industrial
ALKS	Alkermes, Inc.	Biotechnology
ALKSP	Alkermes, Inc.	Biotechnology
SEMI	All American Semiconductor, Inc.	Industrial
ALCI	Allcity Insurance Company	Insurance
ALGX	Allegiance Telecom, Inc.	Telecommunications
ALLE	Allegiant Bancorp, Inc.	Other Finance
AORGB	Allen Organ Company	Industrial
ASTI	Allergan Specialty Therapeutics, Inc.	Biotechnology
ABCL	Alliance Bancorp	Other Finance
ALLIF	Alliance Communications Corp.	Industrial

Symbol	Company Name	Sector
ALLY	Alliance Gaming Corporation	Industrial
ALLP	Alliance Pharmaceutical Corp.	Biotechnology
ALSC	Alliance Semiconductor Corporation	Industrial
ALLC	Allied Capital Corporation	Other Finance
ALDV	Allied Devices Corporation	Industrial
AHPI	Allied Healthcare Products, Inc.	Industrial
AWIN	Allied Waste Industries, Inc.	Industrial
ALLN	Allin Communications Corporation	Industrial
ALLS	Allstar Systems, Inc.	Industrial
ASFN	Allstate Financial Corporation	Other Finance
ALHY	Alpha Hospitality Corporation	Industrial
AHAA	Alpha Industries, Inc.	Industrial
ALMI	Alpha Microsystems	Computer
ATGI	Alpha Technologies Group, Inc.	Computer
ABTI	Alpha-Beta Technology, Inc.	Biotechnology
ALPH	AlphaNet Solutions, Inc.	Industrial
AILP	ALPNET, Inc.	Computer
ALTA	Alta Gold Co.	Industrial
ALTIF	Altair International, Inc	Industrial
ALTN	Alteon Inc.	Biotechnology
ALTR	Altera Corporation	Computer
ALTM	Alternate Marketing Networks, Inc.	Industrial
ALRC	Alternative Resources Corp.	Computer
ALRN	Altron Incorporated	Industrial
ALYD	Alydaar Software Corporation	Industrial
ALYN	Alyn Corporation	Industrial
AMAR	Amarillo Biosciences, Inc.	Industrial
AMZN	Amazon.com, Inc.	Computer
AMFC	AMB Financial Corp.	Other Finance
AHCI	Ambanc Holding Co., Inc.	Other Finance
AMIE	Ambassadors International, Inc.	Transportation
AMBI	AMBI Inc.	Biotechnology
DIST	AMCON Distributing Company	Industrial
AMCPF	Amcor Limited	Industrial
AMCRY	Amcor Limited	Industrial
AMFI	Amcore Financial, Inc.	Other Finance
UHAL	AMERCO	Other Finance
ASBI	Ameriana Bancorp	Bank
APROZ	America First Apartment Investors, L.P.	Other Finance
AFTXZ	America First Tax Exempt Mortgage Fund L.P.	Other Finance
ASGR	America Service Group Inc.	Industrial
AIRS	American Aircarriers Support, Inc.	Industrial

Symbol	Company Name	Sector
AMBC	American Bancorporation	Bank
AMBCP	American Bancorporation	Bank
ABAN	American Bancshares, Inc.	Other Finance
BNGO	American Bingo & Gaming Corp.	Industrial
ABMC	American Bio Medica Corp.	Industrial
MABXA	American Biogenetic Sciences, Inc.	Biotechnology
ABCO	American Buildings Company	Industrial
ABFI	American Business Financial Services, Inc.	Other Finance
ACAS	American Capital Strategies, Ltd.	Other Finance
ACEI	American Champion Entertainment, Inc.	Industrial
AMCE	American Claims Evaluation, Inc.	Insurance
AMCV	American Classic Voyages Co.	Industrial
AMCN	American Coin Merchandising, Inc.	Industrial
ACHI	American Country Holdings Inc.	Industrial
ADPI	American Dental Partners, Inc.	Industrial
ADLI	American Dental Technologies, Inc.	Industrial
AEOS	American Eagle Outfitters, Inc.	Industrial
ECGOF	American Eco Corporation	Industrial
ECOL	American Ecology Corporation	Industrial
AMEP	American Educational Products, Inc.	Industrial
AFWY	American Freightways Corporation	Transportation
AHEPZ	American Health Properties, Inc.	Industrial
AMHC	American Healthcorp, Inc.	Industrial
AHOM	American HomePatient, Inc.	Industrial
HSTR	American Homestar Corporation	Industrial
AIFC	American Indemnity Financial Corporation	Other Finance
AIPN	American International Petroleum Corporation	Industrial
ALGI	American Locker Group, Inc.	Industrial
AMSY	American Management Systems, Incorporated	Computer
AMAC	American Medical Alert Corp.	Industrial
SKYC	American Mobile Satellite Corporation	Telecommunications
ANAT	American National Insurance Company	Insurance
AORI	American Oncology Resources, Inc.	Industrial
AMPBB	American Pacific Bank	Other Finance
APFC	American Pacific Corporation	Industrial
APPM	American Physician Partners, Inc.	Industrial
AMPH	American Physicians Service Group, Inc.	Industrial
APCC	American Power Conversion Corporation	Computer
GASS	American Resources of Delaware, Inc.	Industrial
AMSFF	American Safety Insurance Group, Ltd.	Insurance
RAZR	American Safety Razor Company	Industrial
AMSWA	American Software, Inc.	Computer

Symbol	Company Name	Sector
AMSC	American Superconductor Corporation	Industrial
ACES	American Vantage Companies	Industrial
BETM	American Wagering, Inc.	Industrial
AMWD	American Woodmark Corporation	Industrial
AXTI	American Xtal Technology	Industrial
AGDM	Americana Gold & Diamond Holdings, Inc.	Industrial
ARGNA	Amerigon Incorporated	Industrial
HOST	Amerihost Properties, Inc.	Industrial
ALNK	AmeriLink Corporation	Industrial
AMRN	Amerin Corporation	Insurance
PATH	AmeriPath, Inc.	Industrial
ASCA	Ameristar Casinos, Inc.	Industrial
AMTD	AmeriTrade Holding Corporation	Other Finance
AMVP	AmeriVest Properties, Inc.	Other Finance
AMES	Ames Department Stores, Inc.	Industrial
AMGN	Amgen Inc.	Biotechnology
AMTA	Amistar Corporation	Industrial
AMKR	Amkor Technology, Inc.	Computer
AMLJ	AML Communications, Inc.	Industrial
AMXI	AMNEX, Inc.	Telecommunications
AMPI	Amplicon, Inc.	Computer
AMPD	Amplidyne, Inc.	Industrial
AMCT	AMRESCO Capital Trust	Other Finance
AMMB	AMRESCO, INC.	Industrial
AMSGA	Amsurg Corp.	Industrial
AMSGB	Amsurg Corp.	Industrial
ASYS	Amtech Systems, Inc.	Industrial
AMTR	Amtran, Inc.	Transportation
AMXX	AMX Corporation	Industrial
AMLN	Amylin Pharmaceuticals, Inc.	Biotechnology
ANCO	ANACOMP, Inc.	Computer
ANAD	ANADIGICS, Inc.	Computer
ALOG	Analogic Corporation	Industrial
ANLG	Analogy, Inc.	Computer
AATI	Analysis & Technology, Inc.	Industrial
ANLY	Analysts International Corporation	Computer
ANLT	Analytical Surveys, Inc.	Industrial
ASIPY	Anangel-American Shipholdings Limited	Transportation
ANEN	Anaren Microwave, Inc.	Industrial
ANBC	ANB Corporation	Other Finance
ABCW	Anchor BanCorp Wisconsin Inc.	Bank
AFSC	Anchor Financial Corporation	Other Finance

Symbol	Company Name	Sector
SLOT	Anchor Gaming	Industrial
ANCR	Ancor Communications, Inc.	Industrial
ANDA	Andataco Inc.	Computer
ADCC	Andean Development Corporation	Industrial
ANDR	Andersen Group, Inc.	Industrial
ANDE	Andersons, Inc. (The)	Industrial
ANDB	Andover Bancorp, Inc.	Bank
ANDW	Andrew Corporation	Industrial
ADRX	Andrx Corporation	Biotechnology
ANRG	Anergen, Inc.	Industrial
NSTA	Anesta Corp.	Industrial
ANGN	Angeion Corporation	Industrial
AAGIY	Anglo American Gold Investment Co., Ltd	Industrial
ANIC	Anicom, Inc.	Industrial
ANIK	Anika Therapeutics Inc.	Industrial
ANNB	Annapolis National Bancorp, Inc.	Other Finance
ALREF	Annuity and Life Re (Holdings) Ltd.	Insurance
ASIGF	Ansaldo Signal, N.V. c/o Union Switch	Industrial
ANST	Ansoft Corporation	Computer
ANSR	AnswerThink Consulting Group, Inc.	Industrial
ANSS	ANSYS, Inc.	Computer
ANTC	ANTEC Corporation	Industrial
ANTP	Antenna Products Inc.	Industrial
APAT	APA Optics, Inc.	Industrial
APAC	APAC TeleServices, Inc.	Industrial
AMSI	APACHE Medical Systems, Inc.	Computer
APEX	Apex PC Solutions, Inc.	Computer
APHT	Aphton Corp.	Biotechnology
APOG	Apogee Enterprises, Inc.	Industrial
APOL	Apollo Group, Inc.	Industrial
AAPL	Apple Computer, Inc.	Computer
APPB	Applebee's International, Inc.	Industrial
APWDE	Applewoods, Inc.	Industrial
AAII	Applied Analytical Industries, Inc.	Industrial
ABIO	Applied Biometrics, Inc.	Industrial
ACTC	Applied Cellular Technology, Inc.	Computer
ADAX	Applied Digital Access, Inc.	Industrial
AETC	Applied Extrusion Technologies, Inc.	Industrial
AFCO	Applied Films Corporation	Computer
AGTX	Applied Graphics Technologies, Inc.	Industrial
AICX	Applied Imaging Corp.	Industrial
AINN	Applied Innovation Inc.	Industrial

Symbol	Company Name	Sector
AMAT	Applied Materials, Inc.	Industrial
AMCC	Applied Micro Circuits Corporation	Industrial
APMC	Applied Microsystems Corporation	Computer
ASTX	Applied Science and Technology, Inc.	Industrial
APSG	Applied Signal Technology, Inc.	Industrial
APLX	Applix, Inc.	Computer
AQCR	Aqua Care Systems, Inc. New	Industrial
AQLA	Aquila Biopharmaceuticals, Inc	Industrial
ARSD	Arabian Shield Development Company	Industrial
ARDM	Aradigm Corporation	Industrial
ARMXF	Aramex International Limited	Transportation
ARCAF	Arcadis NV	Industrial
APGR	Arch Communications Group, Inc.	Telecommunications
ASYCF	Architel Systems Corporation	Industrial
ACAT	Arctic Cat Inc.	Industrial
ARDNA	Arden Group, Inc.	Industrial
ARDT	ARDENT Software, Inc.	Computer
AREA	Area Bancshares Corporation	Other Finance
ARLCF	Arel Communications & Software Ltd.	Computer
AGII	Argonaut Group, Inc.	Insurance
ARGX	Arguss Holdings, Inc.	Industrial
ARIS	ARI Network Services, Inc.	Computer
ARIA	ARIAD Pharmaceuticals, Inc.	Industrial
ADSP	Ariel Corporation	Computer
ARSC	ARIS Corporation	Computer
ARINA	Arista Investors Corp.	Insurance
AZIC	Arizona Instrument Corporation	Industrial
ARKR	Ark Restaurants Corp.	Industrial
ABFS	Arkansas Best Corporation	Transportation
ABFSP	Arkansas Best Corporation	Transportation
ARMHY	ARM Holdings, plc	Computer
ARMF	Armanino Foods of Distinction, Incorporated	Industrial
AIND	Arnold Industries, Inc.	Transportation
ARNX	Aronex Pharmaceuticals, Inc.	Industrial
ARQL	ArQule, Inc.	Biotechnology
AROW	Arrow Financial Corporation	Other Finance
ARRO	Arrow International, Inc.	Industrial
ARWM	Arrow-Magnolia International, Inc.	Industrial
ARTE	Artecon, Inc.	Computer
AVEI	Arterial Vascular Engineering, Inc.	Industrial
ARTNA	Artesian Resources Corporation	Industrial
ATSN	Artesyn Technologies, Inc.	Computer

Symbol	Company Name	Sector
ARTC	ArthroCare Corporation	Industrial
ATCH	Arthur Treacher's, Inc.	Industrial
ARTI	Artisan Components, Inc.	Industrial
ASFT	Artisoft, Inc.	Computer
ARTW	Art's-Way Manufacturing Co., Inc.	Industrial
ASAI	ASA Holdings, Inc.	Transportation
ASAA	ASA International Ltd.	Computer
ASAM	ASAHI/America, Inc.	Industrial
ASNT	Asante Technologies, Inc.	Industrial
ASBP	ASB Financial Corp.	Other Finance
ASND	Ascend Communications, Inc.	Computer
GOAL	Ascent Entertainment Group, Inc.	Industrial
ASCT	Ascent Pediatrics, Inc.	Biotechnology
ASDG	ASD Group, Inc.	Industrial
ASTSF	ASE Test, Limited	Computer
ASEC	Aseco Corporation	Industrial
ASHA	ASHA Corporation	Industrial
ASHW	Ashworth, Inc.	Industrial
ASIS	ASI Solutions Incorporated	Industrial
AEHCF	Asia Electronics Holding Co., Inc.	Industrial
APQCF	Asia Pacific Resources, Ltd.	Industrial
ASMIF	ASM International N.V.	Industrial
ASMLF	ASM Lithography Holding N.V.	Industrial
ASPCE	Aspec Technology, Inc.	Computer
ASDV	Aspect Development, Inc.	Computer
ASPT	Aspect Telecommunications Corporation	Industrial
AZPN	Aspen Technology, Inc.	Computer
ASBC	Associated Banc-Corp	Other Finance
SIDE	Associated Materials Corporation	Industrial
ASFI	Asta Funding, Inc.	Other Finance
ATEA	Astea International, Inc.	Computer
ASTE	Astec Industries, Inc.	Industrial
ASFC	Astoria Financial Corporation	Other Finance
ALOT	Astro-Med, Inc.	Industrial
ATRO	Astronics Corporation	Industrial
APWR	ASTROPOWER, Inc.	Computer
ASYM	Asymetrix Learning Systems, Inc.	Computer
ASYT	Asyst Technologies, Inc.	Industrial
ATHM	At Home Corporation	Computer
ATEC	ATEC Group Inc.	Industrial
ATGC	ATG Inc.	Industrial
ATPC	Athey Products Corporation	Industrial

Symbol	Company Name	Sector
AAME	Atlantic American Corporation	Other Finance
ATLB	Atlantic Bank and Trust Company	Bank
ACAI	Atlantic Coast Airlines Holdings, Inc.	Transportation
ADSC	Atlantic Data Services, Inc.	Computer
AGLF	Atlantic Gulf Communities Corporation	Other Finance
AGLFP	Atlantic Gulf Communities Corporation	Other Finance
ATLC	Atlantic Pharmaceuticals, Inc.	Industrial
ATLRS	Atlantic Realty Trust	Other Finance
APCFY	Atlas Pacific Limited	Industrial
ATML	Atmel Corporation	Computer
ATMI	ATMI Inc.	Industrial
ATRI	ATRION Corporation	Industrial
ATXI	Atrix International, Inc.	Industrial
ATRX	Atrix Laboratories, Inc.	Industrial
ATSI	ATS Medical, Inc.	Industrial
ABPCA	Au Bon Pain Co., Inc.	Industrial
AUBN	Auburn National Bancorporation, Inc.	Other Finance
AULT	Ault Incorporated	Industrial
AURA	Aura Systems, Inc.	Computer
ABSC	Aurora Biosciences Corporation	Industrial
ASPX	Auspex Systems, Inc.	Computer
ACAM	Autocam Corporation	Industrial
ACYT	AutoCyte, Inc.	Industrial
ADSK	Autodesk, Inc.	Computer
AIMM	AutoImmune Inc.	Biotechnology
AIII	Autologic Information International, Inc.	Industrial
APCO	Automobile Protection Corporation	Industrial
ATCI	Autonomous Technologies Corporation	Industrial
AVDO	Avado Brands Inc.	Industrial
AVDOP	Avado Brands Inc.	Industrial
MIST	Avalon Capital, Inc.	Other Finance
CITY	Avalon Community Services, Inc.	Industrial
AVAN	Avant Immunotherapeutics, Inc.	Industrial
AVNT	Avant! Corporation	Computer
AVTR	Avatar Holdings Inc.	Other Finance
AVXT	AVAX Technologies, Inc.	Industrial
AVEC	AVECOR Cardiovascular Inc.	Industrial
AVRT	Avert, Inc.	Industrial
AVII	AVI BioPharma, Inc.	Industrial
AVGE	Aviation General, Inc.	Industrial
AVGP	Aviation Group, Inc.	Transportation
AVID	Avid Technology, Inc.	Industrial

Symbol	Company Name	Sector
AVGN	Avigen, Inc.	Industrial
AVIR	Aviron	Biotechnology
AVND	Avondale Financial Corp.	Other Finance
AVDL	Avondale Industries, Inc.	Industrial
AVTC	AVT Corporation	Industrial
AVTM	AVTEAM, Inc.	Industrial
AWRE	Aware, Inc.	Computer
AXNT	AXENT Technologies, Inc.	Computer
AXHM	Axiohm Transaction Solutions Inc.	Computer
AXIM	Axiom, Inc.	Industrial
AXYS	Axsys Technologies, Inc.	Industrial
AXPH	AxyS Pharmaceuticals Inc.	Industrial
AZTC	Aztec Technology Partners, Inc.	Industrial
AZUR	Azurel Ltd.	Industrial
BHIKF	B.H.I. Corporation	Other Finance
BOSCF	B.O.S. Better Online Solutions	Computer
BAANF	Baan Company N.V.	Computer
BAGL	BAB Holdings, Inc.	Industrial
PAPA	Back Bay Restaurant Group, Inc.	Industrial
BYBI	Back Yard Burgers, Inc.	Industrial
BPMI	Badger Paper Mills, Inc.	Industrial
BBAR	Balance Bar Company	Industrial
BWINA	Baldwin & Lyons, Inc.	Insurance
BWINB	Baldwin & Lyons, Inc.	Insurance
BPAO	Baldwin Piano & Organ Company	Industrial
BLDPF	Ballard Power Systems, Inc.	Industrial
BTEK	Baltek Corporation	Industrial
QDRMY	Banca Quadrum S.A.	Other Finance
BANF	BancFirst Corporation	Bank
BFOH	BancFirst Ohio Corp.	Other Finance
BCIS	Bancinsurance Corporation	Insurance
BGALY	Banco de Galicia y Buenos Aires S.A.	Bank
BKCT	Bancorp Connecticut Inc.	Bank
BMCC	Bando McGlocklin Capital Corporation	Other Finance
BMCCP	Bando McGlocklin Capital Corporation	Other Finance
BCOM	Bank of Commerce	Bank
BSXT	Bank of Essex	Bank
GRAN	Bank of Granite Corporation	Bank
BNSC	Bank of Santa Clara	Bank
BKSC	Bank of South Carolina Corp.	Bank
OZRK	Bank of the Ozarks	Bank
BPLS	Bank Plus Corporation	Bank

Symbol	Company Name	Sector
BARI	Bank Rhode Island	Bank
BNKU	Bank United Corporation	Other Finance
BWFC	Bank West Financial Corporation	Other Finance
BANC	BankAtlantic Bancorp, Inc.	Other Finance
BANCP	BankAtlantic Bancorp, Inc.	Other Finance
BKFR	BankFirst Corporation	Bank
BKNG	Banknorth Group, Inc.	Other Finance
BKUNA	BankUnited Financial Corporation	Other Finance
BKUNZ	BankUnited Financial Corporation	Other Finance
BNTA	Banta Corporation	Industrial
BSRTS	Banyan Strategic Realty Trust SBI	Other Finance
BNYN	Banyan Systems Incorporated	Computer
BBQZY	Barbeques Galore Limited	Industrial
BBHF	Barbers, Hairstyling for Men & Women, Inc.	Industrial
BNTT	Barnett Inc.	Industrial
BARZ	BARRA, Inc.	Computer
BBSI	Barrett Business Services, Inc.	Industrial
BARR	Barringer Technologies Inc.	Industrial
BASEA	Base Ten Systems, Inc.	Industrial
BSNX	Basin Exploration, Inc.	Industrial
BSET	Bassett Furniture Industries, Incorporated	Industrial
BATS	Batteries Batteries, Inc.	Industrial
BAYB	Bay Bancshares, Inc.	Bank
BVCC	Bay View Capital Corporation	Bank
FSNJ	Bayonne Bancshares, Inc.	Other Finance
BCSB	BCSB Bankcorp, Inc.	Bank
BCTI	BCT International Inc.	Industrial
BEAV	BE Aerospace, Inc.	Industrial
BESIF	BE Semiconductor Industries NV	Computer
BEAS	BEA Systems, Inc.	Computer
BUTI	BeautiControl Cosmetics, Inc.	Industrial
BEBE	bebe stores, inc.	Industrial
BBBY	Bed Bath & Beyond Inc.	Industrial
BFSB	Bedford Bancshares, Inc.	Other Finance
BMED	BEI Medical Systems Company, Inc.	Industrial
BEIQ	BEI Technologies, Inc.	Industrial
BELFA	Bel Fuse Inc.	Industrial
BELFB	Bel Fuse Inc.	Industrial
BCICF	Bell Canada International, Inc.	Telecommunications
BELM	Bell Microproducts Inc.	Industrial
BELW	Bellwether Exploration Company	Industrial
BLMT	Belmont Bancorp.	Bank

Symbol	Company Name	Sector
BJICA	Ben & Jerry's Homemade, Inc.	Industrial
BNHN	Benihana Inc.	Industrial
BNHNA	Benihana Inc.	Industrial
BTHS	Benthos, Inc.	Industrial
BGRH	Berger Holdings, Ltd.	Industrial
BERW	Beringer Wine Estates Holdings, Inc.	Industrial
BGAS	Berkshire Gas Company (The)	Industrial
BEST	Best Software, Inc.	Industrial
BSTW	Bestway, Inc.	Industrial
BFEN	BF Enterprises, Inc.	Other Finance
BHAG	BHA Group Holdings, Inc.	Industrial
BIAC	BI Incorporated	Industrial
BCORY	Biacore International AB	Industrial
BBUC	Big Buck Brewery & Steakhouse Inc.	Industrial
BIGCD	Big City Bagels, Inc.	Industrial
BDOG	Big Dog Holding, Inc.	Industrial
BIGE	Big Entertainment, Inc.	Industrial
BFFC	Big Foot Financial Corp.	Bank
BEERF	Big Rock Brewery Ltd.	Industrial
BGMR	Bigmar, Inc.	Industrial
BIKR	Bikers Dream, Inc.	Industrial
BILL	Billing Concepts Corp.	Computer
BVEW	Bindview Development Corporation	Computer
BFSC	Bingham Financial Services Corporation	Other Finance
BASI	Bioanalytical Systems, Inc.	Industrial
BCHE	Biochem Pharma Inc.	Biotechnology
BCRX	BioCryst Pharmaceuticals, Inc.	Industrial
BZET	Biofield Corp.	Industrial
BGEN	Biogen, Inc.	Biotechnology
BITI	Bio-Imaging Technologies, Inc.	Industrial
BJCT	Bioject Medical Technologies Inc.	Industrial
BLTI	BioLase Technology, Inc.	Industrial
BLSC	Bio-Logic Systems Corp.	Industrial
BMRA	Biomerica Inc.	Industrial
BMET	Biomet, Inc.	Industrial
BIOMF	Biomira Inc.	Biotechnology
BIME	Biomune Systems, Inc.	Biotechnology
BNRX	Bionutrics, Inc.	Industrial
BINX	Bionx Implants, Inc.	Industrial
BPLX	Bio-Plexus, Inc.	Industrial
BIPL	Biopool International, Inc.	Industrial
BIORY	Biora AB	Industrial

Symbol	Company Name	Sector
BRLI	Bio-Reference Laboratories, Inc.	Industrial
BREL	BioReliance Corporation	Industrial
BSEP	BioSepra Inc.	Industrial
BSTE	Biosite Diagnostics, Inc.	Industrial
BIOI	BioSource International Inc.	Industrial
BSTC	BioSpecifics Technologies Corp	Industrial
BINC	Biospherics Incorporated	Industrial
BTGC	Bio-Technology General Corp.	Biotechnology
BTIM	BioTime, Inc.	Industrial
BTRN	BioTransplant, Inc.	Biotechnology
BVAS	Bio-Vascular, Inc.	Industrial
BIPRY	BIPER, S.A. de C.V.	Telecommunications
BMAN	Birman Managed Care, Inc.	Other Finance
BIRM	Birmingham Utilities, Inc.	Industrial
BDMS	Birner Dental Management Services, Inc.	Industrial
BSYS	BISYS Group, Inc. (The)	Computer
BITS	Bitstream Inc.	Computer
BTWS	Bitwise Designs, Inc.	Industrial
BBOX	Black Box Corporation	Industrial
BHWK	Black Hawk Gaming & Development Co	Industrial
BLOCA	Block Drug Company, Inc.	Industrial
BLWT	Blowout Entertainment, Inc.	Industrial
BDCO	Blue Dolphin Energy Company	Industrial
RINO	Blue Rhino Corporation	Industrial
BRBI	Blue River Bancshares, Inc.	Bank
BWSI	Blue Wave Systems Inc.	Computer
BFLY	Bluefly, Inc.	Industrial
BMCS	BMC Software, Inc.	Computer
BONS	BMJ Medical Management, Inc.	Industrial
BNCM	BNC Mortgage, Inc.	Other Finance
BNCC	BNCCORP, INC.	Other Finance
BOBE	Bob Evans Farms, Inc.	Industrial
BOCI	Boca Research, Inc.	Industrial
BOGN	Bogen Communications International Inc.	Industrial
BOKF	BOK Financial Corporation	Other Finance
BOLD	Bolder Technologies Corporation	Industrial
BEYE	Bolle Inc.	Industrial
BMTR	Bonded Motors, Inc.	Industrial
BCII	Bone Care International, Inc.	Industrial
BNSOF	Bonso Electronics International, Inc.	Industrial
BOTX	Bontex Inc.	Industrial
BONT	Bon-Ton Stores, Inc. (The)	Industrial

Symbol	Company Name	Sector
BAMM	Books-A-Million, Inc.	Industrial
BOOL	Boole & Babbage, Inc.	Computer
BORAY	Boral Limited	Industrial
BLCA	Borel Bank & Trust Company	Bank
BLPG	Boron, LePore & Associates, Inc.	Industrial
BOSA	Boston Acoustics, Inc.	Industrial
BBII	Boston Biomedica, Inc.	Biotechnology
BOSTQ	Boston Chicken, Inc.	Industrial
BCGI	Boston Communications Group, Inc.	Telecommunications
BLSI	Boston Life Sciences, Inc.	Biotechnology
BPFH	Boston Private Financial Holdings, Inc.	Other Finance
BRAI	Boston Restaurant Associates, Inc.	Industrial
BDLS	Boundless Corporation	Computer
BOYD	Boyd Bros. Transportation Inc.	Transportation
BPRX	Bradley Pharmaceuticals, Inc.	Industrial
BRCOA	Brady Corporation	Industrial
BHQU	Brake Headquarters U.S.A., Inc.	Industrial
BBDC	Brantley Capital Corporation	Other Finance
XTRM	Brass Eagle, Inc.	Industrial
BFCI	Braun's Fashions Corporation	Industrial
BOBS	Brazil Fast Food Corp.	Industrial
BRCP	BRC Holdings, Inc.	Computer
BRBK	Brenton Banks, Inc.	Other Finance
BPTM	Bridgeport Machines, Inc.	Industrial
BEDS	BridgeStreet Accommodations, Inc.	Industrial
BRID	Bridgford Foods Corporation	Industrial
BEXP	Brigham Exploration Company	Industrial
BFAM	Bright Horizons Family Solutions Inc.	Industrial
CELL	Brightpoint, Inc.	Industrial
BTSR	BrightStar Information Technology Group, Inc.	Industrial
BRIOF	Brio Industries Inc.	Industrial
BRYO	Brio Technology, Inc.	Computer
BRTL	Bristol Retail Solutions, Inc.	Industrial
BVSI	Brite Voice Systems, Inc.	Computer
BBIOY	British Biotech plc	Industrial
BKBK	Britton & Koontz Capital Corporation	Other Finance
BNBC	Broad National Bancorporation	Other Finance
BNBCP	Broad National Bancorporation	Other Finance
BBTK	BroadBand Technologies, Inc.	Industrial
BCST	Broadcast.com inc.	Computer
BRCM	Broadcom Corporation	Computer
BVSN	BroadVision, Inc.	Computer

Symbol	Company Name	Sector
BSIS	Broadway & Seymour, Inc.	Computer
BYFC	Broadway Financial Corporation	Bank
BLCI	Brookdale Living Communities, Inc.	Industrial
BRKL	Brookline Bancorp, Inc.	Bank
BRKS	Brooks Automation, Inc.	Industrial
BKST	Brookstore, Inc.	Industrial
BRKT	Brooktrout Technology, Inc.	Computer
MILK	Broughton Foods Company	Industrial
BTIC	Brunswick Technologies, Inc.	Industrial
BCMDE	Brush Creek Mining and Development Co., Inc.	Industrial
BMTC	Bryn Mawr Bank Corporation	Bank
BSBN	BSB Bancorp, Inc.	Bank
BTFC	BT Financial Corporation	Other Finance
BTBTY	BT Shipping Limited	Transportation
BTGI	BTG, Inc.	Computer
BTUI	BTU International, Inc.	Industrial
BUCK	Buckhead America Corporation	Industrial
BOCB	Buffets, Inc.	Industrial
BMHC	Building Materials Holding Corporation	Industrial
BOSS	Building One Services Corporation	Industrial
BNBGA	Bull & Bear Group, Inc.	Other Finance
BULL	Bull Run Corporation	Industrial
BMLS	Burke Mills, Inc.	Industrial
BURMY	Burmah Castrol PLC-ADR	Industrial
BBRC	Burr-Brown Corporation	Computer
BOBJY	Business Objects S.A.	Computer
BRGP	Business Resource Group	Industrial
BUTL	Butler International, Inc.	Industrial
BUKS	Butler National Corporation	Industrial
BWCF	BWC Financial Corporation	Bank
BOYL	BYL Bancorp	Bank
CFFI	C&F Financial Corporation	Other Finance
CATX	C*ATS Software Inc.	Computer
CBHI	C. Brewer Homes, Inc.	Industrial
CHRW	C.H. Robinson Worldwide, Inc.	Transportation
CPCL	C.P. Clare Corporation	Industrial
CTWO	C2i Solutions, Inc.	Industrial
CTHR	C3, Inc.	Industrial
CABL	Cable Michigan, Inc.	Telecommunications
CACH	Cache, Inc.	Industrial
CACI	CACI International, Inc.	Computer
CADE	Cade Industries, Inc.	Industrial

Symbol	Company Name	Sector
CLCI	Cadiz, Inc.	Industrial
CDMS	Cadmus Communications Corporation	Computer
KDUS	Cadus Pharmaceutical Corporation	Industrial
CAER	Caere Corporation	Computer
CDIS	Cal Dive International, Inc.	Industrial
CLCP	CalComp Technology, Inc.	Industrial
CLBR	Caliber Learning Network, Inc.	Industrial
CAMP	California Amplifier, Inc.	Industrial
CALC	California Coastal Communities Inc	Industrial
COOK	California Culinary Academy, Inc.	Industrial
CALGZ	California Federal Bank, FSB	Bank
CIBN	California Independent Bancorp	Bank
CAMD	California Micro Devices Corporation	Industrial
CMIC	California Microwave, Inc.	Industrial
CALP	California Pro Sports, Inc.	Industrial
CNEBF	Call-Net Enterprises Inc.	Telecommunications
CLWY	Calloway's Nursery, Inc.	Industrial
CALM	Cal-Maine Foods, Inc.	Industrial
CBCI	Calumet Bancorp, Inc.	Bank
CALY	Calypte Biomedical Corporation	Industrial
CADA	CAM Data Systems, Inc.	Computer
CMDA	CAM Designs Inc.	Industrial
CAMH	Cambridge Heart, Inc.	Industrial
CNSI	Cambridge NeuroScience, Inc.	Industrial
CATP	Cambridge Technology Partners, Inc.	Computer
CAFI	Camco Financial Corporation	Other Finance
CMRN	Cameron Financial Corporation	Bank
CSPLF	Canada Southern Petroleum Ltd.	Industrial
CBRNA	Canandaigua Brands, Inc.	Industrial
CBRNB	Canandaigua Brands, Inc.	Industrial
GUSH	CanArgo Energy Corporation	Industrial
CLZR	Candela Corporation	Industrial
CAND	Candie's, Inc.	Industrial
CNDL	Candlewood Hotel Company, Inc.	Industrial
CANR	Canisco Resources Inc. (DE)	Industrial
BIKE	Cannondale Corporation	Industrial
CANNY	Canon Inc.	Industrial
CNTBY	Cantab Pharmaceuticals plc	Industrial
CNTL	Cantel Industries, Inc.	Industrial
CITI	Canterbury Information Technology, Inc.	Industrial
TRAK	Canterbury Park Holding Corporation	Industrial
CCBT	Cape Cod Bank and Trust Company	Bank

Symbol	Company Name	Sector
CAII	Capital Associates, Inc.	Industrial
CARS	Capital Automotive REIT	Other Finance
CBKN	Capital Bank	Bank
CBEV	Capital Beverage Corporation	Industrial
CCBG	Capital City Bank Group	Other Finance
CCOW	Capital Corp of the West	Other Finance
CAPF	Capital Factors Holding, Inc.	Other Finance
CSWC	Capital Southwest Corporation	Other Finance
CTGI	Capital Title Group, Inc.	Industrial
CBCL	Capitol Bancorp Ltd.	Other Finance
CBCLP	Capitol Bancorp Ltd.	Other Finance
CATA	Capitol Transamerica Corporation	Insurance
CAPR	Caprius Inc.	Industrial
CPRK	CapRock Communications Corp.	Industrial
CRRR	Captec Net Lease Realty, Inc.	Other Finance
CSAR	Caraustar Industries, Inc.	Industrial
CRBO	Carbo Ceramics Inc.	Industrial
CPWY	Cardiac Pathways Corporation	Industrial
CRDM	Cardima, Inc.	Industrial
CFNL	Cardinal Financial Corporation	Bank
CDIC	CardioDynamics International Corporation	Industrial
CGCP	CardioGenesis Corporation	Industrial
CTSI	CardioThoracic Systems, Inc.	Industrial
CVDI	Cardiovascular Diagnostics, Inc.	Industrial
CCVD	Cardiovascular Dynamics, Inc.	Industrial
CECO	Career Education Corporation	Industrial
CTND	Caretenders Health Corp.	Industrial
CARY	Carey International, Inc.	Transportation
CIGR	Caribbean Cigar Company	Industrial
BDRY	Caring Products International, Inc.	Industrial
CARL	Carleton Corporation	Computer
CCTVY	Carlton Communications Plc	Industrial
CGIX	Carnegie Group, Inc.	Computer
CFNC	Carolina Fincorp, Inc.	Bank
CAFC	Carolina First Corporation	Other Finance
CSBK	Carolina Southern Bank	Bank
CANI	Carreker-Antinori, Inc.	Computer
CACS	Carrier Access Corporation	Telecommunications
CARN	Carrington Laboratories, Inc.	Biotechnology
CRZO	Carrizo Oil & Gas, Inc.	Industrial
CRRB	Carrollton Bancorp	Other Finance
CASA	Casa Ole' Restaurants, Inc.	Industrial

Symbol	Company Name	Sector
CACB	Cascade Bancorp	Other Finance
CASB	Cascade Financial Corp	Industrial
CASC	Casco International Inc.	Industrial
CWST	Casella Waste Systems, Inc.	Industrial
CASY	Casey's General Stores, Inc.	Industrial
CHNG	Cash Technologies, Inc.	Industrial
CSDS	Casino Data Systems	Computer
CSNR	Casino Resource Corporation	Industrial
CASS	Cass Commercial Corporation	Other Finance
CSTL	Castelle	Industrial
CASL	Castle Dental Centers, Inc.	Industrial
CECX	Castle Energy Corporation	Industrial
CLYS	Catalyst International, Inc.	Computer
CTAL	Catalytica, Inc.	Industrial
CATY	Cathay Bancorp, Inc.	Other Finance
CATH	Catherines Stores Corporation	Industrial
CACOA	Cato Corporation (The)	Industrial
CATB	Catskill Financial Corporation	Bank
CAVB	Cavalry Bancorp, Inc.	Bank
CWCOF	Cayman Water Company, Ltd.	Industrial
CBBI	CB Bancshares, Inc.	Other Finance
CBES	CBES Bancorp, Inc.	Bank
CBTSY	CBT Group, Plc. CBT Systems U.S.A., Inc.	Computer
RIPEE	CCA Companies Inc.	Industrial
CCAM	CCA Industries, Inc.	Industrial
CCAR	CCAIR, Inc.	Transportation
CCCG	CCC Information Services Group Inc.	Industrial
CCFH	CCF Holding Company	Bank
CCBL	C-COR Electronics, Inc.	Industrial
CUBE	C-Cube Microsystems Inc.	Industrial
CDRD	CD Radio Inc.	Industrial
CDWI	CD Warehouse, Inc.	Industrial
CDNW	CDnow, Inc.	Industrial
CDWC	CDW Computer Centers, Inc.	Industrial
CESH	CE Software Holdings, Inc.	Computer
CECE	CECO Environmental Corp.	Industrial
CEDR	Cedar Income Fund, Ltd.	Other Finance
CLDN	Celadon Group, Inc.	Transportation
FLWR	Celebrity, Inc.	Industrial
CLTK	Celeritek, Inc.	Computer
CLTY	Celerity Solutions Inc.	Industrial
CLRT	Celerity Systems, Inc.	Industrial

Symbol	Company Name	Sector
CTEA	Celestial Seasonings, Inc.	Industrial
CELG	Celgene Corporation	Industrial
CEGE	Cell Genesys, Inc.	Biotechnology
CTIC	Cell Therapeutics, Inc.	Biotechnology
CLGY	Cellegy Pharmaceuticals, Inc.	Industrial
CNDS	CellNet Data Systems, Inc.	Telecommunications
CLST	Cellstar Corporation	Industrial
CCIL	Cellular Communications International, Inc.	Telecommunications
CLRP	Cellular Communications of Puerto Rico, Inc.	Telecommunications
CTSC	Cellular Technical Services Company, Inc.	Computer
CVUS	CellularVision USA, Inc.	Telecommunications
CELT	Celtic Investment, Inc.	Industrial
CTRX	Celtrix Pharmaceuticals, Inc.	Biotechnology
CEMX	CEM Corporation	Industrial
CNIT	CENIT Bancorp, Inc	Bank
CEBC	Centennial Bancorp	Other Finance
CYCL	Centennial Cellular Corp.	Telecommunications
CTEN	Centennial HealthCare Corp.	Industrial
CNBC	Center Bancorp, Inc.	Bank
CGRM	Centigram Communications Corporation	Industrial
CNTO	Centocor, Inc.	Biotechnology
CCBN	Central Coast Bancorp	Bank
CEBK	Central Co-Operative Bank	Bank
CEDC	Central European Distribution Corporation	Industrial
CETV	Central European Media Enterprises Ltd.	Telecommunications
CFAC	Central Financial Acceptance Corporation	Other Finance
CENT	Central Garden & Pet Company	Industrial
CPMNY	Central Pacific Minerals N.L.	Industrial
CRLC	Central Reserve Life Corporation	Insurance
CNSP	Central Sprinkler Corporation	Industrial
CVBK	Central Virginia Bankshares, Inc.	Other Finance
CNTR	Centura Software Corporation	Computer
CENX	Century Aluminum Company	Industrial
CENB	Century Bancorp, Inc.	Bank
CNBKA	Century BanCorp, Inc.	Bank
CNBKP	Century BanCorp, Inc.	Bank
CTRY	Century Bancshares, Inc.	Bank
CBIZ	Century Business Services, Inc	Industrial
CNTY	Century Casinos, Inc.	Industrial
CTYA	Century Communications Corp.	Telecommunications
CSBI	Century South Banks, Inc.	Other Finance
CEPH	Cephalon, Inc.	Biotechnology

Symbol	Company Name	Sector
CRDN	Ceradyne, Inc.	Industrial
CERB	CERBCO, Inc.	Industrial
CEON	Cerion Technologies, Inc.	Computer
CERN	Cerner Corporation	Computer
CRPB	Cerprobe Corporation	Industrial
CERS	Cerus Corporation	Biotechnology
CFCI	CFC International, Inc.	Industrial
CFIM	CFI Mortgage Inc.	Other Finance
PROI	CFI ProServices, Inc.	Industrial
CFMT	CFM Technologies, Inc.	Industrial
CITZ	CFS Bancorp, Inc.	Other Finance
CFSB	CFSB Bancorp, Inc.	Other Finance
CFWC	CFW Communications Company	Telecommunications
CCCFF	Chai-Na-Ta Corp.	Industrial
CHLN	Chalone Wine Group, Ltd. (The)	Industrial
CHMP	Champion Industries, Inc.	Industrial
AMFM	Chancellor Media Corporation	Telecommunications
CHANF	Chandler Insurance Company, Ltd.	Insurance
CHNL	Channell Commercial Corporation	Industrial
CHAR	Chaparral Resources, Inc.	Industrial
CMAN	Chapman Holdings, Inc.	Other Finance
CRAI	Charles River Associates Incorporated	Industrial
CHRS	Charming Shoppes, Inc.	Industrial
COFI	Charter One Financial, Inc.	Other Finance
CHAS	Chastain Capital Corporation	Other Finance
CHTT	Chattem, Inc.	Industrial
FLYAF	CHC Helicopter Corporation	Transportation
CHKPF	Check Point Software Technologies, Ltd.	Computer
CTCQ	Check Technology Corporation	Computer
CHKR	Checkers Drive-In Restaurants, Inc.	Industrial
CKFR	CheckFree Holdings Corporation	Insurance
CAKE	Cheesecake Factory Incorporated (The)	Industrial
CHEF	Chefs International, Inc.	Industrial
CXIL	Chem International, Inc.	Industrial
CHFC	Chemical Financial Corporation	Other Finance
CHEX	Cheniere Energy, Inc.	Industrial
CHERA	Cherry Corporation (The)	Industrial
CHERB	Cherry Corporation (The)	Industrial
CBLI	Chesapeake Biological Laboratories, Inc.	Biotechnology
CNBA	Chester Bancorp, Inc.	Bank
CVAL	Chester Valley Bancorp Inc.	Other Finance
CHGO	Chicago Pizza & Brewery, Inc.	Industrial

Symbol	Company Name	Sector
CHCS	Chico's FAS, Inc.	Industrial
CFCM	Chief Consolidated Mining Company	Industrial
AAHS	Children's Broadcasting Corp.	Industrial
KIDS	Childrens Comprehensive Services Inc.	Industrial
CTIM	Childtime Learning Centers, Inc.	Industrial
CHNA	China Pacific, Inc.	Other Finance
CHRB	China Resources Development, Inc.	Industrial
CHRX	ChiRex Inc.	Biotechnology
CHIR	Chiron Corporation	Biotechnology
PHON	ChoiceTel Communications, Inc.	Telecommunications
CTEC	Cholestech Corporation	Industrial
CCSI	Chromatics Color Sciences International, Inc.	Industrial
CVSN	ChromaVision Medical Systems, Inc.	Industrial
CHMD	Chronimed Inc.	Industrial
CRLS	Chrysalis International Corporation	Industrial
CHDN	Churchill Downs, Incorporated	Industrial
CDCO	Cidco Incorporated	Industrial
CIEN	Ciena Corporation	Industrial
CIMA	CIMA LABS INC.	Biotechnology
CIMTF	Cimatron, Limited	Computer
CINRF	Cinar Films, Inc.	Industrial
CINF	Cincinnati Financial Corporation	Other Finance
LUXY	Cinemastar Luxury Theaters, Inc.	Industrial
CNRMF	Cinram International Inc.	Industrial
CTAS	Cintas Corporation	Industrial
CPCI	Ciprico Inc.	Computer
CINS	Circle Income Shares, Inc.	Other Finance
CRCL	Circle International Group, Inc.	Transportation
CCON	Circon Corporation	Industrial
CSYI	Circuit Systems, Inc.	Industrial
CRUS	Cirrus Logic, Inc.	Computer
CSCO	Cisco Systems, Inc.	Computer
CITA	CITATION Computer Systems, Inc.	Computer
CAST	Citation Corporation	Industrial
CBCF	Citizens Banking Corporation	Other Finance
CNFL	Citizens Financial Corporation	Other Finance
CTXS	Citrix Systems, Inc.	Computer
CHCO	City Holding Company	Other Finance
CNVLZ	City Investing Company Liquidating Trust	Other Finance
CVCLF	CityView Energy Corporation Limited	Industrial
CIVC	Civic BanCorp	Other Finance
CKFB	CKF Bancorp, Inc.	Bank

Symbol	Company Name	Sector
CKSG	CKS Group, Inc.	Computer
CLFY	Clarify, Inc.	Computer
CLKB	Clark/Bardes Holdings, Inc.	Insurance
CLRS	Clarus Corporation	Computer
CLAS	Classic Bancshares, Inc.	Bank
CWEI	Clayton Williams Energy, Inc.	Industrial
CLHB	Clean Harbors, Inc.	Industrial
CLCDF	Clearly Canadian Beverage Corp.	Industrial
CLNTF	Clearnet Communications Inc.	Telecommunications
CLEV	Cleveland Indians Baseball Company, Inc.	Industrial
CCHE	CliniChem Development, Inc.	Biotechnology
CCRO	ClinTrials Research Inc.	Industrial
CLSR	CLOSURE Medical Corporation	Industrial
CMCI	CMC Industries, Inc.	Industrial
CMGI	CMG Information Services, Inc.	Industrial
CMPX	CMP Media Inc.	Industrial
CNBI	CN Biosciences, Inc.	Biotechnology
CNBF	CNB Financial Corp.	Other Finance
CCNE	CNB Financial Corporation	Bank
CNBT	CNBT Bancshares Inc.	Bank
CNWK	CNET, Inc.	Industrial
CNSB	CNS Bancorp, Inc.	Bank
CNXS	CNS, Inc.	Industrial
CNYF	CNY Financial Corporation	Bank
CTBP	Coast Bancorp	Other Finance
CDEN	Coast Dental Services, Inc.	Industrial
CCPRZ	Coast Federal Litigation Contingent Pymnt	Other Finance
CBSA	Coastal Bancorp Inc.	Bank
CBSAP	Coastal Bancorp Inc.	Bank
CFCP	Coastal Financial Corporation	Other Finance
COBR	Cobra Electronics Corporation	Industrial
COKE	Coca-Cola Bottling Co. Consolidated	Industrial
COCN	CoCensys, Inc.	Industrial
COMT	Coda Music Technology, Inc.	Computer
CVLY	Codorus Valley Bancorp, Inc.	Bank
MOKA	Coffee People, Inc.	Industrial
CXIPY	Coflexip	Industrial
CGCA	Cogeneration Corporation of America	Industrial
CGNX	Cognex Corporation	Computer
COGIF	Cognicase Inc.	Computer
CTSH	Cognizant Technology Solutions Corporation	Computer
COGNF	Cognos Incorporated	Computer

Symbol	Company Name	Sector
COHR	Coherent, Inc.	Industrial
COHT	Cohesant Technologies Inc.	Industrial
CSON	Cohesion Technologies, Inc.	Industrial
COHO	Coho Energy, Inc.	Industrial
CHRI	COHR Inc.	Industrial
COHU	Cohu, Inc.	Industrial
WDRY	Coinmach Laundry Corporation	Industrial
CSTR	Coinstar, Inc.	Industrial
CWTR	Coldwater Creek, Inc.	Industrial
CCLR	Collaborative Clinical Research, Inc.	Industrial
CGEN	Collagen Aesthetics Inc.	Industrial
CGPI	CollaGenex Pharmaceuticals, Inc.	Biotechnology
CLTX	Collateral Therapeutics, Inc.	Biotechnology
UCTN	College Television Network, Inc.	Industrial
COLL	Collins Industries, Inc.	Industrial
CCOM	Colonial Commercial Corp.	Industrial
CDWN	Colonial Downs Holdings, Inc.	Industrial
CBAN	Colony Bankcorp, Inc.	Other Finance
COBZ	Colorado Business Bancshares, Inc.	Bank
CCRI	Colorado Casino Resorts, Inc.	Industrial
CMED	Colorado MEDtech, Inc.	Industrial
COLTY	COLT Telecom Group plc	Telecommunications
CBMD	Columbia Bancorp	Other Finance
COLB	Columbia Banking System, Inc.	Other Finance
CFKY	Columbia Financial of Kentucky Inc.	Bank
COLM	Columbia Sportswear Company	Industrial
CMCO	Columbus McKinnon Corporation	Industrial
CMTO	Com21, Inc.	Computer
COMR	Comair Holdings, Inc.	Transportation
CMRO	COMARCO, Inc.	Computer
CCHM	CombiChem, Incorporated	Industrial
CMCSA	Comcast Corporation	Telecommunications
CMCSK	Comcast Corporation	Telecommunications
CMDL	Comdial Corporation	Industrial
CCBP	Comm Bancorp, Inc.	Bank
CMMD	Command Security Corporation	Industrial
CMND	Command Systems, Inc.	Industrial
CBSH	Commerce Bancshares, Inc.	Other Finance
COBH	Commerce Bank/Harrisburg	Bank
CGCO	Commerce Group Corp.	Industrial
CBNY	Commercial Bank of New York	Bank
CLBK	Commercial Bankshares, Inc.	Bank

Symbol	Company Name	Sector
CNAF	Commercial National Financial Corporation	Bank
CELS	CommNet Cellular Inc.	Telecommunications
CCLNF	Commodore Holdings Limited	Transportation
CXOT	Commodore Separation Technologies, Inc.	Industrial
CXOTP	Commodore Separation Technologies, Inc.	Industrial
CMSB	Commonwealth Bancorp, Inc.	Bank
CBTE	Commonwealth Biotechnologies, Inc.	Industrial
CMIN	Commonwealth Industries, Inc.	Industrial
CTCO	Commonwealth Telephone Enterprises, Inc.	Telecommunications
CTCOB	Commonwealth Telephone Enterprises, Inc.	Telecommunications
CICI	Communication Intelligence Corporation	Computer
CSII	Communications Systems, Inc.	Industrial
CBIN	Community Bank Shares of Indiana, Inc.	Other Finance
CBIV	Community Bankshares Incorporated	Bank
CCSE	Community Care Services, Inc.	Industrial
CFTP	Community Federal Bancorp, Inc.	Other Finance
CFFC	Community Financial Corp.	Bank
CFIC	Community Financial Corp.	Other Finance
CFGI	Community Financial Group Inc.	Bank
CFBC	Community First Banking Company	Other Finance
CFBX	Community First Bankshares, Inc.	Bank
CFBXL	Community First Bankshares, Inc.	Bank
CFBXZ	Community First Bankshares, Inc.	Bank
CIBI	Community Investors Bancorp, Inc.	Other Finance
CMTI	Community Medical Transport, Inc.	Transportation
CMSV	Community Savings Bankshares, Inc.	Bank
CTBI	Community Trust Bancorp, Inc.	Other Finance
CTBIP	Community Trust Bancorp, Inc.	Other Finance
CWBC	Community West Bancshares	Bank
CCUUY	Compania Cervecerias Unidas S.A.	Industrial
COGE	Compare Generiks, Inc.	Industrial
CBSS	Compass Bancshares, Inc.	Other Finance
CMPS	Compass International Services Corporation	Computer
CPTI	Compass Plastics & Technologies, Inc.	Industrial
CPDN	CompDent Corporation	Other Finance
CBSI	Complete Business Solutions, Inc.	Computer
CMWL	Complete Wellness Centers, Inc.	Industrial
CTEK	Compositech Ltd.	Industrial
CMPC	CompuCom Systems, Inc.	Computer
CODI	Compu-Dawn, Inc.	Computer
CMPD	CompuMed, Inc.	Computer
CLTDF	Computalog Ltd.	Industrial

Symbol	Company Name	Sector
CCEE	Computer Concepts Corp.	Computer
CHRZ	Computer Horizons Corp.	Computer
CLCX	Computer Learning Centers, Inc.	Industrial
CMSX	Computer Management Sciences, Inc.	Computer
RBOT	Computer Motion, Inc.	Industrial
CMNT	Computer Network Technology Corporation	Computer
COSI	Computer Outsourcing Services, Inc.	Computer
CMPTC	Computone Corporation	Industrial
CPWR	Compuware Corporation	Computer
CSRE	Comshare, Incorporated	Computer
LODE	Comstock Bancorp	Bank
CMTL	Comtech Telecommunications Corp.	Industrial
COMX	Comtrex Systems Corporation	Computer
CMVT	Comverse Technology, Inc.	Computer
CTRA	Concentra Corporation	Computer
CCMC	Concentra Managed Care Inc.	Industrial
CNCX	Concentric Network Corporation	Telecommunications
CDIR	Concepts Direct, Inc.	Industrial
CPTS	Conceptus, Inc.	Industrial
LENS	Concord Camera Corp.	Industrial
CCRD	Concord Communications, Inc.	Computer
CEFT	Concord EFS, Inc.	Computer
CPLNY	Concordia Paper Holdings, Ltd.	Industrial
CCUR	Concurrent Computer Corporation	Computer
CNDR	Condor Technology Solutions, Inc.	Industrial
CDTS	Conductus, Inc.	Industrial
CENI	Conestoga Enterprises, Inc.	Telecommunications
CNMD	CONMED Corporation	Industrial
CNKT	Connect, Inc.	Industrial
CTWS	Connecticut Water Service, Inc.	Industrial
CNCT	Connetics Corporation	Biotechnology
CNNG	Conning Corporation	Other Finance
CNLG	Conolog Corporation	Industrial
CSEP	Consep, Inc.	Industrial
CSIM	Consilium, Inc.	Computer
CNSO	Conso Products Company	Industrial
CDLI	Consolidated Delivery & Logistics, Inc.	Transportation
CFWY	Consolidated Freightways Corporation	Transportation
GQRVF	Consolidated Golden Quail Resources Ltd.	Industrial
CSLMF	Consolidated Mercantile Corp.	Other Finance
CSLR	Consulier Engineering, Inc.	Industrial
CPSS	Consumer Portfolio Services, Inc.	Industrial

Symbol	Company Name	Sector
CONW	Consumers Water Company	Industrial
CSGI	ConSyGen, Inc.	Industrial
CCCI	Continental Choice Care, Inc.	Industrial
CISC	Continental Information Systems Corporation	Industrial
CMETS	Continental Mortgage and Equity Trust	Other Finance
DIGM	Control Chief Holdings, Inc.	Industrial
SNSR	Control Devices, Inc.	Industrial
ZAPS	Cooper Life Sciences Inc.	Industrial
COOP	Cooperative Bankshares, Inc.	Other Finance
CPRT	Copart, Inc.	Industrial
CPLY	Copley Pharmaceutical, Inc.	Industrial
COPY	Copytele, Inc.	Industrial
CORR	COR Therapeutics, Inc.	Biotechnology
CORE	CORE, Inc.	Industrial
COMMF	CoreComm Limited	Telecommunications
COSFF	Corel Corporation	Computer
CRXA	Corixa Corporation	Biotechnology
CNRS	Cornerstone Internet Solutions Company	Industrial
CEXP	Corporate Express, Inc.	Industrial
CREN	Corporate Renaissance Group, Inc.	Other Finance
CSCQ	Correctional Services Corporation	Industrial
CAIR	Corsair Communications, Inc.	Industrial
DLVRY	Cortecs plc	Biotechnology
CORX	Cortex Pharmaceuticals, Inc.	Industrial
CORS	CORUS Bankshares, Inc.	Bank
CVAS	Corvas International, Inc.	Industrial
CRVL	CorVel Corp.	Insurance
COSC	Cosmetic Center, Inc. (The)	Industrial
CPWM	Cost Plus, Inc.	Industrial
COST	Costco Companies, Inc.	Industrial
COSE	Costilla Energy, Inc.	Industrial
CULS	Cost-U-Less, Inc.	Industrial
COTTF	Cott Corporation	Industrial
CSLI	Cotton States Life Insurance Company	Insurance
CLTR	Coulter Pharmaceutical, Inc.	Biotechnology
CXSNF	Counsel Corporation	Other Finance
CRRC	Courier Corporation	Industrial
CVGR	Covalent Group, Inc.	Industrial
CVTI	Covenant Transport, Inc.	Transportation
CVTY	Coventry Health Care Inc	Industrial
COVN	Coventry Industries Corporation	Industrial
COVR	Cover-All Technologies Inc.	Computer

Symbol	Company Name	Sector
COVB	CoVest Bancshares, Inc.	Bank
CVOL	Covol Technologies, Inc.	Industrial
CWLZ	Cowlitz Bancorporation	Industrial
COYT	Coyote Sports, Inc.	Industrial
CPAK	CPAC, Inc.	Industrial
CPBI	CPB Inc.	Other Finance
CFON	C-Phone Corporation	Industrial
CPIA	CPI Aerostructures, Inc.	Industrial
CBRL	Cracker Barrel Old Country Store, Inc.	Industrial
CRFT	Craftmade International, Inc.	Industrial
CRZY	Crazy Woman Creek Bancorp Incorporated	Bank
CBMI	Creative BioMolecules, Inc.	Biotechnology
MALL	Creative Computers, Inc.	Industrial
CHST	Creative Host Services, Inc.	Industrial
CREAF	Creative Technology Ltd.	Computer
CMOS	Credence Systems Corporation	Industrial
CACC	Credit Acceptance Corporation	Other Finance
CMSS	Credit Management Solutions, Inc.	Computer
CRDT	Creditrust Corporation	Industrial
CRED	Credo Petroleum Corporation	Industrial
CREE	Cree Research, Inc.	Industrial
CNDO	Crescendo Pharmaceuticals Corporation	Industrial
COPI	Crescent Operating, Inc.	Other Finance
CRESY	Cresud S.A.C.I.F. y A.	Industrial
CRHCY	CRH, public limited company	Industrial
CXIM	Criticare Systems, Inc.	Industrial
CKEYF	CrossKeys Systems Corporation	Computer
CROS	Crossmann Communities, Inc.	Industrial
CRAN	Crown Andersen Inc.	Industrial
TWRS	Crown Castle International Corp.	Telecommunications
CNGR	Crown Group Inc.	Industrial
CRRS	Crown Resources Corporation	Industrial
CVAN	Crown Vantage Inc.	Industrial
CRSB	Crusader Holding Corporation	Other Finance
CRWF	CRW Financial, Inc.	Industrial
CCEL	Cryo-Cell International, Inc.	Industrial
CMSI	Cryomedical Sciences, Inc.	Industrial
CRYSF	Crystal Systems Solutions, Ltd.	Computer
CSBF	CSB Financial Group, Inc.	Other Finance
CSGS	CSG Systems International, Inc.	Computer
CSKKY	CSK Corporation	Computer
CSPI	CSP Inc.	Computer

Symbol	Company Name	Sector
CTBC	CTB International Corp.	Industrial
CPTL	CTC Communications Corp.	Industrial
CTIB	CTI Industries Corporation	Industrial
CBST	Cubist Pharmaceuticals, Inc.	Biotechnology
CUCO	Cucos Inc.	Industrial
CUIS	Cuisine Solutions, Inc.	Industrial
CUMB	Cumberland Technologies Inc.	Insurance
CDSC	Cumetrix Data Systems Corp.	Industrial
CMLS	Cumulus Media Inc.	Telecommunications
CGII	Cunningham Graphics International, Inc.	Industrial
CUNO	CUNO Incorporated	Industrial
CRGN	CuraGen Corporation	Industrial
CURE	Curative Health Services, Inc.	Industrial
CUST	CustomTracks Corporation	Industrial
CBUK	Cutter & Buck Inc.	Industrial
CVTX	CV Therapeutics, Inc.	Industrial
CYAN	Cyanotech Corporation	Industrial
CYCH	CyberCash, Inc.	Computer
CYBGE	CyberGuard Corporation	Computer
COOL	Cyberian Outpost, Inc.	Industrial
CYBX	Cyberonics, Inc.	Industrial
CYBE	CyberOptics Corporation	Industrial
CYSP	Cybershop International, Inc.	Industrial
CBXC	Cybex Computer Products Corporation	Industrial
CYGN	Cygnus, Inc.	Industrial
CYLK	Cylink Corporation	Industrial
CYMI	Cymer, Inc.	Industrial
CYPB	Cypress Bioscience Inc.	Industrial
CYRK	Cyrk, Inc.	Industrial
CYTL	Cytel Corporation	Biotechnology
CYPH	Cytoclonal Pharmaceutics Inc.	Biotechnology
CYTO	Cytogen Corporation	Biotechnology
CTII	CytoTherapeutics, Inc.	Industrial
CYTR	CytRx Corporation	Biotechnology
CYTC	CYTYC Corporation	Industrial
DKWD	D & K Healthcare Resources Inc	Industrial
DECC	D&E Communications, Inc.	Telecommunications
DNFC	D&N Financial Corporation	Bank
DNFCP	D&N Financial Corporation	Bank
DGJLF	D.G. Jewellery of Canada Ltd.	Industrial
DIYH	D.I.Y. Home Warehouse, Inc.	Industrial
DACG	DA Consulting Group, Inc.	Industrial

Symbol	Company Name	Sector
DAIEY	Dai'ei, Inc.	Industrial
DALY	Dailey International Inc.	Industrial
DJCO	Daily Journal Corp. (S.C.)	Industrial
DZTK	Daisytek International Corporation	Industrial
DAKT	Daktronics, Inc.	Industrial
DLOV	Daleco Resources Corporation New	Industrial
DMRK	Damark International, Inc.	Industrial
DFIN	Damen Financial Corporation	Other Finance
DAGR	Daniel Green Company	Industrial
DANKY	Danka Business Systems PLC	Industrial
DAOU	DAOU Systems, Inc.	Industrial
DASTY	Dassault Systemes, S.A.	Industrial
DBCC	Data Broadcasting Corporation	Other Finance
DDIM	Data Dimensions, Inc.	Computer
DAIO	Data I/O Corporation	Computer
DPRC	Data Processing Resources Corporation	Computer
RACE	DATA RACE, Inc.	Industrial
DRAI	Data Research Associates, Inc.	Computer
DSSI	Data Systems & Software Inc.	Computer
DATX	Data Translation Inc.	Computer
DTLN	Data Transmission Network Corporation	Computer
DKEY	Datakey, Inc.	Computer
DSCP	Datascope Corp.	Industrial
DSTM	Datastream Systems, Inc.	Computer
DATC	Datatec Systems, Inc.	Industrial
DWTI	Dataware Technologies, Inc.	Computer
DWCH	Datawatch Corporation	Computer
DWRX	DataWorks Corporation	Computer
DTSI	Datron Systems Incorporated	Industrial
DATM	Datum, Inc.	Industrial
NGASF	Daugherty Resources, Inc.	Industrial
DANB	Dave & Buster's, Inc.	Industrial
DAVL	Davel Communications Group, Inc.	Industrial
DAVX	Davox Corporation	Industrial
DAWK	Daw Technologies, Inc.	Industrial
DWSN	Dawson Geophysical Company	Industrial
DAYR	Day Runner, Inc.	Industrial
DBRSY	De Beers Consolidated Mines	Industrial
DEAR	Dearborn Bancorp, Inc.	Other Finance
DEBS	Deb Shops, Inc.	Industrial
DOCI	DecisionOne Holdings Corporation	Computer
DECK	Deckers Outdoor Corporation	Industrial

Symbol	Company Name	Sector
DECAF	Decoma International, Inc.	Industrial
DECO	Decora Industries, Inc.	Industrial
DECTF	Dectron International, Inc.	Industrial
DEFI	Defiance, Inc.	Industrial
DGTC	Del Global Technologies Corp.	Industrial
DLIA	dELIA*s Inc.	Industrial
DELL	Dell Computer Corporation	Computer
DLPH	Delphi Information Systems, Inc.	Computer
DLTDF	Delphi International Ltd.	Insurance
DCBI	Delphos Citizens Bancorp, Inc.	Other Finance
DGAS	Delta Natural Gas Company, Inc.	Industrial
DPTR	Delta Petroleum Corporation	Industrial
DLTK	Deltek Systems, Inc.	Computer
DNLI	Denali Incorporated	Industrial
DRTE	Dendrite International, Inc.	Computer
DENHY	Denison International plc	Industrial
DPAC	Dense-Pac Microsystems, Inc.	Computer
DENT	Dental Care Alliance, Inc.	Industrial
DMDS	Dental/Medical Diagnostic Systems, Inc.	Industrial
XRAY	DENTSPLY International Inc.	Industrial
DPMD	DepoMed, Inc.	Industrial
DEPO	DepoTech Corporation	Biotechnology
DSCI	Derma Sciences, Inc.	Industrial
DCBK	Desert Community Bank	Bank
DESI	Designs, Inc.	Industrial
DSWLF	Deswell Industries, Inc.	Industrial
DETC	Detection Systems, Inc.	Industrial
DTRX	Detrex Corporation	Industrial
DEVC	Devcon International Corp.	Industrial
DVLG	DeVlieg-Bullard, Inc.	Industrial
DCRN	Diacrin, Inc.	Biotechnology
DHSM	Diagnostic Health Services, Inc.	Industrial
DLGC	Dialogic Corporation	Industrial
DCAI	Dialysis Corporation of America	Industrial
DMED	Diametrics Medical, Inc.	Industrial
DHMS	Diamond Home Services, Inc.	Industrial
DIMD	Diamond Multimedia Systems, Inc.	Computer
DTPI	Diamond Technology Partners Incorporated	Industrial
DIAN	DIANON Systems, Inc.	Industrial
DIYS	DiaSys Corporation	Industrial
DITI	Diatide, Inc.	Biotechnology
DCPI	dick clark productions, inc.	Industrial

Symbol	Company Name	Sector
AMEN	Didax Inc.	Computer
DDRX	Diedrich Coffee	Industrial
DIEG	Diehl Graphsoft, Inc.	Computer
DIGE	Digene Corporation	Industrial
DGII	Digi International Inc.	Computer
DBII	Digital Biometrics, Inc.	Computer
DCTI	Digital Courier Technologies, Inc.	Industrial
DGIT	Digital Generation Systems, Inc.	Industrial
DIGL	Digital Lightwave, Inc.	Industrial
DLNK	Digital Link Corporation	Industrial
DMIC	Digital Microwave Corporation	Industrial
TBUS	Digital Recorders, Inc.	Telecommunications
DRIV	Digital River, Inc.	Computer
DGSI	Digital Solutions, Inc.	Industrial
DVID	Digital Video Systems, Inc.	Industrial
DTAGY	Digitale Telekabel AG	Telecommunications
DIIG	DII Group, Inc.	Industrial
DCOM	Dime Community Bancshares, Inc.	Bank
DNEX	Dionex Corporation	Industrial
DIPL	Diplomat Corporation	Industrial
DSGR	Disc Graphics, Inc.	Industrial
DCSR	DISC Inc.	Computer
DSCS	Discas, Inc.	Industrial
DSCO	Discovery Laboratories Inc.	Industrial
DSLGF	Discreet Logic, Inc.	Computer
DMSC	Dispatch Management Services Corp.	Transportation
DTEK	Display Technologies Inc.	Industrial
DISS	Diversified Senior Services, Inc.	Industrial
DVNTF	Diversinet Corp.	Industrial
PUTT	Divot Golf Corporation	Industrial
DMMC	DM Management Company	Industrial
DMIF	DMI Furniture, Inc.	Industrial
DNAP	DNAP Holding Corporation	Industrial
DOCDF	DOCdata N.V.	Industrial
DOCU	DocuCon, Incorporated	Industrial
DOCX	Document Sciences Corporation	Computer
DCTM	Documentum, Inc.	Computer
DLTR	Dollar Tree Stores, Inc.	Industrial
DOMZ	Dominguez Services Corporation	Industrial
DHOM	Dominion Homes Inc.	Industrial
DGIC	Donegal Group, Inc.	Insurance
DNKY	Donnkenny, Inc.	Industrial

Symbol	Company Name	Sector
DORL	Doral Financial Corporation	Other Finance
DHULZ	Dorchester Hugoton, Ltd.	Industrial
DIIBF	Dorel Industries, Inc.	Industrial
DOTX	Dotronix, Inc.	Computer
DBLE	Double Eagle Petroleum and Mining Company	Industrial
DCLK	DoubleClick Inc.	Industrial
DOBQ	Doughtie's Foods, Inc.	Industrial
DCPCF	Dransfield China Paper Corporation	Industrial
DRAXF	Draxis Health Inc.	Industrial
DBRN	Dress Barn, Inc. (The)	Industrial
DRXR	Drexler Technology Corporation	Industrial
DRYR	Dreyer's Grand Ice Cream, Inc.	Industrial
DRFNY	Driefontein Consolidated, Ltd.	Industrial
DROV	Drovers Bancshares Corporation	Bank
DEMP	Drug Emporium, Inc.	Industrial
DYPR	Drypers Corporation	Industrial
DSET	DSET Corporation	Computer
DSGIF	DSG International Limited	Industrial
DSIT	DSI Toys, Inc.	Industrial
DSPG	DSP Group, Inc.	Industrial
DSPT	DSP Technology Inc.	Industrial
DTII	DT Industries, Inc.	Industrial
DTMC	DTM Corporation	Industrial
DSTR	DualStar Technologies Corporation	Industrial
DUCK	Duckwall-Alco Stores, Inc.	Industrial
DNCC	Dunn Computer Corporation	Industrial
DPMI	DuPont Photomasks, Inc.	Industrial
DRRA	Dura Automotive Systems, Inc.	Industrial
DRRAP	Dura Automotive Systems, Inc.	Industrial
DURA	Dura Pharmaceuticals, Inc.	Biotechnology
DRKN	Durakon Industries, Inc.	Industrial
DRMD	Duramed Pharmaceuticals, Inc.	Biotechnology
DROOY	Durban Roodepoort Deep, Ltd	Industrial
DUSA	DUSA Pharmaceuticals, Inc.	Industrial
DWYR	Dwyer Group, Inc. (The)	Other Finance
DXPE	DXP Enterprises, Inc.	Industrial
DYII	Dynacq International, Inc.	Industrial
DYMX	Dynamex, Inc.	Transportation
DHTI	Dynamic Healthcare Technologies Inc.	Computer
DYHM	Dynamic Homes, Inc.	Industrial
BOOM	Dynamic Materials Corporation	Industrial
DRCO	Dynamics Research Corporation	Computer

Symbol	Company Name	Sector
DYMTF	DynaMotive Technologies Corp.	Industrial
DYNX	Dynatec International, Inc.	Industrial
DYNT	Dynatronics Corporation	Industrial
DXCPN	Dynex Capital Inc.	Other Finance
DXCPO	Dynex Capital Inc.	Other Finance
DXCPP	Dynex Capital Inc.	Other Finance
EGRP	E*TRADE Group, Inc.	Other Finance
ESPI	e.spire Communications, Inc.	Telecommunications
EACO	EA Engineering, Science, and Technology, Inc.	Industrial
EGLB	Eagle BancGroup, Inc.	Other Finance
EBSI	Eagle Bancshares, Inc.	Other Finance
EGLE	Eagle Food Centers, Inc.	Industrial
EGEO	Eagle Geophysical, Inc.	Industrial
EAGL	Eagle Hardware & Garden, Inc.	Industrial
EGPT	Eagle Point Software Corporation	Computer
EUSA	Eagle USA Airfreight, Inc.	Transportation
ESCI	Earth Sciences, Inc.	Industrial
ELNK	Earthlink Network, Inc.	Telecommunications
ERTH	EarthShell Corporation	Industrial
ESCO	Easco, Inc.	Industrial
ETFS	East Texas Financial Services, Inc.	Other Finance
EASEC	Eastbrokers International Incorporated	Industrial
ESTO	Eastco Industrial Safety Corp.	Industrial
EESI	Eastern Environmental Services, Inc.	Industrial
EVBS	Eastern Virginia Bankshares, Inc.	Bank
EATS	Eateries, Inc.	Industrial
EBAY	eBay Inc.	Computer
ECCS	ECCS, Inc.	Computer
ELON	Echelon Corporation	Computer
ECHTA	EchoCath, Inc.	Industrial
DISH	EchoStar Communications Corporation	Industrial
DISHP	EchoStar Communications Corporation	Industrial
ECILF	ECI Telecom Ltd.	Industrial
ESTI	Eclipse Surgical Technologies, Inc.	Industrial
ECLP	Eclipsys Corporation	Computer
ESSI	Eco Soil Systems, Inc.	Industrial
EECN	Ecogen Inc.	Industrial
ECSC	EcoScience Corporation	Industrial
ECSGY	ECsoft Group plc	Computer
EDAC	Edac Technologies Corporation	Industrial
EDAPY	EDAP TMS S.A.	Industrial
EDEL	Edelbrock Corporation	Industrial

Symbol	Company Name	Sector
EPEX	Edge Petroleum Corporation	Industrial
EDFY	Edify Corporation	Computer
EDBR	Edison Brothers Stores, Incorporated	Industrial
EDCO	Edison Control Corporation	Industrial
EDMC	Education Management Corporation	Industrial
EDUC	Educational Development Corporation	Industrial
EDIN	Educational Insights, Inc.	Industrial
EDUSF	EduSoft Ltd.	Computer
EDUT	EduTrek International, Inc.	Industrial
EMSI	Effective Management Systems, Inc.	Industrial
EFIC	EFI Electronics Corporation	Industrial
EFTC	EFTC Corporation	Industrial
EGGS	Egghead.com, Inc.	Industrial
EIDSY	Eidos plc	Computer
ENBX	Einstein/Noah Bagel Corporation	Industrial
EISI	EIS International, Inc.	Computer
ELAMF	Elamex S.A. de C.V.	Industrial
ELNT	Elantec Semiconductor, Inc.	Computer
ELBTF	Elbit Ltd.	Computer
EMITF	Elbit Medical Imaging Ltd.	Industrial
ESLTF	Elbit Systems Ltd.	Industrial
EVSNF	Elbit Vision Systems, Limited	Industrial
ELCO	Elcom International, Inc.	Computer
ECTL	Elcotel, Inc.	Industrial
ELGT	Electric & Gas Technology, Inc.	Industrial
EFCX	Electric Fuel Corporation	Industrial
ELIX	Electric Lightwave, Inc.	Telecommunications
ELRC	Electro Rent Corporation	Industrial
ESIO	Electro Scientific Industries, Inc.	Industrial
EPLTF	Electrocon International Inc.	Industrial
EGLS	Electroglas, Inc.	Industrial
ELMG	Electromagnetic Sciences, Inc.	Industrial
ERTS	Electronic Arts Inc.	Computer
ECHO	Electronic Clearing House, Inc.	Industrial
EPIQ	Electronic Processing, Inc.	Industrial
ERSI	Electronic Retailing Systems International, Inc.	Computer
ETCIA	Electronic Tele-Communications Inc.	Industrial
ELBO	Electronics Boutique Holdings Corp.	Industrial
EFII	Electronics for Imaging, Inc.	Computer
ELSE	Electro-Sensors, Inc.	Industrial
ELSI	Electrosource, Inc.	Industrial
EILL	Elegant Illusions, Inc.	Industrial

Symbol	Company Name	Sector
PUBSF	Elephant & Castle Group, Inc.	Industrial
EKFG	Elk Associates Funding Corporation	Other Finance
ELET	Ellett Brothers, Inc.	Industrial
ELMS	Elmer's Restaurants, Inc.	Industrial
ESBK	Elmira Savings Bank, FSB (The)	Bank
ELRNF	Elron Electronic Industries Ltd.	Industrial
ELTKF	Eltek Ltd.	Industrial
ELTX	Eltrax Systems, Inc.	Industrial
ELXS	ELXSI Corporation	Industrial
EMBX	Embrex, Inc.	Industrial
EMCI	EMC Insurance Group, Inc.	Insurance
ECIN	EMCEE Broadcast Products Inc.	Industrial
EMLTF	EMCO Limited	Industrial
MCON	EMCON	Industrial
EMCG	EMCOR Group, Inc.	Industrial
EMKR	EMCORE Corporation	Industrial
EMLD	Emerald Financial Corp.	Bank
EMIS	Emisphere Technologies, Inc.	Industrial
EMMS	Emmis Communications Corporation	Telecommunications
EMON	Emons Transportation Group, Inc.	Transportation
EMPI	Empi, Inc.	Industrial
EFBC	Empire Federal Bancorp, Inc.	Other Finance
ESOL	Employee Solutions, Inc.	Industrial
EMLX	Emulex Corporation	Computer
ENPT	En Pointe Technologies, Inc.	Industrial
ENML	Enamelon, Inc.	Industrial
ENBRF	Enbridge Inc.	Transportation
ENCD	ENCAD, Inc.	Industrial
ENMC	Encore Medical Corporation	Industrial
WIRE	Encore Wire Corporation	Industrial
ECSI	Endocardial Solutions, Inc.	Industrial
ENDO	Endocare, Inc.	Industrial
ENDG	Endogen, Inc.	Industrial
ESON	Endosonics Corporation	Industrial
ENGSY	Energis Plc	Telecommunications
ENBC	Energy BioSystems Corporation	Industrial
ENER	Energy Conversion Devices, Inc.	Industrial
EGAS	Energy Search, Incorporated	Industrial
EWST	Energy West, Inc.	Industrial
ENSI	EnergySouth, Inc.	Industrial
ETEL	e-Net, Inc.	Industrial
ENGEF	Engel General Developers Ltd.	Industrial

Symbol	Company Name	Sector
EASI	Engineered Support Systems, Inc.	Industrial
EAII	Engineering Animation, Inc.	Computer
EMCO	Engineering Measurements Company	Industrial
ENGL	Engle Homes, Inc.	Industrial
ESVS	Enhanced Services Company, Inc.	Industrial
SFTW	ENlighten Software Solutions, Inc.	Computer
ENSR	ENStar Inc.	Industrial
EFBI	Enterprise Federal Bancorp, Inc.	Other Finance
ENSW	Enterprise Software, Inc.	Industrial
ENMD	EntreMed, Inc.	Biotechnology
ENTU	Entrust Technologies, Inc.	Computer
ENVG	Envirogen, Inc.	Industrial
POWR	Environmental Power Corporation	Industrial
EVTC	Environmental Technologies Corp.	Industrial
ENSO	Envirosource, Inc.	Industrial
ENVY	ENVOY Corporation	Telecommunications
ENZN	Enzon, Inc.	Biotechnology
EPMD	EP MedSystems, Inc.	Industrial
EPTO	Epitope, Incorporated	Industrial
EPIX	EPIX Medical, Inc.	Biotechnology
EPTG	EPL Technologies, Inc.	Industrial
ENET	Equalnet Communications Corp.	Telecommunications
EQNX	Equinox Systems Inc.	Computer
EQSB	Equitable Federal Savings Bank	Bank
EQTX	Equitex, Inc.	Industrial
ETRC	Equitrac Corporation	Computer
EMAK	Equity Marketing, Inc.	Industrial
EQTY	Equity Oil Company	Industrial
EQUI	Equivest Finance, Inc.	Other Finance
EQUUS	Equus Gaming Company L.P.	Other Finance
ERCI	ERC Industries, Inc.	Industrial
ERGO	Ergo Science Corporation	Biotechnology
ERIE	Erie Indemnity Company	Insurance
ESATY	Esat Telecom Group plc	Telecommunications
ESBF	ESB Financial Corporation	Bank
ESBFP	ESB Financial Corporation	Bank
ESCMF	ESC Medical Systems, Limited	Industrial
ESCA	Escalade, Incorporated	Industrial
ESMC	Escalon Medical Corp.	Industrial
ESNJ	Esenjay Exploration Incorporated	Industrial
ESREF	ESG Re Limited	Other Finance
ROBOF	Eshed Robotec (1982) Ltd.	Industrial

Symbol	Company Name	Sector
EPIE	Eskimo Pie Corporation	Industrial
ESFT	eSoft, Inc.	Computer
ESPRY	Esprit Telecom Group plc	Telecommunications
ESQS	Esquire Communications Ltd.	Industrial
ESST	ESS Technology, Inc	Computer
ESSF	ESSEF Corporation	Industrial
ETEC	Etec Systems, Inc.	Industrial
ETHYD	Ethical Holdings plc	Industrial
EUFA	Eufaula BancCorp, Inc.	Bank
EUPH	Euphonix, Inc.	Industrial
CLWTF	Euro Tech Holdings Company Limited	Industrial
EEFT	Euronet Services, Inc.	Bank
KRUZ	Europa Cruises Corporation	Transportation
EMCC	European Micro Holdings, Inc.	Industrial
EWEB	Euroweb International Corp.	Industrial
ESCC	Evans & Sutherland Computer Corporation	Computer
EVSI	Evans Systems, Inc.	Industrial
EVANC	Evans, Inc.	Industrial
EVMD	Everest Medical Corporation	Industrial
EVGN	Evergreen Bancorp, Inc.	Other Finance
EVER	Evergreen Resources, Inc.	Industrial
EVOL	Evolving Systems, Inc.	Industrial
EXBT	Exabyte Corporation	Computer
EXAC	Exactech, Inc.	Industrial
EXAR	Exar Corporation	Industrial
EXCA	Excalibur Technologies Corporation	Computer
XLSW	Excel Switching Corporation	Industrial
XLTC	Excel Technology, Inc.	Industrial
BIGX	Excelsior-Henderson Motorcycle Mfg	Industrial
XCIT	Excite, Inc.	Computer
EXCO	EXCO Resources, Inc.	Industrial
EXEC	Executay Corporation	Industrial
EGLO	Executive TeleCard, Ltd.	Industrial
XTON	EXECUTONE Information Systems, Inc.	Industrial
EXDS	Exodus Communications	Telecommunications
EXGN	Exogen, Inc.	Industrial
EXPD	Expeditors International of Washington, Inc.	Transportation
XPRT	Expert Software, Inc.	Computer
EXPO	Exponent, Inc.	Industrial
ESRX	Express Scripts, Inc.	Industrial
XTND	Extended Systems Incorporated	Computer
EZPW	EZCORP, Inc.	Industrial

Symbol	Company Name	Sector
FMBN	F & M Bancorp	Bank
FMBK	F & M Bancorporation, Inc.	Bank
FBAN	F.N.B. Corporation	Other Finance
FYII	F.Y.I. Incorporated	Industrial
FCPY	Factory Card Outlet Corp.	Industrial
FDCC	Factual Data Corp.	Industrial
FBRK	Fallbrook National Bank	Bank
FBAR	Family Bargain Corporation	Industrial
FBARP	Family Bargain Corporation	Industrial
FGCI	Family Golf Centers, Inc.	Industrial
RYFL	Family Steak Houses of Florida, Inc.	Industrial
DAVE	Famous Dave's of America, Inc.	Industrial
FTMTF	Fantom Technologies Inc.	Industrial
FARM	Farmer Brothers Company	Industrial
FFKT	Farmers Capital Bank Corporation	Other Finance
FARO	FARO Technologies, Inc.	Industrial
FDJA	Faroudja, Inc.	Industrial
FARC	Farr Company	Industrial
FARL	Farrel Corporation	Industrial
FAST	Fastenal Company	Industrial
FAXX	FaxSav Incorporated	Telecommunications
FCBF	FCB Financial Corp.	Other Finance
FCNB	FCNB Corp.	Bank
FCNBP	FCNB Corp.	Bank
FDPC	FDP Corp.	Computer
FTHR	Featherlite, Inc.	Industrial
FAMCA	Federal Agricultural Mortgage Corporation	Other Finance
FAMCK	Federal Agricultural Mortgage Corporation	Other Finance
FSCR	Federal Screw Works	Industrial
FEIC	FEI Company	Industrial
FMRX	FemRx, Inc.	Industrial
FERO	Ferrofluidics Corporation	Industrial
FFDF	FFD Financial Corporation	Bank
FFLC	FFLC Bancorp, Inc.	Other Finance
FFWC	FFW Corporation	Bank
FFYF	FFY Financial Corp.	Bank
FBST	Fiberstars, Inc.	Industrial
FBCI	Fidelity Bancorp, Inc.	Other Finance
FSBI	Fidelity Bancorp, Inc.	Bank
FSBIP	Fidelity Bancorp, Inc.	Bank
FFFL	Fidelity Bankshares, Inc.	Other Finance
FFFLP	Fidelity Bankshares, Inc.	Other Finance

Symbol	Company Name	Sector
FFED	Fidelity Federal Bancorp	Bank
FFOH	Fidelity Financial of Ohio, Inc.	Other Finance
FDHG	Fidelity Holdings, Inc.	Industrial
LION	Fidelity National Corporation	Other Finance
FASI	Fields Aircraft Spares, Inc.	Industrial
FWRX	FieldWorks, Inc.	Computer
FITB	Fifth Third Bancorp	Other Finance
BSMT	Filene's Basement Corp.	Industrial
FILE	FileNet Corporation	Computer
ROMN	Film Roman, Inc.	Industrial
FIBC	Financial Bancorp, Inc.	Other Finance
FNIN	Financial Industries Corporation	Insurance
FSVP	FIND/SVP, Inc.	Industrial
FDOT	fine.com International Corporation	Computer
FNHC	Finet Holdings Corporation	Other Finance
SBFL	Finger Lakes Financial Corp.	Bank
FINL	Finish Line, Inc. (The)	Industrial
FMST	FinishMaster, Inc.	Industrial
FNLY	Finlay Enterprises, Inc.	Industrial
FATS	Firearms Training Systems, Inc.	Industrial
FTEC	Firetector Inc.	Industrial
FACT	First Albany Companies, Inc.	Other Finance
FACO	First Alliance Corporation	Other Finance
FAHC	First American Health Concepts, Inc.	Industrial
FAVS	First Aviation Services, Inc.	Industrial
FBNC	First Bancorp	Other Finance
FBSI	First Bancshares, Inc.	Other Finance
FBKP	First Bank of Philadelphia	Bank
FBCG	First Banking Company of Southeast Georgia	Other Finance
FBNKO	First Banks, Inc.	Other Finance
FBBC	First Bell Bancorp, Inc.	Other Finance
BUSE	First Busey Corporation	Bank
SKBOD	First Carnegie Deposit	Other Finance
PAWN	First Cash, Inc.	Industrial
FCTR	First Charter Corporation	Other Finance
FCNCA	First Citizens BancShares, Inc.	Other Finance
FSTC	First Citizens Corporation	Bank
FCBK	First Coastal Bankshares Inc.	Other Finance
FCME	First Coastal Corporation	Other Finance
FTCG	First Colonial Group, Inc.	Bank
FCBIA	First Commerce Bancshares, Inc.	Other Finance
FCBIB	First Commerce Bancshares, Inc.	Other Finance

Symbol	Company Name	Sector
FCWI	First Commonwealth, Inc.	Insurance
FCGI	First Consulting Group, Inc.	Industrial
FDEF	First Defiance Financial Corp.	Bank
FESX	First Essex Bancorp, Inc.	Other Finance
FFBZ	First Federal Bancorp, Inc.	Industrial
BDJI	First Federal Bancorporation	Bank
FFBH	First Federal Bancshares of Arkansas, Inc.	Other Finance
FTFC	First Federal Capital Corp.	Other Finance
FFKY	First Federal Financial Corporation of Ky	Other Finance
FFES	First Federal Savings and Loan Association	Other Finance
FFSX	First Federal Savings Bank of Siouxland	Other Finance
FFBC	First Financial Bancorp.	Other Finance
FFIN	First Financial Bankshares, Inc.	Other Finance
FTFN	First Financial Corp.	Bank
THFF	First Financial Corporation Indiana	Bank
FFCH	First Financial Holdings, Inc.	Other Finance
FFHS	First Franklin Corporation	Other Finance
FGHC	First Georgia Holding, Inc.	Other Finance
FHWN	First Hawaiian, Inc.	Other Finance
FHCC	First Health Group Corp.	Industrial
FFSL	First Independence Corporation	Bank
FISB	First Indiana Corporation	Bank
FNCE	First International Bancorp, Inc.	Other Finance
FIFS	First Investors Financial Services Group	Other Finance
FKAN	First Kansas Financial Corporation	Bank
FKFS	First Keystone Financial, Inc.	Other Finance
FLKY	First Lancaster Bancshares, Inc.	Bank
FLPB	First Leesport Bancorp, Inc.	Other Finance
FLFC	First Liberty Financial Corp.	Other Finance
FMFC	First M & F Corporation	Other Finance
FMAR	First Mariner Bancorp	Other Finance
FRME	First Merchants Corporation	Other Finance
FMBI	First Midwest Bancorp, Inc.	Other Finance
CASH	First Midwest Financial, Inc.	Other Finance
FMBD	First Mutual Bancorp, Inc.	Other Finance
FMSB	First Mutual Savings Bank	Bank
FNFI	First Niles Financial, Inc.	Bank
FNGB	First Northern Capital Corporation	Other Finance
FOBBA	First Oak Brook Bancshares, Inc.	Other Finance
FLIC	First of Long Island Corporation (The)	Other Finance
FPGP	First Priority Group, Inc.	Industrial
FRGB	First Regional Bancorp	Other Finance

Symbol	Company Name	Sector
SOPN	First Savings Bancorp Inc.	Other Finance
FSCO	First Security Corporation	Other Finance
FSFF	First SecurityFed Financial Inc.	Other Finance
FSFH	First Sierra Financial, Inc.	Other Finance
FSLA	First Source Bancorp, Inc.	Bank
FSACF	First South Africa Corp., Ltd.	Industrial
FSTH	First Southern Bancshares, Inc	Other Finance
FSNM	First State Bancorporation	Other Finance
FSLB	First Sterling Banks, Inc.	Bank
FTSP	First Team Sports, Inc.	Industrial
FTEN	First Tennessee National Corporation	Other Finance
UNTD	First United Bancshares, Inc.	Other Finance
FUNC	First United Corporation	Other Finance
FVHI	First Virtual Holdings Incorporated	Industrial
FWWB	First Washington Bancorp, Inc.	Other Finance
FWBI	First Western Bancorp, Inc.	Bank
KIDD	First Years, Inc. (The)	Industrial
FBNW	FirstBank Corp.	Bank
FCFC	FirstCity Financial Corporation	Other Finance
FCFCO	FirstCity Financial Corporation	Other Finance
FCLX	FirstCom Corporation	Telecommunications
FFDB	FirstFed Bancorp, Inc.	Bank
FLCI	FirstLink Communications, Inc.	Telecommunications
FIRM	Firstmark Corp.	Insurance
FMER	FirstMerit Corporation	Bank
FSRVF	FirstService Corporation	Computer
FSPT	FirstSpartan Financial Corp.	Bank
FSTW	Firstwave Technologies Inc.	Computer
FIMG	Fischer Imaging Corporation	Industrial
FISV	Fiserv, Inc.	Computer
FLAG	FLAG Financial Corporation	Other Finance
FLGS	Flagstar Bancorp, Inc.	Bank
FLGSP	Flagstar Bancorp, Inc.	Bank
FLMLY	Flamel Technologies S.A.	Industrial
FAME	Flamemaster Corporation (The)	Industrial
FLDR	Flanders Corporation	Industrial
FLCHF	Fletcher's Fine Foods Ltd.	Industrial
FLXI	FlexiInternational Software, Inc.	Computer
FLXS	Flexsteel Industries, Inc.	Industrial
FLEX	Flextronics International Ltd.	Industrial
FLIR	FLIR Systems, Inc.	Industrial
FIIF	Florafax International, Inc.	Industrial

Symbol	Company Name	Sector
FLBK	Florida Banks, Inc.	Bank
FLSC	Florsheim Group Inc.	Industrial
FCIN	Flour City International, Inc.	Industrial
FLOW	Flow International Corporation	Industrial
FDGT	Fluor Daniel GTI, Inc.	Industrial
FFIC	Flushing Financial Corporation	Other Finance
FMCO	FMS Financial Corporation	Other Finance
FNBN	FNB Corp.	Other Finance
FNBP	FNB Corporation	Bank
FNBF	FNB Financial Services Corporation	Other Finance
FNBR	FNB Rochester Corp.	Other Finance
FMXI	Foamex International, Inc.	Industrial
FOCL	Focal, Inc.	Industrial
FCSE	FOCUS Enhancements, Inc.	Computer
FLMK	Foilmark, Inc.	Industrial
FONR	Fonar Corporation	Industrial
FONX	Fonix Corporation	Industrial
FDLNA	Food Lion, Inc.	Industrial
FDLNB	Food Lion, Inc.	Industrial
VIFL	Food Technology Service, Inc.	Industrial
FOOT	Foothill Independent Bancorp	Other Finance
FORE	FORE Systems, Inc.	Computer
FORL	Foreland Corporation	Industrial
FORTY	Formula Systems (1985) Ltd.	Computer
FNCLY	Formulab Neuronetics Corporation Limited	Industrial
FORR	Forrester Research, Inc.	Industrial
FORSF	Forsoft Ltd.	Computer
FBHC	Fort Bend Holding Corp.	Other Finance
FTSB	Fort Thomas Financial Corporation	Other Finance
FRTE	Forte Software, Inc.	Computer
FRTG	Fortress Group, Inc. (The)	Industrial
FWRD	Forward Air Corporation	Transportation
FORD	Forward Industries, Inc.	Industrial
FOSL	Fossil, Inc.	Industrial
FUSA	Fotoball USA, Inc.	Industrial
FPWR	Fountain Powerboat Industries, Inc.	Industrial
FOUR	Four Media Company	Industrial
FSFT	FOURTH SHIFT Corporation	Computer
FPIC	FPIC Insurance Group, Inc.	Other Finance
FMAX	Franchise Mortgage Acceptance Company	Other Finance
FKKY	Frankfort First Bancorp, Inc.	Other Finance
FSVB	Franklin Bank, National Association	Other Finance

Symbol	Company Name	Sector
FSVBP	Franklin Bank, National Association	Other Finance
FELE	Franklin Electric Co., Inc.	Industrial
BLUE	Frederick Brewing Co.	Industrial
FRED	Fred's, Inc.	Industrial
FREEY	Freepages Group plc	Industrial
BYCL	Fremont Corporation	Industrial
FRAG	French Fragrances, Inc.	Industrial
FRES	Fresh America Corp.	Industrial
SALD	Fresh Choice, Inc.	Industrial
FOOD	Fresh Foods, Inc.	Industrial
FRSH	Fresh Juice Company, Inc. (The)	Industrial
FSVC	Freshstart Venture Capital Corp.	Other Finance
FGII	Friede Goldman International, Inc.	Industrial
FRDM	Friedman's Inc.	Industrial
FRND	Friendly Ice Cream Corporation	Industrial
FRIZ	Frisby Technologies, Inc.	Industrial
FBAYF	Frisco Bay Industries Ltd.	Industrial
FRTZ	Fritz Companies, Inc.	Transportation
FRNT	Frontier Airlines, Inc.	Transportation
FTBK	Frontier Financial Corporation	Other Finance
FCCN	Frontline Communications Corporation	Computer
FRONY	Frontline Ltd.	Transportation
FFEX	Frozen Food Express Industries, Inc.	Transportation
FRPP	FRP Properties, Inc.	Transportation
FFHH	FSF Financial Corp.	Other Finance
FSII	FSI International, Inc.	Computer
FTIC	FTI Consulting Inc	Industrial
FTEKF	Fuel-Tech, N.V.	Industrial
FUSE	Fuisz Technologies Ltd.	Industrial
FUJIY	Fuji Photo Film Co., Ltd.	Industrial
FHRI	Full House Resorts, Inc.	Industrial
FTNB	Fulton Bancorp, Inc.	Bank
FULT	Fulton Financial Corporation	Other Finance
FNCO	Funco, Inc.	Industrial
FNDTF	Fundtech Ltd.	Computer
FSON	Fusion Medical Technologies, Inc.	Industrial
VITK	Futurebiotics, Inc.	Industrial
FMDAY	Futuremedia Public Limited Company	Industrial
FVCX	FVC.COM, Inc.	Computer
FVNB	FVNB Corporation	Bank
FXEN	FX Energy, Inc.	Industrial
GKSRA	G&K Services, Inc.	Industrial

Symbol	Company Name	Sector
WILCF	G. Willi-Food International, Ltd.	Industrial
GADZ	Gadzooks, Inc.	Industrial
GGEN	GalaGen Inc.	Biotechnology
GALX	Galaxy Foods Company	Industrial
GAEO	Galileo Corporation	Industrial
GALTF	Galileo Technology Ltd.	Industrial
HIST	Gallery of History, Inc.	Industrial
SIZL	Galveston's Steakhouse Corp.	Industrial
GMTC	GameTech International, Inc.	Industrial
GLCCF	Gaming Lottery Corporation	Industrial
GTOS	Gantos, Inc.	Industrial
GBOT	Garden Botanika, Inc.	Industrial
LTUS	Garden Fresh Restaurant Corp.	Industrial
GRDG	Garden Ridge Corporation	Industrial
GBUR	Gardenburger, Inc.	Industrial
GRTS	Gart Sports Company	Industrial
GSNX	GaSonics International	Industrial
GBNK	Gaston Federal Bancorp, Inc.	Other Finance
GBCB	GBC Bancorp	Other Finance
GEER	Geerlings & Wade, Inc.	Industrial
GEHL	Gehl Company	Industrial
GELX	GelTex Pharmaceuticals, Inc.	Biotechnology
GMSTF	Gemstar International Group, Limited	Industrial
GLGC	Gene Logic Inc.	Industrial
GNLB	Genelabs Technologies, Inc.	Biotechnology
GMED	GeneMedicine, Inc.	Biotechnology
GNRL	General Bearing Corporation	Industrial
GBND	General Binding Corporation	Computer
GCABY	General Cable, PLC	Telecommunications
GNCMA	General Communication, Inc.	Telecommunications
GMGC	General Magic, Inc.	Computer
GMCC	General Magnaplate Corporation	Industrial
GNCI	General Nutrition Companies, Inc.	Industrial
GSCN	General Scanning Inc.	Industrial
GSII	General Surgical Innovations, Inc.	Industrial
GNWR	Genesee & Wyoming Inc.	Transportation
GENBB	Genesee Corporation	Industrial
GDCOF	Genesis Development and Construction, Ltd.	Industrial
GNSSF	Genesis Microchip Inc.	Industrial
GCTI	Genesys Telecommunications Lab., Inc.	Computer
GECM	GENICOM Corporation	Computer
GENS	Genisys Reservation Systems, Inc.	Industrial

Symbol	Company Name	Sector
GLYT	Genlyte Group Incorporated (The)	Industrial
GENE	Genome Therapeutics, Corp	Industrial
GENXY	Genset	Industrial
GNSA	Gensia Sicor, Inc.	Biotechnology
GNSM	Gensym Corporation	Computer
GNTA	Genta Incorporated	Biotechnology
GNTX	Gentex Corporation	Industrial
GNTIY	Gentia Software plc	Computer
GNTL	Gentle Dental Service Corporation	Industrial
GTNR	Gentner Communications Corp.	Industrial
GGNS	Genus, Inc.	Industrial
GENZ	Genzyme General	Biotechnology
GZTC	Genzyme Transgenics Corporation	Industrial
GCTY	GeoCities	Industrial
GEOI	GeoResources, Inc.	Industrial
GSCI	GeoScience Corporation	Industrial
GEOC	GeoTel Communications Corporation	Industrial
GEOW	GeoWaste Incorporated	Industrial
GWRX	Geoworks Corporation	Computer
GABC	German American Bancorp	Other Finance
GERN	Geron Corporation	Biotechnology
GETY	Getty Images, Inc.	Industrial
GUPB	GFSB Bancorp, Inc.	Bank
GCHI	Giant Cement Holding, Inc.	Industrial
GBSE	Gibbs Construction, Inc.	Industrial
PACK	Gibraltar Packaging Group, Inc.	Industrial
ROCK	Gibraltar Steel Corporation	Industrial
GIBG	Gibson Greetings, Inc.	Industrial
GIGX	GIGA Information Group, Inc.	Industrial
GIGA	Giga-tronics Incorporated	Industrial
GIII	G-III Apparel Group, LTD.	Industrial
GICOF	Gilat Communications Ltd.	Industrial
GILTF	Gilat Satellite Networks Ltd.	Telecommunications
GILD	Gilead Sciences, Inc.	Biotechnology
GTAX	Gilman & Ciocia, Inc.	Industrial
GISH	Gish Biomedical, Inc.	Industrial
GBCI	Glacier Bancorp, Inc.	Bank
GLAR	Glas-Aire Industries Group, Ltd.	Industrial
GLMA	Glassmaster Company	Industrial
GLBK	GLB Bancorp, Inc.	Other Finance
GEMS	Glenayre Technologies, Inc.	Industrial
GFCO	Glenway Financial Corp.	Other Finance

Symbol	Company Name	Sector
GLIA	Gliatech Inc.	Biotechnology
GBCS	Global Casinos Inc.	Industrial
GBLX	Global Crossing Ltd	Telecommunications
GISX	Global Imaging Systems, Inc.	Industrial
GLBL	Global Industries, Ltd.	Industrial
CSTM	Global Motorsport Group, Inc.	Industrial
GPTX	Global Payment Technologies, Inc.	Industrial
GLPC	Global Pharmaceutical Corporation	Industrial
GSPT	Global Sports, Inc.	Industrial
GTSG	Global TeleSystems Group, Inc.	Telecommunications
GSTRF	Globalstar Telecommunications, Limited	Telecommunications
GLBE	Globe Business Resources, Inc.	Industrial
GCOM	Globecomm Systems Inc.	Industrial
GBIX	Globix Corporation	Computer
GLCBY	Globo Cabo S.A.	Telecommunications
GNET	go2net, Inc.	Computer
GLDB	Gold Banc Corporation, Inc.	Other Finance
GLDBP	Gold Banc Corporation, Inc.	Other Finance
GLDFY	Gold Fields of South Africa Limited	Industrial
GLDR	Gold Reserve Corporation	Industrial
GSTD	Gold Standard, Inc.	Industrial
GBFE	Golden Books Family Entertainment, Inc.	Industrial
GEGP	Golden Eagle Group, Inc.	Transportation
GLDC	Golden Enterprises, Inc.	Industrial
GGGO	Golden Genesis Company	Industrial
GIFH	Golden Isles Financial Holdings, Inc.	Other Finance
GTII	Golden Triangle Industries, Inc.	Industrial
GGUY	Good Guys, Inc. (The)	Industrial
GTIM	Good Times Restaurants Inc.	Industrial
GDPAP	Goodrich Petroleum Corporation	Industrial
GDYS	Goody's Family Clothing, Inc.	Industrial
GNCNF	Goran Capital, Inc.	Insurance
GOTH	Gothic Energy Corporation	Industrial
GTSI	Government Technology Services, Inc.	Industrial
GRDL	Gradall Industries, Inc.	Industrial
GRCO	Gradco Systems, Inc.	Computer
GATT	Grand Adventures Tour & Travel Publishing	Industrial
GSLM	Grand Central Silver Mines, Inc.	Industrial
GCLI	Grand Court Lifestyles, Inc.	Industrial
GPFI	Grand Premier Financial, Inc.	Other Finance
GRIN	Grand Toys International, Inc.	Industrial
GBTVK	Granite Broadcasting Corporation	Telecommunications

Symbol	Company Name	Sector
GSBI	Granite State Bankshares, Inc.	Other Finance
GTPS	Great American Bancorp, Inc.	Other Finance
GTCMY	Great Central Mines Ltd	Industrial
GLUX	Great Lakes Aviation, Ltd.	Transportation
PEDE	Great Pee Dee Bancorp, Inc.	Bank
GPSI	Great Plains Software, Inc.	Industrial
GSBC	Great Southern Bancorp, Inc.	Other Finance
GTRN	Great Train Store Company (The)	Industrial
GBBK	Greater Bay Bancorp	Other Finance
GBBKP	Greater Bay Bancorp	Other Finance
GFLS	Greater Community Bancorp	Bank
GFLSP	Greater Community Bancorp	Bank
ALLB	Greater Delaware Valley Savings Bank	Bank
GMCR	Green Mountain Coffee, Inc.	Industrial
GSFC	Green Street Financial Corp.	Bank
GMTI	GreenMan Technologies, Inc.	Industrial
GMAI	Greg Manning Auctions, Inc.	Industrial
GBCOA	Greif Bros. Corporation	Industrial
GBCOB	Greif Bros. Corporation	Industrial
GREY	Grey Advertising Inc.	Industrial
GRIF	Griffin Land & Nurseries, Inc.	Industrial
GRIL	Grill Concepts Inc.	Industrial
GSOF	Group 1 Software Inc.	Computer
GLDI	Group Long Distance, Inc.	Telecommunications
GBIZ	Grow Biz International, Inc.	Industrial
GRYP	Gryphon Holdings Inc.	Insurance
GSLA	GS Financial Corp.	Bank
GOSB	GSB Financial Corporation	Bank
GSES	GSE Systems, Inc.	Computer
GSTX	GST Telecommunications	Telecommunications
GTIS	GT Interactive Software Corp.	Computer
GGTI	GTI Corporation	Computer
DRTK	GTS Duratek Inc.	Industrial
GUAR	Guarantee Life Companies (The)	Other Finance
GNTY	Guaranty Bancshares, Inc.	Other Finance
GFED	Guaranty Federal Bancshares, Inc.	Other Finance
GSLC	Guaranty Financial Corporation	Bank
GRDN	Guardian Technologies International, Inc.	Industrial
GLFD	Guilford Pharmaceuticals Inc.	Industrial
GTRC	Guitar Center, Inc.	Industrial
GIFI	Gulf Island Fabrication, Inc.	Industrial
GWBK	Gulf West Banks, Inc.	Other Finance

Symbol	Company Name	Sector
GMRK	GulfMark Offshore, Inc.	Transportation
GULF	GulfWest Oil Company	Industrial
GUMM	GumTech International, Inc.	Industrial
GYMB	Gymboree Corporation (The)	Industrial
GYRO	Gyrodyne Company of America, Inc.	Other Finance
GZEA	GZA GeoEnvironmental Technologies, Inc.	Industrial
FULL	H. B. Fuller Company	Industrial
HDVS	H.D. Vest, Inc.	Industrial
HTEI	H.T.E., Inc.	Computer
HABC	Habersham Bancorp	Other Finance
HACH	Hach Company	Industrial
HACHA	Hach Company	Industrial
HDCO	Hadco Corporation	Industrial
HGGR	Haggar Corp.	Industrial
HBIX	Hagler Bailly, Inc,	Industrial
HAHN	Hahn Automotive Warehouse, Inc.	Industrial
HAKI	Hall, Kinion & Associates, Inc.	Industrial
HALL	Hallmark Capital Corp.	Other Finance
HCRC	Hallwood Consolidated Resources Corp	Industrial
HSRCD	Halstead Energy Corp.	Industrial
HABK	Hamilton Bancorp, Inc.	Other Finance
HAMP	Hampshire Group, Limited	Industrial
HBHC	Hancock Holding Company	Other Finance
HVGO	Hanover Gold Company, Inc.	Industrial
HANS	Hansen Natural Corporation	Industrial
HKID	Happy Kids Inc.	Industrial
HRBC	Harbinger Corporation	Computer
HRBF	Harbor Federal Bancorp, Inc.	Other Finance
HARB	Harbor Florida Bancshares Inc	Bank
HFSA	Hardin Bancorp, Inc.	Bank
HRDG	Harding Lawson Associates Group, Inc.	Industrial
HDNG	Hardinge, Inc.	Industrial
HGIC	Harleysville Group Inc.	Insurance
HNBC	Harleysville National Corporation	Other Finance
HARL	Harleysville Savings Bank	Other Finance
HRMN	Harmon Industries, Inc.	Industrial
HLIT	Harmonic Lightwaves, Inc.	Industrial
HGMCY	Harmony Gold Mining Co., Ltd. c/o Randgold	Industrial
HAHO	Harmony Holdings, Inc.	Industrial
HFGI	Harrington Financial Group, Inc.	Other Finance
HHGP	Harris & Harris Group, Inc.	Industrial
HARS	Harris Financial, Inc.	Bank

Symbol	Company Name	Sector
HFFB	Harrodsburg First Financial Bancorp, Inc.	Other Finance
HARY	Harry's Farmers Market, Inc.	Industrial
HHFC	Harvest Home Financial Corporation	Other Finance
HRVE	Harvey Electronics, Inc.	Industrial
HRVY	Harvey Entertainment Company	Industrial
HSKL	Haskel International, Inc.	Industrial
HAST	Hastings Entertainment, Inc.	Industrial
HATH	Hathaway Corporation	Industrial
HAUP	Hauppauge Digital, Inc.	Industrial
HAUS	Hauser, Inc.	Industrial
HAVN	Haven Bancorp, Inc.	Bank
HNWC	Hawaiian Natural Water Company, Inc.	Industrial
HPAC	Hawker Pacific Aerospace	Industrial
HWKN	Hawkins Chemical, Inc.	Industrial
HAWK	Hawks Industries, Inc. New	Industrial
HTHR	Hawthorne Financial Corporation	Other Finance
HBOC	HBO & Company	Computer
HCBBE	HCB Bancshares, Inc.	Bank
HCIA	HCIA Inc.	Industrial
HDLD	Headlands Mortgage Company	Other Finance
HDWY	Headway Corporate Resources, Inc.	Industrial
HFIT	Health Fitness Corporation	Industrial
HMSY	Health Management Systems, Inc.	Computer
HPWR	Health Power, Inc.	Insurance
HRMI	Health Risk Management, Inc.	Industrial
HSDC	Health Systems Design Corporation	Computer
HCFP	HealthCare Financial Partners, Inc.	Other Finance
HISS	HealthCare Imaging Services, Inc.	Industrial
HCRI	Healthcare Recoveries, Inc.	Industrial
HCSG	Healthcare Services Group, Inc.	Industrial
HCORE	HealthCor Holdings, Inc.	Industrial
HMSI	HealthCore Medical Solutions, Inc.	Industrial
HDSK	HealthDesk Corporation	Computer
HDIE	Healthdyne Information Enterprises, Inc.	Computer
HLRT	HealthRite, Inc.	Industrial
HEAL	HealthWatch, Inc.	Industrial
HWLD	Healthworld Corporation	Industrial
HTLD	Heartland Express, Inc.	Transportation
HPRT	Heartport, Inc.	Industrial
HBCCA	Heftel Broadcasting Corporation	Telecommunications
HEII	HEI, Inc.	Industrial
HELE	Helen of Troy Limited	Industrial

Symbol	Company Name	Sector
HELX	Helix Technology Corporation	Industrial
HELO	Hello Direct, Inc.	Industrial
HAHI	Help At Home, Inc.	Industrial
HEMA	HemaCare Corporation	Industrial
HMGN	Hemagen Diagnostics, Inc.	Industrial
HMLK	Hemlock Federal Financial Corporation	Other Finance
HENL	Henley Healthcare Inc.	Industrial
HSIC	Henry Schein, Inc.	Industrial
HERBA	Herbalife International, Inc.	Industrial
HERBB	Herbalife International, Inc.	Industrial
HERBL	Herbalife International, Inc.	Industrial
HBVA	Heritage Bancorp Inc. (VA)	Bank
HBSC	Heritage Bancorp, Inc.	Bank
HTBK	Heritage Commerce Corp	Bank
HFWA	Heritage Financial Corporation	Bank
HRLY	Herley Industries, Inc.	Industrial
MLHR	Herman Miller, Inc.	Industrial
HERZD	Hertz Technology Group, Inc.	Computer
CUBA	Herzfeld Caribbean Basin Fund, Inc. (The)	Other Finance
HSKA	Heska Corporation	Biotechnology
IFIT	Heuristic Development Group, Inc.	Industrial
HEMT	HF Bancorp, Inc.	Other Finance
HFFC	HF Financial Corp.	Other Finance
HIBB	Hibbett Sporting Goods, Inc.	Industrial
HICKA	Hickok Incorporated	Industrial
HTCO	Hickory Tech Corporation	Telecommunications
HCBC	High Country Bancorp, Inc.	Bank
HIPC	High Plains Corporation	Industrial
HPFC	High Point Financial Corp.	Other Finance
HBNK	Highland Bancorp, Inc.	Other Finance
HSVLY	Highveld Steel and Vanadium Corporation Ltd	Industrial
HIHOF	Highway Holdings Limited	Industrial
HWYM	HighwayMaster Communications, Inc.	Telecommunications
HIWDF	Highwood Resources Ltd.	Industrial
HILI	Hilite Industries, Inc.	Industrial
HORT	Hines Horticulture, Inc.	Industrial
HIFS	Hingham Institution for Savings	Other Finance
HIRI	Hi-Rise Recycling Systems, Inc.	Industrial
HRSH	Hirsch International Corp.	Industrial
HITK	Hi-Tech Pharmacal Co., Inc.	Industrial
HTXA	Hitox Corporation of America	Industrial
HLMD	HLM Design, Inc.	Industrial

Symbol	Company Name	Sector
HMGC	HMG Worldwide Corporation	Industrial
HMII	HMI Industries, Inc.	Industrial
HMNF	HMN Financial, Inc.	Other Finance
HMTT	HMT Technology Corporation	Industrial
HNCS	HNC Software, Inc.	Computer
HOEN	Hoenig Group Inc.	Other Finance
RVEE	Holiday RV Superstores, Incorporated	Industrial
HLGCF	Hollinger Inc.	Industrial
HEPH	Hollis-Eden Pharmaceuticals, Inc.	Biotechnology
HWCC	Hollywood Casino Corporation	Industrial
HLYW	Hollywood Entertainment Corporation	Industrial
FILM	Hollywood Productions, Inc.	Industrial
HOLX	Hologic, Inc.	Industrial
HOLO	HoloPak Technologies, Inc.	Industrial
HOLT	Holt's Cigar Holdings, Inc.	Industrial
HBFW	Home Bancorp	Other Finance
HBEI	Home Bancorp of Elgin, Inc.	Bank
HOMEF	Home Centers, (DIY), Limited	Industrial
HMCH	Home Choice Holdings Inc.	Industrial
HCFC	Home City Financial Corporation	Bank
HOMF	Home Federal Bancorp	Bank
HWEN	Home Financial Bancorp	Bank
HHCA	Home Health Corporation of America, Inc.	Industrial
HLFC	Home Loan Financial Corporation	Bank
HPBC	Home Port Bancorp, Inc.	Other Finance
HPII	Home Products International, Inc.	Industrial
HCAPD	HomeCapital Investment Corporation	Other Finance
HCOM	HomeCom Communications, Inc.	Computer
HGFN	HomeGold Financial, Inc.	Other Finance
HMLD	Homeland Holding Corporation	Industrial
HSOG	Home-Stake Oil & Gas Company	Industrial
HFBC	HopFed Bancorp, Inc.	Bank
HZWV	Horizon Bancorp, Inc.	Other Finance
HRZB	Horizon Financial Corp.	Bank
HZFS	Horizon Financial Services Corporation	Bank
HGPI	Horizon Group Properties, Inc.	Other Finance
HORC	Horizon Health Corporation	Industrial
HMPS	Horizon Medical Products, Inc.	Industrial
HOFF	Horizon Offshore, Inc.	Industrial
HVNV	Horizontal Ventures, Inc.	Industrial
CAFE	Host America Corporation	Industrial
HOTT	Hot Topic, Inc.	Industrial

Symbol	Company Name	Sector
HWLLP	Howell Corporation	Industrial
HOWT	Howtek, Inc.	Computer
HPSC	HPSC, Inc.	Industrial
HUBG	Hub Group, Inc.	Transportation
HUBC	HUBCO, Inc.	Bank
HUDS	Hudson Hotels Corporation	Industrial
HRBT	Hudson River Bancorp, Inc.	Bank
HDSN	Hudson Technologies, Inc.	Industrial
HGSI	Human Genome Sciences, Inc.	Industrial
EROX	Human Pheromone Sciences Inc.	Industrial
HMSC	HumaScan Inc.	Industrial
HUMCF	Hummingbird Communications, Limited	Computer
HUMP	Humphrey Hospitality Trust, Inc.	Other Finance
HBCO	Hungarian Broadcasting Corp.	Telecommunications
HBAN	Huntington Bancshares Incorporated	Other Finance
HURC	Hurco Companies, Inc.	Industrial
HHLAF	Hurricane Hydrocarbons Ltd.	Industrial
HTCH	Hutchinson Technology Incorporated	Computer
HMAR	Hvide Marine Incorporated	Transportation
HYALF	Hyal Pharmaceutical Corporation	Biotechnology
HYBRE	Hybrid Networks, Inc.	Industrial
HYBD	Hycor Biomedical Inc.	Industrial
HTECD	Hydron Technologies, Inc.	Industrial
HYSL	Hyperion Solutions Corporation	Computer
HYPT	Hyperion Telecommunications, Inc.	Telecommunications
HDII	Hypertension Diagnostics, Inc.	Industrial
HYSQ	Hyseq, Inc.	Biotechnology
HTEK	Hytek Microsystems, Inc.	Computer
IVCO	I V C Industries, Inc.	Industrial
ISAC	I.C. Isaacs & Company, Inc.	Industrial
IISLF	I.I.S. Intelligent Information Systems Limited	Computer
ISGTF	I.S.G. Technologies Inc.	Computer
ITWO	i2 Technologies, Inc.	Computer
IACP	IA Corporation	Computer
IATA	IAT Multimedia, Inc.	Computer
IBIS	Ibis Technology Corporation	Industrial
IBSX	IBS Interactive, Inc.	Computer
RRRR	ICC Technologies, Inc.	Industrial
ICGX	ICG Communications, Inc.	Telecommunications
ICHR	ICHOR Corporation	Industrial
ICOGF	ICO Global Communications Holdings Limited	Telecommunications
ICOC	ICO, Inc.	Industrial

Symbol	Company Name	Sector
ICMT	Icon CMT Corp.	Computer
ICLRY	ICON plc	Industrial
ICOS	ICOS Corporation	Biotechnology
IVISF	ICOS Vision Systems Corporation N.V.	Computer
ICTG	ICT Group, Inc.	Industrial
ICTSF	ICTS International N.V.	Industrial
ICUI	ICU Medical, Inc.	Industrial
IDBEF	ID Biomedical Corporation	Biotechnology
IDPH	IDEC Pharmaceuticals Corporation	Industrial
IDXX	IDEXX Laboratories, Inc.	Industrial
IDGB	IDG Books Worldwide, Inc.	Industrial
IDMC	IDM Environmental Corp.	Industrial
IDTC	IDT Corporation	Computer
IDXC	IDX Systems Corporation	Computer
IECE	IEC Electronics Corp.	Industrial
IFLO	I-Flow Corporation	Industrial
IFRS	IFR Systems, Inc.	Industrial
MNYC	IFS International, Inc.	Industrial
MNYCP	IFS International, Inc.	Industrial
FUTR	IFX Corporation	Other Finance
IGEN	IGEN International Inc.	Industrial
IHOP	IHOP Corp.	Industrial
IICR	IIC Industries Inc. New	Industrial
IIVI	II-VI Incorporated	Industrial
IKOS	IKOS Systems, Inc.	Industrial
ILFO	IL Fornaio (America) Corporation	Industrial
ILXO	ILEX Oncology, Inc.	Industrial
ILNK	I-Link Incorporated	Industrial
ISCO	Illinois Superconductor Corporation	Industrial
ILOGY	ILOG S.A.	Computer
DISK	Image Entertainment, Inc.	Industrial
IGTI	Image Guided Technologies, Inc.	Industrial
ISNS	Image Sensing Systems, Inc.	Industrial
IMSG	Image Systems Corporation	Industrial
IMCX	ImageMatrix Corporation	Computer
IMAG	ImageMAX, Inc.	Industrial
ITEC	Imaging Technologies Corporation	Industrial
IMTI	Imagyn Medical Technologies, Inc.	Industrial
IMAL	iMall, Inc.	Industrial
IMAT	Imatron Inc.	Industrial
IMAXF	Imax Corporation	Industrial
IMCC	IMC Mortgage Company	Other Finance

Symbol	Company Name	Sector
IMCL	ImClone Systems Incorporated	Industrial
ICCC	ImmuCell Corporation	Industrial
BLUD	Immucor, Inc.	Industrial
IMUL	ImmuLogic Pharmaceutical Corporation	Biotechnology
IMNR	Immune Response Corporation (The)	Biotechnology
IMNX	Immunex Corporation	Biotechnology
IMGN	ImmunoGen, Inc.	Biotechnology
IMMU	Immunomedics, Inc.	Biotechnology
IMNT	IMNET Systems, Inc.	Computer
IMPX	IMP, Inc.	Industrial
IMPH	IMPATH Inc.	Industrial
IMCO	IMPCO Technologies, Inc	Industrial
ICMI	Imperial Credit Commercial Mortgage Invest.	Other Finance
ICII	Imperial Credit Industries, Inc.	Other Finance
IGPFF	Imperial Ginseng Products, Limited	Industrial
IMTC	Imtec, Inc.	Computer
INFS	In Focus Systems, Inc.	Industrial
IHHI	In Home Health, Inc.	Industrial
INHM	Inco Homes Corporation	Industrial
ICNT	INCOMNET Inc.	Computer
INCY	Incyte Pharmaceuticals, Inc.	Biotechnology
IBCO	Independence Brewing Company	Industrial
ICBC	Independence Community Bank Corp.	Bank
IFSB	Independence Federal Savings Bank	Bank
INHO	Independence Holding Co.	Other Finance
ISIS	Independence Square Income Securities, Inc.	Other Finance
INDB	Independent Bank Corp.	Other Finance
INDBP	Independent Bank Corp.	Other Finance
IBCP	Independent Bank Corporation	Other Finance
IBCPP	Independent Bank Corporation	Other Finance
INDYY	Independent Energy Holdings plc	Industrial
IUBC	Indiana United Bancorp	Other Finance
IUBCP	Indiana United Bancorp	Other Finance
IAABY	Indigo Aviation AB	Industrial
INDGF	Indigo N.V.	Industrial
INDI	Individual Investor Group, Inc	Industrial
IINT	Indus International, Inc.	Computer
INBI	Industrial Bancorp, Inc.	Other Finance
IHII	Industrial Holdings, Inc.	Industrial
INRB	Industrial Rubber Products, Inc.	Industrial
ISCX	Industrial Scientific Corporation	Industrial
IDSA	Industrial Services of America, Inc.	Industrial

Symbol	Company Name	Sector
IMIC	Industri-Matematik International Corporation	Computer
INFR	Inference Corporation	Computer
IMCI	Infinite Machines Corp.	Industrial
IFNY	Infinity, Inc.	Industrial
INFM	Infinium Software, Inc.	Computer
INFD	Infodata Systems Inc.	Computer
INFO	Infonautics, Inc.	Computer
IACO	Information Advantage, Inc.	Industrial
IAIC	Information Analysis Inc.	Computer
IMAA	Information Management Associates, Inc.	Computer
IMRS	Information Management Resources, Inc.	Computer
IMTKA	Information Management Technologies Corp.	Industrial
IREG	Information Resource Engineering, Inc.	Industrial
IRIC	Information Resources, Inc.	Computer
ISDI	Information Storage Devices, Inc.	Computer
IFMX	Informix Corporation	Computer
SEEK	Infoseek Corporation	Computer
IUSAA	infoUSA, Inc.	Industrial
IUSAB	infoUSA, Inc.	Industrial
INFU	Infu-Tech, Inc.	Industrial
IMKTA	Ingles Markets, Incorporated	Industrial
INHL	Inhale Therapeutic Systems, Inc.	Industrial
INTO	Initio, Inc.	Industrial
INKP	Inkine Pharmaceutical Company Inc.	Industrial
INKT	Inktomi Corporation	Computer
INLD	Inland Entertainment Corporation	Industrial
INLN	Inland Resources Inc.	Industrial
IMKE	Inmark Enterprises, Inc.	Industrial
IDYN	InnerDyne, Inc.	Industrial
INOD	Innodata Corporation	Computer
INOC	Innotrac Corporation	Industrial
IDEA	Innovasive Devices, Inc.	Industrial
IGCA	Innovative Gaming Corporation of America	Industrial
PURE	Innovative Medical Services	Industrial
IVTC	Innovative Valve Technologies Inc.	Industrial
INVX	Innovex, Inc.	Computer
INNO	Innovo Group, Inc.	Industrial
INPR	Inprise Corporation	Computer
INPT	Input Software Inc.	Computer
INSI	INSCI Corp.	Computer
NSIT	Insight Enterprises, Inc.	Industrial
IHSC	InSight Health Services Corp.	Industrial

Symbol	Company Name	Sector
INSGY	Insignia Solutions, plc	Computer
ISIG	Insignia Systems, Inc.	Industrial
INEI	Insituform East, Incorporated	Industrial
INSUA	Insituform Technologies, Inc.	Industrial
INSO	INSO Corporation	Industrial
NSPR	INSpire Insurance Solutions, Inc.	Computer
ILABY	Instrumentation Laboratory SpA	Computer
IAAI	Insurance Auto Auctions, Inc.	Industrial
INTAF	Intasys Corporation	Telecommunications
NTEG	Integ Incorporated	Industrial
IART	Integra LifeSciences Corporation	Industrial
ISYS	Integral Systems, Inc.	Computer
INMD	IntegraMed America, Inc.	Industrial
ICST	Integrated Circuit Systems, Inc.	Computer
IDTI	Integrated Device Technology, Inc.	Computer
IMSC	Integrated Measurement Systems, Inc.	Industrial
IMRI	Integrated Medical Resources, Inc.	Industrial
IPAC	Integrated Packaging Assembly Corporation	Computer
IPEC	Integrated Process Equipment Corp.	Industrial
IZZI	Integrated Security Systems, Inc.	Industrial
ISNR	Integrated Sensor Solutions, Inc.	Industrial
ISSI	Integrated Silicon Solution, Inc.	Computer
RDOC	Integrated Surgical Systems, Inc.	Industrial
ISCG	Integrated Systems Consulting Group, Inc.	Computer
INTS	Integrated Systems, Inc.	Computer
ITGR	Integrity Incorporated	Industrial
IGLC	Intek Global Corporation	Industrial
INTC	Intel Corporation	Computer
ICOM	Intelect Communications, Inc.	Industrial
INTD	InteliData Technologies Corporation	Computer
FONE	Intellicell Corp.	Industrial
INAI	IntelliCorp Inc.	Computer
IMII	Intelligent Medical Imaging, Inc.	Industrial
ITIG	Intelligroup, Inc.	Industrial
IQST	IntelliQuest Information Group, Inc.	Industrial
IHCC	Intensiva HealthCare Corporation	Computer
IELSF	Interactive Entertainment Ltd.	Industrial
FLYTD	Interactive Flight Technologies, Inc.	Computer
IMGK	Interactive Magic, Inc.	Computer
ITRC	Intercardia, Inc.	Industrial
ICAR	Intercargo Corporation	Insurance
ILCO	Intercontinental Life Corporation	Insurance

Symbol	Company Name	Sector
RENEF	Intercorp Excelle Inc.	Industrial
INTF	Interface Systems, Inc.	Computer
IFSIA	Interface, Inc.	Industrial
IFSC	Interferon Sciences, Inc.	Biotechnology
INGR	Intergraph Corporation	Computer
INTG	Intergroup Corporation (The)	Other Finance
INTXA	Interiors, Inc.	Industrial
INTXP	Interiors, Inc.	Industrial
LEAF	Interleaf, Inc.	Computer
INLK	Interlink Computer Sciences, Inc.	Computer
LINK	Interlink Electronics	Industrial
INLQ	INTERLINQ Software Corporation	Computer
ICIX	Intermedia Communications Inc.	Telecommunications
INMT	Intermet Corporation	Industrial
IAIS	International Aircraft Investors	Industrial
IAAC	International Assets Holding Corporation	Other Finance
IBOC	International Bancshares Corporation	Bank
IBHVF	International Briquettes Holding	Industrial
ICIQ	International CompuTex, Inc.	Computer
IEIBC	International Electronics, Inc.	Industrial
IFCI	International FiberCom, Inc.	Industrial
ICUB	International Integration Incorporated	Computer
INIS	International Isotopes Inc.	Industrial
ITSIC	International Lottery & Totalizator Systems, Inc.	Computer
IMSX	International Manufacturing Services, Inc.	Industrial
IMSI	International Microcomputer Software, Inc.	Industrial
INSS	International Network Services	Computer
ISCA	International Speedway Corporation	Industrial
ISWI	International Sports Wagering Inc.	Computer
ITSW	International Total Services, Inc.	Transportation
YOCM	International Yogurt Company	Industrial
ICCSA	Internet Commerce Corp.	Industrial
INCC	Internet Communications Corporation	Industrial
IPIC	Interneuron Pharmaceuticals, Inc.	Industrial
INPH	Interphase Corporation	Computer
IPLY	Interplay Entertainment Corp.	Computer
BONZ	Interpore International	Industrial
ISTN	Interstate National Dealer Services, Inc.	Industrial
INTL	Inter-Tel, Incorporated	Industrial
IBCA	Intervest Bancshares Corp.	Bank
IVBK	Intervisual Books, Inc.	Industrial
INTV	InterVoice, Inc.	Computer

Symbol	Company Name	Sector
ITVU	InterVU Inc.	Computer
IWBK	InterWest Bancorp Inc.	Bank
IWHM	Interwest Home Medical, Inc.	Industrial
INTT	inTest Corporation	Industrial
IVAC	Intevac, Inc.	Industrial
ITDS	Intl. Telecommunications Data Systems	Computer
INRS	IntraNet Solutions Inc.	Industrial
TRAV	Intrav, Inc.	Transportation
INET	Intrenet, Inc.	Transportation
INTU	Intuit Inc.	Computer
IVCR	Invacare Corporation	Industrial
ITGI	Investment Technology Group, Inc.	Computer
IFIN	Investors Financial Services Corp.	Other Finance
ITIC	Investors Title Company	Insurance
INVN	InVision Technologies, Inc.	Industrial
SAFE	Invivo Corporation	Industrial
IONAY	IONA Technologies PLC	Computer
IFTI	Ionic Fuel Technology, Inc.	Industrial
IONCY	Ionica Group plc	Telecommunications
IPCRF	IPC Holdings, Limited	Insurance
INST	IPI, Inc.	Industrial
IPSW	Ipswich Savings Bank	Bank
IRATE	IRATA, Inc.	Industrial
IRIX	IRIDEX Corporation	Industrial
IRIDF	Iridium World Communications Ltd.	Telecommunications
IMTN	Iron Mountain Incorporated	Transportation
IROQ	Iroquois Bancorp, Inc.	Other Finance
IRSN	Irvine Sensors Corporation	Computer
IRWN	Irwin Financial Corporation	Other Finance
IRWNP	Irwin Financial Corporation	Other Finance
HHHH	Irwin Naturals/4Health, Inc.	Industrial
ISBF	ISB Financial Corporation	Other Finance
ISKO	Isco, Inc.	Industrial
SISGF	ISG International Software Group Ltd.	Computer
ISIP	Isis Pharmaceuticals, Inc.	Biotechnology
ISLE	Isle of Capris Casinos, Inc.	Industrial
ICOR	ISOCOR	Computer
OREX	Isolyser Company, Inc.	Industrial
IOMT	Isomet Corporation	Industrial
ILDCY	Israel Land Development Company Limited	Other Finance
ISRL	Isramco, Inc.	Industrial
ISSX	ISS Group, Inc.	Industrial

Symbol	Company Name	Sector
STAT	i-STAT Corporation	Industrial
ITCD	ITC DeltaCom, Inc.	Telecommunications
ITCC	ITC Learning Corporation	Industrial
ITEQ	ITEQ, Inc.	Industrial
ITEX	ITEX Corporation	Industrial
ITII	ITI Technologies, Inc.	Industrial
ITLA	ITLA Capital Corporation	Bank
IYCOY	Ito-Yokado Co., Ltd.	Industrial
ITRI	Itron, Inc.	Industrial
CMIV	IVI Checkmate Corp.	Industrial
IWRK	Iwerks Entertainment, Inc.	Industrial
IIXC	IXC Communications, Inc.	Telecommunications
XOSY	iXOS Software AG	Computer
SYXI	IXYS Corporation	Industrial
JJSF	J & J Snack Foods Corp.	Industrial
JBAK	J. Baker, Inc.	Industrial
MAYS	J. W. Mays, Inc.	Industrial
JBHT	J.B. Hunt Transport Services, Inc.	Transportation
JDEC	J.D. Edwards & Company	Computer
JTWOD	J2 Communications	Industrial
JKHY	Jack Henry & Associates, Inc.	Computer
JXVL	Jacksonville Bancorp, Inc.	Bank
JXSB	Jacksonville Savings Bank	Bank
JACO	Jaco Electronics, Inc.	Industrial
JCBS	Jacobson Stores Inc.	Industrial
JCOR	Jacor Communications, Inc.	Telecommunications
JAKK	JAKKS Pacific, Inc.	Industrial
JRBK	James River Bankshares, Inc.	Bank
JAMS	Jameson Inns, Inc.	Other Finance
JAMSP	Jameson Inns, Inc.	Other Finance
JANNF	Jannock Limited	Industrial
JAGI	Janus American Group, Inc.	Industrial
JAPNY	Japan Air Lines Company, Ltd.	Transportation
JASN	Jason Incorporated	Industrial
JVLN	Javelin Systems, Inc.	Industrial
JACCQ	Jayhawk Acceptance Corporation	Other Finance
JBOH	JB Oxford Holdings, Inc.	Other Finance
JDAS	JDA Software Group, Inc.	Industrial
JEAN	Jean Philippe Fragrances, Inc.	Industrial
JEFF	JeffBanks, Inc.	Bank
JEFFP	JeffBanks, Inc.	Bank
JSBA	Jefferson Savings Bancorp, Inc	Other Finance

Symbol	Company Name	Sector
JJSC	Jefferson Smurfit Corporation	Industrial
JFBC	Jeffersonville Bancorp	Bank
JNKN	Jenkon International, Inc.	Computer
JLNY	Jenna Lane, Inc.	Industrial
DELI	Jerry's Famous Deli, Inc.	Industrial
JTFX	JetFax, Inc.	Industrial
FORMF	JetForm Corporation	Computer
JEVC	Jevic Transportation, Inc.	Transportation
JCTCF	Jewett-Cameron Trading Company	Industrial
JHPC	JLM Couture Inc.	Industrial
JLMI	JLM Industries, Inc.	Industrial
JMAR	JMAR Technologies, Inc.	Industrial
JMCG	JMC Group, Inc.	Other Finance
JBSS	John B. Sanfilippo & Son, Inc.	Industrial
JWAIA	Johnson Worldwide Associates, Inc.	Industrial
JAII	Johnstown America Industries, Inc.	Industrial
JOIN	Jones Intercable, Inc.	Telecommunications
JOINA	Jones Intercable, Inc.	Telecommunications
JMED	Jones Pharma Incorporated	Industrial
JOSB	Jos. A. Bank Clothiers, Inc.	Industrial
JPMX	JPM Company (The)	Computer
JPSP	JPS Packaging Company	Industrial
JPST	JPS Textile Group, Inc.	Industrial
JUNI	Juniper Group, Inc.	Industrial
JUNO	Juno Lighting, Inc.	Industrial
FEET	Just For Feet, Inc.	Industrial
JSTN	Justin Industries, Inc.	Industrial
MENS	K & G Men's Center, Inc.	Industrial
KTWO	K2 Design, Inc.	Industrial
KRSC	Kaiser Ventures, Inc.	Industrial
KAMNA	Kaman Corporation	Industrial
KCLI	Kansas City Life Insurance Company	Insurance
KARR	Karrington Health, Inc.	Industrial
KINT	Karts International Incorporated	Industrial
KASP	Kasper A.S.L., Ltd.	Industrial
KAYE	Kaye Group Inc.	Insurance
KTIC	Kaynar Technologies Inc.	Industrial
KOGC	Kelley Oil & Gas Corporation	Industrial
KOGCP	Kelley Oil & Gas Corporation	Industrial
KELL	Kellstrom Industries, Inc.	Industrial
KELYA	Kelly Services, Inc.	Industrial
KELYB	Kelly Services, Inc.	Industrial

Symbol	Company Name	Sector
KMET	KEMET Corporation	Industrial
KTCO	Kenan Transport Company	Transportation
KNDL	Kendle International Inc.	Industrial
KWIC	Kennedy-Wilson, Inc.	Other Finance
KNSY	Kensey Nash Corporation	Industrial
KENT	Kent Financial Services, Inc.	Industrial
KNTK	Kentek Information Systems, Inc.	Computer
KESI	Kentucky Electric Steel, Inc.	Industrial
KERA	KeraVision, Inc.	Industrial
KEST	Kestrel Energy, Inc.	Industrial
KVCO	Kevco, Inc.	Industrial
KEQU	Kewaunee Scientific Corporation	Industrial
KTEC	Key Technology, Inc.	Industrial
KTCC	Key Tronic Corporation	Computer
KEYS	Keystone Automotive Industries, Inc.	Industrial
KSTN	Keystone Financial, Inc.	Other Finance
KBALB	Kimball International, Inc.	Industrial
KING	King Pharmaceuticals, Inc.	Industrial
KREN	Kings Road Entertainment, Inc.	Industrial
KINN	Kinnard Investments, Inc.	Other Finance
KILN	Kirlin Holding Corporation	Other Finance
KTTY	Kitty Hawk, Inc.	Transportation
KFBI	Klamath First Bancorp, Inc.	Other Finance
KLAC	KLA-Tencor Corporation	Industrial
KLLM	KLLM Transport Services, Inc.	Transportation
KMGB	KMG Chemicals, Inc.	Industrial
KNAP	Knape & Vogt Manufacturing Company	Industrial
KNGT	Knight Transportation, Inc.	Transportation
NITE	Knight/Trimark Group, Inc.	Other Finance
VLCCF	Knightsbridge Tankers, Limited	Transportation
KARE	Koala Corporation	Industrial
KOFX	Kofax Image Products, Inc.	Industrial
KMAG	Komag, Incorporated	Computer
KKRE	Koo Koo Roo Enterprises, Inc.	Industrial
KOPN	Kopin Corporation	Industrial
KOSP	Kos Pharmaceuticals, Inc.	Biotechnology
KOSS	Koss Corporation	Industrial
KRSL	Kreisler Manufacturing Corporation	Industrial
KRON	Kronos Incorporated	Computer
KSBK	KSB Bancorp, Inc.	Other Finance
KSWS	K-Swiss Inc.	Industrial
KTEL	K-tel International, Inc.	Industrial

Symbol	Company Name	Sector
KTIE	KTI, Inc.	Industrial
KTII	K-Tron International, Inc.	Industrial
KUAL	Kuala Healthcare Inc.	Industrial
KLIC	Kulicke and Soffa Industries, Inc.	Industrial
KVHI	KVH Industries, Inc.	Industrial
KYZN	Kyzen Corporation	Industrial
FSTR	L. B. Foster Company	Industrial
LABH	Lab Holdings Inc.	Other Finance
LABS	LabOne, Inc.	Industrial
LABZ	Laboratory Specialists of America, Inc.	Industrial
LCLD	Laclede Steel Company	Industrial
BOOT	LaCrosse Footwear, Inc.	Industrial
LADF	LADD Furniture, Inc.	Industrial
LDSH	Ladish Co., Inc.	Industrial
LUCK	Lady Luck Gaming Corporation	Industrial
LJPC	LaJolla Pharmaceutical Company	Biotechnology
LABN	Lake Ariel Bancorp, Inc.	Other Finance
LKFN	Lakeland Financial Corporation	Bank
LKFNP	Lakeland Financial Corporation	Bank
LAKE	Lakeland Industries, Inc.	Industrial
LVSB	Lakeview Financial Corp.	Other Finance
LRCX	Lam Research Corporation	Industrial
LAIX	Lamalie Associates, Inc.	Industrial
LAMR	Lamar Advertising Company	Industrial
LMAR	Lamaur Corporation	Industrial
LAMT	Laminating Technologies, Inc.	Industrial
LANC	Lancaster Colony Corporation	Industrial
LNCE	Lance, Inc.	Industrial
LANZ	Lancer Orthodontics, Inc.	Industrial
LAND	Landair Corporation	Transportation
LNDC	Landec Corporation	Industrial
LARK	Landmark Bancshares, Inc.	Bank
LDMK	Landmark Systems Corporation	Industrial
LDRY	Landry's Seafood Restaurants, Inc.	Industrial
LSTR	Landstar System, Inc.	Transportation
GAIT	Langer Biomechanics Group, Inc. (The)	Industrial
LNOPF	LanOptics Ltd.	Computer
LANV	LanVision Systems, Inc.	Computer
LARS	Larscom Incorporated	Industrial
LDII	Larson-Davis Incorporated	Industrial
LVDG	Las Vegas Discount Golf & Tennis, Inc.	Industrial
LVEND	Las Vegas Entertainment Network, Inc.	Industrial

Symbol	Company Name	Sector
LPWR	Laser Power Corporation	Industrial
LVCI	Laser Vision Centers, Inc.	Industrial
LPAC	Laser-Pacific Media Corporation	Industrial
LSCP	Laserscope	Industrial
LASE	LaserSight Incorporated	Industrial
AXSI	Lasertechnics, Inc.	Computer
LSON	Lason, Inc.	Industrial
LACI	Latin American Casinos Inc.	Industrial
LSCC	Lattice Semiconductor Corporation	Computer
LARL	Laurel Capital Group, Inc.	Other Finance
LSBX	Lawrence Savings Bank	Bank
LAWS	Lawson Products, Inc.	Industrial
LAYN	Layne Christensen Company	Industrial
LCAV	LCA-Vision Inc.	Industrial
LCCI	LCC International, Inc.	Telecommunications
LCSI	LCS Industries, Inc.	Computer
LEPI	Leading Edge Packaging, Inc.	Industrial
LWIN	Leap Wireless International, Inc.	Industrial
LTRE	Learning Tree International, Inc.	Industrial
LECE	LEC Technologies, Inc.	Computer
LECEP	LEC Technologies, Inc.	Computer
LECH	Lechters, Inc.	Industrial
LCRY	LeCroy Corporation	Industrial
LECT	LecTec Corporation	Industrial
LFED	Leeds Federal Bankshares, Inc.	Bank
LGCY	Legacy Software, Inc.	Computer
LGTO	Legato Systems, Inc.	Computer
LHSPF	Lernout & Hauspie Speech	Computer
LSCO	LESCO, Inc.	Industrial
LEBC	Letchworth Independent Bancshares Corp	Other Finance
LTCW	Let's Talk Cellular & Wireless, Inc.	Industrial
LKST	LeukoSite, Inc.	Industrial
LVLT	Level 3 Communications, Inc.	Telecommunications
LVEL	Level 8 Systems, Inc.	Computer
LEVL	Level One Communications, Incorporated	Industrial
LXMO	Lexington B & L Financial Corporation	Bank
LGAM	Lexington Global Asset Managers, Inc.	Other Finance
LEXI	Lexington Healthcare Group, Inc.	Industrial
LHSG	LHS Group, Inc.	Computer
LIBB	Liberty Bancorp, Incorporated	Other Finance
LIBHA	Liberty Homes, Inc.	Industrial
LIBHB	Liberty Homes, Inc.	Industrial

Symbol	Company Name	Sector
LDAKA	LIDAK Pharmaceuticals	Biotechnology
LFCO	Life Financial Corporation	Bank
LTEK	Life Technologies, Inc.	Industrial
LUSA	Life USA Holding, Inc.	Insurance
LIFC	LifeCell Corporation	Industrial
LCBM	Lifecore Biomedical, Inc.	Industrial
LIFE	Lifeline Systems, Inc.	Industrial
LQMD	LifeQuest Medical, Inc.	Industrial
LCUT	Lifetime Hoan Corporation	Industrial
LWAY	Lifeway Foods, Inc.	Industrial
LIFF	Lifschultz Industries, Inc.	Industrial
LGND	Ligand Pharmaceuticals Incorporated	Biotechnology
LTBG	Lightbridge, Inc.	Telecommunications
LPTHA	LightPath Technologies, Inc.	Industrial
LIHRY	Lihir Gold, Limited	Industrial
LNCC	LINC Capital, Inc.	Industrial
LNCR	Lincare Holdings, Inc.	Industrial
LECO	Lincoln Electric Holdings, Inc.	Industrial
SNAX	Lincoln Snacks Company	Industrial
LNDL	Lindal Cedar Homes, Inc.	Industrial
LIND	Lindberg Corporation	Industrial
LLTC	Linear Technology Corporation	Computer
LIPO	Liposome Company, Inc. (The)	Biotechnology
LIQB	Liqui-Box Corporation	Industrial
LIQWF	Liquidation World, Inc.	Industrial
LTCH	Litchfield Financial Corporation	Other Finance
LMTR	Lithia Motors, Inc.	Industrial
LFUS	Littelfuse, Inc.	Industrial
LFBI	Little Falls Bancorp, Inc.	Other Finance
LSVI	Little Switzerland, Inc.	Industrial
LSKI	Liuski International, Inc.	Industrial
LVNTF	Livent, Inc.	Industrial
LJLB	LJL Biosystems, Inc.	Industrial
ERICY	LM Ericsson Telephone Company	Telecommunications
LMIA	LMI Aerospace, Inc.	Industrial
LNET	LodgeNet Entertainment Corporation	Telecommunications
LOEH	Loehmann's Inc.	Industrial
LOGLF	Logal Educational Software & Systems, Ltd	Computer
RDHS	Logan's Roadhouse, Inc.	Industrial
LOGN	Logansport Financial Corp.	Other Finance
LOGC	Logic Devices Incorporated	Computer
LGTY	Logility, Inc.	Industrial

Symbol	Company Name	Sector
LOGIY	Logitech International S.A.	Industrial
LOJN	LoJack Corporation	Industrial
LONDY	London International Group plc	Industrial
LPGLY	London Pacific Group, Limited	Insurance
STAR	Lone Star Steakhouse & Saloon, Inc.	Industrial
LBFC	Long Beach Financial Corporation	Other Finance
LGCB	Long Island Commercial Bank	Bank
LORX	Loronix Information Systems, Inc.	Computer
LEIX	Lowrance Electronics, Inc.	Industrial
LXBK	LSB Bancshares, Inc.	Other Finance
LSBI	LSB Financial Corp.	Other Finance
LYTS	LSI Industries Inc.	Industrial
LTXX	LTX Corporation	Industrial
LUCY	Lucille Farms, Inc.	Industrial
LUCR	Lucor, Inc.	Industrial
LUFK	Lufkin Industries, Inc.	Industrial
LUMI	Lumisys Incorporated	Industrial
LUNR	Lunar Corporation	Industrial
LUND	Lund International Holdings, Inc.	Industrial
LOILY	Lundin Oil AB GDS	Industrial
LUTH	Luther Medical Products, Inc.	Industrial
LVMHY	LVMH Moet Hennessy Louis Vuitton	Industrial
LCOS	Lycos, Inc.	Computer
LYNX	Lynx Therapeutics, Inc.	Biotechnology
MHMY	M. H. Meyerson & Co., Inc.	Other Finance
MSCA	M.S. Carriers, Inc.	Transportation
MARC	M/A/R/C Inc.	Industrial
MACC	MACC Private Equities Inc.	Other Finance
MACE	Mace Security International, Inc.	Industrial
MKFCF	Mackenzie Financial Corporation	Other Finance
MKIE	Mackie Designs, Inc.	Industrial
MMBLF	MacMillan Bloedel Limited	Industrial
MCHM	MacroChem Corporation	Industrial
MACR	Macromedia, Inc.	Industrial
MXICY	Macronix International Co. Ltd	Computer
MVSN	Macrovision Corporation	Industrial
MTMS	Made2Manage Systems, Inc.	Computer
MADGF	Madge Networks, N. V.	Computer
MADB	Madison Bancshares Group, Ltd.	Other Finance
MDSN	Madison Gas and Electric Company	Industrial
MAFB	MAF Bancorp, Inc.	Other Finance
MAGN	Magainin Pharmaceuticals Inc.	Biotechnology

Symbol	Company Name	Sector
MAGSF	Magal Security Systems Ltd.	Industrial
MGICF	Magic Software Enterprises Ltd	Computer
OSKY	Mahaska Investment Company	Other Finance
MGNB	Mahoning National Bancorp, Inc	Other Finance
MAIN	Main Street and Main Incorporated	Industrial
MBNK	Main Street Bancorp, Inc.	Bank
MSBC	MainStreet Financial Corporation	Other Finance
MKTAY	Makita Corp.	Industrial
MLRC	Mallon Resources Corporation	Industrial
MCSX	Managed Care Solutions, Inc.	Industrial
MANA	Manatron, Inc.	Computer
MANC	Manchester Equipment Co., Inc.	Industrial
MANH	Manhattan Associates, Inc.	Computer
BGLSQ	Manhattan Bagel Company, Inc.	Industrial
MANS	Mansur Industries Inc.	Industrial
MANU	Manugistics Group, Inc.	Computer
MAPX	MAPICS Inc.	Computer
MAPS	MapInfo Corporation	Industrial
MFCV	Marathon Financial Corporation	Other Finance
MRCM	Marcam Solutions, Inc.	Computer
MGAS	Marcum Natural Gas Services, Inc.	Industrial
CGUL	Margate Industries, Inc.	Industrial
MRGO	Margo Caribe Inc.	Industrial
MARPS	Marine Petroleum Trust	Other Finance
MTLX	Marine Transport Corporation	Transportation
MARN	Marion Capital Holdings, Inc.	Bank
MRSA	Marisa Christina, Incorporated	Industrial
MCSI	Mark Solutions, Inc.	Industrial
MVII	Mark VII, Inc.	Transportation
MFAC	Market Facts, Inc.	Industrial
MRKF	Market Financial Corporation	Bank
MARG	Market Guide Inc.	Industrial
MSGI	Marketing Services Group, Inc.	Industrial
MBJI	Marks Bros. Jewelers, Inc.	Industrial
MWHX	MarkWest Hydrocarbon, Inc.	Industrial
MARQ	Marquette Medical Systems, Inc.	Industrial
MARSA	Marsh Supermarkets, Inc.	Industrial
MARSB	Marsh Supermarkets, Inc.	Industrial
MRIS	Marshall & Ilsley Corporation	Other Finance
MATK	Martek Biosciences Corporation	Industrial
MRTN	Marten Transport, Ltd.	Transportation
MRCF	Martin Color-Fi, Inc.	Industrial

Symbol	Company Name	Sector
MTIN	Martin Industries, Inc.	Industrial
MSDX	Mason-Dixon Bancshares, Inc.	Bank
MSDXO	Mason-Dixon Bancshares, Inc.	Bank
MSDXP	Mason-Dixon Bancshares, Inc.	Bank
MASB	MASSBANK Corp.	Other Finance
MAST	Mastech Corporation	Computer
MAGR	Master Graphics, Inc.	Industrial
MATVY	Matav-Cable Systems Media Ltd.	Industrial
MATE	Matewan BancShares, Inc.	Other Finance
MATEP	Matewan BancShares, Inc.	Other Finance
MATH	MathSoft, Inc.	Computer
MATR	Matria Healthcare, Inc	Industrial
NMPS	Matritech, Inc.	Industrial
MTXC	Matrix Capital Corporation	Other Finance
MATX	Matrix Pharmaceutical, Inc.	Industrial
MTRX	Matrix Service Company	Industrial
MATW	Matthews International Corporation	Industrial
MATT	Matthews Studio Equipment Group	Industrial
MTSN	Mattson Technology, Inc.	Industrial
MAVK	Maverick Tube Corporation	Industrial
MAXE	Max & Erma's Restaurants, Inc.	Industrial
MAXC	Maxco, Inc.	Industrial
MAXF	Maxcor Financial Group Inc.	Other Finance
MAXI	Maxicare Health Plans, Inc.	Insurance
MXIM	Maxim Integrated Products, Inc.	Industrial
MAXS	Maxwell Shoe Company Inc.	Industrial
MXWL	Maxwell Technologies, Inc.	Industrial
MFLR	Mayflower Co-operative Bank	Bank
MOIL	Maynard Oil Company	Industrial
MAZL	Mazel Stores, Inc.	Industrial
MBLF	MBLA Financial Corporation	Other Finance
MCCL	McClain Industries, Inc.	Industrial
MCCRK	McCormick & Company, Incorporated	Industrial
MGRC	McGrath RentCorp	Industrial
MCICP	MCI WORLDCOM, Inc.	Telecommunications
WCOM	MCI WORLDCOM, Inc.	Telecommunications
MCLD	McLeodUSA Incorporated	Telecommunications
MOXY	McMoRan Oil & Gas Co.	Industrial
MDCAF	MDC Communications Corporation	Telecommunications
MDSIF	MDSI Mobile Data Solutions, Inc.	Computer
MEAD	Meade Instruments Corp.	Industrial
MVCO	Meadow Valley Corporation	Industrial

Symbol	Company Name	Sector
MECH	MECH Financial Inc.	Bank
MDII	Mechanical Dynamics, Inc.	Industrial
MECK	Mecklermedia Corporation	Industrial
MECN	Mecon, Inc.	Computer
MWDS	Med/Waste, Inc.	Industrial
TAXI	Medallion Financial Corp.	Other Finance
MEDM	MedAmicus, Inc.	Industrial
MEDA	Medaphis Corporation	Computer
MDXR	Medar, Inc.	Industrial
MEDX	Medarex, Inc.	Industrial
MCAR	MedCare Technologies, Inc.	Industrial
MEDC	Med-Design Corporation (The)	Industrial
MDERF	Med-Emerg International, Inc.	Industrial
MEDRF	medEra Life Science Corporation	Industrial
MDBK	Medford Bancorp, Inc.	Other Finance
MDEA	Media 100 Inc.	Computer
ARTS	Media Arts Group, Inc.	Industrial
MDLK	Medialink Worldwide Incorporated	Telecommunications
MDCI	Medical Action Industries Inc.	Industrial
MAII	Medical Alliance, Inc.	Industrial
MDCL	Medical Control, Inc.	Insurance
MEDY	Medical Dynamics, Inc.	Industrial
MGCC	Medical Graphics Corporation	Industrial
MIOA	Medical Industries of America Inc.	Industrial
MMGR	Medical Manager Corporation	Computer
MRII	Medical Resources, Inc.	Industrial
MSSI	Medical Science Systems, Inc.	Industrial
MDKI	Medicore, Inc.	Industrial
MEDJ	Medi-Ject Corporation	Industrial
MEDI	Medimmune, Inc.	Biotechnology
MDMD	Medirisk, Inc.	Industrial
MDSLF	Medis El Ltd.	Industrial
MEDW	MEDIWARE Information Systems, Inc.	Computer
MEDP	MedPlus, Inc.	Industrial
MEDQ	MedQuist, Inc.	Industrial
MEDS	Medstone International Inc.	Industrial
MDWV	Medwave, Inc.	Industrial
MBIO	Megabios Corp.	Industrial
MEGO	Mego Financial Corp.	Other Finance
MMGC	Mego Mortgage Corporation	Other Finance
MELI	Melita International Corporation	Industrial
MBRS	MemberWorks, Inc.	Industrial

Symbol	Company Name	Sector
MEMCF	Memco Software Limited	Computer
MENJ	Menley & James, Inc.	Industrial
SUIT	Men's Wearhouse, Inc. (The)	Industrial
MNTR	Mentor Corporation	Industrial
MENT	Mentor Graphics Corporation	Computer
MTSLF	MER Telemanagement Solutions Ltd.	Industrial
MRBK	Mercantile Bankshares Corporation	Other Finance
MERCS	Mercer International Inc.	Other Finance
MBIA	Merchants Bancorp, Inc.	Bank
MBVT	Merchants Bancshares, Inc.	Other Finance
MBNY	Merchants New York Bancorp, Inc.	Bank
MRCY	Mercury Computer Systems	Computer
MERQ	Mercury Interactive Corporation	Industrial
MWSI	Mercury Waste Solutions, Inc.	Industrial
MRGE	Merge Technologies Inc.	Industrial
MDCD	Meridian Data, Inc.	Computer
KITS	Meridian Diagnostics, Inc.	Industrial
MIGI	Meridian Insurance Group, Inc.	Insurance
MTEC	Meridian Medical Technologies Inc.	Industrial
MPTBS	Meridian Point Realty Trust 83	Other Finance
MSEL	Merisel, Inc.	Industrial
MRET	Merit Holding Corporation	Other Finance
MMSI	Merit Medical Systems, Inc.	Industrial
MERX	Merix Corporation	Computer
MRLL	Merrill Corporation	Industrial
MERB	Merrill Merchants Bancshares, Inc.	Other Finance
MRYP	Merry Land Properties, Inc.	Other Finance
MESA	Mesa Air Group, Inc.	Transportation
MLAB	Mesa Laboratories, Inc.	Industrial
MAIR	Mesaba Holdings, Inc.	Transportation
METG	META Group, Inc.	Industrial
MCRE	MetaCreations Corporation	Computer
MTLM	Metal Management, Inc.	Computer
MTLC	Metalclad Corporation	Industrial
METLF	Metallica Resources Inc.	Industrial
MMWW	Metamor Worldwide Inc.	Industrial
META	Metatec Corporation	Industrial
METR	Meteor Industries, Inc.	Industrial
MEOHF	Methanex Corporation	Industrial
METHA	Methode Electronics, Inc.	Industrial
METHB	Methode Electronics, Inc.	Industrial
MTRA	Metra Biosystems, Inc.	Industrial

Symbol	Company Name	Sector
MCOM	Metricom, Inc.	Industrial
MTRS	Metris Companies Inc.	Other Finance
MGMA	Metro Global Media, Inc.	Industrial
MISI	Metro Information Services, Inc.	Computer
MTNT	Metro Networks, Inc.	Telecommunications
MTON	Metro One Telecommunications, Inc.	Industrial
METB	MetroBanCorp	Bank
MCLL	Metrocall, Inc.	Telecommunications
MTLG	Metrologic Instruments, Inc.	Computer
MFNX	Metromedia Fiber Network, Inc.	Telecommunications
METNF	MetroNet Communications Corp.	Telecommunications
METF	Metropolitan Financial Corp.	Bank
METFP	Metropolitan Financial Corp.	Bank
MDPA	Metropolitan Health Networks, Inc.	Industrial
MTRO	Metro-Tel Corp.	Industrial
MTRN	Metrotrans Corporation	Industrial
MTWKF	Metrowerks Corporation	Computer
MWBX	MetroWest Bank	Bank
METZ	Metzler Group, Inc. (The)	Industrial
MFBC	MFB Corp.	Other Finance
MXBIF	MFC Bancorp Ltd.	Other Finance
MFRI	MFRI, Inc.	Industrial
MGCX	MGC Communications, Inc.	Telecommunications
MOGN	MGI PHARMA, Inc.	Industrial
MCSC	Miami Computer Supply Corporation	Industrial
SUBS	Miami Subs Corporation	Industrial
MIKL	Michael Foods, Inc.	Industrial
MIKE	Michaels Stores, Inc.	Industrial
MFCB	Michigan Financial Corporation	Bank
MCRL	Micrel, Incorporated	Computer
MICN	Micrion Corporation	Industrial
MCTI	Micro Component Technology, Inc.	Industrial
MIFGY	Micro Focus Group PLC	Computer
MLIN	Micro Linear Corporation	Industrial
MTIX	Micro Therapeutics, Inc.	Industrial
MWHS	Micro Warehouse, Inc.	Industrial
MICA	MicroAge, Inc.	Industrial
MICTF	Microcell Telecommunications Inc.	Telecommunications
MCHP	Microchip Technology Incorporated	Industrial
MCDE	Microcide Pharmaceuticals, Inc.	Industrial
MCDY	Microdyne Corporation	Computer
MICG	Microfield Graphics, Inc.	Industrial

Symbol	Company Name	Sector
MFIC	Microfluidics International Corporation	Industrial
MCFR	Microframe, Inc.	Industrial
MGXI	Micrografx, Inc.	Computer
MINT	Micro-Integration Corp.	Industrial
MLOG	Microlog Corporation	Industrial
MUSE	Micromuse, Inc.	Computer
MUEI	Micron Electronics, Inc.	Computer
NOIZ	Micronetics Wireless, Inc.	Industrial
MCRS	MICROS Systems, Inc.	Computer
MTMC	Micros to Mainframes, Inc.	Industrial
MSCC	Microsemi Corporation	Industrial
MSFT	Microsoft Corporation	Computer
MSFTP	Microsoft Corporation	Computer
MSTR	Microstrategy Incorporated	Computer
MCTL	MicroTel International, Inc.	Industrial
MTST	Microtest, Inc.	Industrial
MTSI	MicroTouch Systems, Inc.	Computer
MVIS	Microvision, Inc.	Computer
MWAR	Microware Systems Corporation	Computer
MFCO	Microwave Filter Company, Inc.	Industrial
MPDI	Microwave Power Devices, Inc.	Industrial
MABG	Mid-Atlantic Community BankGroup, Inc.	Bank
MCBN	Mid-Coast Bancorp, Inc.	Other Finance
MBOC	Middle Bay Oil Company, Inc.	Industrial
MIDD	Middleby Corporation (The)	Industrial
MSEX	Middlesex Water Company	Industrial
MIFC	Mid-Iowa Financial Corp.	Industrial
MDST	Mid-State Bancshares	Other Finance
MDWY	Midway Airlines Corporation	Transportation
MBHI	Midwest Banc Holdings, Inc.	Bank
MWBI	Midwest Bancshares, Inc.	Bank
MWGP	Midwest Grain Products, Inc.	Industrial
MIKN	Mikohn Gaming Corporation	Industrial
MIKR	Mikron Instrument Company, Inc.	Industrial
MILM	Millennium Electronics, Inc.	Industrial
MLNM	Millennium Pharmaceuticals, Inc.	Industrial
MSPT	Millennium Sports Management, Inc.	Industrial
MBSI	Miller Building Systems, Inc.	Industrial
MEXP	Miller Exploration Company	Industrial
MICCF	Millicom International Cellular S.A.	Telecommunications
MFFC	Milton Federal Financial Corporation	Other Finance
MILT	Miltope Group, Inc.	Computer

Symbol	Company Name	Sector
MIMS	MIM Corporation	Industrial
MSPG	MindSpring Enterprises, Inc.	Industrial
MNES	Mine Safety Appliances Company	Industrial
MNMD	MiniMed Inc.	Industrial
MSIX	Mining Services International Corporation	Industrial
MBRW	Minnesota Brewing Company	Industrial
MNTX	Minntech Corporation	Industrial
MNRCY	Minorco	Industrial
MMAN	Minuteman International Inc.	Industrial
MIPS	MIPS Technology, Inc.	Computer
MAENF	Miramar Mining Corporation	Industrial
MRVT	Miravant Medical Technologies	Biotechnology
MSON	MISONIX, Inc.	Industrial
MVBI	Mississippi Valley Bancshares, Inc.	Other Finance
MVBIP	Mississippi Valley Bancshares, Inc.	Other Finance
MGLCF	Misty Mountain Gold, Limited	Industrial
MIND	Mitcham Industries, Inc.	Industrial
MBSP	Mitchell Bancorp, Inc.	Bank
MITK	Mitek Systems, Inc.	Computer
MITSY	Mitsui & Company, Ltd.	Industrial
MITY	Mity-Lite, Inc.	Industrial
MKAU	MK Gold Company	Industrial
MLCH	MLC Holdings, Inc.	Other Finance
MMCN	MMC Networks, Inc.	Computer
MNBB	MNB Bancshares Inc.	Bank
MAME	Mobile America Corporation	Insurance
MINI	Mobile Mini, Inc.	Industrial
MOBI	Mobius Management Systems, Inc.	Computer
MODA	ModaCAD, Inc.	Computer
MOCO	Modern Controls, Inc.	Industrial
MODM	Modern Medical Modalities Corporation	Industrial
MTGNY	Modern Times Group MTG AB	Telecommunications
MODI	Modine Manufacturing Company	Industrial
MODT	Modtech, Inc.	Industrial
MDCC	Molecular Devices Corporation	Industrial
MOLX	Molex Incorporated	Industrial
MOLXA	Molex Incorporated	Industrial
MCCO	Monaco Coach Corporation	Industrial
MONFA	Monaco Finance, Inc.	Other Finance
MAHI	Monarch Avalon, Inc.	Industrial
MCRI	Monarch Casino & Resort, Inc.	Industrial
MDDS	Monarch Dental Corporation	Industrial

Symbol	Company Name	Sector
MONM	Monmouth Capital Corporation	Other Finance
MNRTA	Monmouth Real Estate Investment Corp	Other Finance
MNOC	Monocacy Bancshares, Inc.	Bank
MNRO	Monro Muffler Brake, Inc.	Industrial
MBBC	Monterey Bay Bancorp, Inc.	Other Finance
PSTA	Monterey Pasta Company	Industrial
MONT	Montgomery Financial Corporation	Other Finance
MORP	Moore Products Co.	Industrial
MHCO	Moore-Handley, Inc.	Industrial
MFUN	Morgan FunShares, Inc.	Other Finance
MRRW	Morrow Snowboards, Inc.	Industrial
MGRP	Morton Industrial Group, Inc.	Industrial
MOSX	Mosaix, Inc.	Industrial
MWRK	Mothers Work, Inc.	Industrial
MOTO	Moto Photo, Inc.	Industrial
CRGO	Motor Cargo Industries, Inc.	Transportation
MOTR	Motor Club of America	Insurance
MPAA	Motorcar Parts & Accessories, Inc.	Industrial
MVAC	MotorVac Technologies, Inc.	Industrial
MPVIF	Mountain Province Mining, Inc. New	Industrial
MOVA	Movado Group Inc.	Industrial
MOVI	Movie Gallery, Inc.	Industrial
MOFN	MovieFone, Inc.	Telecommunications
MOYC	Moyco Technologies, Inc.	Industrial
MPML	MPM Technologies, Inc.	Industrial
MPSI	MPSI Systems, Inc.	Industrial
MPWG	MPW Industrial Services Group, Inc.	Industrial
MRSIQ	MRS Technology, Inc.	Industrial
MRVC	MRV Communications, Inc.	Industrial
MSBF	MSB Financial, Inc.	Other Finance
FLSHF	M-Systems Flash Disk Pioneers Ltd.	Industrial
MTIC	MTI Technology Corporation	Industrial
MNTG	MTR Gaming Group, Inc.	Industrial
MTSC	MTS Systems Corporation	Industrial
LABL	Multi-Color Corporation	Industrial
MMAC	MultiMedia Access Corporation	Industrial
MGAM	Multimedia Games, Inc.	Industrial
MZON	Multiple Zones International, Inc.	Industrial
MSTGC	Mustang Software, Inc.	Computer
MSBK	Mutual Savings Bank, f.s.b., A Stock Co	Bank
MVSI	MVSI, Inc.	Industrial
MWAV	M-WAVE, Inc.	Industrial

Symbol	Company Name	Sector
MYCO	Mycogen Corporation	Industrial
MYLX	Mylex Corporation	Computer
MYGN	Myriad Genetics, Inc.	Industrial
MYSW	MySoftware Company	Computer
MYST	Mystic Financial, Inc.	Bank
NTKI	N2K Inc.	Computer
NABC	NAB Asset Corporation	Bank
NABI	NABI	Biotechnology
NATL	NAI Technologies, Inc.	Computer
NAMC	NAM Corporation	Industrial
NTAIF	Nam Tai Electronics, Inc.	Computer
NMCOF	Namibian Minerals Corporation	Industrial
NGEN	Nanogen, Inc.	Industrial
NANO	Nanometrics Incorporated	Industrial
NANX	Nanophase Technologies Corporation	Industrial
NSSC	Napco Security Systems, Inc.	Industrial
NPRO	NaPro BioTherapeutics, Inc.	Industrial
NARA	Nara Bank, National Association	Bank
NAFC	Nash-Finch Company	Industrial
NSTK	Nastech Pharmaceutical Company, Inc.	Industrial
NATH	Nathan's Famous, Inc.	Industrial
NAFI	National Auto Finance Company, Inc.	Other Finance
NBAK	National Bancorp of Alaska, Inc.	Other Finance
NCBM	National City Bancorporation	Other Finance
NCBE	National City Bancshares, Inc.	Bank
NCBEP	National City Bancshares, Inc.	Bank
NCBC	National Commerce Bancorporation	Other Finance
NLCS	National Computer Systems, Inc.	Computer
NADX	National Dentex Corporation	Industrial
NEGX	National Energy Group, Inc.	Industrial
NESC	National Environmental Service Co.	Industrial
NHMCF	National Healthcare Manufacturing Corp	Industrial
NHCI	National Home Centers, Inc.	Industrial
NHHC	National Home Health Care Corp.	Industrial
NIRTS	National Income Realty Trust	Other Finance
NAIG	National Information Group	Insurance
NATI	National Instruments Corporation	Industrial
NMFS	National Medical Financial Services Corp	Computer
MBLA	National Mercantile Bancorp	Other Finance
NPBC	National Penn Bancshares, Inc.	Other Finance
NPBCP	National Penn Bancshares, Inc.	Other Finance
NRVH	National R.V. Holdings, Inc.	Industrial

Symbol	Company Name	Sector
NRMI	National Record Mart, Inc.	Industrial
NRID	National Registry Inc. (The)	Computer
NRCI	National Research Corporation	Industrial
NSEC	National Security Group, Inc.	Insurance
NTSC	National Technical Systems, Inc.	Industrial
TEAM	National TechTeam, Inc.	Computer
NVAL	National Vision Associates, Ltd.	Industrial
NWLIA	National Western Life Insurance Company	Insurance
NWIR	National Wireless Holdings Inc.	Industrial
NTOL	Natrol, Inc.	Biotechnology
NAII	Natural Alternatives International, Inc.	Industrial
NHTCC	Natural Health Trends Corp.	Industrial
NMSS	Natural MicroSystems Corporation	Industrial
NATW	Natural Wonders, Inc.	Industrial
NATR	Nature's Sunshine Products, Inc.	Industrial
NAUT	Nautica Enterprises, Inc.	Industrial
NAVR	Navarre Corporation	Industrial
NVDC	NAVIDEC, Inc.	Computer
FLYR	Navigant International, Inc.	Industrial
NAVG	Navigators Group, Inc. (The)	Insurance
NBTB	NBT Bancorp Inc.	Bank
NBTY	NBTY, Inc.	Industrial
NCOG	NCO Group, Inc.	Industrial
NCSS	NCS HealthCare, Inc.	Industrial
NCTI	NCT Group, Inc.	Industrial
NIPNY	NEC Corporation	Computer
NEMA	Nematron Corporation	Industrial
NEOG	Neogen Corporation	Industrial
NMGC	NeoMagic Corporation	Industrial
NEOM	NeoMedia Technologies, Inc.	Industrial
NPTH	NeoPath, Inc.	Computer
NEOP	Neoprobe Corporation	Industrial
NERX	NeoRx Corporation	Biotechnology
NTEC	Neose Technologies, Inc.	Industrial
NEOT	NeoTherapeutics, Inc.	Industrial
NWRE	Neoware Systems Inc.	Industrial
NERAY	Nera AS	Telecommunications
NTBK	Net.B@nk, Inc.	Other Finance
NECSY	Netcom AB ADS	Telecommunications
NETE	Netegrity, Inc.	Industrial
NETG	NetGravity, Inc.	Computer
NETM	NetManage, Inc.	Computer

Symbol	Company Name	Sector
NTPA	Netopia, Inc.	Industrial
NTRX	Netrix Corporation	Industrial
NSCP	Netscape Communications Corporation	Computer
NTST	Netsmart Technologies, Inc.	Industrial
NSPK	NetSpeak Corporation	Computer
NETT	Netter Digital Entertainment, Inc.	Industrial
NTAP	Network Appliance, Inc.	Industrial
NETA	Network Associates, Inc.	Computer
NCDI	Network Computing Devices, Inc.	Computer
TNCX	Network Connection, Inc. (The)	Computer
NETS	Network Event Theater, Inc.	Telecommunications
NPIX	Network Peripherals, Inc.	Computer
NWSS	Network Six, Inc.	Computer
NSOL	Network Solutions, Inc.	Computer
NESI	Network Systems International, Inc.	Computer
NETN	Networks North Inc.	Telecommunications
NBIX	Neurocrine Biosciences, Inc.	Industrial
NRGN	Neurogen Corporation	Biotechnology
NSIX	Neuromedical Systems, Inc.	Industrial
NTRL	Neutral Posture Ergonomics, Inc.	Industrial
NVST	NevStar Gaming Corporation	Industrial
NBSC	New Brunswick Scientific Co., Inc.	Industrial
NCEN	New Century Financial Corp.	Other Finance
DDDDF	New Dimension Software Ltd.	Computer
NECB	New England Community Bancorp, Inc.	Other Finance
NEON	New Era Networks, Inc.	Industrial
NOOF	New Frontier Media, Inc.	Industrial
NHTB	New Hampshire Thrift Bancshares, Inc.	Other Finance
KIDQ	New Horizon Kids Quest, Inc.	Industrial
NEWH	New Horizons Worldwide, Inc.	Industrial
NWCI	New World Coffee & Bagels, Inc	Industrial
NYBS	New York Bagel Enterprises, Inc.	Industrial
NYHC	New York Health Care, Inc.	Industrial
NWCA	NewCare Health Corporation	Industrial
NWCM	NEWCOM, Inc.	Industrial
NEWC	Newcor, Inc.	Industrial
NHCH	Newmark Homes Corp.	Industrial
NMSB	NewMil Bancorp, Inc.	Other Finance
NEWP	Newport Corporation	Industrial
NCOME	News Communications, Inc.	Industrial
NEWZ	NewsEDGE Corporation	Computer
NSBC	NewSouth Bancorp, Inc.	Bank

Symbol	Company Name	Sector
NWSTC	NewStar Media Inc.	Industrial
NERIF	Newstar Resources, Inc.	Industrial
NEXR	Nexar Technologies, Inc.	Computer
NXTR	NeXstar Pharmaceuticals, Inc.	Industrial
NXTL	Nextel Communications, Inc.	Telecommunications
NEXT	NextHealth, Inc.	Industrial
NXLK	NEXTLINK Communications, Inc.	Telecommunications
NXUSF	Nexus Telecommunications Systems, Ltd	Telecommunications
NHAN	NHancement Technologies Inc.	Computer
NBCP	Niagara Bancorp, Inc.	Bank
NIAG	Niagara Corporation	Industrial
NICEY	NICE-Systems Limited	Computer
NICKF	Nicholas Financial, Inc.	Other Finance
NRES	Nichols Research Corporation	Industrial
NSATF	NII Norsat International Inc.	Computer
NSANY	Nissan Motor Co., Ltd.	Industrial
NICH	Nitches, Inc.	Industrial
NMTI	Nitinol Medical Technologies, Inc.	Industrial
NMBT	NMBT CORP	Bank
NNBR	NN Ball & Roller, Inc.	Industrial
NEDI	Nobel Education Dynamics, Inc.	Industrial
NOBLF	Nobel Insurance Limited	Insurance
NOBH	Nobility Homes, Inc.	Industrial
NOEL	Noel Group, Inc.	Industrial
NOGAF	Noga Electro-Mechanical Industries Ltd	Industrial
NOLD	Noland Company	Industrial
NKID	Noodle Kidoodle, Inc.	Industrial
NRTI	Nooney Realty Trust, Inc.	Other Finance
NORPF	Nord Pacific Limited	Industrial
NDSN	Nordson Corporation	Industrial
NOBE	Nordstrom, Inc.	Industrial
NRRD	Norstan, Inc.	Industrial
NSYS	Nortech Systems Incorporated	Industrial
NASI	North American Scientific, Inc.	Industrial
NATK	North American Technologies Group, Inc.	Industrial
NBSI	North Bancshares, Inc.	Bank
FFFD	North Central Bancshares, Inc.	Other Finance
NCEB	North Coast Energy, Inc.	Industrial
NCBH	North County Bancorp	Bank
NEIC	North East Insurance Company	Insurance
NPSI	North Pittsburgh Systems, Inc.	Telecommunications
NOVB	North Valley Bancorp	Other Finance

Symbol	Company Name	Sector
GSMI	Northeast Digital Networks, Inc.	Telecommunications
NEIB	Northeast Indiana Bancorp, Inc.	Bank
NOPT	NorthEast Optic Network, Inc.	Telecommunications
NBOC	Northern Bank of Commerce	Bank
NSFC	Northern States Financial Corporation	Other Finance
NTRS	Northern Trust Corporation	Other Finance
NFLD	Northfield Laboratories, Inc.	Industrial
CBRYA	Northland Cranberries, Inc.	Industrial
NRIM	Northrim Bank	Bank
NSCF	Northstar Computer Forms, Inc.	Industrial
NWFI	Northway Financial Inc.	Bank
NWAC	Northwest Airlines Corporation	Transportation
NWSB	Northwest Bancorp, Inc.	Bank
NWEQ	Northwest Equity Corp.	Bank
NWNG	Northwest Natural Gas Company	Industrial
NWPX	Northwest Pipe Company	Industrial
NWSW	Northwestern Steel and Wire Company	Industrial
NORT	Norton Drilling Services, Inc.	Industrial
NRTY	Norton McNaughton, Inc.	Industrial
NWFL	Norwood Financial Corp.	Bank
NPPI	Norwood Promotional Products, Inc.	Industrial
NTFY	Notify Corporation	Industrial
NCES	NovaCare Employee Services, Inc.	Industrial
NVDM	Novadigm, Inc.	Computer
TONSF	Novamerican Steel, Inc.	Industrial
NMTX	Novametrix Medical Systems Inc.	Industrial
NGPSF	NovAtel Inc.	Industrial
NVLDF	Novel Denim Holdings Limited	Industrial
NOVL	Novell, Inc.	Computer
NVLS	Novellus Systems, Inc.	Industrial
NOVN	Noven Pharmaceuticals, Inc.	Industrial
NOVI	Novitron International, Inc.	Industrial
NOVT	Novoste Corporation	Industrial
NPCI	NPC International, Inc.	Industrial
NPSP	NPS Pharmaceuticals, Inc.	Biotechnology
NSLB	NS&L Bancorp, Inc.	Bank
NSCC	NSC Corporation	Industrial
NSDB	NSD Bancorp, Inc.	Bank
NSSY	NSS Bancorp, Inc.	Bank
NTLI	NTL Incorporated	Telecommunications
NUHC	Nu Horizons Electronics Corp.	Industrial
NUCO	NuCo2 Inc.	Industrial

Symbol	Company Name	Sector
NINE	Number Nine Visual Technology Corporation	Industrial
NUMD	NuMED Home Health Care, Inc.	Industrial
NMRX	Numerex Corp.	Industrial
NURTF	Nur Macroprinters, Ltd	Industrial
NTMG	Nutmeg Federal Savings & Loan Association	Bank
NUTR	Nutraceutical International Corporation	Industrial
NMPC	NutraMax Products, Inc.	Industrial
NFLI	Nutrition For Life International, Inc.	Industrial
NMSCA	Nutrition Management Services Company	Industrial
NMED	Nutrition Medical, Inc.	Industrial
WAVE	NuWave Technologies, Inc.	Industrial
NVUE	nVIEW Corporation	Industrial
NVIC	N-Viro International Corporation	Industrial
NVSN	n-Vision, Inc.	Industrial
NYER	Nyer Medical Group, Inc.	Industrial
NYMXF	Nymox Pharmaceutical Corporation	Industrial
OICO	O. I. Corporation	Industrial
OCIS	Oacis Healthcare Holdings Corporation	Computer
OAKF	Oak Hill Financial, Inc.	Other Finance
OAKT	Oak Technology, Inc.	Industrial
OAOT	OAO Technology Solutions, Inc.	Computer
OBIE	Obie Media Corporation	Industrial
ODIS	Object Design, Inc.	Computer
OCOM	Objective Communications, Inc.	Industrial
OSII	Objective Systems Integrators, Inc.	Computer
OBJS	ObjectShare Inc	Industrial
OSFT	ObjectSoft Corporation	Industrial
OCAL	Ocal, Inc.	Industrial
OHRI	Occupational Health & Rehabilitation Inc.	Industrial
OBCI	Ocean Bio-Chem, Inc.	Industrial
OCFC	Ocean Financial Corp.	Bank
CHUX	O'Charley's Inc.	Industrial
OCLR	Ocular Sciences, Inc.	Industrial
ODETA	Odetics, Inc.	Industrial
ODETB	Odetics, Inc.	Industrial
ODSI	ODS Networks, Inc.	Computer
ODWA	Odwalla, Inc.	Industrial
OFLDF	Officeland Inc.	Industrial
OLOG	Offshore Logistics, Inc.	Transportation
OGLE	Oglebay Norton Company	Transportation
OCAS	Ohio Casualty Corporation	Insurance
OVBC	Ohio Valley Banc Corp.	Other Finance

Symbol	Company Name	Sector
OHSL	OHSL Financial Corp.	Bank
OLGR	Oilgear Company (The)	Industrial
OVONE	OIS Optical Imaging Systems, Inc.	Industrial
ODFL	Old Dominion Freight Line, Inc.	Transportation
OGGI	Old Guard Group, Inc.	Insurance
OKEN	Old Kent Financial Corporation	Other Finance
OLDB	Old National Bancorp	Other Finance
OSBC	Old Second Bancorp, Inc.	Other Finance
OLCMF	Olicom A/S	Industrial
OLSAY	OLS Asia Holdings, Limited	Industrial
NATS	Olympic Cascade Financial Corporation	Other Finance
ZEUS	Olympic Steel, Inc.	Industrial
OMEF	Omega Financial Corporation	Bank
OHSI	Omega Health Systems, Inc.	Industrial
ORTH	Omega Orthodontics, Inc.	Industrial
OMGA	Omega Research	Computer
OWWI	Omega Worldwide, Inc.	Other Finance
OMNI	OMNI Energy Services Corp.	Industrial
OUSA	Omni U.S.A., Inc.	Industrial
XMIT	OmniAmerica, Inc.	Industrial
OMPT	Omnipoint Corporation	Telecommunications
OMQP	OmniQuip International, Inc.	Industrial
OMTL	Omtool, Ltd.	Computer
ASGN	On Assignment, Inc.	Industrial
ONCO	On Command Corporation	Computer
ONST	On Stage Entertainment, Inc.	Industrial
ONTC	ON Technology Corporation	Computer
ONPR	One Price Clothing Stores, Inc.	Industrial
OWLD	OneWorld Systems Inc.	Industrial
ONHN	OnHealth Network Company	Industrial
WEBB	Online System Services, Inc.	Computer
ONPT	On-Point Technology Systems, Inc.	Industrial
ONSL	ONSALE, Inc.	Industrial
ONSS	On-Site Sourcing, Inc.	Industrial
ONDI	Ontrack Data International, Inc.	Computer
ONTR	Ontro, Inc.	Industrial
ONYX	Onyx Acceptance Corporation	Other Finance
ONXX	ONYX Pharmaceuticals, Inc.	Biotechnology
OMKT	Open Market, Inc.	Computer
PLAN	Open Plan Systems, Inc.	Industrial
OTEXF	Open Text Corporation	Computer
OPEN	OpenROUTE Networks, Inc.	Computer

Symbol	Company Name	Sector
OPHD	Ophidian Pharmaceuticals, Inc.	Industrial
ORCI	Opinion Research Corporation	Industrial
OPTS	Opta Food Ingredients, Inc.	Industrial
OPTT	Optek Technology, Inc.	Industrial
OPTC	Optelecom, Inc.	Industrial
OPTI	OPTi Inc.	Industrial
OCCF	Optical Cable Corporation	Industrial
OCLI	Optical Coating Laboratory, Inc.	Industrial
OPSC	Optical Security Group, Inc.	Industrial
OPSI	Optical Sensors Incorporated	Industrial
OPTK	Optika Imaging Systems, Inc.	Computer
OPMRF	Optimal Robotics Corp.	Computer
OPTN	OPTION CARE, Inc.	Industrial
OPTLF	OptiSystems Solutions, Ltd.	Computer
ORCL	Oracle Corporation	Computer
OLAB	Oralabs Holding Corp.	Industrial
OGNB	Orange National Bancorp	Bank
ORNGY	Orange, plc	Telecommunications
ORVX	OraVax, Inc.	Biotechnology
ORBT	Orbit International Corporation	Industrial
ORFR	ORBIT/FR, Inc.	Industrial
ORBKF	Orbotech Ltd.	Computer
OCAD	OrCAD, Inc.	Industrial
ORCTF	Orckit Communications, Limited	Industrial
OTFC	Oregon Trail Financial Corp.	Bank
ORLY	O'Reilly Automotive, Inc.	Industrial
OFPI	Organic Food Products, Inc.	Industrial
OROA	OroAmerica, Inc.	Industrial
ORPH	Orphan Medical, Inc.	Industrial
ORTC	Ortec International, Inc.	Industrial
ORTL	Ortel Corporation	Industrial
ORAL	OrthAlliance, Inc.	Industrial
OTIX	Orthodontix, Inc.	Industrial
OFIXF	Orthofix International N.V.	Industrial
OLGC	Orthologic Corp.	Industrial
ORYX	Oryx Technology Corp.	Industrial
OSHSF	Oshap Technologies Ltd.	Industrial
GOSHA	Oshkosh B'Gosh, Inc.	Industrial
OTRKB	Oshkosh Truck Corporation	Industrial
OSIP	OSI Pharmaceuticals Inc.	Biotechnology
OSIS	OSI Systems, Inc.	Computer
FIBR	Osicom Technologies, Inc.	Industrial

Symbol	Company Name	Sector
OSTE	Osteotech, Inc.	Industrial
OSTX	Ostex International, Inc.	Industrial
OTRX	OTR Express, Inc.	Transportation
OFCP	Ottawa Financial Corporation	Other Finance
OTTR	Otter Tail Power Company	Industrial
OSSI	Outback Steakhouse, Inc.	Industrial
OUTL	Outlook Group Corp.	Industrial
OSIX	Outsource International, Inc.	Industrial
OVRL	Overland Data, Inc.	Industrial
OVID	Ovid Technologies, Inc.	Computer
OWOS	Owosso Corporation	Industrial
OMED	Oxboro Medical International, Inc.	Industrial
OXHP	Oxford Health Plans, Inc.	Industrial
OXGN	OXiGENE, Inc.	Industrial
OXISD	Oxis International, Inc.	Industrial
OYOG	OYO Geospace Corporation	Industrial
OZEMY	OzEmail, Limited	Computer
PFINA	P & F Industries, Inc.	Industrial
PGWCZ	P G Energy, Inc.	Industrial
PTSI	P.A.M. Transportation Services, Inc.	Transportation
PSNRY	P.T. Pasifik Satelit Nusantara	Telecommunications
PAZZF	Pacalta Resources, Ltd.	Industrial
PCAR	PACCAR Inc	Industrial
PTCH	Pacer Technology	Industrial
PCTH	Pacific Aerospace & Electronics, Inc.	Computer
PBMI	Pacific Biometrics, Inc.	Industrial
PABN	Pacific Capital Bancorp	Other Finance
PCCI	Pacific Crest Capital, Inc.	Bank
PCCIP	Pacific Crest Capital, Inc.	Bank
PDLPY	Pacific Dunlop Limited	Industrial
PGEX	Pacific Gateway Exchange, Inc.	Telecommunications
PSUN	Pacific Sunwear of California, Inc.	Industrial
PAMM	PacificAmerica Money Center, Inc.	Other Finance
PHSYA	PacifiCare Health Systems, Inc.	Industrial
PHSYB	PacifiCare Health Systems, Inc.	Industrial
PHLI	PacificHealth Laboratories, Inc.	Industrial
PMWI	PageMart Wireless, Inc.	Computer
PAGE	Paging Network, Inc.	Telecommunications
PPAR	Paging Partners Corporation	Telecommunications
PAIR	PairGain Technologies, Inc.	Industrial
PLTN	Palatin Technologies, Inc.	Biotechnology
PALX	PalEx, Inc.	Industrial

Symbol	Company Name	Sector
PHHM	Palm Harbor Homes, Inc.	Industrial
PMTI	Palomar Medical Technologies, Inc.	Industrial
PBCI	Pamrapo Bancorp, Inc.	Other Finance
PAASF	Pan American Silver Corp.	Industrial
PANA	PANACO, Inc.	Industrial
SPOT	PanAmSat Corporation	Telecommunications
PAMX	Pancho's Mexican Buffet, Inc.	Industrial
PANRA	Panhandle Royalty Company	Industrial
PZZA	Papa John's International, Inc.	Industrial
PWHS	Paper Warehouse, Inc.	Industrial
PGEOF	Paradigm Geophysical Ltd.	Computer
PMED	Paradigm Medical Industries, Inc.	Industrial
PRDQE	Paradise Holdings Inc.	Industrial
PDSE	Paradise Music & Entertainment Inc.	Industrial
PLLL	Parallel Petroleum Corporation	Industrial
PMTC	Parametric Technology Corporation	Computer
PARA	Paramount Financial Corporation	Computer
PVAT	Paravant Inc.	Computer
PRXL	PAREXEL International Corporation	Industrial
PBFI	Paris Corporation	Industrial
PFED	Park Bancorp, Inc.	Bank
PRKR	ParkerVision, Inc.	Industrial
PKOH	Park-Ohio Holdings Corp.	Industrial
PVSA	Parkvale Financial Corporation	Other Finance
PRLX	Parlex Corporation	Industrial
PARL	Parlux Fragrances, Inc.	Industrial
PCTY	Party City Corporation	Industrial
PBHC	Pathfinder Bancorp, Inc.	Bank
PGNS	PathoGenesis Corporation	Biotechnology
PTHW	Pathways Group, Inc. (The)	Computer
PATI	Patient Infosystems, Inc.	Industrial
PATK	Patrick Industries, Inc.	Industrial
PBIX	Patriot Bank Corp.	Bank
PNBK	Patriot National Bank	Bank
PDCO	Patterson Dental Company	Industrial
PTEN	Patterson Energy, Inc.	Industrial
PAUH	Paul Harris Stores, Inc.	Industrial
MUEL	Paul Mueller Company	Industrial
PFCO	PAULA Financial	Insurance
PLCC	Paulson Capital Corp.	Other Finance
PSON	Paul-Son Gaming Corporation	Industrial
PMRT	PawnMart, Inc.	Industrial

Symbol	Company Name	Sector
PAYX	Paychex, Inc.	Industrial
PBOC	PBOC Holdings, Inc.	Bank
PCCC	PC Connection, Inc.	Industrial
DOCSF	PC DOCS Group International	Computer
PCSS	PC Service Source, Inc.	Industrial
PCFR	PC411, Inc.	Computer
PCCG	PCC Group, Inc.	Industrial
PCDI	PCD Inc.	Industrial
PCMS	P-COM, Inc.	Industrial
PDKL	PDK Labs, Inc.	Industrial
PDKLP	PDK Labs, Inc.	Industrial
PDSF	PDS Financial Corporation	Other Finance
PEAKF	Peak International Limited	Industrial
PPOD	Peapod, Inc.	Industrial
WPOG	Pease Oil & Gas Company	Industrial
PSAI	Pediatric Services of America, Inc.	Industrial
PEEK	Peekskill Financial Corporation	Other Finance
PLSS	Peerless Group, Inc.	Industrial
PMFG	Peerless Manufacturing Company	Industrial
PRLS	Peerless Systems Corporation	Industrial
PGTV	Pegasus Communications Corporation	Industrial
PEGS	Pegasus Systems, Inc.	Industrial
PEGA	Pegasystems Inc.	Industrial
PENC	Pen Interconnect, Inc.	Industrial
PENX	Penford Corporation	Industrial
PENN	Penn National Gaming, Inc.	Industrial
POCC	Penn Octane Corporation	Industrial
PTAC	Penn Treaty American Corporation	Insurance
PFSB	PennFed Financial Services, Inc.	Other Finance
PFSBP	PennFed Financial Services, Inc.	Other Finance
PNNW	Pennichuck Corporation	Industrial
PMFRA	Pennsylvania Manufacturers Corporation	Insurance
PWBK	Pennwood Bancorp, Inc.	Bank
SPWY	Penske Motorsports, Inc.	Industrial
PNTK	Pentech International, Inc.	Industrial
PPCO	Penwest Pharmaceuticals Co.	Industrial
PFDC	Peoples Bancorp	Other Finance
PEBO	Peoples Bancorp Inc.	Other Finance
TSBS	People's Bancorp, Inc.	Bank
PBKB	People's Bancshares, Inc.	Bank
PBTC	Peoples BancTrust Company, Inc. (The)	Bank
PEBK	Peoples Bank	Bank

Symbol	Company Name	Sector
PBCT	People's Bank	Other Finance
PPLS	Peoples Bank Corporation of Indianapolis	Bank
PFFC	Peoples Financial Corporation	Other Finance
PHBK	Peoples Heritage Financial Group, Inc.	Bank
PHSB	Peoples Home Savings Bank	Bank
PPCCP	People's Preferred Capital Corporation	Other Finance
PSFT	PeopleSoft, Inc.	Computer
PSFC	Peoples-Sidney Financial Corporation	Other Finance
PRCP	Perceptron, Inc.	Industrial
PERC	Perclose, Inc.	Industrial
PRCN	Percon Incorporated	Industrial
PRGN	Peregrine Systems, Inc.	Computer
PERF	PerfectData Corporation	Industrial
PFGC	Performance Food Group Company	Industrial
PTIX	Performance Technologies, Incorporated	Computer
PRFM	Perfumania, Inc.	Industrial
PSEM	Pericom Semiconductor Corporation	Computer
PERI	Periphonics Corporation	Industrial
PTUS	Peritus Software Services, Inc.	Computer
PERLF	Perle Systems Limited	Industrial
PESI	Perma-Fix Environmental Services, Inc.	Industrial
PERM	Permanent Bancorp, Inc.	Other Finance
PCBC	Perry County Financial Corporation	Bank
PVSW	Pervasive Software Inc.	Computer
PETC	Petco Animal Supplies, Inc.	Industrial
PGEI	Petroglyph Energy, Inc.	Industrial
PETD	Petroleum Development Corporation	Industrial
HEAT	Petroleum Heat and Power Co., Inc.	Industrial
PHEL	Petroleum Helicopters, Inc.	Transportation
PHELK	Petroleum Helicopters, Inc.	Transportation
PNTGF	Petromet Resources Limited	Industrial
PTRO	Petrominerals Corporation	Industrial
PQUE	Petroquest Energy Inc	Industrial
PETM	PETsMART, Inc.	Industrial
PFFB	PFF Bancorp, Inc.	Bank
PMRX	Pharmaceutical Marketing Services Inc.	Computer
PPDI	Pharmaceutical Product Development, Inc.	Industrial
PCOP	Pharmacopeia, Inc.	Industrial
PCYC	Pharmacyclics, Inc.	Biotechnology
PPRT	PharmaPrint Inc.	Industrial
PCHM	PharmChem Laboratories, Inc.	Industrial
DOSE	PharMerica, Inc.	Industrial

Symbol	Company Name	Sector
PHSE	Pharmhouse Corp.	Industrial
PMOR	Phar-Mor, Inc.	Industrial
PARS	Pharmos Corporation	Industrial
PIHC	PHC, Inc.	Industrial
PHLY	Philadelphia Consolidated Holding Corp.	Insurance
PGLD	Phoenix Gold International, Inc.	Industrial
PHXX	Phoenix International Ltd., Inc.	Industrial
PTEC	Phoenix Technologies Ltd.	Computer
PHOC	Photo Control Corporation	Industrial
PECX	Photoelectron Corporation	Industrial
PHRX	Photomatrix, Inc.	Computer
PHTN	Photon Dynamics, Inc.	Industrial
PTRN	Photran Corporation	Industrial
PLAB	Photronics, Inc.	Industrial
PHYC	PhyCor, Inc.	Industrial
PHMX	PhyMatrix Corporation	Industrial
PHYN	Physician Reliance Network, Inc.	Industrial
ENTS	Physicians' Specialty Corp.	Industrial
PHYX	Physiometrix, Inc.	Industrial
PIAM	PIA Merchandising Services, Inc.	Industrial
PICO	PICO Holdings Inc.	Other Finance
PCTL	Picture Tel Corporation	Industrial
PIFI	Piemonte Foods, Inc.	Industrial
PGDA	Piercing Pagoda, Inc.	Industrial
PACC	Pilgrim America Capital Corporation	Other Finance
PILT	Pilot Network Services, Inc.	Computer
PINN	Pinnacle Banc Group, Inc.	Other Finance
PCLE	Pinnacle Systems, Inc.	Industrial
PCFC	Pioneer Commercial Funding Corp.	Bank
PIONA	Pioneer Companies, Inc.	Industrial
PRRR	Pioneer Railcorp	Transportation
PIOS	Pioneer-Standard Electronics, Inc.	Industrial
PRAN	Piranha Interactive Publishing Inc.	Computer
PHFC	Pittsburgh Home Financial Corp.	Bank
PHFCP	Pittsburgh Home Financial Corp.	Bank
PIXR	Pixar	Industrial
PIXT	PixTech, Inc.	Computer
PZZI	Pizza Inn, Inc.	Industrial
PJAM	PJ America, Inc.	Industrial
LANPF	Plaintree Systems Inc.	Computer
PLNR	Planar Systems, Inc.	Industrial
POLY	Planet Polymer Technologies, Inc.	Industrial

Symbol	Company Name	Sector
PTIS	Plasma-Therm, Inc.	Industrial
PTET	Platinum Entertainment, Inc.	Industrial
PSQL	Platinum Software Corporation	Computer
PLAT	PLATINUM technology, inc.	Computer
PBYP	Play By Play Toys & Novelties, Inc.	Industrial
PLAY	Players International, Inc.	Industrial
PLDI	PLD Telekom Inc.	Telecommunications
PLXS	Plexus Corp.	Industrial
PMCS	PMC-Sierra, Inc.	Computer
PMRP	PMR Corporation	Industrial
PNBF	PNB Financial Group	Bank
PFSL	Pocahontas Bancorp, Inc.	Bank
POSIF	Point of Sale Limited	Industrial
PWCC	Point West Capital Corporation	Industrial
PNTE	Pointe Financial Corporation	Bank
PRCC	Pollution Research and Control Corp.	Industrial
PLCM	Polycom, Inc.	Industrial
POLXF	Polydex Pharmaceuticals Limited	Industrial
PROA	Polymer Research Corp. of America	Industrial
PMRY	Pomeroy Computer Resources, Inc.	Industrial
PNDR	Ponder Industries, Inc.	Industrial
PESC	Pool Energy Services Co.	Industrial
POOR	Poore Brothers, Inc.	Industrial
POPEZ	Pope Resources	Industrial
BPOP	Popular, Inc.	Other Finance
BPOPP	Popular, Inc.	Other Finance
POSS	Possis Medical, Inc.	Industrial
PTRS	Potters Financial Corporation	Other Finance
POWL	Powell Industries, Inc.	Industrial
POWI	Power Integrations, Inc.	Computer
PCRV	Powercerv Corporation	Industrial
PWRH	Powerhouse Technologies, Inc.	Industrial
PWER	Power-One, Inc.	Industrial
PTEL	Powertel, Inc.	Telecommunications
PWAV	Powerwave Technologies, Inc.	Industrial
PPTV	PPT Vision Inc.	Computer
PGTZ	Praegitzer Industries, Inc.	Computer
PBSIA	Precept Business Services, Inc.	Industrial
PACI	Precision Auto Care, Inc.	Industrial
POCI	Precision Optics Corporation, Inc.	Industrial
PRRC	Precision Response Corporation	Industrial
PCSN	Precision Standard, Inc.	Industrial

Symbol	Company Name	Sector
PSYS	Precision Systems, Inc.	Computer
PEGI	Preferred Employers Holding, Inc.	Insurance
PFNT	Preferred Networks, Inc.	Industrial
FAUX	Premier Concepts, Inc.	Industrial
PFBI	Premier Financial Bancorp, Inc.	Other Finance
PFBIP	Premier Financial Bancorp, Inc.	Other Finance
PLSIA	Premier Laser Systems, Inc.	Industrial
PRWW	Premier Research Worldwide, Inc.	Industrial
PTEK	Premiere Technologies, Inc.	Telecommunications
PRMS	Premisys Communications, Inc.	Industrial
PCIG	Premium Cigars International, Ltd.	Industrial
PREZ	President Casinos, Inc.	Industrial
PLFE	Presidential Life Corporation	Insurance
PRST	Presstek, Inc.	Industrial
PRBC	Prestige Bancorp, Inc.	Other Finance
PRFN	Prestige Financial Corp.	Other Finance
PTVL	Preview Travel, Inc.	Transportation
PRIA	PRI Automation, Inc.	Industrial
PREN	Price Enterprises, Inc.	Other Finance
PRENP	Price Enterprises, Inc.	Other Finance
PSMT	PriceSmart, Inc.	Industrial
LEAS	Pride Automotive Group, Inc.	Industrial
PENG	Prima Energy Corporation	Industrial
PRMA	Primadonna Resorts, Inc.	Industrial
PBNK	Prime Bancorp, Inc.	Other Finance
PBTX	Prime Bancshares, Inc.	Bank
PMCP	Prime Capital Corporation	Industrial
PMSI	Prime Medical Services, Inc.	Industrial
PNRG	PrimeEnergy Corporation	Industrial
PSRC	PrimeSource Corporation	Industrial
PRMX	Primex Technologies, Inc.	Industrial
PMIX	PRIMIX Solutions, Inc.	Computer
PRTL	Primus Telecommunications Group, Inc.	Telecommunications
PMGIF	Princeton Media Group, Inc.	Industrial
PNBC	Princeton National Bancorp, Inc.	Other Finance
PVII	Princeton Video Image, Inc.	Industrial
AFIS	Printrak International Inc.	Computer
PTNX	Printronix, Inc.	Computer
PRTW	Printware, Inc.	Industrial
PHCC	Priority Healthcare Corporation	Industrial
PRZM	Prism Solutions, Inc.	Computer
PRBZ	ProBusiness Services, Inc.	Computer

Symbol	Company Name	Sector
PRCT	Procept, Inc.	Industrial
PRCM	Procom Technology Incorporated	Industrial
PRCY	ProCyte Corporation	Biotechnology
PDEX	Pro-Dex, Inc.	Industrial
TPEG	Producers Entertainment Group Ltd. (The)	Industrial
PRAC	Productivity Technologies Corp.	Industrial
PFACP	Pro-Fac Cooperative, Inc.	Industrial
PDII	Professional Detailing, Inc.	Industrial
PSTFY	Professional Staff, plc	Industrial
TRUC	Professional Transportation Group Ltd., Inc.	Transportation
PICM	Professionals Group, Inc.	Insurance
PRTK	Profile Technologies, Inc.	Industrial
PGLAF	Progen Industries Limited	Industrial
PGNX	Progenics Pharmaceuticals Inc.	Biotechnology
PGEN	Progenitor, Inc.	Industrial
PROG	Programmer's Paradise, Inc.	Industrial
PFNC	Progress Financial Corporation	Other Finance
PRGS	Progress Software Corporation	Computer
PSDI	Project Software & Development, Inc.	Computer
PJTV	Projectavision, Inc.	Industrial
PMCO	ProMedCo Management Company	Industrial
PXXI	Prophet 21, Inc.	Industrial
POSO	Prosoft I-Net Solutions, Inc.	Industrial
ALRM	Protection One, Inc.	Industrial
PDLI	Protein Design Labs, Inc.	Biotechnology
PPTI	Protein Polymer Technologies, Inc.	Industrial
PCOL	Protocol Systems, Inc.	Industrial
PSCO	ProtoSource Corporation	Industrial
POVT	Provant, Inc.	Industrial
PBKS	Provident Bankshares Corporation	Other Finance
PFGI	Provident Financial Group, Inc.	Other Finance
PROV	Provident Financial Holdings, Inc.	Bank
PRHC	Province Healthcare Company	Industrial
PROX	Proxim, Inc.	Industrial
PILL	ProxyMed, Inc.	Industrial
PRTG	PRT Group Inc.	Computer
PSFI	PS Financial, Inc.	Bank
PSBI	PSB Bancorp, Inc.	Bank
PSCX	PSC Inc.	Industrial
PSIX	PSINet Inc.	Telecommunications
PSSI	PSS World Medical Inc.	Industrial
PSWT	PSW Technologies, Inc.	Industrial

Symbol	Company Name	Sector
PTII	PTI Holding Inc.	Industrial
PUBO	Pubco Corporation	Industrial
PCNA	Publishing Company of North America, Inc.	Industrial
PULB	Pulaski Bank, A Federal Savings Bank	Bank
PLFC	Pulaski Furniture Corporation	Industrial
PLSK	Pulaski Savings Bank	Bank
PULS	Pulse Bancorp, Inc.	Other Finance
PLPT	PulsePoint Communications	Industrial
PUMA	Puma Technology, Inc.	Computer
PURW	Pure World, Inc.	Industrial
PVCC	PVC Container Corporation	Industrial
PVFC	PVF Capital Corp.	Bank
PMID	Pyramid Breweries, Inc.	Industrial
QEPC	Q.E.P. Co., Inc.	Industrial
QADI	QAD Inc.	Computer
QCFB	QCF Bancorp, Inc.	Other Finance
QGENF	QIAGEN N.V.	Industrial
QLGC	QLogic Corporation	Industrial
QLTIF	QLT Phototherapeutics, Inc.	Industrial
QEKG	Q-Med, Inc.	Industrial
QRSI	QRS Corporation	Computer
QSNDF	Qsound Labs, Inc.	Computer
QCHI	Quad City Holdings, Inc.	Other Finance
QSYS	Quad Systems Corporation	Industrial
QMDC	QuadraMed Corporation	Computer
QCBC	Quaker City Bancorp, Inc.	Other Finance
QFAB	Quaker Fabric Corporation	Industrial
QCOM	QUALCOMM Incorporated	Industrial
QDIN	Quality Dining, Inc.	Industrial
QUAL	Quality Semiconductor, Inc.	Computer
QSII	Quality Systems, Inc.	Industrial
FTSW	Qualix Group, Inc.	Computer
QMRK	QualMark Corporation	Industrial
QNTM	Quantum Corporation	Computer
QSRI	Queen Sand Resources, Inc.	Industrial
QCSB	Queens County Bancorp, Inc.	Bank
QUOB	QueryObject Systems Corporation	Computer
QEDC	Quest Education Corporation	Industrial
QIXXF	Quest International Resources Corporation	Industrial
QUES	Questa Oil & Gas Co.	Industrial
QTEC	QuesTech, Inc.	Computer
QUST	Questron Technology, Inc.	Industrial

Symbol	Company Name	Sector
QKTN	Quickturn Design Systems, Inc.	Industrial
QDEL	Quidel Corporation	Industrial
QTEL	Quintel Communications, Inc.	Industrial
QTRN	Quintiles Transnational Corp.	Industrial
QUIP	Quipp, Inc.	Industrial
QUIX	Quixote Corporation	Industrial
QUIZ	Quizno's Corporation (The)	Industrial
QHGI	Quorum Health Group, Inc.	Industrial
QWST	Qwest Communications International Inc.	Telecommunications
RBIN	R & B, Inc.	Industrial
RGFC	R&G Financial Corporation	Other Finance
RGFCP	R&G Financial Corporation	Other Finance
RHPS	R.H. Phillips, Inc.	Industrial
RACN	Racing Champions Corporation	Industrial
RCOM	Racom Systems, Inc.	Industrial
RADIF	Rada Electronic Industries Limited	Industrial
RDCMF	RADCOM LTD.	Industrial
RADS	Radiant Systems, Inc.	Industrial
RADAF	Radica Games Limited	Industrial
RSYS	RadiSys Corporation	Industrial
RDUS	Radius Inc. New	Computer
RAGS	Rag Shops, Inc.	Industrial
RAIL	RailAmerica, Inc.	Transportation
RTEX	RailTex, Inc.	Transportation
RWKS	Railworks Corporation	Transportation
RBOW	Rainbow Rentals, Inc.	Computer
RNBO	Rainbow Technologies, Inc.	Computer
RAIN	Rainforest Cafe, Inc.	Industrial
RLLY	Rally's Hamburgers, Inc.	Industrial
RMPO	Ramapo Financial Corporation	Other Finance
RMBS	Rambus, Inc.	Industrial
RHCI	Ramsay Health Care, Inc.	Industrial
RMTR	Ramtron International Corporation	Industrial
RAND	Rand Capital Corporation	Other Finance
RANGY	Randgold & Exploration Company, Limited	Industrial
RAVE	Rankin Automotive Group, Inc.	Industrial
RARE	RARE Hospitality International Inc.	Industrial
RARB	Raritan Bancorp Inc.	Other Finance
RATL	Rational Software Corporation	Industrial
RAVN	Raven Industries, Inc.	Industrial
RAWL	Rawlings Sporting Goods Company, Inc.	Industrial
RTEL	Raytel Medical Corporation	Industrial

Symbol	Company Name	Sector
RBBR	R-B Rubber Products, Inc.	Industrial
RCMT	RCM Technologies, Inc.	Industrial
RCNC	RCN Corporation	Telecommunications
RDGE	Reading Entertainment Inc.	Industrial
RDRT	Read-Rite Corporation	Computer
RDMMF	Real del Monte Mining Corporation	Industrial
RGTC	Real Goods Trading Corporation	Industrial
RLAXY	Realax Software AG	Industrial
RLCO	Realco, Inc.	Industrial
RNWK	RealNetworks, Inc.	Computer
RIGX	Realty Information Group, Inc.	Computer
RESY	Reconditioned Systems, Inc.	Industrial
RCOT	Recoton Corporation	Industrial
REIN	Recovery Engineering, Inc.	Industrial
RECY	Recycling Industries, Inc.	Industrial
REDB	Red Brick Systems, Inc.	Computer
RHCS	Red Hot Concepts, Inc.	Industrial
HOOK	Redhook Ale Brewery, Incorporated	Industrial
REFN	Regency Bancorp	Bank
REGN	Regeneron Pharmaceuticals, Inc.	Biotechnology
RGNT	Regent Assisted Living, Inc.	Industrial
RGBK	Regions Financial Corporation	Other Finance
RGIS	Regis Corporation	Industrial
RHBC	RehabCare Group, Inc.	Industrial
REHB	Rehabilicare Inc.	Industrial
REAL	Reliability Incorporated	Industrial
RELY	Reliance Bancorp, Inc.	Other Finance
RELI	Reliance Bancshares, Inc.	Bank
RELV	Reliv' International, Inc.	Industrial
RELM	RELM Wireless Corporation	Industrial
REMC	REMEC, Inc.	Industrial
RMDY	Remedy Corporation	Computer
REMX	RemedyTemp, Inc.	Industrial
ROILA	Remington Oil and Gas Corporation	Industrial
ROILB	Remington Oil and Gas Corporation	Industrial
RENN	Renaissance Capital Growth & Income	Other Finance
FAIRC	Renaissance Entertainment Corporation	Industrial
REGI	Renaissance Worldwide Inc.	Computer
RCGI	Renal Care Group, Inc.	Industrial
RENX	Renex Corporation	Industrial
RENO	Reno Air, Inc.	Transportation
RENOP	Reno Air, Inc.	Transportation

Symbol	Company Name	Sector
RAWA	Rent-A-Wreck of America, Inc.	Industrial
RNTK	Rentech, Inc.	Industrial
RCII	Renters Choice, Inc.	Industrial
RENT	Rentrak Corporation	Industrial
RGEN	Repligen Corporation	Biotechnology
REPT	Reptron Electronics, Inc.	Industrial
RBNC	Republic Bancorp Inc.	Other Finance
RBCAA	Republic Bancorp, Inc.	Bank
REPB	Republic Bancshares, Inc.	Other Finance
REPBP	Republic Bancshares, Inc.	Other Finance
RBCF	Republic Banking Corporation of Florida	Bank
FRBK	Republic First Bancorp, Inc.	Other Finance
RSFC	Republic Security Financial Corporation	Other Finance
RSCR	Res-Care, Inc.	Industrial
RENG	Research Engineers, Inc.	Computer
REFR	Research Frontiers Incorporated	Industrial
RPII	Research Partners International Inc.	Other Finance
RESR	Research, Incorporated	Industrial
RESM	ResMed, Inc.	Industrial
RSND	ReSound Corporation	Industrial
REXI	Resource America, Inc.	Industrial
RBMG	Resource Bancshares Mortgage Group, Inc.	Other Finance
RESP	Respironics, Inc.	Industrial
ROIX	Response Oncology, Inc.	Industrial
RSPN	Response USA, Inc.	Industrial
RSTO	Restoration Hardware, Inc.	Industrial
RTRK	Restrac, Inc.	Computer
RPIA	Resurgence Properties, Inc.	Other Finance
RTRO	Retrospettiva, Inc.	Industrial
RUNI	Reunion Industries Inc.	Industrial
RTRSY	Reuters Group PLC	Industrial
RPCLF	Revenue Properties Company Limited	Other Finance
RXSD	Rexall Sundown, Inc.	Industrial
REXL	Rexhall Industries, Inc.	Industrial
RFIL	RF Industries, Inc.	Industrial
RFMD	RF Micro Devices, Inc.	Industrial
RFMI	RF Monolithics, Inc.	Computer
RIBI	Ribi ImmunoChem Research, Inc.	Biotechnology
RZYM	Ribozyme Pharmaceuticals, Inc.	Industrial
RICA	Rica Foods, Inc.	Industrial
RELL	Richardson Electronics, Ltd.	Industrial
RCHY	Richey Electronics, Inc.	Industrial

Symbol	Company Name	Sector
RCBK	Richmond County Financial Corp.	Bank
RICK	Rick's Cabaret International, Inc.	Industrial
RIDL	Riddell Sports Inc.	Industrial
RIDE	Ride, Inc.	Industrial
RIDG	Ridgeview, Inc.	Industrial
RIGS	Riggs National Corporation	Other Finance
RMCI	Right Management Consultants, Inc.	Industrial
RTST	Right Start, Inc. (The)	Industrial
RIMG	Rimage Corporation	Industrial
RCHI	Risk Capital Holdings, Inc.	Insurance
RITTF	RIT Technologies Ltd.	Industrial
RIVL	Rival Company (The)	Industrial
RIVR	River Valley Bancorp.	Other Finance
RSGIC	Riverside Group, Inc.	Industrial
RVSB	Riverview Bancorp Inc	Other Finance
RVFD	Riviana Foods Inc.	Industrial
RMHT	RMH Teleservices, Inc.	Industrial
GRLL	Roadhouse Grill, Inc.	Industrial
ROAD	Roadway Express, Inc.	Transportation
RESC	Roanoke Electric Steel Corporation	Industrial
RGCO	Roanoke Gas Company	Industrial
RBDS	Roberds, Inc.	Industrial
MOND	Robert Mondavi Corporation (The)	Industrial
RNIC	Robinson Nugent, Inc.	Industrial
RIMS	Robocom Systems Inc.	Industrial
ROBV	Robotic Vision Systems, Inc.	Industrial
ROCM	Rochester Medical Corporation	Industrial
BREW	Rock Bottom Restaurants, Inc.	Industrial
RCCK	Rock Financial Corporation	Other Finance
ROAC	Rock of Ages Corporation	Industrial
ROCF	Rockford Industries, Inc.	Other Finance
RSHX	RockShox, Inc.	Industrial
RMTI	Rockwell Medical Technologies, Inc.	Industrial
RMCF	Rocky Mountain Chocolate Factory, Inc.	Industrial
RMII	Rocky Mountain Internet, Inc.	Industrial
RCKY	Rocky Shoes & Boots, Inc.	Industrial
RSTI	Rofin-Sinar Technologies, Inc.	Industrial
RWAV	Rogue Wave Software, Inc.	Computer
ROHN	ROHN Industries Inc.	Industrial
ROLL	Rollerball International, Inc.	Industrial
ROMT	Rom Tech, Inc.	Computer
ROMC	Romac International, Inc.	Industrial

Symbol	Company Name	Sector
RONC	Ronson Corporation	Industrial
PLUS	Room Plus, Inc.	Industrial
TRSEF	Rose Corporation, The	Other Finance
ROSDF	Rosedale Decorative Products, Ltd.	Industrial
RSLN	Roslyn Bancorp, Inc.	Bank
ROST	Ross Stores, Inc.	Industrial
ROSS	Ross Systems, Inc.	Computer
WSTNA	Roy F. Weston, Inc.	Industrial
RBPAA	Royal Bancshares of Pennsylvania, Inc.	Other Finance
RGLD	Royal Gold, Inc.	Industrial
ROCLF	Royal Olympic Cruise Lines, Inc.	Transportation
RIFL	Royal Precision, Inc.	Industrial
ROYL	Royale Energy, Inc.	Industrial
FUND	Royce Global Trust Inc.	Other Finance
OTCM	Royce Micro-Cap Trust, Inc.	Other Finance
RSIS	RSI Systems, Inc.	Computer
RSLCF	RSL Communications, Ltd.	Telecommunications
RTWI	RTW, Inc.	Insurance
RCCC	Rural Cellular Corporation	Telecommunications
RURL	Rural/Metro Corporation	Transportation
RUSH	Rush Enterprises, Inc.	Industrial
RFGI	Rushmore Financial Group, Inc.	Industrial
RUSMF	Russel Metals, Inc.	Industrial
RMOC	Rutherford-Moran Oil Corporation	Industrial
RWDT	RWD Technologies, Inc.	Industrial
RYAAY	Ryanair Holdings plc	Transportation
RYAN	Ryan's Family Steak Houses, Inc.	Industrial
SKFB	S & K Famous Brands, Inc.	Industrial
SISI	S I Technologies Inc.	Industrial
WINS	S M & A Corporation	Industrial
STMI	S T M Wireless, Inc.	Industrial
STBA	S&T Bancorp, Inc.	Bank
GOLF	S2 Golf Inc.	Industrial
SIII	S3 Incorporated	Industrial
SBTK	Sabratek Corporation	Industrial
SACM	SAC Technologies, Inc.	Industrial
SAESY	SAES Getters S.p.A.	Industrial
LOCK	Saf T Lok, Inc.	Computer
SAFC	SAFECO Corporation	Insurance
SFGD	Safeguard Health Enterprises, Inc.	Insurance
SAFS	SafeScience, Inc.	Industrial
SFSK	Safeskin Corporation	Industrial

Symbol	Company Name	Sector
SAFT	Safety 1st, Inc.	Industrial
ABAG	Safety Components International, Inc.	Industrial
SAGC	Saint Andrews Golf Corporation	Industrial
STCIA	Salient 3 Communications, Inc.	Industrial
SALT	Salton/Maxim Housewares, Inc.	Industrial
SAMC	Samsonite Corporation	Industrial
SCAI	Sanchez Computer Associates, Inc.	Computer
SNDCF	Sand Technology Systems International Inc.	Industrial
SAND	Sandata, Inc.	Computer
SAFM	Sanderson Farms, Inc.	Industrial
SNDK	SanDisk Corporation	Computer
SNDS	Sands Regent (The)	Industrial
SASR	Sandy Spring Bancorp, Inc.	Other Finance
SANG	SangStat Medical Corporation	Industrial
SANM	Sanmina Corporation	Industrial
SABB	Santa Barbara Bancorp	Bank
SBRG	Santa Barbara Restaurant Group, Inc.	Industrial
SCOC	Santa Cruz Operation, Inc. (The)	Computer
SFEF	Santa Fe Financial Corporation	Industrial
STOSY	Santos, Ltd.	Industrial
SPNSF	Sapiens International Corporation N.V.	Computer
SAPE	Sapient Corporation	Computer
TOGA	Saratoga Beverage Group Inc.	Industrial
STGA	Saratoga Brands, Inc.	Industrial
SASOY	Sasol Ltd.	Industrial
SATC	SatCon Technology Corporation	Industrial
SCNYA	Saucony, Inc.	Industrial
SCNYB	Saucony, Inc.	Industrial
SAVB	Savannah Bancorp, Inc. (The)	Other Finance
SAVLY	Saville Systems, plc	Computer
SVTG	Savoir Technology Group, Inc.	Industrial
SWKOY	Sawako Corporation	Industrial
SAWS	Sawtek Inc.	Computer
SXTN	Saxton Incorporated	Other Finance
SBEI	SBE, Inc.	Industrial
SBSE	SBS Technologies, Inc.	Industrial
SBTVF	Scandinavian Broadcasting System SA	Telecommunications
SCNG	Scan-Graphics, Inc.	Industrial
SOCR	Scan-Optics, Inc.	Computer
SCSC	ScanSource, Inc.	Industrial
SVECF	ScanVec Company (1990), Ltd.	Computer
SCBI	SCB Computer Technology, Inc.	Computer

Symbol	Company Name	Sector
SCCX	SCC Communications Corp.	Industrial
SVIN	Scheid Vineyards, Inc.	Industrial
SCHR	Scherer Healthcare, Inc.	Industrial
SCHK	Schick Technologies, Inc.	Industrial
BUNZ	Schlotzsky's, Inc.	Industrial
SMIT	Schmitt Industries, Inc.	Industrial
SCHN	Schnitzer Steel Industries, Inc.	Industrial
SCHL	Scholastic Corporation	Industrial
SCHS	School Specialty, Inc.	Industrial
SHUF	Schuff Steel Company	Industrial
SHLR	Schuler Homes, Inc.	Industrial
SAVO	Schultz Sav-O Stores, Inc.	Industrial
SCLN	SciClone Pharmaceuticals, Inc.	Biotechnology
SIDY	Science Dynamics Corporation	Industrial
STIZ	Scientific Technologies, Incorporated	Industrial
SCIO	Scios, Inc.	Biotechnology
SCIXF	Scitex Corporation Ltd.	Computer
SCMM	SCM Microsystems, Inc.	Industrial
SCOT	Scott & Stringfellow Financial, Inc.	Other Finance
SCTTA	Scott Technologies, Inc.	Industrial
SCTTB	Scott Technologies, Inc.	Industrial
POOL	SCP Pool Corporation	Industrial
SDLI	SDL, Inc.	Computer
SEAC	SeaChange International, Inc.	Industrial
SBCFA	Seacoast Banking Corporation of Florida	Other Finance
SEMD	SeaMED Corporation	Industrial
FOTO	Seattle FilmWorks, Inc.	Industrial
SEWY	Seaway Food Town, Inc.	Industrial
SECM	Secom General Corporation	Industrial
SECD	Second Bancorp, Incorporated	Other Finance
SECT	Sector Communications Inc.	Industrial
SCUR	Secure Computing Corporation	Computer
SBCM	Security Bank Corporation	Bank
SBHC	Security Bank Holding Company	Other Finance
SDTI	Security Dynamics Technologies, Inc.	Industrial
SONE	Security First Technologies Corporation	Other Finance
SNFCA	Security National Financial Corporation	Insurance
SECX	SED International Holdings Inc	Industrial
SEEC	SEEC, Inc.	Industrial
SEEQ	SEEQ Technology Incorporated	Industrial
SEGU	Segue Software, Inc.	Computer
SEIC	SEI Investments Company	Computer

Symbol	Company Name	Sector
SBIG	Seibels Bruce Group, Inc. (The)	Insurance
SELAY	Select Appointments (Holdings)	Industrial
SLCTY	SELECT Software Tools PLC	Computer
SIGI	Selective Insurance Group, Inc.	Insurance
SELBD	Sel-Leb Marketing, Inc.	Industrial
SMGS	SEMCO Energy, Inc.	Industrial
VSLF	Semele Group Inc.	Other Finance
SLIC	Semiconductor Laser International Corp.	Industrial
SMTL	Semitool, Inc.	Industrial
SMTC	Semtech Corporation	Computer
SEMX	SEMX Corp.	Industrial
SENEA	Seneca Foods Corp.	Industrial
SENEB	Seneca Foods Corp.	Industrial
SNTO	Sento Corporation	Industrial
SEPR	Sepracor Inc.	Industrial
SQNT	Sequent Computer Systems, Inc.	Computer
SEQU	SEQUUS Pharmaceuticals, Inc.	Biotechnology
SERO	Serologicals Corporation	Biotechnology
SEVN	Sevenson Environmental Services, Inc.	Industrial
SFED	SFS Bancorp, Inc.	Other Finance
SFXE	SFX Entertainment	Telecommunications
SGVB	SGV Bancorp, Inc.	Other Finance
SHMN	Shaman Pharmaceuticals, Inc.	Industrial
STCL	Shared Technologies Cellular, Inc.	Telecommunications
SHRP	Sharper Image Corporation	Industrial
SHEL	Sheldahl, Inc.	Industrial
SHLL	Shells Seafood Restaurants, Inc.	Industrial
SHDN	Sheridan Energy, Inc.	Industrial
SHCR	Sheridan Healthcare, Inc.	Industrial
SHLO	Shiloh Industries, Inc.	Industrial
SHPGY	Shire Pharmaceuticals Group, plc	Biotechnology
SHVA	Shiva Corporation	Industrial
SCVL	Shoe Carnival, Inc.	Industrial
SHOE	Shoe Pavilion, Inc	Industrial
LODG	ShoLodge, Inc.	Industrial
SATH	Shop at Home, Inc.	Industrial
SHBK	Shore Financial Corporation	Bank
SLFC	Shoreline Financial Corporation	Other Finance
SHFL	Shuffle Master, Inc.	Industrial
SIHS	SI Handling Systems, Inc.	Industrial
SIBI	SIBIA Neurosciences, Inc.	Biotechnology
SEBL	Siebel Systems, Inc.	Computer

Symbol	Company Name	Sector
SIEB	Siebert Financial Corp.	Industrial
SWBS	SierraWest Bancorp	Other Finance
SGPH	SIGA Pharmaceuticals, Inc.	Industrial
VISN	Sight Resource Corp.	Industrial
SIGM	Sigma Designs, Inc.	Computer
SIAL	Sigma-Aldrich Corporation	Industrial
SGMA	SigmaTron International, Inc.	Industrial
SGNL	Signal Corporation	Other Finance
SGNLO	Signal Corporation	Other Finance
SEYE	Signature Eyewear, Inc.	Industrial
SGNS	Signature Inns, Inc.	Industrial
SGNSP	Signature Inns, Inc.	Industrial
SIGYY	Signet Group plc	Industrial
SLGN	Silgan Holdings, Inc.	Industrial
SILCF	Silicom Ltd	Industrial
SGIC	Silicon Gaming, Inc.	Industrial
SSTI	Silicon Storage Technology, Inc.	Computer
SIVB	Silicon Valley Bancshares	Other Finance
SVGI	Silicon Valley Group, Inc.	Industrial
SVRI	Silicon Valley Research	Computer
SILI	Siliconix Incorporated	Computer
SLVR	Silver Diner, Inc.	Industrial
SSRIF	Silver Standard Resources, Inc	Industrial
SCHI	Simione Central Holdings, Inc.	Industrial
SFNCA	Simmons First National Corporation	Other Finance
SFNCP	Simmons First National Corporation	Other Finance
SIMN	Simon Transportation Services, Inc.	Transportation
SMPS	Simpson Industries, Inc.	Industrial
SIMS	SIMS Communications, Inc.	Industrial
SIMU	Simulations Plus, Inc.	Computer
SIMWF	Simware Inc.	Computer
SBGI	Sinclair Broadcast Group, Inc.	Telecommunications
SBGIP	Sinclair Broadcast Group, Inc.	Telecommunications
SIPX	SIPEX Corporation	Computer
SIRC	Sirco International Corp.	Industrial
SIRN	Sirena Apparel Group, Inc. (The)	Industrial
SISB	SIS Bancorp, Inc.	Bank
SIXR	Six Rivers National Bank	Bank
SJNB	SJNB Financial Corp.	Other Finance
SKAN	Skaneateles Bancorp Inc.	Bank
SKYF	Sky Financial Group, Inc.	Bank
NZSKY	Sky Network Television Limited	Telecommunications

Symbol	Company Name	Sector
SKYEY	SkyePharma PLC	Biotechnology
SKCB	Skylands Community Bank	Bank
SKYL	Skyline Multimedia Entertainment, Inc.	Industrial
SKYM	SkyMall, Inc.	Industrial
SKYT	SkyTel Communications, Inc.	Telecommunications
SKYW	SkyWest, Inc.	Transportation
SFBC	Slade's Ferry Bancorp	Bank
SMCH	Smart Choice Automotive Group, Inc.	Industrial
SMOD	SMART Modular Technologies, Inc.	Computer
SMTK	SmarTalk TeleServices, Inc.	Telecommunications
SFLX	Smartflex Systems, Inc.	Computer
SMCC	SMC Corporation	Industrial
SMEDF	SMED International Inc.	Industrial
SCCO	Smith Corona Corporation	Industrial
SMSI	Smith Micro Software, Inc.	Industrial
HAMS	Smithfield Companies, Inc. (The)	Industrial
SFDS	Smithfield Foods, Inc.	Industrial
SMID	Smith-Midland Corporation	Industrial
SMXC	Smithway Motor Xpress Corp.	Transportation
SNBJ	SNB Bancshares, Inc.	Bank
SOBI	Sobieski Bancorp, Inc.	Bank
SODK	Sodak Gaming, Inc.	Industrial
SOFT	SofTech, Inc.	Computer
SPCOC	Software Publishing Corporation Holdings, Inc.	Computer
SSPE	Software Spectrum, Inc.	Industrial
BYND	software.net Corporation	Industrial
SWRX	SOFTWORKS, Inc.	Computer
SOLP	Solomon-Page Group Ltd. (The)	Industrial
SLPT	SoloPoint, Inc.	Industrial
SMTS	Somanetics Corporation	Industrial
SOMN	Somnus Medical Technologies, Inc.	Industrial
SNSTA	Sonesta International Hotels Corporation	Industrial
SONC	Sonic Corp.	Industrial
SNIC	Sonic Solutions	Industrial
SIMA	Sonics & Materials, Inc.	Industrial
SONO	SonoSight, Inc.	Industrial
SNUS	SONUS Pharmaceuticals, Inc.	Biotechnology
SOSS	SOS Staffing Services, Inc.	Industrial
SUND	Sound Advice, Inc.	Industrial
SFFS	Sound Federal Bancorp	Bank
SSII	Sound Source Interactive, Inc.	Industrial
SOCC	Source Capital Corporation	Industrial

Symbol	Company Name	Sector
SRCM	Source Media, Inc.	Telecommunications
SABC	South Alabama Bancorporation, Inc.	Other Finance
SCCB	South Carolina Community Bancshares, Inc.	Other Finance
SSFC	South Street Financial Corporation	Bank
UMPQ	South Umpqua Bank	Bank
SBAN	SouthBanc Shares, Inc.	Bank
STBF	Southeastern Thrift and Bank Fund, Inc. (The)	Other Finance
SCBS	Southern Community Bancshares, Inc.	Bank
SEHI	Southern Energy Homes, Inc.	Industrial
SFFB	Southern Financial Bancorp, Inc.	Other Finance
SMIN	Southern Mineral Corporation	Industrial
SMBC	Southern Missouri Bancorp, Inc.	Other Finance
SPPTY	Southern Pacific Petroleum N.L	Industrial
SSLI	Southern Security Life Insurance Company	Insurance
SLCM	Southland Corporation (The)	Industrial
SBCO	Southside Bancshares Corp.	Other Finance
SBSI	Southside Bancshares, Inc.	Bank
SBSIP	Southside Bancshares, Inc.	Bank
SOTR	SouthTrust Corporation	Other Finance
SWTX	Southwall Technologies, Inc.	Industrial
OKSB	Southwest Bancorp, Inc.	Bank
OKSBO	Southwest Bancorp, Inc.	Bank
SWBT	Southwest Bancorporation of Texas, Inc.	Other Finance
SWPA	Southwest National Corporation	Other Finance
SWWC	Southwest Water Company	Industrial
SVRN	Sovereign Bancorp, Inc.	Bank
SPAB	SPACEHAB, Incorporated	Industrial
SLMD	Spacelabs Medical, Inc.	Industrial
SIMC	Spacetec IMC Corporation	Computer
SPAN	Span-America Medical Systems, Inc.	Industrial
SPLK	Spanlink Communications, Inc.	Industrial
SPFO	Sparta Foods, Inc.	Industrial
SPTA	Sparta Pharmaceuticals, Inc.	Industrial
SPAR	Spartan Motors, Inc.	Industrial
SPAZ	Spatializer Audio Laboratories, Inc.	Industrial
SDII	Special Devices, Inc.	Industrial
SMCX	Special Metals Corporation	Industrial
SHPI	Specialized Health Products International, Inc.	Industrial
SCNI	Specialty Care Network, Inc.	Industrial
CTLG	Specialty Catalog Corp.	Industrial
SPEQ	Specialty Equipment Companies, Inc.	Industrial
DIAGF	Spectral Diagnostics Inc.	Biotechnology

Symbol	Company Name	Sector
SLNK	SpectraLink Corporation	Industrial
SPTR	SpecTran Corporation	Industrial
SPNC	Spectranetics Corporation (The)	Industrial
SPLI	Spectra-Physics Lasers, Inc.	Industrial
SPSI	SpectraScience, Inc.	Industrial
SPCT	Spectrian Corporation	Industrial
SPEC	Spectrum Control, Inc.	Industrial
SSPIF	Spectrum Signal Processing Inc.	Computer
SPRX	Spectrx, Inc.	Industrial
SFAM	SpeedFam International, Inc.	Industrial
SPZN	Speizman Industries, Inc.	Industrial
SPZE	Spice Entertainment Companies, Inc.	Telecommunications
SPGLA	Spiegel, Inc.	Industrial
SPIR	Spire Corporation	Industrial
SPLH	Splash Technology Holdings, Inc.	Industrial
SPCH	Sport Chalet, Inc.	Industrial
SPOR	Sport-Haley, Inc.	Industrial
SPLN	Sportsline USA, Inc.	Industrial
SPRI	SPR Inc.	Industrial
SPSS	SPSS Inc.	Computer
SPYG	Spyglass, Inc.	Industrial
SRSL	SRS Labs, Inc.	Other Finance
SSNC	SS&C Technologies, Inc.	Computer
SSET	SSE Telecom, Inc.	Industrial
STFR	St. Francis Capital Corporation	Bank
MARY	St. Mary Land & Exploration Company	Industrial
SPBC	St. Paul Bancorp, Inc.	Other Finance
STAA	STAAR Surgical Company	Industrial
STAC	Stac, Inc.	Computer
SBLI	Staff Builders, Inc.	Industrial
STFF	Staff Leasing, Inc.	Industrial
STAF	StaffMark, Inc.	Industrial
STKLF	Stake Technology Ltd.	Industrial
SFUN	Standard Funding Corp.	Other Finance
SMAN	Standard Management Corporation	Insurance
SMSC	Standard Microsystems Corporation	Computer
STII	Stanford Telecommunications, Inc.	Industrial
STLY	Stanley Furniture Company, Inc.	Industrial
SPLS	Staples, Inc.	Industrial
STRZ	Star Buffet, Inc.	Industrial
SMCS	Star Multi Care Services, Inc.	Industrial
STRX	STAR Telecommunications, Inc.	Telecommunications

Symbol	Company Name	Sector
SBAS	StarBase Corporation	Industrial
SBUX	Starbucks Corporation	Industrial
STCR	Starcraft Corporation	Industrial
STMT	Starmet Corporation	Industrial
STGC	Startec Global Communications Corporation	Telecommunications
STFC	State Auto Financial Corporation	Insurance
STBC	State Bancorp, Inc.	Other Finance
SFSW	State Financial Services Corporation	Other Finance
SFFC	StateFed Financial Corporation	Bank
SFIN	Statewide Financial Corp.	Other Finance
STBI	STB Systems, Inc.	Computer
SLHN	Stearns & Lehman, Inc.	Industrial
STLD	Steel Dynamics, Inc.	Industrial
SWVA	Steel of West Virginia, Inc.	Industrial
STTX	Steel Technologies Inc.	Industrial
SMRT	Stein Mart, Inc.	Industrial
STNRF	Steiner Leisure Limited	Industrial
SRCL	Stericycle, Inc.	Industrial
STER	Sterigenics International, Inc	Industrial
STRC	Sterile Recoveries, Inc.	Industrial
STRL	STERIS Corporation	Industrial
SBIB	Sterling Bancshares, Inc.	Bank
SBIBP	Sterling Bancshares, Inc.	Bank
SLFI	Sterling Financial Corporation	Other Finance
STSA	Sterling Financial Corporation	Bank
STSAO	Sterling Financial Corporation	Bank
ISEE	Sterling Vision, Inc.	Industrial
STHLY	STET Hellas Telecommunications S.A.	Telecommunications
SHOO	Steven Madden, Ltd.	Industrial
SSSS	Stewart & Stevenson Services, Inc.	Industrial
STEI	Stewart Enterprises, Inc.	Industrial
STIM	Stimsonite Corporation	Industrial
SCBHF	Stirling Cooke Brown Holdings Limited	Insurance
STKR	Stocker & Yale, Inc.	Industrial
SCSWF	Stolt Comex Seaway S.A.	Industrial
STLBY	Stolt-Nielsen S.A. c/o Stolt-Nielsen S.A.	Transportation
STLTF	Stolt-Nielsen S.A. c/o Stolt-Nielsen S.A.	Transportation
STMDQ	StorMedia Incorporated	Industrial
SSYS	Stratasys, Inc.	Industrial
SDIX	Strategic Diagnostics Inc.	Industrial
STRD	Strategic Distribution, Inc.	Industrial
STRT	Strattec Security Corporation	Industrial

Symbol	Company Name	Sector
STRS	Stratus Properties, Inc.	Industrial
STRA	Strayer Education, Inc.	Industrial
FUEL	Streicher Mobile Fueling, Inc.	Industrial
SKRI	Striker Industries, Inc.	Industrial
STRO	Strouds, Inc.	Industrial
SDRC	Structural Dynamics Research Corp.	Computer
STVI	STV Group, Inc.	Industrial
STYL	Styling Technology Corporation	Industrial
SBNK	Suburban Bancshares, Inc.	Other Finance
SLAM	Suburban Lodges of America, Inc.	Industrial
SXNB	Success Bancshares, Inc.	Bank
SXNBP	Success Bancshares, Inc.	Bank
SCES	Successories Inc.	Industrial
SUBK	Suffolk Bancorp	Other Finance
SUGN	SUGEN, Inc.	Biotechnology
SUMA	Summa Four, Inc.	Industrial
SUMX	SUMMA INDUSTRIES	Industrial
SBIT	Summit Bancshares, Inc.	Other Finance
SBGA	Summit Bank Corporation	Bank
SMMT	Summit Design, Inc.	Computer
SUMM	Summit Financial Corporation	Other Finance
SUMT	Summit Medical Systems, Inc.	Computer
BEAM	Summit Technology, Inc.	Industrial
SNBC	Sun Bancorp, Inc.	Bank
SNBCP	Sun Bancorp, Inc.	Bank
SUBI	Sun Bancorp, Inc. (SUN)	Bank
SNHY	Sun Hydraulics Corporation	Industrial
SUNW	Sun Microsystems, Inc.	Computer
SNBS	Sunbase Asia, Inc.	Industrial
SUNH	Sundance Homes, Inc.	Industrial
RAYS	Sunglass Hut International, Inc.	Industrial
SUNP	SunPharm Corporation	Industrial
SUNQ	Sunquest Information Systems, Inc.	Computer
SNRZ	Sunrise Assisted Living Inc.	Industrial
SUNL	Sunrise International Leasing Corporation	Computer
SUNS	SunStar Healthcare, Inc.	Industrial
SUPVA	Super Vision International, Inc.	Industrial
SCON	Superconductor Technologies Inc.	Industrial
SUPG	SuperGen, Inc.	Biotechnology
SUPC	Superior Consultant Holdings Corporation	Industrial
SESI	Superior Energy Services, Inc.	Industrial
SNTL	Superior National Insurance Group, Inc.	Insurance

Symbol	Company Name	Sector
SUPR	Superior Services, Inc.	Industrial
SPPR	Supertel Hospitality, Inc.	Industrial
SUPX	Supertex, Inc.	Computer
CHEZ	Suprema Specialties, Inc.	Industrial
SUPI	Supreme International Corporation	Industrial
SRGE	Surge Components, Inc.	Industrial
SLTI	Surgical Laser Technologies, Inc.	Industrial
SRDX	SurModics, Inc.	Industrial
SOAP	Surrey, Inc.	Industrial
SUSQ	Susquehanna Bancshares, Inc.	Other Finance
STTZF	Sutton Resources, Ltd.	Industrial
SVBF	SVB Financial Services, Inc.	Bank
SNKI	Swank, Inc.	Industrial
SWMAY	Swedish Match, AB	Industrial
SWFT	Swift Transportation Co., Inc.	Transportation
SABI	Swiss Army Brands Inc.	Industrial
SYBS	Sybase, Inc.	Computer
SYKE	Sykes Enterprises, Incorporated	Computer
SYLN	Sylvan Inc.	Industrial
SLVN	Sylvan Learning Systems, Inc.	Industrial
SYMC	Symantec Corporation	Computer
SYMBA	Symbollon Corporation	Industrial
SYMX	Symix Systems, Inc.	Computer
SYMM	Symmetricom, Inc.	Industrial
SIGC	Symons International Group, Inc.	Insurance
SMPX	Symphonix Devices, Inc.	Industrial
SYGR	Synagro Technologies, Inc.	Industrial
SYNC	Synalloy Corporation	Industrial
SNAP	Synaptic Pharmaceutical Corporation	Biotechnology
SBIO	Synbiotics Corporation	Industrial
SYNX	Sync Research, Inc.	Industrial
SCOR	Syncor International Corporation	Industrial
SYBR	Synergy Brands Inc.	Industrial
SNTC	Synetic, Inc.	Industrial
SNPS	Synopsys, Inc.	Computer
SYBBF	SYNSORB Biotech Inc.	Biotechnology
SYNT	Syntel, Inc.	Computer
SYNL	Syntellect Inc.	Industrial
NZYM	Synthetech, Inc.	Industrial
SIND	Synthetic Industries, Inc	Industrial
SYNM	Syntroleum Corporation	Industrial
SYPR	Sypris Solutions, Inc.	Computer

Symbol	Company Name	Sector
SYQT	SyQuest Technology, Inc.	Computer
SYCM	Syscomm International Corporation	Industrial
SSAX	System Software Associates, Inc.	Computer
SCTC	Systems & Computer Technology Corporation	Computer
SYSF	SystemSoft Corporation	Computer
TWFC	T & W Financial Corporation	Other Finance
ROSE	T R Financial Corp.	Bank
TROW	T. Rowe Price Associates, Inc.	Other Finance
AXLE	T.J.T., Inc.	Industrial
TVGTF	T.V.G. Technologies Ltd.	Computer
TACO	Taco Cabana, Inc.	Industrial
TDEO	Tadeo Holdings Inc.	Industrial
TTELF	Tadiran Telecommunications, Limited	Telecommunications
TAIT	Taitron Components Incorporated	Industrial
TTWO	Take-Two Interactive Software, Inc.	Computer
TALX	TALX Corporation	Computer
TAMR	TAM Restaurants, Inc.	Industrial
TBAC	Tandy Brands Accessories, Inc.	Industrial
TESI	Tangram Enterprise Solutions, Inc.	Industrial
TNSU	Tanisys Technology, Inc.	Industrial
TGEN	Targeted Genetics Corporation	Biotechnology
VIPT	Tarragon Realty Investors, Inc.	Other Finance
TAGS	Tarrant Apparel Group	Industrial
TATTF	TAT Technologies Ltd.	Computer
TOFF	Tatham Offshore, Inc.	Industrial
TAVA	TAVA Technologies Inc.	Industrial
TAYD	Taylor Devices, Inc.	Industrial
TBAE	TBA Entertainment Corporation	Industrial
TBCC	TBC Corporation	Industrial
TCAT	TCA Cable TV, Inc.	Telecommunications
TCICP	TCI Communications, Inc.	Telecommunications
TCII	TCI International, Inc.	Industrial
TUNE	TCI Music, Inc.	Telecommunications
TSATA	TCI Satellite Entertainment, Inc.	Telecommunications
TSATB	TCI Satellite Entertainment, Inc.	Telecommunications
TCSI	TCSI Corporation	Computer
TMAM	TEAM America Corporation	Industrial
TMTV	Team Communications Group, Inc.	Industrial
TDRP	TearDrop Golf Company	Industrial
TECD	Tech Data Corporation	Industrial
TELE	Tech Electro Industries, Inc.	Industrial
TCDN	Techdyne, Inc.	Industrial

Symbol	Company Name	Sector
TFRC	TechForce Corporation	Computer
TECH	Techne Corporation	Biotechnology
TCPI	Technical Chemicals and Products, Inc.	Industrial
TCCO	Technical Communications Corporation	Industrial
TCLN	Techniclone Corporation	Industrial
TSRC	Technisource, Inc.	Industrial
TRCI	Technology Research Corporation	Industrial
TSCC	Technology Solutions Company	Computer
TCNOF	Tecnomatix Technologies Ltd.	Computer
TECUA	Tecumseh Products Company	Industrial
TECUB	Tecumseh Products Company	Industrial
TGAL	Tegal Corporation	Industrial
TANK	TEI, Inc.	Industrial
TKLC	TEKELEC	Industrial
TKGFA	Tekgraf, Inc.	Industrial
TELC	Telco Systems, Inc.	Industrial
TLCM	TelCom Semiconductor, Inc.	Computer
TCTV	Tel-Com Wireless Cable TV Corporation	Industrial
TBFC	TeleBanc Financial Corporation	Bank
TBFCP	TeleBanc Financial Corporation	Bank
TINTA	Tele-Communications International, Inc.	Telecommunications
LBTYA	Tele-Communications, Inc.	Telecommunications
LBTYB	Tele-Communications, Inc.	Telecommunications
TCIVA	Tele-Communications, Inc.	Telecommunications
TCIVB	Tele-Communications, Inc.	Telecommunications
TCOMA	Tele-Communications, Inc.	Telecommunications
TCOMB	Tele-Communications, Inc.	Telecommunications
TCOMP	Tele-Communications, Inc.	Telecommunications
TLDCF	Teledata Communications Ltd	Industrial
TGRP	Telegroup, Inc.	Telecommunications
TPADA	TelePad Corporation	Computer
TPARY	Telepartner A/S	Industrial
TSCN	Telescan, Inc.	Industrial
TSFT	Telesoft Corp.	Computer
TLSP	Telespectrum Worldwide, Inc.	Industrial
TIWIF	Telesystem International Wireless Inc.	Telecommunications
TTEC	TeleTech Holdings, Inc.	Industrial
TELV	TeleVideo Inc.	Computer
TWSTY	Telewest Communications plc	Telecommunications
TLDT	Telident, Inc.	Industrial
TGNT	Teligent, Inc.	Industrial
TLAB	Tellabs, Inc.	Industrial

Symbol	Company Name	Sector
TALK	Tel-Save Holdings, Inc.	Telecommunications
TSCP	Telscape International Inc.	Industrial
TLTN	Teltrend Inc.	Industrial
TELT	Teltronics, Inc.	Industrial
WRLS	Telular Corporation	Industrial
TLXN	Telxon Corporation	Computer
TMPL	Template Software, Inc.	Computer
TMTX	Temtex Industries, Inc.	Industrial
TANT	Tennant Company	Industrial
TERA	Tera Computer Company	Industrial
TERN	Terayon Communication Systems, Inc.	Telecommunications
TESOF	Tesco Corporation	Industrial
TSMAF	Tesma International, Inc.	Industrial
TESS	TESSCO Technologies Incorporated	Industrial
WATR	Tetra Tech, Inc.	Industrial
TEVIY	Teva Pharmaceutical Industries Limited	Biotechnology
TEXM	Texas Micro Inc.	Computer
TRBS	Texas Regional Bancshares, Inc.	Bank
TXLI	Texoil, Inc.	Industrial
THRD	TF Financial Corporation	Other Finance
TFCE	TFC Enterprises, Inc.	Other Finance
TGCIC	TGC Industries, Inc.	Industrial
TGCPC	TGC Industries, Inc.	Industrial
TACX	The A Consulting Team, Inc.	Computer
ARTL	The Aristotle Corporation	Industrial
ASTN	The Ashton Technology Group, Inc.	Computer
AGRPA	The Associated Group, Inc.	Telecommunications
AGRPB	The Associated Group, Inc.	Telecommunications
CGGI	The Carbide/Graphite Group, Inc.	Industrial
PLCE	The Children's Place Retail Stores, Inc.	Industrial
COLO	The Colonel's International, Inc.	Industrial
CBNJ	The Community Bank of New Jersey	Bank
CRNSF	The Cronos Group	Industrial
DIALY	The Dialog Corporation plc ADR	Computer
DXYN	The Dixie Group, Inc.	Industrial
EBSC	The Elder-Beerman Stores Corp.	Industrial
TXCO	The Exploration Company	Industrial
HAIN	The Hain Food Group, Inc.	Industrial
JUDG	The Judge Group, Inc.	Computer
KROG	The Kroll-O'Gara Company	Industrial
KLOC	The Kushner-Locke Company	Industrial
KNIC	The L.L. Knickerbocker Company, Inc.	Industrial

Symbol	Company Name	Sector
LEAP	The Leap Group, Inc.	Industrial
MALT	The Lion Brewery, Inc.	Industrial
MILB	The Millbrook Press, Inc.	Industrial
NTPL	The Netplex Group, Inc.	Computer
TNFI	The North Face, Inc.	Industrial
PRED	The Orlando Predators Entertainment, Inc.	Industrial
PBSF	The Pacific Bank, National Association	Bank
PNDA	The Panda Project, Inc.	Computer
ACEP	The Parts Source, Inc.	Industrial
PIOG	The Pioneer Group, Inc.	Other Finance
PRGX	The Profit Recovery Group International, Inc.	Industrial
QGLY	The Quigley Corporation	Industrial
RNET	The Recovery Network, Inc.	Industrial
SWCB	The Sandwich Bancorp, Inc.	Other Finance
SOMR	The Somerset Group, Inc.	Industrial
SORC	The Source Information Management Co	Industrial
SGDE	The Sportsman's Guide, Inc.	Industrial
TSST	The TesseracT Group, Inc.	Industrial
TODDA	The Todd-AO Corporation	Industrial
ULTI	The Ultimate Software Group, Inc.	Computer
UNMG	The UniMark Group, Inc.	Industrial
IQIQ	The viaLink Company	Computer
WIDEF	The WideCom Group, Inc.	Industrial
WMFG	The WMF Group, Ltd.	Other Finance
YRKG	The York Group, Inc.	Industrial
THRT	TheraTech, Inc.	Industrial
VCLL	Thermacell Technologies, Inc.	Industrial
TMXI	Thermatrix, Inc.	Industrial
TTRIF	Thermo Tech Technologies, Inc.	Industrial
KOOL	THERMOGENESIS Corp.	Industrial
THNK	THINK New Ideas, Inc.	Industrial
THTL	Thistle Group Holdings, Co.	Bank
TGIS	Thomas Group, Inc.	Industrial
TMSTA	Thomaston Mills, Inc.	Industrial
TMSTB	Thomaston Mills, Inc.	Industrial
THOR	Thoratec Laboratories Corporation	Industrial
TAVI	Thorn Apple Valley, Inc.	Industrial
THRNY	Thorn plc	Industrial
THQI	THQ Inc.	Industrial
TMSR	ThrustMaster, Inc.	Industrial
TXHI	THT Inc.	Industrial
TIBB	TIB Financial Corporation	Other Finance

Symbol	Company Name	Sector
ATMS	Tidel Technologies, Inc.	Industrial
TIER	Tier Technologies, Inc.	Computer
TIII	TII Industries, Inc.	Industrial
TSBK	Timberland Bancorp, Inc.	Bank
TMBS	Timberline Software Corporation	Computer
TEXP	Titan Exploration, Inc.	Industrial
TTNP	Titan Pharmaceuticals, Inc.	Industrial
TVLI	Tivoli Industries, Inc.	Industrial
TJCO	TJ International, Inc.	Industrial
TBDI	TMBR/Sharp Drilling, Inc.	Industrial
TMEI	TMCI Electronics, Inc.	Industrial
TMPW	TMP Worldwide Inc.	Industrial
TNTX	T-NETIX Inc.	Telecommunications
TMAN	Today's Man, Inc.	Industrial
TKIOY	Tokio Marine & Fire Insurance Company, Ltd	Insurance
TLGD	Tollgrade Communications, Inc.	Industrial
TMBR	Tom Brown, Inc.	Industrial
TLXAF	Toolex International N.V.	Industrial
TISAF	Top Image Systems, Ltd.	Computer
TOPP	Topps Company, Inc. (The)	Industrial
TOPS	Tops Appliance City, Inc.	Industrial
TRGL	Toreador Royalty Corporation	Industrial
TCIX	Total Containment, Inc.	Industrial
TCPS	Total Control Products, Inc.	Industrial
TENT	Total Entertainment Restaurant Corp.	Industrial
TOTL	Total Research Corporation	Industrial
TELU	Total-Tel USA Communications, Inc.	Industrial
TASA	Touchstone Applied Science Associates, Inc.	Industrial
TSSW	TouchStone Software Corporation	Industrial
TOWR	Tower Air, Inc.	Transportation
TSEMF	Tower Semiconductor Ltd.	Computer
TTMT	Tower Tech, Inc.	Industrial
TWNE	Towne Services, Inc.	Computer
TMAX	Toymax International, Inc.	Industrial
TOYOY	Toyota Motor Corporation	Industrial
TRAC	Track Data Corporation	Computer
TKTL	Track 'n Trail	Industrial
TSCO	Tractor Supply Company	Industrial
TRBR	Trailer Bridge, Inc.	Transportation
TRKA	Trak Auto Corporation	Industrial
TSRG	Trans Energy, Inc. New	Industrial
TGSI	Trans Global Services, Inc.	Industrial

Symbol	Company Name	Sector
TWMC	Trans World Entertainment Corp.	Industrial
TACT	TransAct Technologies Incorporated	Industrial
TNSI	Transaction Network Services, Inc.	Telecommunications
TSAI	Transaction Systems Architects, Inc.	Industrial
TRCR	Transcend Services, Inc.	Industrial
TSND	Transcend Therapeutics, Inc.	Biotechnology
TCMS	TransCoastal Marine Services, Inc.	Industrial
TRIXY	Transcom International, Limited	Industrial
TRGNY	TRANSGENE S.A.	Biotechnology
TGBRY	Trans-Global Resources N.L.	Industrial
TRNI	Trans-Industries, Inc.	Industrial
TRGP	Transit Group Inc.	Transportation
TSIX	Transition Systems, Inc.	Computer
TKTX	Transkaryotic Therapies, Inc.	Industrial
TRNS	Transmation, Inc.	Industrial
MBTA	Transmedia Asia Pacific, Inc.	Industrial
TCAM	Transport Corporation of America, Inc.	Transportation
TXCC	TranSwitch Corporation	Industrial
TWHH	Transworld HealthCare Inc.	Industrial
TNZRY	Tranz Rail Holdings, Limited	Transportation
TPOA	Travel Ports of America, Inc.	Industrial
TRVL	Travel Services International, Inc.	Transportation
TRVS	Travis Boats & Motors, Inc.	Industrial
TRED	Treadco, Inc.	Industrial
TRES	TreeSource Industries, Inc.	Industrial
TREV	TREEV Inc.	Computer
TREVP	TREEV Inc.	Industrial
TRGA	Trega Biosciences Inc.	Industrial
TRND	Trend-Lines, Inc.	Industrial
TWRI	Trendwest Resorts, Inc.	Other Finance
TREN	Trenwick Group Inc.	Insurance
TGIC	Triad Guaranty Inc.	Insurance
VIRS	Triangle Pharmaceuticals, Inc.	Biotechnology
TBCOA	Triathlon Broadcasting Company	Telecommunications
TCBK	TriCo Bancshares	Other Finance
TMAR	Trico Marine Services, Inc.	Transportation
TRCD	Tricord Systems, Inc.	Computer
TRIC	Tri-County Bancorp, Inc.	Bank
TRDT	Trident International, Inc.	Computer
TRID	Trident Microsystems, Inc.	Computer
TRGI	Trident Rowan Group Inc.	Industrial
TRDX	Tridex Corporation	Industrial

Symbol	Company Name	Sector
TRKN	Trikon Technologies, Inc.	Industrial
TLNOF	Trillion Resources Ltd.	Industrial
TMRK	Trimark Holdings, Inc.	Industrial
TRMB	Trimble Navigation Limited	Industrial
TMED	Trimedyne, Inc.	Industrial
TRMS	Trimeris, Inc.	Industrial
TRIBY	Trinity Biotech PLC	Biotechnology
TRON	Trion, Inc.	Industrial
TPPPF	Triple P, N.V.	Computer
TSSS	Triple S Plastics, Inc.	Industrial
TRPS	Tripos, Inc.	Computer
TQNT	TriQuint Semiconductor, Inc.	Industrial
TRSM	TRISM, Inc.	Transportation
TSAR	TRISTAR Corporation	Industrial
TRMM	TRM Corporation	Industrial
TUTR	TRO Learning, Inc.	Industrial
TSIC	Tropical Sportswear Int'l Corporation	Industrial
TRUV	Truevision, Inc.	Computer
TCNJ	Trust Company of New Jersey (The)	Other Finance
TRST	TrustCo Bank Corp NY	Other Finance
TRMK	Trustmark Corporation	Other Finance
TSNG	Tseng Labs, Inc.	Computer
TSII	TSI Incorporated	Industrial
TSFW	TSI International Software Ltd	Computer
TSRI	TSR, Inc.	Computer
TSTI	TST/Impreso, Inc.	Industrial
TTILF	TTI Team Telecom International Ltd.	Computer
TUBY	Tubby's, Inc.	Industrial
TFCO	Tufco Technologies, Inc.	Industrial
TRBO	TurboChef Technologies, Inc.	Industrial
TRBD	Turbodyne Technologies, Inc.	Industrial
TUSC	Tuscarora Incorporated	Industrial
PYTV	TV Filme, Inc.	Telecommunications
TWTR	Tweeter Home Entertainment Group, Inc	Industrial
TWIN	Twin City Bancorp, Inc.	Bank
TWLB	Twinlab Corporation	Biotechnology
OFIS	U.S. Office Products Company	Industrial
USPL	U.S. Plastic Lumber Corporation	Industrial
USAM	U.S. Automotive Manufacturing Inc.	Industrial
USDL	U.S. Diagnostic Inc.	Industrial
USEG	U.S. Energy Corp.	Industrial
USEY	U.S. Energy Systems, Inc.	Industrial

Symbol	Company Name	Sector
USFS	U.S. Franchise Systems, Inc.	Industrial
GROW	U.S. Global Investors, Inc.	Other Finance
USHG	U.S. Home & Garden, Inc.	Industrial
USPN	U.S. Pawn, Inc.	Industrial
USPH	U.S. Physical Therapy, Inc.	Industrial
TIMBZ	U.S. Timberlands Company, L.P.	Industrial
USTC	U.S. Trust Corporation	Other Finance
USVI	U.S. Vision, Inc.	Industrial
USWC	U.S. Wireless Corporation	Industrial
XPRSA	U.S. Xpress Enterprises, Inc.	Transportation
ROSI	U.S.A. Floral Products, Inc.	Industrial
CHDX	U.S.-China Industrial Exchange, Inc.	Industrial
UBIX	UBICS, Inc.	Computer
UFPT	UFP Technologies, Inc.	Industrial
UGLY	Ugly Duckling Corporation	Industrial
UICI	UICI	Insurance
ULTE	Ultimate Electronics, Inc.	Industrial
ULTD	Ultradata Corporation	Computer
ULTR	Ultradata Systems, Incorporated	Industrial
ULTK	Ultrak, Inc.	Industrial
ULBI	Ultralife Batteries, Inc.	Industrial
UTEK	Ultratech Stepper, Inc.	Industrial
UMBF	UMB Financial Corporation	Other Finance
UNAM	Unico American Corporation	Insurance
UNRC	Unico, Inc.	Industrial
UCMP	UniComp, Inc.	Industrial
UNDG	Unidigital, Inc.	Industrial
UDYN	UNIDYNE Corporation	Industrial
UFAB	UNIFAB International, Inc.	Industrial
UNFY	Unify Corporation	Computer
UGNE	Unigene Laboratories, Inc.	Industrial
UHLDE	UniHolding Corp.	Industrial
UMED	Unimed Pharmaceuticals, Inc.	Industrial
UACA	Union Acceptance Corporation	Other Finance
UBSH	Union Bankshares Corporation	Other Finance
UBSC	Union Bankshares, Ltd.	Other Finance
UCBC	Union Community Bancorp	Other Finance
UFBS	Union Financial Bancshares, Inc.	Other Finance
UNNL	Union National Bancorp, Inc.	Bank
UPCPO	Union Planters Corporation	Other Finance
UNBC	UnionBanCal Corporation	Bank
UBCD	UnionBancorp, Inc	Other Finance

Symbol	Company Name	Sector
UNPH	Uniphase Corporation	Industrial
UNIQ	Unique Casual Restaurants, Inc	Industrial
UTCI	Uniroyal Technology Corporation	Industrial
UNSRA	Uniservice Corporation	Industrial
UNII	Unit Instruments, Inc.	Industrial
UBCP	United Bancorp, Inc.	Bank
UBSI	United Bankshares, Inc.	Other Finance
UCFC	United Community Financial Corp.	Bank
UBMT	United Financial Corp	Bank
UFCS	United Fire & Casualty Company	Insurance
UHCP	United Heritage Corporation	Industrial
UIHIA	United International Holdings, Inc.	Telecommunications
UIRT	United Investors Realty Trust	Industrial
UTDL	United Leisure Corporation	Industrial
UNBJ	United National Bancorp	Bank
UNFI	United Natural Foods, Inc.	Industrial
UNEWY	United News & Media, p.l.c.	Industrial
UPFC	United PanAm Financial Corporation	Other Finance
UPUP	United Payors & United Providers, Inc.	Insurance
URGI	United Retail Group, Inc.	Industrial
URSI	United Road Services, Inc.	Industrial
USBN	United Security Bancorporation	Bank
USLM	United States Lime & Minerals, Inc.	Industrial
USTR	United Stationers Inc.	Industrial
UTVI	United Television, Inc.	Telecommunications
UTBI	United Tennessee Bankshares, Inc.	Bank
UTIN	United Trust, Inc.	Insurance
UVSGA	United Video Satellite Group, Inc.	Telecommunications
UTOG	Unitog Company	Industrial
UNIT	Unitrin, Inc.	Insurance
UNTY	Unity Bancorp, Inc.	Bank
UNVC	UNIVEC, Inc.	Industrial
UHCO	Universal American Financial Corp.	Insurance
UVSL	Universal Automotive Industries, Inc.	Industrial
PANL	Universal Display Corporation	Industrial
UEIC	Universal Electronics Inc.	Industrial
UFPI	Universal Forest Products, Inc.	Industrial
UFMG	Universal Mfg. Co.	Industrial
USEC	Universal Security Instruments, Inc.	Industrial
USAP	Universal Stainless & Alloy Products, Inc.	Industrial
UHCI	Universal Standard Healthcare Inc.	Industrial
UNIB	University Bancorp, Inc.	Industrial

Symbol	Company Name	Sector
UVEW	uniView Technologies Corporation	Industrial
UOLP	UOL Publishing, Inc.	Industrial
URIX	Uranium Resources, Inc.	Industrial
URBN	Urban Outfitters, Inc.	Industrial
UCOR	UroCor, Inc.	Industrial
ULGX	Urologix, Inc.	Industrial
URMDC	UroMed Corporation	Industrial
UROQ	UroQuest Medical Corporation	Industrial
UTCC	Ursus Telecom Corporation	Telecommunications
USWI	US WATS, INC.	Telecommunications
USBC	USA Biomass Corporation	Industrial
USBRE	USA Bridge Construction of N.Y., Inc.	Industrial
USAD	USA Detergents, Inc.	Industrial
USAI	USA Networks, Inc.	Telecommunications
USAK	USA Truck, Inc.	Transportation
USAB	USABancshares, Inc.	Bank
USBGE	USABG Corporation	Industrial
USNA	USANA, Inc.	Industrial
UBAN	USBANCORP, Inc.	Other Finance
UBANP	USBANCORP, Inc.	Other Finance
USCM	USCI, Inc.	Telecommunications
USCS	USCS International, Inc.	Computer
USDC	USDATA Corporation	Industrial
USFC	USFreightways Corporation	Transportation
USHP	U-Ship, Inc.	Transportation
USNC	USN Communications, Inc.	Telecommunications
USPTS	USP Real Estate Investment Trust	Other Finance
USTB	UST Corp.	Other Finance
USTL	UStel, Inc.	Telecommunications
USTX	USTMAN Technologies, Inc.	Industrial
USWB	USWeb Corporation	Computer
UTLX	UTILX Corporation	Industrial
VITX	V. I. Technologies, Inc.	Biotechnology
VDRY	Vacu-Dry Company	Industrial
VLNC	Valence Technology, Inc.	Industrial
VALN	Vallen Corporation	Industrial
VLFG	Valley Forge Scientific Corp.	Industrial
VNGI	Valley National Gases, Inc.	Industrial
VALE	Valley Systems, Inc.	Industrial
VALM	Valmont Industries, Inc.	Industrial
VALU	Value Line, Inc.	Other Finance
VVTV	ValueVision International, Inc.	Industrial

Symbol	Company Name	Sector
VCELA	Vanguard Cellular Systems, Inc.	Telecommunications
VANS	Vans, Inc.	Industrial
VNTV	Vantive Corporation (The)	Computer
VFLX	Variflex, Inc.	Industrial
VARL	Vari-L Company, Inc.	Industrial
LITE	Vari-Lite International, Inc.	Industrial
VRLN	Varlen Corporation	Industrial
VASO	Vasomedical, Inc.	Industrial
VGHN	Vaughn Communications, Inc.	Industrial
VDIM	VDI Media	Industrial
VTRAO	Vectra Banking Corporation	Other Finance
VECO	Veeco Instruments Inc.	Industrial
VENGF	Vengold, Inc.	Industrial
VMSI	Ventana Medical Systems, Inc.	Industrial
VSEIF	Venture Seismic, Limited	Industrial
VENT	Venturian Corp.	Industrial
VENX	Venus Exploration, Inc.	Industrial
VERA	Veramark Technologies Inc	Industrial
VERD	Verdant Brands, Inc.	Industrial
VRLK	Verilink Corporation	Industrial
VRIO	Verio Inc.	Computer
VRSN	VeriSign, Inc.	Industrial
VRTS	VERITAS Software Corporation	Industrial
VRTY	Verity, Inc.	Computer
VFSC	Vermont Financial Services Corp.	Other Finance
VPUR	Vermont Pure Holdings, Ltd.	Industrial
BEAR	Vermont Teddy Bear Co., Inc. (The)	Industrial
VSNT	Versant Corporation	Computer
VRTL	Vertel Corporation	Computer
VTEX	Vertex Communications Corporation	Industrial
VRTX	Vertex Pharmaceuticals Incorporated	Biotechnology
VESC	Vestcom International, Inc.	Industrial
VCAI	Veterinary Centers of America, Inc.	Industrial
VIAX	ViaGrafix Corporation	Industrial
VSAT	ViaSat, Inc.	Industrial
VIAS	VIASOFT, Inc.	Computer
VYTL	Viatel, Inc.	Telecommunications
VIBC	VIB Corp	Bank
VICL	Vical Incorporated	Biotechnology
VICR	Vicor Corporation	Industrial
VRES	VICORP Restaurants, Inc.	Industrial
VIDA	VidaMed, Inc.	Industrial

Symbol	Company Name	Sector
VIDE	Video Display Corporation	Industrial
VUPDA	Video Update, Inc.	Industrial
VLAB	VideoLabs, Inc.	Industrial
VDNX	Videonics, Inc.	Computer
VSVR	VideoServer, Inc.	Industrial
VUTK	View Tech, Inc.	Industrial
VISG	Viisage Technology, Inc.	Computer
VBNK	Village Bancorp, Inc.	Other Finance
VLGEA	Village Super Market, Inc.	Industrial
VMRX	VIMRx Pharmaceuticals Inc.	Industrial
VCAM	Vincam Group, Inc. (The)	Industrial
VION	Vion Pharmaceuticals Inc.	Industrial
VERP	Viragen (Europe) Ltd.	Industrial
VRGN	Viragen, Inc.	Industrial
VIRGY	Virgin Express Holdings plc	Transportation
VCBK	Virginia Commerce Bank	Bank
VCFC	Virginia Commonwealth Financial Corp	Bank
VGCO	Virginia Gas Company	Industrial
VPHM	ViroPharma Incorporated	Biotechnology
VFND	VirtualFund.com, Inc.	Computer
VGINF	Visible Genetics, Inc.	Industrial
VSIO	Visio Corporation	Computer
EYES	Vision Twenty-One, Inc.	Industrial
VSNR	Visioneer, Inc.	Industrial
VSCI	Vision-Sciences, Inc.	Industrial
VBNJ	Vista Bancorp, Inc.	Other Finance
VINF	Vista Information Solutions Inc.	Computer
VMTI	Vista Medical Technologies, Inc.	Industrial
VSTN	Vistana, Inc.	Other Finance
VDAT	Visual Data Corporation	Industrial
EDGE	Visual Edge Systems Inc.	Industrial
VNWK	Visual Networks, Inc.	Computer
VISX	VISX Incorporated	Industrial
VITL	Vital Signs, Inc.	Industrial
VCOM	VitalCom, Inc.	Industrial
VTCH	Vitech America, Inc.	Computer
VTSS	Vitesse Semiconductor Corporation	Computer
VTNAF	Vitran Corporation, Inc.	Transportation
VVID	Vivid Technologies, Inc.	Industrial
VVUS	Vivus, Inc.	Biotechnology
VLSI	VLSI Technology, Inc.	Computer
VOCLF	VocalTec Communications Ltd	Computer

Symbol	Company Name	Sector
VTEK	Vodavi Technology, Inc.	Industrial
VCSI	Voice Control Systems, Inc.	Industrial
VONE	V-ONE Corporation	Industrial
VOXW	Voxware, Inc.	Computer
VRBA	VRB Bancorp	Bank
VSEC	VSE Corporation	Industrial
VSIN	VSI Enterprises, Inc.	Industrial
VTEL	VTEL Corporation	Industrial
VWRX	VWR Scientific Products Corporation	Industrial
VYSI	Vysis, Inc.	Biotechnology
BKLY	W. R. Berkley Corporation	Insurance
BKLYZ	W. R. Berkley Corporation	Insurance
WAIN	Wainwright Bank & Trust Company	Bank
WALB	Walbro Corporation	Industrial
WALBP	Walbro Corporation	Industrial
WALK	Walker Interactive Systems, Inc.	Computer
WALL	Wall Data Incorporated	Computer
WSDI	Wall Street Deli, Inc.	Industrial
WNUT	Walnut Financial Services, Inc.	Other Finance
WALS	Walshire Assurance Company	Insurance
WANG	Wang Laboratories, Inc.	Industrial
WCRXY	Warner Chilcott Public Limited Company	Industrial
WARPF	Warp 10 Technologies, Inc.	Computer
WTEC	Warrantech Corporation	Industrial
WRNB	Warren Bancorp, Inc.	Bank
WSBI	Warwick Community Bancorp, Inc	Bank
WWVY	Warwick Valley Telephone Company	Telecommunications
WBCO	Washington Banking Company	Other Finance
WFSL	Washington Federal, Inc.	Other Finance
WAMU	Washington Mutual, Inc.	Bank
WSCI	Washington Scientific Industries, Inc.	Industrial
WASH	Washington Trust Bancorp, Inc.	Other Finance
WCNX	Waste Connections Inc.	Industrial
WWIN	Waste Industries, Inc.	Industrial
WSII	Waste Systems International, Inc.	Industrial
WTEK	Waste Technology Corp.	Industrial
WAST	WasteMasters, Inc.	Industrial
WATFZ	Waterford Wedgwood PLC	Industrial
WTRS	Waters Instruments, Inc.	Industrial
WSCC	Waterside Capital Corporation	Other Finance
WAVT	Wave Technologies International, Inc.	Industrial
WAVO	WavePhore, Inc.	Industrial

Symbol	Company Name	Sector
ITEL	Wavetech, Inc.	Industrial
WNNB	Wayne Bancorp, Inc.	Other Finance
WAYN	Wayne Savings Bancshares Inc.	Other Finance
WCMC	WCM Capital Inc.	Industrial
WDFC	WD-40 Company	Industrial
WCFB	Webster City Federal Savings Bank	Bank
WBST	Webster Financial Corporation	Other Finance
WBSTP	Webster Financial Corporation	Other Finance
WGNR	Wegener Corporation	Telecommunications
WLPT	Wellington Properties Trust	Other Finance
WEFC	Wells Financial Corp.	Bank
WERN	Werner Enterprises, Inc.	Transportation
WSBC	WesBanco, Inc.	Other Finance
WCSTF	Wescast Industries Inc.	Industrial
WJCO	Wesley Jessen VisionCare, Inc.	Industrial
WCBO	West Coast Bancorp	Other Finance
WEBK	West Essex Bancorp, Inc.	Bank
WMAR	West Marine, Inc.	Industrial
WTSC	West TeleServices Corporation	Industrial
WSTF	Westaff Inc.	Industrial
WABC	Westamerica Bancorporation	Other Finance
WBKC	WestBank Corporation	Other Finance
WCBI	Westco Bancorp, Inc.	Bank
WSTL	Westell Technologies, Inc.	Industrial
WTBK	Westerbeke Corporation	Industrial
WSTR	WesterFed Financial Corporation	Other Finance
WEBC	Western Bancorp	Other Finance
BEEF	Western Beef, Inc.	Industrial
WCCI	Western Country Clubs, Inc.	Industrial
WOFC	Western Ohio Financial Corporation	Other Finance
WPEC	Western Power & Equipment Corp.	Industrial
WWTR	Western Water Company	Industrial
WWCA	Western Wireless Corporation	Telecommunications
WBPR	Westernbank Puerto Rico	Bank
WGHI	Westmark Group Holdings, Inc.	Other Finance
WPSN	WestPoint Stevens Inc.	Industrial
WNMP	Westwood Corporation	Industrial
WEHO	Westwood Homestead Financial Corp	Other Finance
WONE	Westwood One, Inc.	Telecommunications
WTSLA	Wet Seal, Inc. (The)	Industrial
WEYS	Weyco Group, Inc.	Industrial
WFSI	WFS Financial Inc.	Other Finance

Symbol	Company Name	Sector
WHGB	WHG Bancshares Corporation	Bank
WHCP	White Cap Industries, Inc.	Industrial
WPNE	White Pine Software, Inc.	Computer
WWLI	Whitewing Labs, Inc.	Industrial
WTNY	Whitney Holding Corporation	Bank
WHIT	Whittman-Hart, Inc.	Computer
WFMI	Whole Foods Market, Inc.	Industrial
WIKS	Wickes Inc.	Industrial
OATS	Wild Oats Markets, Inc.	Industrial
WVVI	Willamette Valley Vineyards, Inc.	Industrial
WMCO	Williams Controls, Inc.	Industrial
WMSI	Williams Industries, Inc.	Industrial
WLFC	Willis Lease Finance Corporation	Industrial
WLMR	Wilmar Industries, Inc.	Industrial
WILM	Wilmington Trust Corporation	Bank
WFSG	Wilshire Financial Services Group Inc.	Other Finance
WREI	Wilshire Real Estate Investment Trust Inc.	Other Finance
WLSN	Wilsons The Leather Experts Inc.	Industrial
WIND	Wind River Systems, Inc.	Computer
WCAP	Winfield Capital Corp.	Other Finance
WLET	Winland Electronics, Inc.	Industrial
WLFI	WinsLoew Furniture, Inc.	Industrial
WCII	WinStar Communications, Inc.	Telecommunications
WTFC	Wintrust Financial Corporation	Bank
WCLX	Wisconsin Central Transportation Corp	Transportation
WIZTF	Wiztec Solutions Ltd.	Computer
WLRF	WLR Foods, Inc.	Industrial
WLHN	Wolohan Lumber Company	Industrial
FFWD	Wood Bancorp, Inc.	Other Finance
WDHD	Woodhead Industries, Inc.	Industrial
WGOV	Woodward Governor Company	Industrial
WORK	Workflow Management, Inc.	Industrial
WKGP	Workgroup Technology Corporation	Computer
WRLD	World Acceptance Corporation	Other Finance
WAXS	World Access, Inc.	Telecommunications
WLDA	World Airways, Inc.	Transportation
WHRTF	World Heart Corporation	Industrial
WOSI	World of Science, Inc.	Industrial
WTLK	Worldtalk Communications Corporation	Computer
WWES	Worldwide Entertainment & Sports Corp.	Industrial
WFDS	Worthington Foods, Inc.	Industrial
WTHG	Worthington Industries, Inc.	Industrial

Symbol	Company Name	Sector
WPIC	WPI Group, Inc.	Industrial
WPPGY	WPP Group plc	Industrial
WRPC	WRP Corporation	Industrial
WSFS	WSFS Financial Corporation	Other Finance
WVFC	WVS Financial Corp.	Other Finance
WYNT	Wyant Corporation	Industrial
WYMN	Wyman-Gordon Company	Industrial
XATA	XATA Corporation	Computer
XCED	X-Ceed, Inc.	Industrial
XEIKY	Xeikon, N.V.	Industrial
XNVAY	Xenova Group plc	Industrial
XETA	Xeta Corporation	Computer
XTEL	XeTel Corporation	Industrial
XICO	Xicor, Inc.	Computer
XLNX	Xilinx, Inc.	Industrial
XION	Xionics Document Technologies, Inc.	Industrial
XIOX	XIOX Corporation	Computer
XIRC	Xircom, Inc.	Computer
XOMA	XOMA Corporation	Biotechnology
XOMD	Xomed Surgical Products, Inc.	Industrial
XRIT	X-Rite, Incorporated	Industrial
XSYS	XXsys Technologies, Inc.	Industrial
XYBR	Xybernaut Corporation	Computer
XYLN	Xylan Corporation	Industrial
YHOO	Yahoo! Inc.	Computer
YANB	Yardville National Bancorp	Other Finance
YELL	Yellow Corporation	Transportation
YESS	YES! Entertainment Corporation	Industrial
YILD	YieldUP International Corporation	Industrial
YFCB	Yonkers Financial Corporation	Other Finance
YFED	York Financial Corp.	Other Finance
YORK	York Research Corporation	Industrial
YBTVA	Young Broadcasting, Inc.	Telecommunications
YDNT	Young Innovations, Inc.	Industrial
YSII	Youth Services International, Inc.	Industrial
ZMBA	Zamba Corporation	Telecommunications
ZHOM	Zaring National Corporation	Industrial
ZBRA	Zebra Technologies Corporation	Computer
ZILA	Zila, Inc.	Industrial
ZNDTY	Zindart Limited	Industrial
ZING	Zing Technologies, Inc.	Industrial
ZION	Zions Bancorporation	Other Finance

Symbol	Company Name	Sector
ZITL	Zitel Corporation	Computer
ZMAX	ZMAX Corporation	Industrial
ZOLL	Zoll Medical Corporation	Industrial
ZOLT	Zoltek Companies, Inc.	Industrial
ZOMX	Zomax Optical Media, Inc.	Industrial
ZONA	Zonagen, Inc.	Industrial
ZOOM	Zoom Telephonics, Inc.	Industrial
ZRAN	Zoran Corporation	Computer
ZSEV	Z-Seven Fund, Inc.	Other Finance
ZIGO	Zygo Corporation	Industrial
ZMTX	ZYMETX, Inc.	Biotechnology

glossary

This glossary is not limited to the words I have used in the text. To do so would be a disservice to you. Hopefully, you will use this glossary as a reference while you trade.

Advanced Computerized Execution System (ACES) Customized facility offered by the NASD that permits broker/dealers to automate their internal executions and record-keeping functions.

all-or-none (AON) In brokerage, order instruction, particularly for large orders, to execute the total quantity or none.

arbitrage 1. A financial transaction where an arbitrageur (arb) simultaneously purchases in one market and sells in another where there is a slight price differential. Often it is a full hedge, and therefore, a risk-free transaction. Arbs play an important role in keeping markets liquid and efficient. 2. A rare occurrence when the bid price is higher than the ask price. It usually only lasts for a very short time, because someone is selling a stock for less than someone else is willing to buy it for.

ARCA, ATTN, BTRD, ISLD, STRK ECNs

ask 1. The price at which someone who owns a security offers to sell it; also known as the asked price. It is also referred to as the offer. 2. The ask is the side of the montage where market makers and individuals are offering to sell a stock. This is usually the higher price.

asset allocation The process of deciding what types of assets you want to own, and the percentage of each. Tactical asset allocation is a sophisticated form of market timing in which an investor decides how much to allocate to each asset class based on market indicators, particularly interest rates. As conditions change, the percent allotted to each asset class changes.

assets   Any possessions that have value in an exchange.

auction   A public sale of items to the highest bidders.

average maturity   The average time to maturity of securities held by a mutual fund. Changes in interest rates have greater impact on funds with longer average life.

ax   The key market maker in a stock, who often directs the movement of price.

baby bond   One sold at face amount less than $1,000 to make it attractive to smaller investors. See *bond.*

balanced equities   A mutual fund whose holdings are split fairly evenly between stocks and bonds. Balanced funds can change their asset allocation according to market conditions. Balanced funds seek a relatively steady return.

balance sheet   A listing of all assets and liabilities for an individual or a business. The surplus of assets over liabilities is the net worth, or what is owned free of debt.

balance sheet—cash and debt   A view in the stock database that displays: fiscal year end, quick ratio, debt/equity ratio, current ratio, and cash/share. These items measure the financial health of a company, particularly its assets and liabilities. Click each item in the glossary list for definitions of each of these items.

balance sheet return   A view in the stock database that displays sales/price ratio, price/book ratio, book/share, return on equity, profit margin, and reporting date. These items are all measures of company value and profitability.

bank information   Descriptive information about a given bank. A view in the CDs and money markets database that displays: minimum deposit, city, state, phone, out-of-state indicator.

basis   An accounting term that refers to the cost of an asset, including all adjustments and improvements. For tax purposes, it is the amount you subtract from the net sale price to determine the realized gain or loss. For example, if you paid $150,000 for your home, but added a porch for $25,000, your basis is now $175,000. You have stepped up the basis.

basis point   The smallest measure used in quoting yields and interest rates. One basis point equals .01%, so a 100-basis-point move in a U.S. Treasury bond yield is 1%.

bearer certificate A security whose owner is not registered on the books of the issuer and which is, therefore, payable to the person possessing the certificate. A bearer bond has coupons attached, which the bondholder sends in or presents on the interest date for payment. Bearer stock certificates are negotiable without endorsement.

bearish A trading environment in which the market is declining.

beginning net asset value The market value of a fund share on a pre-determined start date.

best ask The price at which someone who owns a security offers to sell it; also known as the asked price. Please note that the New York Stock Exchange and the American Stock Exchange do not provide ask information on a delayed basis.

best ask The lowest quoted offer of all competing market makers to sell a particular stock at any given time.

best bid 1. The highest quoted bid of all competing market makers to buy a particular stock at any given time. 2. The price a prospective buyer is prepared to pay at a particular time for trading a unit of a given security. Please note that the New York Stock Exchange and the American Stock Exchange do not provide bid information on a delayed basis.

best-execution requirement The obligation of market makers, broker/dealers, and others to execute customer orders at the best price available at the time the trade is entered. The quoted bid at which a market maker is willing to buy a stock.

beta A measure of risk commonly used to compare the volatility of mutual funds or stocks to the overall market. The S&P 500 Index is the base for calculating beta and carries a value of 1. Securities with betas below 1 are less risky than the market as a whole. Betas above 1 are more risky. A beta of 1.3 is 30% more volatile than the S&P 500. Betas with negative values are inversely related to the S&P 500.

bid 1. The price a prospective buyer is prepared to pay at a particular time for trading a unit of a given security. 2. The bid is the side where market makers and individuals are offering to buy a stock. This is usually the lower price.

bid/ask spread The difference between the price at which a market maker is willing to buy a security (bid), and the price at which the firm is willing to sell it (ask). The spread narrows or widens according to the supply and demand for the security being traded.

block trade   Usually, a trade of 10,000 shares or more. For bonds, a $200,000 face amount or more. Block trades are often executed through a special section of a brokerage firm called the Block Desk. Using the Block Desk may result in a better price.

block trade   A purchase or sale of a large quantity of stock, generally 10,000 shares or more.

bond   A debt security that represents the obligation of the issuer to pay interest to the creditor or bond holder and return the principal at maturity. Bonds backed by collateral are termed secured while those that are not secured are called debentures. A sinking-fund bond obligates the issuer to set aside some of its earnings to retire bonds periodically. A bond is usually identified by its maturity date and its coupon rate, which is the interest rate stated on the bond. The price of the bond is equal to its face value when issued, which is called the par price. After that, the price fluctuates in the market. Bonds selling above original price are selling at a premium to par while those selling below original price are selling at a discount to par. Prices vary inversely with interest rates, as the prices of old bonds must adjust so that their current yield will stay competitive with those of newly issued bonds. A bond does not represent ownership. See baby bond, callable, junk bond, municipal bond, U.S. government issues, zero coupon bond, convertible bond, corporate bond.

bond prices   View in the bond database that displays: maturity, outstanding bond amount, latest price, current year high and low prices. For latest price, see *price* (trade) *bonds*.

bond type   The bond pays fixed interest amounts over its term. The bond price, however, can change as prevailing market interest rates change over time. Zero coupon bonds, or zeroes, do not pay interest. They are sold at deep discount to their par value, which is returned at maturity. Interest is internally compounded to produce the stated yield to maturity. With floating rate, the interest rate paid on the bond can change as prevailing market interest rates change.

book/share   The current fiscal year book value (or net equity for the corporation) per share of common stock.

breakdown   A sharp decline in price after the stock has traded sideways for a while.

breakout   A sharp rise in price after the stock has traded sideways for a while.

broker/dealer   In the broadest sense, an agent who facilitates trades between a buyer and a seller and receives a commission for his services. Dealers buy and sell for their own account and keep their own inventory of securities on which they can profit or incur losses. Most stock brokerage firms really act as brokers and dealers. Brokers are also classed as full-service or discount, the former using a commission-based salesforce and the latter using salaried brokers only.

broker call rate Interest rate at which brokerage firms borrow from banks to finance their clients' security positions.

bullet trade A trade that lasts only a few minutes or less.

bullish A trading environment in which the market is rising.

buy(s) A transaction type for the purchase of a security. A buy creates an open lot, which is part of a holding of a given security that you currently own. Buy(s) is also a filter for displaying only buy transactions.

buy-to-cover A transaction type that is a closing transaction for a short sell and that creates a closed lot. Buy-to-cover is also a filter for displaying only buy-to-cover transactions.

buying power Value of margin-eligible securities that may be purchased in a margin account. Determined by doubling the sum of the cash held in the brokerage account and the loan value of margined securities.

buy-side trader An individual, such as a pension or mutual fund portfolio manager, who effects trades for an institutional investor.

call option A call option gives the owner the right, but not the obligation, to buy the underlying stock at a given price (the strike price) by a given time (the expiration date). The owner of the call is speculating that the underlying stock will go up in value, hence, increasing the value of the option. The purpose can be to speculate with the option (hope it goes up and sell for a profit), to invest in the underlying stock at a locked-in price if the stock price goes high enough, or to generate income. Each option contract equals 100 shares of stock. For example, an AAA MAR 65 call, would give the owner the right to buy 100 shares of AAA at $65 (strike price) per share between now and the third Friday in March (expiration date).

callable A security redeemable by the issuer before the scheduled maturity. The issuer must pay the holder a premium price if the security is retired early. Most corporate and municipal bonds are callable. U.S. government issues are generally not callable. They are called when interest rates fall so significantly that the bond issuer can save money by floating new bonds at the lower rate. The first call date is the date to or after which a specific call price will be offered by the issuer, usually a premium price to par, as an incentive to the bondholder to redeem the bond.

canceled order   A buy or sell order that is canceled before it has been executed. In most cases, a limit order can be can be canceled at any time as long as it has not been executed. A market order may only be canceled if the order is placed after market hours and is then canceled before the market opens the following day.

capital gains distribution   Payments to mutual fund shareholders of profits from the sale of securities in a fund's portfolio. Capital gains distributions (if any) are usually made annually.

capital preservation   Maintaining your trading capital by not allowing yourself to lose more than a certain percentage of your capital in any given trade. A good number to use is 3%.

capital stock   Amount of money or property contributed by stockholders to be used as the financial foundation for the corporation. It includes all classes of common and preferred stock.

cash account   Orders placed in a cash account are settled on a cash basis, meaning that cleared funds must be in the account within three (3) business days to cover purchases.

cash available   The amount that may either be withdrawn in cash, or used to purchase additional securities without creating a debit balance. It is a combination of credit balances in all accounts and excess credit balances in margin accounts.

cash balance   Whenever a transaction occurs that affects cash, the cash balance is debited or credited. The cash balance is usually invested in a money market mutual fund that pays interest. Money market funds can be taxable or tax-exempt. In brokerage accounts, the balance in cash is swept into the money market daily.

cash flow   Net income plus depreciation and other noncash charges. A strong cash flow is important for covering interest payments, particularly for highly leveraged companies.

cash/share   The amount of cash divided by total number of common stock shares outstanding for a given stock. A corporation with a high cash/share amount relative to the current price per share is said to be cash rich and may be considered low risk or undervalued.

cash market   A market in which security or commodity transactions occur within a few days of the trade date. Also called the spot market. The opposite is the futures market, where transactions are completed at a specified future date, price, and quantity, which is determined in the present. Stock, bond, and mutual funds trade in the cash market.

cash percent The percentage of a given mutual fund's total assets invested in cash and equivalents. A high cash percent is usually good in a declining market but can result in underperformance in a rising market.

CD rate The current interest rate for a given CD (certificate of deposit).

certificate of deposit Investment created by banks, which pays stated interest at either fixed or variable rates. If sold directly by banks, principal is returned at maturity subject only to penalties for early cashing in. If sold through brokers (called broker CDs), principal value can vary like with bonds, and early cashing in can fetch a principal lower than amount paid.

change (in NAV) The change in the net asset value since the close of the previous trading day. Negative values means the mutual fund has dropped in price; positive values means the mutual fund has appreciated in price.

channel When a stock trades around the same price for a certain period of time, it is said to be in a channel. On a chart, a channel will be recognized as a sideways line.

chasing a stock Buying or shorting a stock after it has already made a large move. Chasing a stock is considered very dangerous, because one may buy at the top.

circuit breaker A procedure that temporarily halts trading on all U.S. stock markets for one hour when the Dow Jones Industrial Average falls 250 points or more within a trading day. The pause is designed to allow time for the markets to absorb the news that precipitated the decline. Should the average fall another 150 points within the same day, trading would again be halted, this time for two hours.

churning (excessive trading) A broker excessively trades an account for the purpose of increasing his or her commissions, rather than to further the customer's investment goals.

Class A/Class B shares Shares of stock issued by the same company but having some difference, such as voting rights, or a dividend preference, or participation.

clearinghouse A computerized facility that compares and reconciles both sides of a brokerage trade.

CLO At the close. By choosing CLO, your order will be executed as near the closing price as possible. Please note that the closing price is not guaranteed as the purchase price.

closed to new accounts The mutual fund is currently closed to new investors. To be sure, call the mutual fund for the latest information.

closing commission The commission deducted from the proceeds before calculating realized gain or loss. It is the fee charged by your broker to execute your trade. It may be a composite of several fees and charges.

closing price The market price you receive when you sell or buy to cover your security.

commercial paper Unsecured short-term debt, usually from 2 to 270 days, issued by banks and corporations, which is generally safe and flexible. It is usually a major component of money market fund investment portfolios.

commission Fee charged by broker to execute your trade. May be a composite of several fees and charges. Commission is taken into account when calculating realized gain or loss. The buy, or opening commission, is added to the cost basis and the sell, or closing commission, is deducted from the proceeds before calculating realized gain or loss; therefore, commissions reduce taxable gains and increase losses. Total commission is the sum of both buy and sell commission. Commission rates take into account the quantity of the purchase, the unit price of the security (low priced stocks may have higher commission rates), and the type of investment (options have higher commissions).

common shares Represents the total number of common shares outstanding, excluding treasury stock (stock issued but reacquired by the company through buybacks). This number is expressed in thousands, so add three zeros.

common stock Security representing partial ownership interest in a corporation. Ownership may also be shares with preferred stock, which has prior claim on any dividends to be paid and, in the event of liquidation, to the distribution of the corporation's assets. Common stockholders assume the primary risk if business is poor, and realize greater gains in the event of success. They also elect the board of directors that controls the company.

computer-assisted execution system (CAES) Nasdaq service that automates order routing and execution for securities listed on domestic exchanges in the Intermarket Trading System (ITS). When linked to ITS, market makers can execute trades in exchange-listed securities through CAES with specialists on an exchange floor.

confirmation A written notification from a broker to a client specifying the details of a securities' transaction.

conversion price The price at which convertible securities, such as bonds and preferred stock, can be converted into common stock at a set conversion ratio. For example, if the conversion ratio is 25 to 1, and you own a $1,000 face value convertible bond, then the conversion price is $40 per share. The conversion value is the value of 25 shares at the current price per share. If you assume $32 per share, then the current value is 25 × $32 = $800. In this example, it is clearly better not to convert.

convertible bond A debt security that is exchangeable for a set number of shares of another type of security, usually common stock, at a predetermined price. See *bond*.

corporate bond A debt security investment in obligations of U.S. corporations. Corporate bonds are taxable and have a specific maturity date. They are often traded on major exchanges. See *bond*.

covered calls A covered call seller or writer is an investor who owns a stock and sells a call option against it to generate additional income, which comes from the premium received for selling the option. If things work out right for the writer, the stock price will stay below the strike price and the writer will retain both the premium and the stock. However, if the stock price rises enough, the stock will be called away by the call buyer who has exercised the option and now gets the stock and pays the writer the strike price. Whether the writer makes a profit or loss on the stock that is called away depends on the purchase price (the cost basis). See *call option*.

covering To cover means getting out of a short position. When one is short in a stock, one needs to buy back the borrowed shares to close out the trade.

credit balance For cash accounts, it is the uninvested money in your account. In a margin account, it is the money on deposit against a short position.

cumulative return (12-month, 10-year) Measures the price change over the period of time indicated, ending at the current date (or the date the price was last updated). This measure includes any dividends paid and reinvested during the period measured. Cumulative return can also be referred to as total return. It is the most useful measure of performance among different asset classes, such as stocks, bonds, cash, and so forth.

current *P/E* ratio   The ratio of current price divided by last two quarters earnings per share (EPS) plus next two estimated quarters EPS. See *price/earnings ratio.*

current year high and low prices   The highest and lowest price for a given bond during the current calendar year.

cumulative return through (year)   Includes the price change over the period of years indicated, ending at the year shown, plus any dividend paid and reinvested over the period shown. The bar graph represents the total value of your portfolio.

cumulative return (1-yr, 3-yr, 5-yr, 10-yr)   The price change over the time period shown, plus any dividend, interest, or capital gains paid and reinvested over the period shown for any given security. Note that for stocks, the periods are complete calendar years, but for mutual funds, periods are rolling up to the current month.

CUSIP number   An industry code which uniquely identifies nearly all traded stocks and bonds.

current ratio   A company's current assets divided by its current liabilities.

current yield   For stock, the annual dividend divided by the current price per share. For bond, the annual interest payment divided by [current price divided by 100 times quantity]. A measure in percentage terms of how much income you can derive from the security. Of great importance to fixed income investors and of minimal importance to growth investors. See *yield to maturity.*

CyberTrader   A dynamic Level II Software with lots of creative features. It's developed by CyberBroker, a subsidiary of CyberCorp.

date of record   The date on which a shareholder must officially own shares to be entitled to a dividend.

day   By choosing day, your order will remain open for one trading day until it is executed or canceled. If the order is placed after market hours it will remain open for the next trading day. If it is placed during market hours it will remain open for the remainder of that trading day.

day trade   A trade that is closed within the same day.

dealer spread Currently, there is also a dealer spread on Nasdaq, reflecting the difference between a market maker's simultaneous bid and ask prices for a stock. NASD rules stipulate that Nasdaq market makers maintain two-sided quotes, even when they are only interested in one side of the market.

deleted A security is no longer included in The Nasdaq Stock Market.

depth of the market The total number of buyers and sellers within the market. Related to the amount of capital committed to a stock. Nasdaq market makers provide depth of market to companies by standing ready to commit capital to stocks in which they are registered and by providing immediate and continuous trading in a company's stock. ECNs further Nasdaq's market depth by delivering additional buyers and sellers to the marketplace.

distribution date Date on which the payout of realized capital gains on securities in the fund portfolio occurred.

dividend Distribution of earnings to shareholders, prorated by the class of security and paid in the form of money, stock, scrip, or, rarely, company products or property. The amount is decided by the board of directors and is usually paid quarterly. Mutual fund dividends are paid out of income, usually on a quarterly basis from the fund's investments.

DOT (designated order turnaround) The NYSE electronic system for order handling, which permits member firms to place day market orders and limit orders.

double witching A term used for the day when both options and futures expire.

Dow Jones Industrial Average—DJIA The *Dow Jones Industrial Average index* (DJIA) is a price-weighted average of 30 actively traded blue-chip stocks, primarily industrials but including American Express Co. and American Telephone and Telegraph Co. Prepared and published by Dow Jones & Co., it is the oldest and most widely quoted of all the market indicators. The components, which change from time to time, represent between 15% and 20% of the market value of NYSE stocks. The DJIA is calculated by adding the closing prices of the component stocks and using a divisor that is adjusted for splits and stock dividends equal to 10% or more of the market value of an issue as well as substitutions and mergers. The average is quoted in points, not in dollars.

downtick A downtick occurs when the bid price drops one level.

earning the spread Due to emergence of alternatives to SOES in recent years, traders are now able to earn the spread by using ECNs instead of SOES. If you buy a stock on the bid (lower price) and sell it on the ask (higher price), you will have earned the spread. This trading technique is also called playing market maker.

ECN Electronic communication network. ARCA, ATTN, BTRD, ISLD, REDI, and STRK are examples of ECNs.

effective annualized seven-day yield Yield for 7-day period including the day reported, calculated by adding 1 to the base period return used in calculating the standard 7-day yield raising the total to the power of 365 divided by 7 and subtracting 1. (Note: To be reported on Wednesday only).

Electronic Data Gathering, Analysis, and Retrieval (EDGAR) An electronic system implemented by the SEC that is used by companies to transmit all documents required to be filed with the SEC in relation to corporate offerings and ongoing disclosure obligations. EDGAR became fully operational mid-1995.

ending net asset value The market value of a fund share on a predetermined end date.

ex-dividend Interval between the announcement and the payment of the next dividend.

ex-dividend date The date on or after which a security begins trading without the dividend (cash or stock) included in the contract price.

excess spread policy The NASD requirement that prohibits market makers from entering quotations on The Nasdaq Stock Market that exceed prescribed limits for maximum allowable spreads.

family of funds Group of mutual funds managed by the same investment management company. Each fund typically has a different objective; one may be a growth-oriented stock fund, whereas another may be a bond fund or money market fund. Shareholders in one of the funds can usually switch their money into any of the family's other funds, sometimes at no charge. Family of funds with no sales charges are called no-load families. Those with sales charges are called load families.

five-minute rule You can only buy up to 1,000 shares of the same stock within 5 minutes if you are using SOES. If you want to buy more than 1,000 shares of the same stock on SOES, you have to wait 5 minutes before you can issue another buy order. However, if you bought 500 shares of a stock using SOES the first time, you may buy up to 500 shares more using SOES within the next 5 minutes. Note that if you use an ECN, such as ISLD, you can always buy as many shares as you like of the same stock. The five-minute rule only applies to SOES! The same five-minute rule applies when selling or shorting a stock.

flat for the day   To close out all your positions before the end of the trading day. Day traders almost never hold positions overnight, because one has no control over which way a stock may gap overnight.

FOK   Fill or kill. By choosing FOK, your order will be executed with an order for immediate purchase or sale of your entire specified quantity of stock, but not necessarily at one price. If the entire order cannot be filled immediately, then it will be automatically canceled.

foreign   A non-U.S. company with securities trading on The Nasdaq Stock Market.

futures   A future contract is an agreement between two parties in which one buys and the other sells something on a prearranged date. What day traders are mostly interested in are the S&P 500 futures. Stock prices follow future prices. So watch the directions of the futures closely.

gaining the spread   See *earning the Spread.*

gap   Difference between the closing price of the last trading day and the opening price of the next.

going high bid   Offering to pay more for a stock than the previous high bidder. This will narrow the spread.

going low ask   Offering to sell a stock for less than the previous lowest seller. This will narrow the spread.

Gold (GOX)   The *CBOE Gold Index* (GOX) is an equal-dollar-weighted index composed of 10 companies involved primarily in gold mining and production. The index is rebalanced after the close of business on expiration Friday on the March quarterly cycle.

grinding   A trading technique that aims to continually grind out small profits such as $\frac{1}{8}$ or $\frac{1}{4}$ while keeping the downside risk under control.

GTC   Good 'til canceled. By choosing GTC, your order will remain open until it is executed or cancelled, regardless of the number of trading days.

held   A situation where a security is temporarily not available for trading (for example, market makers are not allowed to display quotes).

holding the ask   Someone is preventing the price on the ask from going up even though there is a lot of buying of the stock.

holding the bid   Someone is preventing the price on the bid from going down even though there is a lot of selling of the stock.

initial public offering (IPO)   A company's first sale of stock to the public. Companies making an IPO are seeking outside equity capital and a public market for their stock.

inside ask   See *going low ask.*

inside bid   See *going high bid.*

inside market   The highest bid and the lowest offer prices among all competing market makers in a Nasdaq security (that is, the best bid and offer prices).

inside market   The highest bid and the lowest ask (offer) prices among all market makers competing in a Nasdaq security; the best bid and ask prices for a security.

inside spread (inside quote)   The difference between the best bid and best ask among all securities is the highest bid and lowest offer being quoted among all of the market makers competing in a security. Because the spread is the aggregate of individual market maker spreads, it is narrower than an individual dealer spread or quote.

Instinet   Private network that currently handles about 10 to 15% of the volume on Nasdaq. It matches buyers and sellers and often allows traders to buy and sell at prices between the ask and the bid.

institutional investor   A bank, mutual fund, pension fund, or other corporate entity that trades securities in large volumes.

Intermarket Trading System (ITS)   A computer system that interconnects competing exchange markets for the purpose of choosing the best market. ITS is operated by Securities Industry Automation Corporation (SIAC).

IOC   Immediate or Cancel. By choosing IOC, your order will have immediate execution of all or part of the quantity of stock you specified. Any portion of the order that is not executed immediately is automatically canceled.

last sale reporting   An electronic entry by NASD members to The Nasdaq Stock Market of the price and the number of shares involved in a transaction in a Nasdaq security. The trade reported must be submitted to Nasdaq with 90 seconds of the execution of the trade.

Level II   Level II gives the trader much more detailed information than Level I. It lists all MMs and ECNs on the bid and the ask on a given stock, not just the top bid and top ask. One can also get much faster executions by using Level II. Examples of good Level II software programs are Cybertrader and RealTick III.

limit   This is an order in which you can set the maximum price you want to pay for your purchase, or a minimum price you will accept as seller.

limit order   An order to buy or sell a security at a customer-specified price; a customer order to buy or sell a specified number of shares of a security at a specific price. If the stock moves past your price before you get filled at your desired price, you will not get filled.

liquidity   A stock is liquid when it's easy to buy or sell a good amount of a stock without causing a major move in the price.

load fund   Mutual fund that is sold for a sales charge by a brokerage firm or other sales representative. Such funds may be stock, bond, or commodity funds, with conservative or aggressive objectives.

locked or crossed quotations   A temporary and unusual condition where the ask (offer) price of one market maker for a security is the same or lower than the bid (buy) price of another market maker. Locked or crossed quotations may occur in fast-moving markets.

long-term gain   A gain on the sale of a capital asset where the holding period was six months or more and the profit was subject to the long-term capital gains tax.

making the spread   See *earning the spread.*

marketable order   An order that agrees with the market. For a buy order, your price is at or higher than the ask; for a sell order, your price is at or lower than the bid.

market   This is an order that is executed immediately, at the best available price.

market close date   Date on which the closing net asset value (NAV) was last calculated.

market maker   A representative of a brokerage house, like Goldman Sachs or Merrill Lynch, who buys and sells shares for a particular stock. A popular stock like MSFT has market makers from almost all brokerage houses, whereas less popular stocks only have a few market makers from smaller institutions.

market maker spread   The difference between the price at which a market maker is willing to buy a security and the price at which the firm is willing to sell it (that is, the difference between a market maker's bid and ask for a given security). Because each market maker positions itself to either buy or sell inventory at any given time, each individual market maker spread is not indicative of the market as a whole. See also *inside market.*

market makers The NASD member firms that use their own capital, research, retail, and/or systems resources to represent a stock and compete with each other to buy and sell the stocks they represent. There are over 500 member firms that act as Nasdaq market makers. One of the major differences between The Nasdaq Stock Market and other major markets in the United States is Nasdaq's structure of competing market makers. Each market maker competes for customer order flow by displaying buy and sell quotations for a guaranteed number of shares. Once an order is received, the market maker will immediately purchase for or sell from its own inventory, or seek the other side of the trade until it is executed, often in a matter of seconds.

market order 1. An order to buy or sell a stated amount of a security at the best possible price at the time the order is received in the marketplace. 2. An order to buy or sell a stock at given market conditions. Your order may get executed at different prices than what you envisioned.

market surveillance The department responsible for investigating and preventing abusive, manipulative, or illegal trading practices on The Nasdaq Stock Market. Considerable resources are devoted to surveilling The Nasdaq Stock Market. A vast array of sophisticated automated systems reviews each trade and price quotation on an online, real-time basis. Offline, computer-based analyses are conducted to evaluate trading patterns on a monthly, a weekly, and a daily basis.

   Whenever any of these automated systems indicate unusual price or volume in a stock, Nasdaq market surveillance analysts determine if this was the result of legitimate market forces or perhaps a violation of rules. Among other things, analysts review press releases, review historical trading activity, interview brokers, market makers, and Nasdaq-listed company officials. Market surveillance continues its inquiries until unusual movements are adequately explained.

   If legitimate market forces were at work, the case is closed without action. If it appears rule violations have occurred, a disciplinary action is initiated. Where corporate insiders or members of the investing public are involved in a potential violation, the case will be referred to the SEC.

market value   The market price; the price at which buyers and sellers trade similar items in an open marketplace. The current market price of a security as indicated by the latest trade recorded.

material news   News released by a Nasdaq company that might reasonably be expected to affect the value of a company's securities or influence investors' decisions. Material news includes information regarding corporate events of an unusual and nonrecurring nature, news of tender offers, unusually good or bad earnings reports, and a stock split or stock dividend. See also *trading halt.*

maturity date   The date on which the principal amount of a bond is to be paid in full.

member firm   A broker/dealer that is a member of the National Association of Securities Dealers, Inc.

MM   Short for *market maker.*

money market fund   Open-ended mutual fund that invests in commercial paper, banker's acceptances, repurchase agreements, government securities, certificates of deposit, and other highly liquid and safe securities, and pays money market rates of interest. The fund's net asset value remains a constant $1 a share, only the interest rate goes up or down.

most active   Most active Nasdaq National Market stocks.

moving average   Measures the past movement in price and allows one to see whether a stock is currently acting strong or weak compared with its past behavior.

MSCO, GSCO, MONT, MLCO, SLKC, HRZG, FBCO   Symbols for market makers that one can see for Nasdaq stocks using Level II software. Note that stocks traded on the NYSE don't have these market makers.

mutual fund   Fund operated by an investment company that raises money from shareholders and invests it in stocks, bonds, options, commodities, or money market securities.

Nasdaq 100 Index   The Nasdaq 100 Index includes 100 of the largest nonfinancial domestic companies listed on the Nasdaq National Market tier of The Nasdaq Stock Market. Launched in January 1985, each security in the Index is proportionately represented by its market capitalization in relation to the total market value of the Index.

   The Index reflects Nasdaq's largest growth companies across major industry groups. All index components have a minimum market capitalization of $500 million, and an average daily trading volume of at least 100,000 shares.

The number of securities in the Nasdaq 100 Index makes it an effective vehicle for arbitrageurs and securities traders. In October 1993, the Nasdaq 100 Index began trading on the CBOE. On April 10, 1996, the CME began trading futures and futures options on the Nasdaq 100 Index.

As of the end of 1996, the Nasdaq 100 Index has outperformed other major indices. The Nasdaq 100 Index was up 43%, while the Dow Jones Index rose 26%, and the Standard and Poors 500 Index climbed 20%. Individual stocks within the Nasdaq 100 Index varied with 69 stocks finishing the year with higher prices. Dell Computer was the best-performing stock within the Index, with a 206.9% price increase from $17.31 per share to $53.12 per share.

Nasdaq Composite^{SM} Index   A statistical measure that indicates changes in the Nasdaq Stock Market. The Nasdaq Composite Index measures all Nasdaq domestic and foreign common stocks. It is market-value-weighted: each company's security affects the Index in proportion to its market value. Securities in the Nasdaq Composite Index generally are assigned to subindexes based on their Standard Industrial Classification (SIC) codes.

Today, the Nasdaq Composite Index includes over 5,000 companies, more than most other stock market indexes. Because it is so broad-based, the Composite is one of the most widely followed and quoted major market indexes.

Nasdaq International Ltd.   A subsidiary of the NASD headquartered in London, England. Its mission is to support NASD members in London, serve as a liaison to international companies seeking to list securities on Nasdaq, encourage foreign institutional participation in Nasdaq stocks, and to heighten the international image of the NASD and its markets.

Nasdaq International Service   An extension to the Nasdaq Stock Market's trading systems that allows early morning trading from 3:30 to 9:00 A.M. Eastern Standard Time on each U.S. trading day. This Nasdaq service enables participants to monitor trades during London market hours. NASD members are eligible to participate in this session through their U.S. trading facilities or through those of an approved U.K. affiliate.

Nasdaq National Market securities   The Nasdaq National Market consists of over 3,000 companies that have a national or international shareholder base, have applied for listing, meet stringent financial requirements, and agree to specific corporate governance standards. To list initially, companies are required to have significant net tangible assets or operating income, a minimum public float of 500,000 shares, at least 400 shareholders, and a bid price of at least $5. The Nasdaq National Market operates from 9:30 A.M. to 4:00 P.M. EST, with extended trading in SelectNet from 8:00 A.M. to 9:30 A.M. EST and from 4:00 P.M. and 5:15 P.M. EST.

Nasdaq SmallCap Market securities The Nasdaq SmallCap Market comprises over 1,400 companies that want the sponsorship of market makers, have applied for listing, and meet specific and financial requirements. Once a company is approved and listed on this market, market makers are able to quote and trade the company's securities through a sophisticated electronic trading and surveillance system. The Nasdaq SmallCap Market operates from 9:30 A.M. to 4:00 P.M. EST, with extended trading in SelectNet from 8:00 A.M. to 9:30 A.M. EST and from between 4:00 P.M. and 5:15 P.M. EST.

Nasdaq Workstation II™ A computerized trading tool that provides access to all Nasdaq markets for market makers, brokers, and institutions (formerly named Service Delivery Platform).

National Association of Securities Dealers, Inc. (NASD) The self-regulatory organization of the securities industry responsible for the regulation of The Nasdaq Stock Market and the over-the-counter markets. The NASD operates under the authority granted it by the 1938 Maloney Act Amendment to the Securities Exchange Act of 1934.

negotiation The process whereby the purchase price is determined by a public offering.

net asset value (NAV) The market value of a fund share, synonymous with a bid price. In the case of no-load funds, the NAV, market price, and offering price are all the same figure, which the public pays to buy shares; load fund market or offer prices are quoted after adding the sales charge to the net asset value. NAV is calculated by most funds after the close of the exchanges each day by taking the closing market value of all securities owned plus all other assets such as cash, subtracting all liabilities, then dividing the result (total net assets) by the total number of shares outstanding. The number of shares outstanding can vary each day depending on the number of purchases and redemptions.

net change The difference between today's last trade and the previous day's last trade. The difference between today's closing net asset value (NAV) and the previous day's closing net asset value (NAV).

no-load fund Mutual fund offered by an open-end investment company that imposes no sales charge (load) on its shareholders. Investors buy shares in no-load funds directly from the fund companies, rather than through a broker as is done in load funds. Many no-load fund families allow switching of assets between stock, bond, and money market funds. The listing of the price of a no-load fund in the newspaper is accompanied by the designation NL. The net asset value, market price, and offer prices of this type of fund are exactly the same, because there is no sales charge.

no quote (NQ) No market makers making an inside market at this time.

nonmarketable order An order that disagrees with the market. For a buy order, your price is lower than the ask; for a sell order, your price is higher than the bid.

NYSE New York Stock Exchange.

NYSE Composite Index—NYSE The *NYSE Composite Index* (NYSE) is a market value-weighted index that relates all NYSE stocks to an aggregate market value as of December 31, 1965, adjusted for capitalization changes. The base value of the index is $50 and point changes are expressed in dollars and cents.

open order An order to buy or sell a security that remains in effect until it is either canceled by the customer or executed.

options An option is the right to either buy or sell a specified amount or value at a fixed exercise price. An option that gives the right to buy is a call option. An option that gives the right to sell is a put option. One needs to exercise the option before the specified expiration date. Stock options expire every third Friday of the month and can become absolutely worthless.

OPG At the opening. By choosing OPG, your order will be executed at the opening price. If it is not executed at the opening, it will be cancelled automatically.

penalty bid A syndicate penalty bid can be displayed on the Nasdaq System during the period of a registered public offering of a security. Such a bid may be entered by the managing underwriter or a member of the underwriting group acting on its behalf, and is intended to facilitate the offering by stabilizing the price of the security during the distribution period. This activity is permissible under SEC Rule 10b-7.

presyndicate bid A presyndicate bid can be entered in the Nasdaq System to stabilize the price of a Nasdaq security prior to the effective date of a registered secondary offering. This activity is permissible under SEC Rule 10b-7.

previous day's close The previous trading day's last reported trade. The previous day's close on the Nasdaq web site is updated at 3:30 A.M.

principal orders Refers to activity by a broker/dealer when buying or selling for its own account and risk.

range trading Similar to grinding, but one allows for more room for the stock to move. Range trades tend to take a little longer with both the gainers and losers being bigger than when grinding.

RealTick III Level II Software developed by Townsend Analytics and used by many day-trading firms.

real-time trade reporting A requirement imposed on market makers (and in some instances, non–market makers) to report each trade immediately after completion of the transaction. Stocks traded on The Nasdaq Stock Market are subject to real-time trade reporting within 90 seconds of execution.

relative strength An indicator that measures the past behavior of a stock against all other stocks on a scale from 99 to 1, 99 being the strongest and 1 the weakest.

resistance When a stock has trouble breaking through a price area, it is said that a stock is up against resistance (for example, it often trades just below $25, but can't move above $25).

retained earnings Net profits kept for accumulation in a business after dividends are paid.

return of capital A distribution of cash resulting from depreciation tax savings, the sale of a capital asset, or of securities in a portfolio, or any other transaction unrelated to retained earnings.

run When a stock has a quick change of price, it's said to be on a run.

scalping To trade quickly for small gains.

Securities and Exchange Commission (SEC) The federal agency created by the Securities Exchange Act of 1934 to administer that act and the Securities Act of 1933. The statutes administered by the SEC are designed to promote full public disclosure and protect the investing public against fraudulent and manipulative practices in the securities markets. Generally, most issues of securities offered in interstate commerce or through the mails must be registered with the SEC.

SelectNet Operated by Nasdaq. One can try to get a better price than with using SOES, but there is no obligation for the other party to buy or sell the stock that you're interested in. A SelectNet order is an open order. It can be placed anywhere within the market. SelectNet is not a forced order; thus, it will be filled only if a market maker chooses to do so. This order is not a guaranteed fill and has a 10-second minimum time where a day trader cannot cancel his/her order.

seven-day yield Yield for seven-day period including the day reported.

shake out A pullback in price before the stock continues in the same direction. Market makers love to shake traders out of their winning positions by creating wide trading ranges and big pullbacks.

short interest The total number of shares of a security that have been sold short by customers and securities firms.

Short Sale Rule If the last tick was a downtick, you cannot short a stock at or below the bid price. However, you can still try to short the stock at any price above the bid price by offering it out on the ask.

short selling Short selling is the selling of a security that the seller does not own, or any sale that is completed by the delivery of a security borrowed by the seller. Short selling is a legitimate trading strategy. Short sellers assume the risk that they will be able to buy the stock at a more favorable price than the price at which they sold short.

The Nasdaq Short Sale Rule prohibits NASD members from selling a Nasdaq National Market stock at or below the inside best bid when that price is lower than the previous inside best bid in that stock.

short-term gain The loss realized from the sale of securities or other capital assets held six months or less.

shorting a stock Shorting a stock can be very profitable in weak market conditions or when a stock has gotten way ahead of itself. The concept of shorting is that you sell a stock that you don't own (you basically borrow it from your broker) and expect to buy it back later at a lower price.

Small Order Execution System^{SM} (**SOES**^{SM}) Automated execution system for processing small-order agency executions of Nasdaq securities (up to 1,000 shares).

SOES Stands for *Small Order Execution System,* it allows you to buy (or sell) up to 1,000 shares from any market maker.

specialist 1. Member of a stock exchange through which all trades in a given security pass. 2. Someone who handles all the transactions in a stock traded on the NYSE.

split The division of outstanding shares of a corporation into a larger or smaller number of shares. For example: in a 3-for-1 split, each holder of 100 shares before would have 300 shares, although the proportionate equity in the company would remain the same. A reverse split occurs when the company reduces the total number of outstanding shares, but each share is worth more.

spread 1. The difference between the bid price at which a market maker will buy a security, and the ask price at which a market maker will sell a security. 2. The difference in price between the bid and the ask.

Standard and Poor's 500—$SPX The *S&P 500 Index* ($SPX), more formally known as the S&P 500 Composite Stock Price Index, is a European-style, capitalization-weighted index (shares outstanding multiplied by stock price) of 500 stocks that are traded on the New York Stock Exchange, American Stock Exchange, and Nasdaq Stock Market®. The advantage of cap weighting is that each company's influence on index performance is directly proportional to its relative market value. It is this characteristic that makes the S&P 500 such a valuable tool for measuring the performance of actual portfolios.

Standard & Poor's Corporation A company well known for its rating of stocks and bonds according to investment risk (the Standard & Poor's Rating) and for compiling the Standard & Poor's Index—commonly called the Standard & Poor's 500—that tracks 400 industrial stocks, 20 transportation stocks, 40 financial stocks, and 40 public utilities as a measurement indicative of broad changes in the market.

stock An instrument that signifies an ownership position in a corporation.

stock dividend Payment of a corporate dividend in the form of stock rather than cash. The stock dividend may be additional shares in the company, or it may be shares in a subsidiary being spun off to shareholders. Stock dividends are often used to conserve cash needed to operate the business. Unlike a cash dividend, stock dividends are not taxed until sold.

stock symbol A unique four- or five-letter symbol assigned to a Nasdaq security. If a fifth letter appears, it identifies the issue as other than a single issue of common stock or capital stock. A list of fifth-letter identifiers and a description of what each represents follows:

A—Class A
B—Class B
C—Issuer qualifications exceptions*
D—New
E—Delinquent in required filings with the SEC
F—Foreign
G—First convertible bond
H—Second convertible bond, same company
I—Third convertible bond, same company
J—Voting
K—Nonvoting
L—Miscellaneous situations, such as depositary receipts, stubs, additional warrants, and units
M—Fourth preferred, same company
N—Third preferred, same company
O—Second preferred, same company
P—First preferred, same company
Q—Bankruptcy proceedings
R—Rights
S—Shares of beneficial interest
T—With warrants or with rights
U—Units
V—When issued and when distributed
W—Warrants
Y—ADR (American Depositary Receipt)
Z—Miscellaneous situations such as depositary receipts, stubs, additional warrants, and units.

* The letter *C* as a fifth character in a security symbol, indicates that the issuer has been granted a continuance in Nasdaq under an exception to the qualification standards for a limited period.

stock symbol A unique four- or five-letter symbol assigned to a Nasdaq security that is used for identifying it on stock tickers, in newspapers, on online services, and in automated information retrieval systems. If a fifth letter appears, it identifies the issue as other than a single issue of common or capital stock.

stop   This is an order that becomes a market order once the stock trades at or through the stop price you have specified. When this order becomes active you are guaranteed execution of the purchase. However, the execution price cannot be guaranteed.

stop limit   This is an order that combines both the stop and limit order, in that once the stop price is activated your order can be executed up to your limit price. However, in a fast-moving market, your trade may not be executed if the price goes past your limit.

stop loss   The worst price that you are willing to sell a stock for. Stop losses are very important to cut your losses when a trade has gone in the wrong direction!

stop-loss order   A customer order to a broker that sets the sell price of a stock below the current market price, therefore protecting profits that have already been made or preventing further losses if the stock drops.

subindex   Categories of the Nasdaq Composite Index. There are currently 11 subindexes: Bank, Biotechnology, Computer, Industrial, Insurance, Nasdaq ADR (American Depositary Receipts), Nasdaq Regional Indexes, Nasdaq 100® (100 of the largest companies on the Nasdaq National Market), Other Finance, Telecommunications. Note: A way to calculate previous day's closing price, is to subtract the change from the current price—add negative values.

support   When a stock is not falling through a price area, it is said that a stock is sitting on support (for example, it sits just above $25, but doesn't go below $25).

swing trade   A trade that lasts several days, usually from 3 to 5 days.

syndicate bid   A syndicate bid can be entered in the Nasdaq System to stabilize the price of a Nasdaq security prior to the effective date of a registered secondary offering. This activity is permissible under SEC Rule 10b-7.

tick   An important short-time indicator. It's the difference between the number of NYSE stocks that are on an uptick versus the number of NYSE stocks that are on a downtick. For example, if we have 2,000 stocks on an uptick and 1,800 on a downtick, then the tick would read +200.

today's high   The intraday high trading price.

today's low   The intraday low trading price.

trading halt   The temporary suspension of trading in a Nasdaq security, usually for 30 minutes, while material news from the issuer is being disseminated over the news wires. A trading halt gives all investors equal opportunity to evaluate news and make buy, sell, or hold decisions on that basis. A trading halt may also be imposed for purely regulatory reasons, either by The Nasdaq Stock Market or the SEC.

TRIN   Also called the Arms Index, by Richard Arms. Measures the volatility and selling pressure. It's a ratio of the quotient of advancing stocks divided by declining stocks and up volume divided by down volume. Typically, a rising TRIN is bearish, and a falling TRIN bullish.

Treasury Bond 30 Year—TYX   The Treasury Bond Index (TYX) is based on 10 times the yield to maturity on the most recently auctioned 30-year Treasury bond.

two-sided market   The obligation imposed by the NASD that Nasdaq market makers make both firm bids and firm asks in each security in which they make a market.

uptick   An uptick occurs when the bid price moves up a level.

volume   Total volume in each stock reported to The Nasdaq Stock Market from NASD members and exchanges trading Nasdaq securities between the hours of 8:00 A.M. and 5:15 P.M. EST.

yield   In general, a return on an investor's capital investment. For bonds, the coupon rate of interest divided by the purchase price, called current yield. Also, the rate of return on a bond, taking into account the total of annual interest payments, the purchase price, the redemption value, and the amount of time remaining until maturity.

zero-plus tick   A zero-plus tick occurs when a stock upticks on a trade and the following trade is executed at the same price level.

bibliography and sources

Barnes, Robert M. *High-Impact Day Trading.* New York: McGraw-Hill, 1996.

Bernstein, Jake. *The Compleat Day Trader II.* New York: McGraw-Hill, 1998.

Dorsey, Thomas J. *Point & Figure Charting.* New York: John Wiley & Sons, 1995.

Farrell, Christopher A. *Day Trade Online.* New York: John Wiley & Sons, 1999.

Friedfertig, Marc, and George West. *The Electronic Day Trader.* New York: McGraw-Hill, 1998.

Harris, Sunny J. *Trading 101—How to Trade Like a Pro.* New York: John Wiley & Sons, 1996.

Harris, Sunny J. *Trading 102—Getting Down to Business.* New York: John Wiley & Sons, 1998.

Houtkin, Harvey, with David Waldman. *Secrets of the SOES Bandit.* New York: McGraw-Hill, 1999.

Kase, Cynthia A. *Trading with the Odds.* Chicago: Irwin Professional Publishing, 1996.

Kaufman, Perry J. *Trading Systems and Methods, 3rd Edition.* New York: John Wiley & Sons, 1998.

Krutsinger, Joe. *The Trading Systems Toolkit.* Chicago: Probus Publishing Company, 1994.

Murphy, Michael. *Every Investor's Guide to High-Tech Stocks and Mutual Funds, 2nd Edition.* New York: Broadway Books, 1999.

Nassar, David S. *How to Get Started in Electronic Day Trading.* New York: McGraw-Hill, 1999.

Ross, Joe, and Mark Cherlin. *Electronic Trading 'TNT' I—Gorilla Trading Stuff.* Cedar Park, TX: Ross Trading, 1998.

Ross, Joe, and Mark Cherlin. *Electronic Trading 'TNT' II—How-to-Win Trading Stuff.* Cedar Park, TX: Ross Trading, 1998.

Ross, Joe, and Mark Cherlin. *Electronic Trading 'TNT' III—Technical Trading Stuff.* Cedar Park, TX: Ross Trading, 1998.

Ross, Joe, and Mark Cherlin. *Electronic Trading 'TNT' IV—Tips, Tricks and Other Trading Stuff.* Cedar Park, TX: Ross Trading, 1998.

Rudd, Barry. *Stock Patterns for Day Trading.* Greenville, SC: Traders Press, 1998.

index